Old Cars

Questions & Answers

&

Edited by John A. Gunnell

Published by

 **krause
publications**

700 E. State Street • Iola, WI 54990-0001
Telephone: 715/445-2214

Library of Congress Catalog Number: 93-77543
ISBN: 0-87341-255-9
Printed in the United States of America

CONTENTS

INTRODUCTION

When I began working at *OLD CARS WEEKLY* in the fall of 1978, my duties included editing the quarterly *OLD CARS PRICE GUIDE* and writing the "Q & A" (questions and answers) column. Needless to say, the second job took most of my time.

Those who collect and restore old cars, as well as those who just like them or those who inherit them, seem to have an endless stream of questions about their vehicles. How many did they make? How many are left? What color should the engine be painted? How much is it worth?

Over several years of meeting people through their letters to *OLD CARS WEEKLY*, the process of networking with writers, historians, restorers and car owners led to constant enhancement of the column. People volunteered their personal expertise in a variety of topics, such as body work, paint, engines and historical research, to name a few. When a difficult question arose, we learned who we could call for a satisfactory answer.

The initial answer was usually far from the final word, however. Commonly, one specialist after another would add to the general body of knowledge. Often, the bits and pieces of expanded information would trickle in for weeks on end. In a few cases, we received dozens of letters; enough input to write small books on topics such as 1934 Chevrolets built at the Chicago World's Fair, the Fisher Body Craftsman's Guild competition and Chrysler Corporation's six-bank military tank engine.

Later, the job of answering questions was handled by distributing them to several writers for a while. They included Dennis Shrimpf, Bill Siuru, Jim Flammang and Tom Brownell. This scheme had its benefits, but there were drawbacks, too, chiefly in duplication of efforts. Eventually, Tom Brownell took over the column entirely.

This book represents an attempt to bring Tom Brownell's favorite questions and answers together in one book. The material has been organized into 10 separate chapters, as described in the table of contents. The questions and answers have been edited and made timelier. For instance, years have elapsed since some were published, so we've updated the names and addresses of helpful hobby information sources. Also, to protect the privacy of car collectors, we have replaced the use of full names and city addresses with initials and states.

The thing that we find most exciting about this book is that the answers now integrate all of the information that was sent in concerning each question. In other words, the answers are more complete and detailed than they were originally. They reflect the knowledge of everyone who responded to their fellow hobbyists' need for information. In this sense, they go far beyond the initial responses in their scope and depth of research.

I hope that you'll find *OLD CARS Q & A* stimulating and enlightening. I should point out that this popular column still appears weekly in *OLD CARS WEEKLY NEWS & MARKETPLACE* which is available by subscription from Krause Publications.

John A. Gunnell

PHOTO CREDITS

AUTO HISTORY

A 1957 Plymouth is buried in Oklahoma.

Q. Recently, I heard that Oklahoma officials buried a new 1957 Plymouth in a time capsule to mark the state's 50th birthday. The capsule is to be opened in 2007, with the Plymouth going to the person who guessed, in 1957, what Tulsa's population would be when the capsule was opened. Why a Plymouth? What model was it? What condition can one expect the car to be in when the capsule is opened? Are there other "time capsule" cars out there? D.E., Pennsylvania.

A. Hobbyist K.W. Beene advises that a 1957 Plymouth is definitely buried under the courthouse/city hall lawn in downtown Tulsa, along with one or more drums of gasoline. The car was furnished by Cox Motor Company, a long time Chrysler-Plymouth dealer, which probably explains why a Plymouth was selected. The car was buried by a local firm in a water-tight chamber, to be exhumed on its 50th anniversary. There is a plaque marking the site of the time capsule. We are not sure of the model of the car. Most likely, the car will remain in good condition, since it should be well protected from moisture and air inside the sealed chamber. An early Corvette that was sealed inside a room when new or nearly new was featured in a *SPECIAL-INTEREST AUTOS* magazine article in the late-1970s. Some 20 years later, this car was taken out of its basement crypt and found to be in good condition, with some signs of minor paint blistering. While the Corvette's fiberglass body may have been less prone to deterioration,

5

the fact that the Tulsa time capsule was water-tight should help preserve the steel-bodied Plymouth. It's likely that there are other cars buried in time capsules, although we do not have any specific information about how common this practice was.

Q. Could you tell me who made the first four-wheel drive vehicle and when? R.T.L., Maryland.
A. Dozens of inventors in America and Europe were working on the four-wheel drive principle around the turn-of-the-century. As early as 1901, Gustave Hoffman, a German living, in England, filed the first patents for an "equal power" system. On August 1, 1907, Otto Zachow and William Besserdich, of Clintonville, Wisconsin filed patents on a ball-and-socket device designed to provide all-wheel drive. The patents came through in the summer of 1908 and a chassis with four-wheel drive was built. A steam engine was used. In May of 1909, a large touring car body arrived for the chassis. It was described as "a dandy, deep maroon in color, large and roomy, holding eight people all told ... two in front, four in the rear and two extra on folding seats." The car was completed and successfully tested and a second was ordered. Then, the two men started the legwork of organizing a company to build motor vehicles. The first car built for public sale was finished late in the summer of 1911 and sold to a local man. A second was completed late in the winter and not sold until 1912. The Four Wheel Drive Auto Company (evolved from the Badger Four Wheel Drive Auto Company) opened its first factory building on December 20, 1911. Another vehicle ... somewhat a cross between a car and a pickup ... was built for testing by the U.S. Army. Meanwhile, two more touring cars were built, with one sold to M. W. Pinkerton, the famous Chicago detective agency owner. Then, the company began building trucks. Things moved slowly, with FWD spending money to promote its products and picking up sales here and there. In 1914, war broke out in Europe and two trucks were sold to an English import/export company. Within a month, 50 more were ordered for delivery to England in 40 days. By the time 1915 was over, 288 trucks had gone to England and 88 had gone to Russia. The company also had a backlog of orders for 200 trucks per month. Then, on April 6, 1916, an order for 147 trucks arrived from the U.S. Army Quartermaster Corps. They were needed to fight in the Mexican War. The next year, when the U.S. entered World War I, an order for 3,750 trucks arrived from Washington, D.C. The FWD Auto Company was suddenly on the map. By the way, that first four-wheel drive touring car still exists! See the next answer for more information.

Q. In 1937, I worked at the FWD truck factory in Clintonville, Wisconsin. Lots of history was made there. They built a four-wheel drive car before trucks and used this car to get mail in 1937. What happened to it? In 1937, Studebaker put a four-wheel drive car in the Indianapolis 500. The car didn't win, but for 200-300 miles, it did well. G.D., Wisconsin.
A. Otto Zachow and William Besserdich, who founded the Four Wheel Drive Auto Company sold Reo automobiles. Around 1909, they put a Reo body on a chassis equipped with their "ball-and-socket" all-wheel drive system and a steam engine. Later, this test car, nicknamed "The Battleship," was converted to gasoline power. A year or two later, a second vehicle called the "Nancy Hank" was constructed for U.S. Army testing. This may have also been based on a Reo. It was fitted with a wooden dispatch box and used for company chores for about 35 years. In 1930, directors of the company signed a contract with Harry Miller for construction of an FWD race car, which was completed in 1932. It was powered by a 300 horsepower V-8 and could do 175 miles per hour. Barney Oldfield and Harry Miller managed the car, with Bob McDonough driving. It qualified for the 500 in 1932, but left with a hot motor after

seven laps. Frank Brisko drove it in the 1933 race, again experiencing engine problems. In 1934, it ran with a new four-cylinder engine and led the race for the first 177 miles and again at 280 miles. A broken oil tank overflow pipe slowed the car down and, at 322 laps, Rex Mays took over and finished ninth. Mauri Rose drove the car in 1935 and 1936, coming in fourth the latter year. He probably would have won, except that he ran out of gas, which was rationed that year. After World War II, William F. Milliken, Jr. of Cornell Aeronautical Laboratory, borrowed the car to do research on four-wheel drive handling by racing it in hillclimbs and road races. He set a Pike's Peak record in the FWD race car in 1946. It raced as late as 1952, performing well against the era's top sports cars. All three of these FWD cars (as well as the Battleship's original steam engine) survive. Most are still in a small company museum which is no longer regularly open. Also resting there are several early FWD trucks and a second race car built in the 1950s. Check used book stores for a copy of *THE FOUR WHEEL DRIVE STORY* written by Howard William, Troyer. It was published by McGraw-Hill in 1954.

Q. Could you please tell me the names of the 10 oldest makes of automobiles still in production and the year that each of these companies started? L.F., Ohio.
A. Any list is open to revision, but here are 10 automobiles that are at least among the oldest still being manufactured and their founding years: Mercedes Benz (1886); Renault (1898); Fiat (1899); Cadillac (1902); Ford (1903); Oldsmobile (1903); Buick (1903); Rolls-Royce (1904); Lancia (1906); and Dodge (1914).

Q. Can you furnish information on the SPA Truck Corporation, of South Bend, Indiana? I have such a truck with Buick hubcaps on the front axle. V.A.V., Minnesota.
A. Though not shown in several standard references, J.H.M. Jones Jr. found facts about this make in *STUDEBAKER: THE COMPLETE STORY* written by Bill Cameron and Fred Fox. Studebaker and Pierce-Arrow merged briefly in the late 1920s to early 1930s. Studebaker made light- and medium-duty trucks, while Pierce made medium- and heavy-duty models. The SPA Truck Corporation was a combination of the two firms' commercial vehicle divisions. It produced only one truly unique product, the 1930 series S 1-1/2-ton truck using a 70 horsepower Studebaker six. By 1932, SPA gained temporary control of White Motor Company, which built White and Indiana trucks. The economic depression of the 1930s prompted Studebaker to dissolve the SPA conglomerate. White resumed building trucks as a relatively independent manufacturer. Studebaker stayed in the truck market through the 1960s. Obviously, the hubcaps on the truck you have are not original equipment.

Q. Who was the first United States President to ride in an automobile? What kind of car did he ride in? D. Carter, California.
A. Well, it wasn't your uncle Jimmy! According to the Automobile Manufacturers Association, the first U.S. President to go cruising around in a car was William McKinley. In November of 1899, he was seen riding in a steam carriage owned by F.O. Stanley, inventor of the Locomobile and Stanley Steamer. An automotive journal of the time noted, "Now that the horseless carriage has won the approval of the chief magistrate, its popularity will gain decided impetus." However, it wasn't until the administration of Howard Taft that the automobile became a White House institution. Taft replaced the stable of horses with a fleet of automobiles in 1909. As you may have heard, our latest president is a bit of a car hobbyist. Bill Clinton owns a 1967 Ford Mustang convertible.

Q. What year, make and model car had a headlight in the center of the grille that turned as the car was steered around a corner? I know there was such a car, but my friends think I'm crazy. R.S., Michigan.

A. You are thinking of the Tucker, a uniquely styled and designed vehicle marketed for a brief time by entrepreneur Preston Tucker of Ypsilanti, Michigan. Only 51 Tuckers were made before financial regulatory agencies closed the operation down. The late Tom McCahill, one of America's foremost car experts, tested the car and thought it was great. All Tuckers had three headlights. The center "Cyclops" light did turn with the wheels, illuminating the road in the direction in which the driver steered. Although they are rare, Tuckers are easy to see today. Simply go down to your local video rental outlet and borrow a copy of the motion picture "Tucker: The Man and His Dream." It is a romanticized, but well-done history of the company and its founder starring Jeff Bridges as Preston Tucker.

Q. In the 1950s, I understand there was a Mexican Road Race or Pan-American Road race or both. I spoke with the original owner of a 1957 car that I have. He stated he was able to purchase the car since the man originally ordering it did not pick it up because the race was canceled. To verify this story I'm wondering if you have any knowledge of either of these races or any other that may have had its last running in 1956. The car I have was built the last part of April and wouldn't have been delivered until May. I have also considered the possibility that the car was ordered, but not produced in time for some race that may have been run during or prior to April 1957. B.E., California.

A. The Mexican Road Race (also called the La Carrera Panamericana) covered 1,912 miles of tortuous driving from Tuxtla Gutierrez near the Guatemala border to Ciudad Juarez just across the Rio Grande from El Paso, Texas. Altitudes ranged from sea level to 10,500 feet. The race was started in 1950 and immediately became an international event. Crowds were uncontrollable and deaths from cars careening into crowds were numerous. For this reason the Mexican government outlawed the race in 1954. You don't mention the make of your car or whether or not it is equipped with special racing equipment (heavy-duty engine, brakes, suspension). These would give the best clue as to whether your car had been specially ordered and became available at the cancellation of some particular racing event.

Q. I recently purchased a 1964 Dodge Custom Special pickup D100. On the door frame data plate all categories are marked "Special." On the decal it lists, SERT Summary #28327; exhaust systems #13540; engine and transmission #13899; power steering #15737; torque rods #18404; tachometer #56018. The VIN is 118-1343870. This truck appears to have all its original equipment: Brakes, power steering, bucket seats and trim. Is this supposed to be a 426 cubic-inch "street wedge" V-8 truck? If so, what is the code? The truck has had the short block replaced. How or where can I find an original block? Is production known? How many survive? Where can I get copies of the SERT documentation? What value does this truck have when it is returned to its original engine type? S.E., Oregon.

A. The Custom Sport Special was an option package for the D100, D200, W100 and W200 series full-size Dodge pickups in 1964. It could be ordered with either the narrow Utiline box or wide Sweptline box. Trucks with this option package had sporty looks inside and out. Black vinyl bucket seats and a console were borrowed from Dodge passenger cars. Dual armrests and sun visors also contributed to an upscale interior. The Custom Sport Special featured a chrome grille, bumper and roof moldings, as well as four-inch-wide sport-type racing stripes that ran the length of the hood and across the cab roof. The 426 cubic-inch "street wedge" V-8 engine was available. I do not have the code information for the Custom Sports Special and suggest you contact the Light Commercial Vehicle Association, 316 Berkley Court, Jonesboro, Tennessee 37659. Contact MoPar Performance Headquarters, PO Box 2117, Farmington Hills, Michigan 48333 or call (313) 553-4566 regarding sources of an engine block. Production figures are unavailable. Only two of these trucks are known to survive. Dodge truck expert Don Bunn says, "If you stumble on one, especially a 426 powered Custom Sports Special, buy it. It's a rare and valuable truck which will appreciate and be a lot of fun to own and drive."

Q. Were any U.S. passenger autos produced, perhaps for military staff cars, between 1943 and 1945? If so, were they serial numbered as 1942 models? If none were produced here, were any produced elsewhere such as South America? For a number of reasons, 1942 was an unusual automotive year. Is there any plan to do a feature article on this one year? K.H., Kentucky.

A. To fill its staff car needs, the military used cars that had been built in 1941 and 1942 and put into storage. These were serial numbered as 1941 and 1942 models. Although manufacturers, notably Chevrolet, were allowed to build a few light- and medium-duty trucks after mid-1944, we are not aware of any cars being built between early 1942 and VE day here or in other countries. In fact, an interesting tidbit of information that we recently picked up from the new *STANDARD CATALOG OF MILITARY VEHICLES 1940-1965* is that the great bulk of World War II military vehicle production was completed by 1943. Author Tom Berndt indicates that the conversion to wartime production was made so smoothly that the majority of the military's needs were filled by that time. Civilian-type cars used by the military were finished as black-out models with painted trim. Recently, we came across an article in a 1941 edition of *AUTOMOBILE DIGEST* that documented how an American car was blacked-out in England. It said, "By order of His Majesty's Air Raid Prevention Bureau, this Pontiac Special Six sedan has been painted to conform with British black-out regulations. A broad stripe of bright, white paint outlines the car for the safety of pedestrians who might otherwise walk into it during the lightless nights. Bumpers also must be painted white. Headlamps have been painted blue except for thin 'monitor' slots, which deflect the beam downward and reduce it to a few candlepower. Parking lamps are painted out entirely. Specifications for this car were furnished by Kaye Don, well-known speedboat enthusiast and Pontiac's distributor in England, Scotland and North Ireland." Your idea of an article on 1942 automotive history and production is a good one. Maybe one of the automotive journalists will pick up on it.

Q. I have a 1966 Ford F-100 Twin-I-Beam 4x4 extended wheelbase pickup with coil springs in front and leaf springs in back. The transmission is a four-speed manual type. The transfer case tucks up high under the vehicle, which puts the differential on the driver's side. I was told by an old time parts man and Ford employee that this vehicle was one of only 1,000 produced. He knew this through locating steering box parts, which came direct from Detroit. He also said that production was stopped and held up for 10 years. What can you add to his information? F.D., New Jersey.

A. There is nothing in any literature I have seen on Ford's using independent front suspension (Twin-I-Beam) with four-wheel drive. The Bronco, which first appeared in 1966, used coil springs in front like the Twin-I-Beam suspension, but the front end had what Ford called a "Mono-Beam" (rigid) axle. If your truck does indeed have an independent front suspension with a front-drive axle, it would for sure be a very low production unit.

Q. I have a 1957 Oldsmobile Super 88 J-2 that I bought new. The serial number is 578A13031. According to my information, General Motors built 32,155 Super 88s. Since my car was built in Atlanta, Georgia, my question is how many were built in Atlanta? J.C.S., South Carolina.

A. The correct production number for 1957 Oldsmobile Super 88 Holiday coupes is 31,155. According to *THE STANDARD CATALOG OF AMERICAN CARS 1946-1975* the 1957 Oldsmobile Super 88 serial numbers assigned to the Atlanta plant were 578A1001 to 578A13297. As you can see, your car with its 578A13031 serial number was built very near the end of the Atlanta plant's 1957 production run.

Q. I recently acquired a 1957 Lloyd Alexander 600 two-door station wagon and a 1960 Lloyd van. Are any Lloyd clubs or newsletters? Are there other places where I could find spare parts and share information? Do you have production figures, values or other information on these cars? M.H., Michigan.

A. We show a listing for the Lloyd in *THE STANDARD CATALOG OF IMPORTED CARS 1946-1990*. It tells us that the car's German manufacturer has automotive roots dating all the way back to 1906. Dr. Carl Borgward revived the firm, as part of the Hansa and Goliath group, after World War II. Offered in 1949 was the LP300, a mini-car with front-wheel-drive and a two-stroke engine. The first year for the Alexander model was 1957, when your car was built. The catalog does not cover vans, but does give a thumbnail history of the 1960-1961 passenger car models. There is no price guide listing for Lloyd, due to lack of information about actual sales. We cannot find a listing for anyone specializing in these marques, but there are many local shops that repair vintage imported cars that may be of help. Check in your area Yellow Pages. Lloyd lover Rick Bachmann reports that there are two clubs in the United States for owners of Lloyd cars. They are the Borgward Owners Club (attention Dick Livant), 77 New Hampshire Avenue, Bay Shore, New York 11706 and the Microcar and Minicar Club (c/o Rick Bachmann), 2 Second Street, North Arlington, New Jersey 07031. The Microcar and Minicar Club is dedicated to the preservation and restoration of small and unusual cars, foreign and domestic, usually with engine displacements under 1,000 cubic centimeters. A recent club newsletter contained a road test of the Lloyd Alexander.

Q. I have reason to believe that the following car was the first or one of the first of its type to be produced. It is a 1954 Nash Metropolitan convertible with the following information on the data tag: Body number 4729; model number 541; trim number T-1; vehicle number E-4756. If you or your readers can help me authenticate or confirm the production sequence of this car, I would greatly appreciate it. F.C., Wisconsin.

A. The Metropolitan was built for Nash in England, by Austin. There were two series. The series 54, which your car belongs to, was built from 1954 to 1956. The series 56 was built from 1956 to 1957. The basic difference is a larger engine for the series 56 cars, plus a different paint scheme. Also, the later series cars did not carry the fake hood scoop. The Metropolitan sold quite well in its initial model year with 13,095 built. From the vehicle and body numbers you listed, I would have difficulty believing that this car is the first of the series. Manufacturers usually begin a serial number sequence at 0001 or 1000. In either case, your car's serial number of 4756 suggests that it was built approximately a third of the way through the first year model run. The body number 4729 also suggests that the car is not from the start of the production run. Metropolitan bodies came from a separate supplier, hence the slightly different sequence in the body and serial numbers on your car.

10

Q. I believe I have one of the first Ford Broncos made. It is serial number U14FL733991. Could you tell me when it was built? D.L., Montana.

A. According to the *CATALOG OF FORD TRUCK ID NUMBERS 1946-1972* published by *CARS & PARTS*, the 1966 Bronco vehicle identification numbers were carried on a rating plate. The first three symbols identified the series and U14 indicated a Sports Utility model. The fourth digit identified the engine and F indicated a 170 cubic-inch V-8. The fifth symbol indicated the assembly plant and L indicated the factory at Lorain, Ohio. The last six numbers were the sequential production number. Broncos with numbers 732,000 through 745,999 were built during the first month of production, which was August of 1965. Your truck fits within this sequence and was one of the first 2,000.

Q. I own a 1951 Plymouth Concord three-passenger coupe that I have been restoring for the past five years. I have been to many car shows and to date I haven't seen another one like it. I was wondering how many were made and how many still exist? I was told that the three-passenger coupe was selected by NASCAR driver Lee Petty in the 1950s. Is this statement true or false? If an article has been written on NASCAR racing, how can I get a copy? I am also looking for information and parts for this car. W.B., New York.

A. Plymouth built 14,255 Concord three-passenger coupes in 1951, making this a fairly low production car when new. Forty years later it would be unlikely that more than five to 10 percent of these cars have survived. The circumstances where you would be most likely to see another would be at a Plymouth or Chrysler Products collectors meet. It's true that Lee Petty (father of Richard Petty) selected a Plymouth for stock car racing on the NASCAR circuit in 1950. The hot car of that year was the Oldsmobile 88, but Petty reasoned that the Plymouth's lighter weight and better fuel economy would give him the advantage of not having to make as many pit stops for gas and tires as the driver's of larger, heavier cars. The strategy worked and Petty placed second in NASCAR standings that year. Another driver, Johnny Mantz, also chose a Plymouth after he wrecked his Oldsmobile 88. His choice was largely due to the reputation established by Lee Petty. Mantz was able to cut his pit stops to three and replace only right-hand side tires. The Plymouth he drove never blew a tire, although the Oldsmobiles that tried to keep up with him did. You will find this information and more details on early 1950s NASCAR racing in Phil Hall's article "Jalopies Blazed the Trail for Modern Stock Racers" which is reprinted in the *BEST OF OLD CARS,* Volume 1. For information and parts help, I suggest that you contact the Plymouth 4 and 6 Cylinder Owners Club, 203 Main Street East, Box 416, Cavalier, North Dakota 58220.

Q. I have been watching in old car magazines that my son receives and have never seen anything about the Halladay automobile. I bought a farm my grandfather owned and discovered several old car parts. One is a brass foot-feed with the name Halladay cast into it. There is the bottom of a door plate, made of brass, with the Halladay name on it. Also, there is a hood and large magneto. The body has a brass nameplate on it with Briscoe Manufacturing Company, Detroit, Michigan, U.S.A. stamped on it. It has a logo of two wheels with a wing-like fender over each wheel and a big "B" in between. I think it's from a 1909 model. I saw a picture of it long ago. It had right-hand steering with levers on the outside and a squeeze bulb horn. I have been to a lot of old car shows and nobody that I have talked to has even heard of it. I'd be interested to know if there were many of them made. H.B., Minnesota.

A. According to the *STANDARD CATALOG OF AMERICAN CARS 1805-1942*, Halladays were built from 1905 to 1922 and were produced in Illinois and Ohio. In the early years, about 900 cars were produced annually. A note of some historical significance is that Eddie Rickenbacker, who later went on to build a car carrying his name, got his start at Halladay. The Briscoe was a different, unrelated marque. It was produced by Benjamin Briscoe in Jackson, Michigan between 1914 and 1921. An unusual feature of early Briscoes was a center-mounted headlamp in the middle of the radiator shell at the top. Briscoe tried to form United Motors, an "umbrella" corporation of different automobile companies, to compete with General Motors. He joined forces with Jonathan D. Maxwell for a time. United Motors failed. Later, he formed Briscoe Motor Corporation and manufactured some 40,000 Briscoe automobiles over a seven-year period.

The 1915 Halladay Light Six Touring.

Q. Chevrolet and GMC from 1967-1972 had extra-long bed pickups called the Longhorn (Chevrolet) and Sierra Grande (GMC). There was also a long-bed Chevrolet Camper Special. I have developed an interest in these trucks. What can you tell me? W.R.M., California.

A. According to the *STANDARD CATALOG OF AMERICAN LIGHT-DUTY TRUCKS*, Chevrolet built the Longhorn from 1969 to 1972. The C20 3/4-ton Fleetside Longhorn pickup had a special longer 133-inch wheelbase and 8-1/2 foot bed to accommodate oversize loads and pickup campers. The C30 1-ton Fleetside pickup also had a 133-inch wheelbase and an 8.5-foot bed. In this case, the wheelbase wasn't especially long (most C-30 models had the same 133-inch stance), but the Longhorn name was still used. GMC also made Longhorns from at least 1969 on. I think the GMC Longhorn nameplate was on the rear quarter, in the same place that Chevrolet placed it. A Camper Special package RPO Z81 was available for Longhorn trucks. Truck collector Jon Bagley told me about a red 1970 GMC Longhorn in his town. With the 8-1/2-foot bed it is great for hauling long lengths of pipe for a local plumber. Truck buff Joseph Wright owns a 1972 GMC Longhorn 3500 series (1-ton) with Sierra trim and a 1971 Chevrolet Custom 20 Longhorn. The major difference between the GMC and Chevrolet models, besides the grille, is that the GMC does not have the Longhorn script on the bed. Wright believes that all 1-ton GMC pickups (133-in. wheelbase) were Longhorns

12

and that some 3/4-ton models were built as such. He also learned that the exhaust system on these trucks was custom-built at the factory and that no replacement parts were produced. This attests to the limited quantity of these vehicles. The Longhorn pickups are indeed rare and desirable trucks. I am told that occasionally one can be found working on farms in the Great Plains states, but they are not often seen at shows. One Longhorn Chevrolet pickup is owned by the Light Commercial Vehicle Association (a club for pickup and panel truck owners and enthusiasts). Often, the club's newsletter carries articles about this Longhorn pickup. If you want to contact them to learn more about this limited-production pickup, you can write to LCVA, 316 Berkley Court, Jonesborough, Tennessee 37659.

Q. I have a 1957 Cadillac Eldorado Seville with the 365 cubic-inch, 325 horsepower, dual four-barrel carburetor engine. I understand that there were only 2,000 or 2,100 of these 1957 Eldorados made and that only a certain number of these were equipped with double four-barrel carburetors. Can you tell me how I can find out the actual statistics? Also, the seller told me that this car was once owned by movie actress Rita Hayworth. However, he does not have any paperwork to authenticate this statement. Can you tell me how I may be able to verify this ownership? C.J.S. III, Georgia.
A. Production figures are usually listed only by model and not by engine options or other special equipment. Industry trade publications list engine production for different corporations, according to displacement, for later model years. They did not list this information in 1957. The production figure of 2,100 is correct for your 1957 Eldorado Seville Coupe, but none of our sources show how many of these cars were equipped with the optional 325 horsepower dual four-barrel carburetor engine. This motor was optional for the Eldorado Seville and Biarritz only. As to authenticating former ownership, you can sometimes have the state motor vehicle departments do an ownership trace. This can get expensive. If the car has passed through a number of owners, a fee is levied for each owner who turns up.

Q. Recently I purchased a most unusual car. It's a 1974 Cadillac Fleetwood Talisman. What's unique about this car is the interior, four-place individual seating with huge consoles front and rear. The local Cadillac dealer told me these cars are very uncommon, having been built only for two years. Can you elaborate on this? C.G., Florida.
A. The Talisman (a name that means magical or miraculous effects) was a special option in the Fleetwood. It consisted of regal-style seating for four with deeply cushioned armchair seats. The upholstered consoles between the seats contained an illuminated writing set in the front and vanity in the rear (implying that women rode in the back seats?). The front passenger seat had a reclining feature and carpeting was a rich Medici crushed velour. Our STANDARD CATALOG OF AMERICAN CARS 1946-1975 states that a leather trim package was also available on the Talisman for "only $100 less than a brand new 1974 four-cylinder Ford Pinto two-door sedan!" Opulent is the only word to describe this car's interior. A Talisman script on the rear roof quarters and special turbine wheel disks (which were part of the Brougham d'Elegance package) are ways to recognize this special model from the exterior. My information shows that the Talisman was available through 1976, but as a special option model in the Fleetwood series, no production figures are given.

Q. I just purchased a Cadillac. It is a 1947 Cadillac 47-500 with the manufacturer's serial number 8083 built by Hess & Eisenhardt in Ohio. It has six doors and a 15-foot wheelbase. It has dual rear glass, one behind the rear seat and another just above the trunk door. The body has no running boards. The trunk door is completely different from other Cadillacs in that it is streamlined from the roof like a 1940 Plymouth. How many of this model were built? Who was the car built for? P.K., California.

A. The car you describe would be a special model built on the Cadillac series 75 commercial chassis. According to the Crestline book *AMERICAN FUNERAL CARS & AMBULANCES SINCE 1900* the Cincinnati firm Sayers & Scovill Company, established in 1876, changed ownership in the late 1930s and took the corporate name Hess & Eisenhardt in 1942. The Crestline book *80 YEARS OF CADILLAC LaSALLE* shows a car exactly like you are describing on page 272. It identifies it as a 47-500 Airline Coach and says, "This nine-passenger car had an oversized trunk to carry the luggage of eight passengers." The *STANDARD CATALOG OF AMERICAN CARS 1946-1975* tells us that Cadillac built 2,423 commercial chassis in 1947. That's the closest we can get to a figure indicating the rarity of your vehicle. You might want to contact the Professional Car Society, PO Box 09636, Columbus, Ohio 43209.

Q. I have a 1942 GPW Jeep. I plan to restore it. How can I find literature on this vehicle? J.P., Arizona.

A. Look for *THE ALL-AMERICAN WONDER: THE MILITARY JEEP 1941-1945*, Volumes I and II, by Ray Cowdery. These books contain incredible detail, from the history of the Jeep's design and development, to restoration instructions, to correct military markings, to Jeep lore you never even imagined. They are available from Northstar Books, Box 803, Lakeville, Minnesota 55044.

Q. Would you be able to give me information on where I can find a picture of a 1932 Nash? J.H., Arizona.

A. Our *STANDARD CATALOG OF AMERICAN CARS 1805-1942* has two pictures of 1932 Nash models. You may be able to obtain information about sources of 1932 Nash photos by contacting the Nash Car Club of America, 635 Lloyd Street, Hubbard, Ohio 44425. Another source of Nash photos and illustrations is John Conde, 1340 Fieldway Drive, Bloomfield Hills, Michigan 48013. Mr. Conde, an automotive historian and former AMC public relations executive sells books and historic automobile literature. His phone number is (313) 338-4478.

Q. I am considering selling my 1967 Dodge Coronet 440. This car has a special "White Hat Special" option package. It came as a fully-equipped two-door hardtop powered by a 383 cubic-inch V-8 with a two-barrel carburetor. Extras included power steering, power brakes, air conditioning, automatic transmission and a white vinyl top. The VIN code is WH23G77170323. Can you tell me the production number for this specific car? Can you give me a ballpark price in number 2 condition? C.K., Michigan.

A. Chrysler Corporation marketed a number of special option packages. Some were sold in regional or seasonal sales promotions, although the White Hat Special sale was a national promotion. As option packages, rather than models, the promotional specials are not specified in production figures. In fact, Dodge records showing body style break-outs for the 1967 Coronet 440 series aren't public knowledge. The figures we have give a total number of 92,500 Coronet 400s of all body styles. Of these, 83,900 were equipped with V-8 engines. In general, 42.2 percent of all Chrysler products were two-door hardtops and 24.8 percent had the 383 cubic-inch V-8. By applying these percentages to the general totals, you can make a reasonable estimate of production for your body style and engine. Of all Coronets built (including base, Deluxe, 400 and 500 models) 21.4 percent had vinyl tops. This can be worked into your estimate, too. Some information on the VIN number may be of interest to you. The first symbol "W" represents Coronet. The second symbol "H" stands for high-trim class (deluxe model). The third and fourth symbols show that your car is a two-door hardtop and the fifth symbol stands for the 383 cubic-inch V-8. The sixth digit is for the year 1967. The seventh digit indicates the assembly plant, St. Louis for your car. The remaining digits are the sequential production number. According to the latest *OLD CARS PRICE GUIDE* a 1967 Coronet 440 two-door hardtop in number 2 condition has a value of $5,900. We cannot say whether a buyer might be willing to pay a premium for the White Hat Special option package. Our guess would be that its greatest value would be as a contributing factor to the car's overall eye appeal and condition.

Q. I recently purchased a 1956 Chevrolet 150 four-door sedan. It is a six-cylinder car with a column-shifted three-speed transmission. It is also an old U.S. Army staff car. The trunk interior is original olive drab paint and the car has no factory paint code. It even has a flag holder in the rear. I have called three army forts for information, but so far no one has been able to help me as to where the car was used. If you or your readers could help I surely would appreciate it. The serial number is A56A113061. Also, is this a rare car? I have been going to car shows for 20 years and I have never seen a 1956 Chevrolet staff car. B.L., South Carolina.
A. This reminds me of a story I heard about 1957 Chevrolets being used as unmarked military police cars in Germany during the 1960s. It seems that the undercover MPs were easy to spot, since everyone knew they used most of the 1957 Chevrolets in Germany then. Researching your serial number shows the prefix A56 to stand for a 1956 Chevrolet 1500 series (150 model) six-cylinder Chevrolet. The fourth symbol indicates the Atlanta, Georgia assembly plant where the car was built. This suggests that your car may have seen duty on an army base in the South or Southeast. Beyond that, unless you can get access to government motor pool records, it would be difficult to find out where it was used. I don't have figures on Chevrolet production in 1956 for the U.S. Government, but the number of cars purchased by the U.S. Army was probably not extremely large.

Q. I have acquired a 1951 Pontiac six-cylinder sedan-coupe. The serial number is P6UH 1256. The previous owner (who was a member of the Pontiac-Oakland Club International) wondered if this was the oldest six-cylinder 1951 Pontiac still known to be on the highway. Can you help? Also, is it true that all 1951 Pontiacs were considered "Silver Anniversary" models? J.M., Wisconsin.
A. There is probably no way of knowing whether yours is the oldest 1951 Pontiac six still on the highway. However, we can tell you that serial numbers for cars with sixes and stick shift started at serial number P6US 1001 and ended at P6US 24016 and that cars with a six and automatic transmission were numbered P6UH 1001 through P6UH 2406. What these numbers show is that your car was in the early part of the run. How many that were ahead of it are still running would be impossible to ascertain unless the owners of all similar cars that came earlier in the production run could be contacted. The answer to your question about all 1951 Pontiacs being considered "Silver Anniversary" models is yes. Pontiac was introduced in January 1926 as a companion car to the Oakland built in Pontiac, Michigan. Until the Saturn came along, Pontiac was the only new General Motors nameplate introduced after the formation of the corporation in 1908 to survive.

Q. Chevrolet claimed its optional fuel-injected 283 cubic-inch engine of 1957 was "the first mass-production engine with one horsepower per cubic inch." Can anyone explain how Chevrolet could make this claim to fame when Chrysler exceeded one horsepower per cubic inch the year before? F.J.M., New Hampshire.

15

A. In 1956, Chrysler produced the 300B letter car. With 354 cubic inches, 10.0:1 compression heads and dual four-barrel carburetors, this hemi-engined car produced as much as 355 horsepower. The 355 horsepower engine was only available in the 300B with stick shift, while the 283 was optionally available in several models. However, if we're comparing engines, rather than car models, both engines were listed as "optional" and both were available to anyone who had the money. I'd have to believe they were both "mass-produced." So Chevrolet engines were certainly not the first ones to exceed one horsepower per cubic inch, but in the marketplace credit goes to whomever best publicizes an achievement, not to whom it first occurs. I recall seeing the one horsepower per cubic inch ads in sports car magazines in 1957 and being mighty impressed that Chevrolet had done it again. Most who saw those ads did not have the Chrysler 300B specifications in front of them and I don't recall any automotive editors debunking the ads. It'd be nice to think that inaccurate ad claims like this couldn't be put over on the public today, but I'm not so sure that our gullibility has changed all that much. In partial defense of Chevrolet's claim, most Chrysler 300Bs that got the 355 horsepower motor were marketed specifically to those who intended to race them, such as Carl Kiekhaefer and the number of such cars built was quite small.

Q. While recently paging though an old 1925 newspaper, I saw an ad for a Jewett Model 640 car. In the ad it mentioned hydraulic four-wheel brakes and a silent chain front-end drive. Did this car really have front-wheel drive and four-wheel hydraulic brakes? What were the years this car was manufactured and who made it? J.L., Minnesota.

A. The newspaper you found must have been printed near the end of 1925 because Jewett's 1926 line introduced four-wheel hydraulic brakes. The cars in the line were called "New Day" models. They had a six-cylinder 40 horsepower engine. Jewett cars were built by the Paige-Detroit Motor Car Company from 1922 to 1927. They did not feature front-wheel drive. "Silent chain front-end drive" was a reference to the timing chain mechanism. In January of 1927, the Jewett name was dropped and the car continued to be sold under the Paige nameplate. In June of that year, the company was sold to the Graham brothers. The Paige name continued as part of the new Graham-Page Motors Corporation.

Q. I have a 1979 Thunderbird Heritage. This car was supposedly produced in only two colors: blue and dark red. My Heritage model is white with a white roof and side trim. The interior, the bumper impact strips and the grille accents are dark red. The car features gold accent stripes. The previous owner bought the car new at a Ford factory sale in November 1979. He was told that the white Heritage model was made for Ford vice presidents and that only 50 were produced for Ford vice presidents. Do you have any information concerning this? I have not been able to verify the previous owner's claim and wonder if anyone remembers the white Heritage edition. Any help would be useful in authenticating this unusual Thunderbird. V.P., New York.

A. Gene Makrancy, president of The Ranchero Club, says the Heritage Thunderbird was a continuation of the 1978 Diamond Jubilee model with many refinements. It provided Ford dealers with a premium-priced model and gave Ford of Canada a special model for its Diamond Jubilee in 1979. Originally the car's color choices were Light Medium Blue (code 3F) and Maroon (code 2J). The only Heritage options, besides the two color choices, were leather seat surfaces, an eight-track quadra-sonic tape, a moon roof and a 357 cubic-inch V-8. Everything else was standard equipment including a hand-sewn leather crash pad, luxury cloth upholstery, an ebony wood applique for the dash and knobs and 25-ounce cut-pile carpet throughout (even in the luggage compart-

16

ment and the underside of the deck lid.) The blind-quarter roof upholstery was the same color as the body paint, as was the side trim, bumper rub strips, grille inserts and turbine wheel inserts. Makrancy studied the Heritage Thunderbirds closely, since he had purchased a new 1979-1/2 Ford Limited-Production Ranchero, which was created from composites of Heritage parts. While at a dealership in 1979, he spotted a white Heritage Thunderbird, opened the door, and saw the 9D paint code for Polar White. A friend at Ford Motor Company told Makrancy that only two colors were originally planned for these cars, but that an executive viewing a white car felt a spring color should be added to the Heritage and so it was tried. Based on one car found in a salvage yard, Makrancy believes that early-production white Heritage models may have a blank color code indicator instead of one reading 9D. There is no documentation that only 50 cars were made. In fact, Jim Neuhart was a Ford dealer in 1979 and says that the white Heritage Thunderbird was offered to all Ford dealers late in the 1979 production run. He recalls that 1979 came on the heels of two very successful sales seasons, and that the 1979 Fords got caught in a major sales crunch due to a recession. Neuhart says that the factory was pushing Ford Thunderbirds and Mercury Cougars to dealers to clear inventories before the 1980 models came out. As a spring offering, the Heritage was made available in white, as well as the original colors. As to how many were built, Neuhart feels the answer is as many as the dealer body could absorb at the time. Incidentally, the 1979 Lincoln "Collector Series" was also made available in white late in the season. It came complete with a gold grille and Collector Series appliques. Many Ford and Lincoln-Mercury factory representatives drove these future collector cars in 1979, since they were not selling well to the public. This might explain why your Heritage was sold at a closed factory auction. A factory representative was probably assigned to put some miles on it, then sell it through an auction.

Q. I would like to know if you could tell me the value of a 1971 GMC Sprint pickup? It is basically the same as an El Camino. Mine is a base model. It has a 307 cubic-inch engine and Turbo-Hydramatic transmission. It is in number 2 or number 3 condition. There doesn't seem to be much information about trucks like these. M.L., Massachusetts.

A. According to our heavily-revised new second edition of THE *STANDARD CATALOG OF AMERICAN LIGHT-DUTY TRUCKS*, this model is worth $7,400 and $4,200, respectively, in the condition classifications you note. The *ILLUSTRATED CHEVROLET PICKUP BUYER'S GUIDE* offered by Motorbooks International states that the El Camino was an exclusively Chevrolet product until 1971. Then, GMC introduced its El Camino variant called the Sprint. This model differed from the El Camino in trim and nameplates only. From the collector's standpoint, your truck is of some interest because it is considerably rarer than an El Camino.

Q. How many 1968 Dodge Monaco 500 series convertibles were made in 1968? Mine was made in Windsor, Canada and has serial number DP27F8R349751. C.A., Ontario, Canada.

A. Only 3,400 Monacos of all types were built. Your Monaco 500 convertible is even rarer since it was a Canadian-only model. In the United States the Monaco 500 line for 1968 offered only a two-door hardtop. In Canada, both a Monaco 500 hardtop and convertible were offered. Your Monaco 500 convertible uses the same special interior and exterior trim as an American Monaco 500 hardtop combined with the Polara convertible body shell.

Q. I have been going to write you for years regarding a car that I saw in the Los Angeles, California auto salon about 1930. I was sure it was an American car by one of the coach makers of that era. Does anyone remember a car with two seats that had a single door on each side that opened to give access to both seats? Everyone at the show thought it would be the "coming thing" because, in those days of small folding jump seats, it was a real struggle to get in the back seat. I found a picture of a car similar to the one I saw at Los Angeles in the issue of *MOTOR* magazine covering the 1930 London and Paris auto shows. B.M., California.

A. The car in the photocopy you sent us from the show issue of *MOTOR* is a Lancia five-passenger coupe made in Italy. The single wide door can be opened from either end, giving access to the front seat, the back seat or both seats. The illustration shows handles at both ends of the door and the text states, "All that is required is to turn the knob at this end and the mechanism automatically brings the hinges on the other end into action." However, it is not likely that this is the car you saw at the Los Angeles auto salon. According to car buff Jim Griffin, Brunn Custom Body Company created a special "Double Entry Sport Sedan" on a 145-inch wheelbase, 1932 Lincoln KB chassis. It was built for the New York Auto show held in November 1931. This car was scheduled to be shown at a California Salon Show at the Los Angeles Biltmore Hotel shortly thereafter. However, a Rochester, New York doctor insisted on taking immediate delivery of it. This forced Brunn to push through the production of a second Double Entry model for the California show. This car, which was sold right off the Biltmore Hotel show floor, is most likely the car that you saw. It had a large door equipped with hinges, latches and door handles on each end. Collector Bob Bickley adds that both 1932 Lincoln V-12 Double Entry Sport Sedans were pictured in the FORK and BLADE publication of the Lincoln Owners Club in January-March 1992. Historian Jim Petrik notes that, while Brunn called these cars sedans, they were actually two-door models resembling a Club Coupe or Victoria. Automotive historian Herman Sass of Buffalo, New York also remembers a picture of either a Lincoln or a Pierce-Arrow, bodied by Brunn, that had this type of entry system. He suggests that the design was possibly copied from Lancia.

Q. I have a 1956 La Dare (sic) and have been unable to locate any information about this car. It has a fiberglass body sitting on a 1956 Thunderbird drive train and a 327 cubic-inch Chevrolet engine with a two-speed Powerglide transmission. I have been told that this car is not considered to be a kit. It is a two-seater sports car. Could you please ask your readers if they have any information? J.P., Mississippi.

A. The car must be a LaDawri. Two distinctly different types of LaDawris were marketed. According to information in the new third edition of the *STANDARD CATALOG OF AMERICAN CARS 1946-1975*, the LaDawri Conquest was made in 1960 by LaDawri Coachcraft of Los Angeles, California. This sports roadster was the company's first product. Ads indicated that it was built for use on 100-inch wheelbase chassis and that it could be finished with bucket seats or a bench seat. In 1960, the LaDawri Conquest kit sold for $395. Later, LaDawri offered a sports coupe. Both models were marketed as body kits that could be mounted on a variety of chassis to produce instant sports cars. We have personally seen two LaDawris. The first was a roadster that we photographed at a car show in Manitowoc, Wisconsin many years ago. It had mid-1950s Ford running gear. The second was a coupe that we photographed at the Gilmore Museum in Kalamazoo, Michigan three or four years ago. It was owned by a General Motors engineer (not the original builder) and had, of all things, Oldsmobile Toronado running gear.

Q. I am interested in getting more information about my 1957 Borgward Isabella. For example, what years were these cars produced? Would the parts be interchangeable with any other cars? What would the value of this vehicle be in today's market? If the parts are not interchangeable, are parts currently available? Do you have an address for the manufacturer? I have checked with my local library and auto dealers and have not been able to find anything on this car at all. Any information you could give me would be most appreciated. V.T., Arizona.

A. According to the *STANDARD CATALOG OF IMPORTED CARS 1946-1990*, Borgward introduced the Isabella in 1954 and continued to build this model through 1961 when the company declared bankruptcy. In 1957, Borgward built a total of 23,258 Isabellas. This number includes all body styles offered. Since the Isabella was based on the Hansa 1500, many mechanical parts should interchange between these two cars. The catalog values the Isabella TS sport coupe at $3,300 in number three condition, $4,900 in number two and $7,000 in pristine number one condition. For parts help and other information on this attractively styled mid-1950s import, I suggest that you contact the Borgward Owner's Club, 77 Hampshire Avenue, Bay Shore, New York 11706.

A 1957 Borgward Isabella coupe.

Q. Could you tell me when the first convertible sedan was built and who built it? By convertible sedan I mean a car with four doors, a convertible top and roll-up glass windows. R.R., Jr., Delaware.

19

A. Cadillac offered a Town Car with a removable chauffeur's compartment covering and a collapsible rear top in 1926. Although this car would probably qualify as a convertible sedan in the sense that it had four doors, a convertible top and roll-up glass windows (at least in the passenger compartment), it would not be considered a convertible sedan in the usual sense. The earliest car with that body style designation that I've personally encountered is a Dietrich design offered for the 1929 Lincoln. History buff Jim Petrik told me that he has photos of a 1925 Rolls-Royce and a 1928 Stutz with convertible sedan bodies.

Q. I have a 1957 Ford Tudor Sedan, model 300, with a 272 cubic-inch V-8 engine. This car was brought back from Hawaii by a serviceman in 1966. Were not many produced? Should I continue to house it and pamper it or is it a non-collectible? A.L., New York.
A. Ford built a whopping 160,360 Tudor (two-door) sedans in the 300 series in 1957. I remember these cars being almost as plentiful as rainwater in my high school years. Most have fallen prey to the "tin worm" or have just been used up. In my opinion, your car is a very nice representation of a very pleasant era and one you should continue to preserve with loving care. *OLD CARS PRICE GUIDE* values your car at $4,200 in number two condition.

Q. I recently purchased a 1/2-ton Reo Speed Wagon pickup. The title indicates it was the 156th unit built in 1937. I have seen a lot of large Reo trucks, but never a 1/2-ton pickup. How many were built? Are there any other notes of interest about this truck? D.W., Iowa.
A. An article titled "Reo Truck History" written by Raymond W. Wood appeared in the March/April 1987 issue of the Light Commercial Vehicle Association's newsletter. It states that Reo introduced a 1/2-ton pickup with a six-foot express box and a step-up roofed panel (like Dodge's well-known "humpback" panel truck) in 1935. According to Wood, a suburban station wagon was also available on this chassis. These models were continued in 1936 virtually unchanged. For 1937, Reo reworked its light truck line, moving the engine and cab forward on the frame. The restyled cab was wider and had a veed windshield. The front fenders had full shields behind the wheels and the truck sported a chrome grille with vertical bars giving a "waterfall" appearance. Reo offered this 1/2-ton pickup through 1939. With a four-cylinder engine it was called the model 450. With a six-cylinder engine it was model 650. Both were available on either a short 114-inch wheelbase or a longer 120-inch wheelbase. Wheelbase length is noted by either an "S" or an "L" after the model (i.e., 450S or 450L). The engines were supplied by Continental and both the four- and six-cylinder versions are called Silver Crown engines. The four-cylinder displaced 140 cubic inches and carried a 45 horsepower rating. The six-cylinder displaced 209 cubic inches and produced 70 horsepower. No production figures are given for Reo's light trucks, but I can tell you that very few exist today. Rarer still is a version of this pickup that Reo built for Mack called the Mack Junior. These trucks, which Mack contracted Reo to build between 1936 and 1938, were identical to the Reo-badged versions in all respects, except for their Mack nameplates, the famous Mack bulldog perched atop the grille and two chrome bars that wrapped around the grille and extended along the sides of the hood. Many feel that these bars interrupt Reo's otherwise clean frontal styling. Mack also offered buyers a choice of the Continental four- or six-cylinder engines. They called a short-wheelbased four-cylinder Mack Junior the 2M4A. In long wheelbase form, a six-cylinder version of this truck would be designated 2M6B. Mack also offered an up-rated 3/4-ton model with a heavier-duty rear end and 6.50 x 16 tires. In 1938, Mack introduced its own 1/2-ton ED model. It was possible that a Mack dealer, in 1938,

could have had two very different 1/2-ton pickups on display at the same time. One would have been built by Reo and the other by Mack.

Q. When the Ford Skyliner retractable hardtop came out in 1957, were there more Sunliners (the standard convertible) or more Skyliners (the retractable model) made? J.W., Oregon.
A. In 1957, Ford built 77,728 Sunliner convertibles and 20,766 Skyliner retractables. Although it was a uniquely designed automobile, there were several reasons for the lower sales of the retractable. First, the Skyliner cost about $350 more than the Sunliner. As a proportion of the base price, this represented almost a 15 percent premium on purchase price. Second, there were a lot of stories about the retractable's top not working on inconvenient occasions. Some reports claimed that Skyliner owners were stranded when the top stuck mid-way in its raising or lowering cycle. Others told of owners being caught in downpours unable to raise the top. A friend got a ride home from college in a new Skyliner, but was unable to get at her luggage stored in the trunk, because the top mechanism wouldn't unlatch the trunk lid. A third problem was that of very limited luggage space when the Skyliner's retractable hardtop was lowered. Whatever their problems as everyday drivers, as collectibles, Skyliners are wonderful novelties.

Q. I am restoring a car which was imported from South America and sold as a 1908 Studebaker. Having a copy of the *STANDARD CATALOG OF AMERICAN CARS 1805-1942*, I would think that the car is more likely to be an Everitt. The engine appears to have a displacement of approximately 1,700 cubic-centimeters. It is fitted with electrics. The carburetor is a Zenith with a December 1908 patent registration. The word Studebaker is on the hubcaps, which are cast and turned in brass. T.H., England.
A. The profile view of a 1910 Everitt inside-drive coupe shown in the catalog bears a close resemblance to your opera coupe body. However, I suggest that you contact the Studebaker National Museum, 520 South Lafayette Street, South Bend, Indiana 46601. They may be able to provide information or photocopies of 1908 sales catalogs in exchange for a reasonable research fee.

Q. The first Model A Ford was the 1928 Model, but the title for my car shows it as a 1927 model. Is it a rare car or a prototype? Did all early "AR" type Model As have shock absorbers? Mine does not have the frame drilled for shock absorbers. Did all Model A Fords come with pop-out switches? Mine has a Ford Model T type lock and key. J.E.S., Indiana.
A. You own an early 1928 Model A Ford (number 4406). Your paperwork indicates that it was sold on December 16, 1927. Indiana did not issue titles with new model years until after January 1. If the car had been sold after January 1, it would have been titled as a 1928 model. I have heard the designation AR applied to early Model As, specifically those built before mid-June in 1928. This designation comes from an AR stamping on some of the parts. One of the most notable AR features was the absence of a separate emergency brake system. When the driver pulled back on the emergency brake lever (located to the left of the clutch pedal), he moved the rear service brake shoes against the brake drums. Laws in several states and some foreign countries required a separate braking mechanism for the emergency brakes. The Model T had met the requirement because it had two braking systems. There was a brake mechanism on the rear wheels, which the driver engaged by a lever. It could be locked into position, thereby serving as an emergency brake. The Model Ts' second braking mech-

anism was in the planetary transmission. As to how Ford could sell Model As in violation of the laws, my response is that enforcement was much more lax than today. When word came to Ford Motor Company that sales would be prohibited in states where the AR brake design violated the law, Ford quickly changed to a separate parking brake. This required redesigning the rear brake drums and using different wheels. The earliest Model A passenger cars did not have shocks. Accordingly, the spring perches on these cars did not have an attachment ball for the shock link. Approximately the first 200 Model As were assembled without shocks, but it's believed that none of these were released to dealers. Model A club judging standards state that all Model As had pop-out style ignition switches. No mention is made of the use of Model T locks and keys on early cars, though with Ford's obsession with using up leftover parts, this would not be unusual. Ford owner Max Riebenack tells us that Ray Miller's book HENRY'S LADY has fairly comprehensive coverage of early 1928 Model AR features. One feature is a single shaft brake system, which was illegal in some states.

Q. A friend claims that the first Cadillac V-8 was offered in 1942. I claim that Cadillac came out with a V-8 in the year 1915. Who's right? J.L., Illinois.
A. You're closest, though Cadillac actually introduced its V-8 in September 1914. Over the next several decades, Cadillac would refine the V-8 into a masterpiece of smoothness and power.

Q. I recently purchased a 1959 Ford F-100 pickup with a factory installed four-wheel drive system. Is this the first year for four-wheel drive Fords? How many were made? Should I use it as a farm truck or should it be a "keeper?" L.F., Washington.
A. Prior to 1959, which was the first year that Ford equipped its pickups with four-wheel drive at the factory, Ford trucks could be fitted with an aftermarket four-wheel drive setup built by Marmon-Herrington. The increasing sales of four-wheel drive led Ford to engineer its own system. We don't have production figures for the number of Ford trucks built in 1959 with four-wheel drive. The F-100 production figures for that year are 26,616 Flareside narrow box pickups and 112,082 Styleside wide box pickups. A relatively small number of these were fitted with four-wheel drive. Personally, I would consider a solid truck with the useful and unusual four-wheel drive feature to be a keeper. You might want to contact the Light commercial Vehicle Association (a club devoted to light duty trucks of all makes), 316 Berkley Court, Jonesboro, Tennessee 37659 for information about events and activities you may wish to participate in with your collectible truck.

Q. I recently became the owner of a 1939 LaSalle opera coupe. The engine and transmission are not original and I would like very much to find the proper replacements. Also, the dash needs some original parts. The body is wonderful and the interior is complete. I would very much like to see this car back in its original condition. Can you help me find the information or parts I need? E.A., Minnesota.
A. Typically, the best place to start looking for original parts is to contact a club for your make and model car. In your case this would be the Cadillac LaSalle Club, Incorporated, 3083 Howard Road, Petosky, Michigan 49770. Clubs often allow members to place ads in their newsletters. They can also put you in touch with owners of similar cars who can help you locate needed parts.

Q. I go to auto museums whenever I travel. I have been looking for two cars in particular. One is my namesake, a Murray. I also wanted to find a 1929 Moon, which was my first. Is it possible none exist? I also own a 1952 Ford convertible. How many of these are left? J.L.M., California.

A. According to the *STANDARD CATALOG OF AMERICAN CARS 1805-1942*, six Murray car manufacturers existed in the start-up years of the automobile. In 1969, automotive historian Willard Prentice took a photo of a 1902 Murray then on display at Bellm's Cars and Music of Yesterday, 5500 North Tamiami Trail, Sarasota, Florida 34234. According to hobbyist David O. Lyon, a Murray car was built in Aldrin, Michigan in 1902 and 1903. One of these was among the first dozen cars to arrive in Kalamazoo, Michigan. It was purchased in July 1903 by Reverend Blekkink of the Second Reformed Church. He wanted to use it in his pastoral duties, but the good Reverend wrecked the car within 24 hours. He turned the steering gear in the wrong direction and ended up on a pile of rocks. Lyon notes that no Michigan museums have an example, but a collector car dealer had one for sale on May 28, 1992. He was asking $20,000 for it. We also received a fax message indicating that a Washington restoration shop has one and that it's restored. The Moon was built from 1905 to 1929, with peak production of 13,000 cars occurring in 1925. As recently as 1989, Mr. Prentice personally saw a 1928 Model 8-75 Moon roadster exhibited at the Johns Hopkins University Spring Fair in Baltimore. There is also a Moon on exhibit at a Texas car museum, according to Nancy Ragland of the Central Texas Museum of Automotive History on Highway 304 in the town of Rosanky. As to how many 1952 Fords remain, a ballpark estimate might be 10 percent of the 22,534 cars originally built.

Q. I own a 1960 Chevrolet Bel Air two-door hardtop Sports Coupe. This car was purchased new by family members. The car's actual mileage is 31,875. It is powered by a 283 with Powerglide. The *STANDARD CATALOG OF AMERICAN CARS 1946-1975* lists the production figure of Sports Coupes as 204,467, with no breakdown as to series, model, or engine. Some "experts" have told me that five to 10 percent of all Sports Coupes were the Bel Air models. Could you give me an indication of the accuracy of these figures? D.N., Colorado.

A. In 1960, Chevrolet built 381,517 Bel Air series cars of all models and 511,925 Impalas. Since the Impala series lacked the two-door sedan and had only one station wagon (compared to two station wagon models in the Bel Air series) these figures might be worked around a bit to show that Chevrolet sold somewhere in the neighborhood of two Impalas to every one Bel Air on a model-for-model basis. However, the sporty models were the bigger sellers in up-class Impala trim, so it's more likely that 80 or so percent of 1960 Chevrolet Sports Coupes were sold in the Impala series. Why not contact the Late Great Chevrolet Club, PO Box 607824, Orlando, Florida 32860 to see if this group has more definitive figures on 1960 Bel Air Sports Coupe production.

Q. I came across a book titled *KING MIDGET SPORT AND UTILITY: WORLD'S MOST EXCITING SMALL CAR.* Where can I get more information on the King Midget? Is there a club for King Midgets? Are they still being made? Where could I buy one? This looks like a car I could afford. M.F., Nebraska.

A. The *STANDARD CATALOG OF AMERICAN CARS 1946-1975* covers the King Midget, a truly pint-sized car built by an Athens, Ohio firm originally called Midget Motors Supply Company and later known as Midget Motors Corporation. They were produced between the years of 1947 and 1969. Apparently, early King Midgets were built from parts recycled from World War II military vehicles. Even Crosley couldn't compete with the King Midgets' low price. In 1947, they cost only $270. However, the buyer had to assemble the car upon delivery. Early King Midgets were styled to resemble dirt track race cars. Later examples looked more like shrunken Jeeps. Machinists

Claud Dry and Dale Orcutt began production of the later design in 1951. To promote their midget automobile, they used the slogan, "A car that a schoolboy can afford to own and drive." In a 1992 *COUNTRY LIVING* magazine interview with the son of Dale Orcutt, the interviewer was told that Mrs. Orcutt sewed the canvas tops, side curtains, and seat upholstery for all the King Midgets in her basement. This made her a busy woman in peak production periods. The King Midget measured four feet wide by eight feet long. It was small enough for two King Midgets to fit into a normal one-car parking space. The cars were shipped disassembled in a crate, requiring the buyer to put them together. After assembly, the crate could be used as a garage. Wisconsin one-cylinder engines displacing 23 cubic inches were used through 1966, with the very late cars using 29 cubic-inch Kohler one-cylinder engines. According to articles, federal safety regulations caused the King Midget's demise in 1970. King Midgets are cute cars. The greatest pleasure of owning one is seeing the expressions on people's faces as you drive by listening to onlookers trying to guess the make. The King Midget Registry, PO Box 549, Westport, Indiana 47283 was formed in 1974. You can call them at (812) 591-2719 after 7 pm Central Standard Time. A related business selling parts and literature via mail order is King Midget Auto Works, 306 E. Main Street, Westport, Indiana at the same phone number. In 1992, the *WALL STREET JOURNAL* chronicled King Midget homecoming in Athens, Ohio. It noted that one owner drove a King Midget 8,500 miles towing a 12-foot boat trailer. He spent $63.40 on gas and oil for the entire trip to the homecoming. Another owner reported having travelled 115,000 total miles in his King Midget. The article recited a prank played on one King Midget owner. His boss and fellow workers hoisted his car onto a garbage dumpster. The owner would have lost his car to the trash collector had not the pranksters helped him get the car back down.

Q. Recent trips to the Henry Ford Museum in Dearborn, Michigan and the Imperial Palace in Las Vegas, Nevada have shown that President John F. Kennedy had several Lincoln Continental convertibles. What ever happened to the car in which President Kennedy was riding when he was assassinated? N.J., California.
A. According to *THE NEW ROADSIDE AMERICA: THE MODERN TRAVELER'S GUIDE TO THE WILD AND WONDERFUL WORLD OF AMERICA'S TOURIST ATTRACTIONS* published by Fireside/Simon & Schuster, the Presidential Lincoln in which John F. Kennedy was shot is in the Henry Ford Museum at Dearborn, Michigan. Coincidentally, so is the chair from Ford's Theater in which President Abraham Lincoln was shot.

Q. I have a friend who has a 1932 Ford coupe which has been chopped and hopped up. I have never seen another "Deuce" with suicide doors. Is this a late 1932 model or is someone mistaken about the correct year? M.P., Oregon.
A. The 1932 Ford "Deuce" three-window coupe had front-opening "suicide" doors. In addition to the standard five-window coupe (with small quarter windows behind the doors), Ford also built a deluxe three-window coupe in 1932-1936. To hot rodders, the three-window coupe is a highly-desirable prize, ranking up there with a "highboy" roadster. Production of three-window coupes was only a fraction of the production of the more common five-window coupe.

Q. Do you know of any identification on the body of a 1927 Ford Model A Tudor sedan? On the crossmember supporting the front seats the number 1064 appears in rather large characters. M.D.M., Nevada.

A. On Ford Model As assembled from 1928 and through mid-1929, the date of manufacture is stamped on the engine side of the gas tank in the lower left (driver's side). I do not believe this date stamping was done in 1927, but check the gas tank. The numbers might be nearly obscured by repainting.

Q. Is the 1963 Ford Sprint Falcon convertible a rare car? What is the amount that the last one sold for? S.K., Illinois.

A. As a top-of-the-line model in 1963, only 4,602 Falcon Sprint convertibles were built. The *OLD CARS PRICE GUIDE* lists a value of $12,000 for a car in number 1 condition.

Q. I acquired a Jowett Jupiter. Is there a club? There were two convertible top frames with the car. One top doesn't fit. It has a tag inside with Reutter-Verdeck NR77891 marked on it. The main bracket is cast aluminum, as is the main bow. The rest is steel, except for a wood portion where it attaches to the windshield. The car appears to have a Ford flathead V-8 and three-speed transmission. It has an aluminum two-barrel intake manifold and the 17-stud heads. I can't find any Ford markings. Is it a Ford V-8? D.B., Connecticut.

A. The Jowett shows up in the *STANDARD CATALOG OF IMPORTED CARS 1946-1990*. It tells us that the Jupiter, a sports convertible, was introduced in 1950. About five were sold here that year. United States sales jumped to 46 in 1951; 110 in 1952; and 66 in 1953. There was no V-8. Your car has undergone an engine transplant. The original engine was a flat four-cylinder with an aluminum block and cast iron cylinder heads (very unique). The radiator was mounted behind the engine and the exhaust pipes ran forward to the front. America's pre-eminent car tester Tom McCahill wrote his driving impressions of a Jowett Jupiter in the September 1951 issue of *MECHANIX ILLUSTRATED*. The car was shown on the cover. It was same issue in which "Uncle" Tom McCahill tested a 1914 Stutz Bearcat, which is probably why I remembered the Jowett article. According to Tom McCahill's article, the Jowett Javelin Jupiter's pancake-style engine made the 1,500-pound car run like a "baby wildcat." However, actual performance figures suggest the wildcat comparison was a little overstated. McCahill's best 0-to-60 miles per hour time was 15.3 seconds and the car topped out at 89 miles per hour. In 1951, this performance pleased McCahill. However, he sharply criticized the car's handling. It was described as "...worse than any Detroit family bus I have driven since the advent of those dangerous blugger (balloon) tires." Of the Jowett's handling, Uncle Tom went on to say, "This reluctant torpedo dives into corners like a porpoise with heartburn and the steering is like winding up an eight-day clock with a broken mainspring." If you can locate a copy, the article and photos might provide some restoration information you need. The North American Jowett Register, PO Box 4131, Burbank, California 91503 lists a telephone number of (818) 842-5798. Jowett expert Rodger Airy knows of two other clubs: The Jowett Car Club, 45 Station Road, Stoke Mandeville, Bucks HP22-5UE, England and the Jupiter Owner's Club, 16 Empress Avenue, Woudford Green, Essex, England. Airy notes that several articles about Jowetts recently appeared in *THOROUGHBRED AND CLASSIC CARS*, a British publication. The November 1991 issue of this magazine included an article describing a Jupiter rebuild. This article is a must for the would-be restorer, as it very clearly shows the car in various stages of restoration. You should be able to obtain copies of the article from magazine vendors at any large old car swap meet.

Q. I recently purchased your *STANDARD CATALOG OF AMERICAN LIGHT-DUTY TRUCKS* in hopes of identifying what year Chevrolet pickup I own. Here is my dilemma. My title reads as follows: 1945 truck, serial number BD714498; weight 3,050/5,499 pounds. The plate on the firewall reads: Weight not to exceed 4,600 lbs.; chassis BK 3992. According to your book, the serial number on the title corresponds to Chevrolet trucks built in 1942. However, the BK 41 on the plate confuses me. Can you clarify? G.B.S. III, West Virginia.

A. According to recent research for the new third edition of the *STANDARD CATALOG OF AMERICAN LIGHT-DUTY TRUCKS* after nearly all military vehicle production was completed by mid-1943, Chevrolet got permission to put 1942 models back into limited production. This was done to turn out trucks for essential users on the homefront. So, Chevrolet BK 1/2-ton trucks were actually built in two series. The factory called the prewar-built units "early 1942" models and referred to the wartime-built trucks as "late 1942" models. Technically, BK trucks built between January 1, 1944 and August 31, 1945 are a continuation of the prewar series. There are virtually no product changes. However, many of the late 1942 trucks were registered as new vehicles according to the calendar year in which they were sold. The beginning serial number for these units was BK-2127. Normally, a Chevrolet serial number should start with a digit indicating assembly plant code. Next comes a two-letter series designator, then an alphabetical month code, then the consecutive unit number. However, since the series lasted more than 12 months, this system was modified in late 1941. For trucks built from August 1941 to July 1943, both single and double digit numerical date codes were used (in place of a single alphabetical code). The new truck catalog lists the specific codes for each month of production. Judging by the chassis number, your truck seems to be an example of the "late 1942" BK series (built in late 1944 or early 1945), which would have been titled as a 1945 vehicle in many states.

Q. I am enclosing a photo of an International model 1210. How many of these were made? Are they worthwhile restoring? Do you know the year or value? J.R., New York.

A. Your truck is an International Travelall converted into an airport limousine. Somewhere on the truck you may find a plate identifying the shop that did the conversion. I have no idea how many International Travelalls were lengthened like this, but I'll bet the answer is very few. The open grille and placement of the International nameplate in the grille's lower left corner makes your truck a 1971. It's hard to place a dollar value on a special model like this, which may be a one-of-a-kind. You may want to contact the Scout and IH Light Truck Association, c/o Wanda Ray, 4026 Senour Road, Indianapolis, Indiana 46239 to inquire whether any of their members own or have information on a stretch-Travelall. I have attended several all-International shows and have not seen another truck like yours.

Q. Have any of your die-hard Ford readers ever heard of a full-size Ford Falcon factory drag race car produced in 1969 or 1970? A person told me he had one, but I didn't believe it until I saw the car. It looks a little like a Torino. It has a 428 cubic-inch Cobra-Jet engine, a front seat only and a factory roll bar. P.F., Illinois.

A. A 1970-1/2 Ford Falcon 429-CJ high-performance model is shown in our *STANDARD GUIDE TO AMERICAN MUSCLE CARS*. According to this book, Ford moved the Falcon name to the three lowest priced models in the Fairlane/Torino sub-series in the middle of the 1969 model year. A handful of these cars were sold with the 429-CJ engine with 11.3:1 compression and 375 horsepower at 5600 rpm. This engine was also available with ram air induction. Zero-to-60 performance for these cars was in the six second bracket, with 14.5-second quarter-mile runs possible. We cannot confirm a factory-issued model without a back seat and with a roll bar.

Q. I have been an old car enthusiast from the age of six in 1932. I have mentally filed away lots of useless auto trivia. There are two types of cars which I never see a picture of or hear about. They are early 1940s Checker taxis and Yellow Cabs. On a special trip to Chicago around 1941, I remember Checker cabs that had open front fenders, triangular shaped headlights and a steel clam-shell landau rear roof that retracted into the lower body. There was also a lot of checkerboard trim used around the lights and beltline. It was a heady remembrance of a warm summer evening in the downtown loop area of Chicago with bright lights, lots of activity and cabs scooting around the town with their special taxi lights on, filled with laughing couples sitting in the open air racing to their destination. Where are any of these cabs? Or did I dream the whole thing? D.D., Colorado.

A. The cabs you remember were real and looked very much as you describe them. You can find pictures of them in the *STANDARD CATALOG OF AMERICAN CARS 1805-1942*. You are correct about their distinctive features, notably the cut-away front fenders and clam-shell style landau top. Checkers were built in Kalamazoo, Michigan. I am told that there is still a museum in that city with a number of Checker cabs on display. I don't know the museum's hours, but if you are ever visiting in the Midwest, you might want to put Kalamazoo and the Checker museum on your itinerary.

Q. I have a 1953 Chevrolet rack body pickup. It has a six-cylinder engine, a four-speed transmission, 17-inch wheels and single, heavy-duty rear tires. The truck has a 5,800-pound maximum gross vehicle weight (GVW) rating. I was told this is a 3600 series or 3/4-ton. Is that correct? The engine number is 3835849 and the serial number is J53T018149. Please break down these numbers for me so that I know what I have. A friend said my engine number was the first produced, but should be in a panel truck only. Is this correct? I would also like to know about matching numbers. As you can see, both my truck's engine and serial numbers end in "49." Does this indicate matching numbers? T.B., Pennsylvania.

A. Your information that your truck is a 3600 series 3/4-ton model is correct. The GVW and J prefix in the serial number indicates this. The rest of the serial number tells that your truck was built in 1953 at the Tarrytown, New York plant and is number 18149 in the production sequence there. According to the *HEAVYWEIGHT BOOK OF AMERICAN LIGHT-DUTY TRUCKS*, the engine number matches a Chevrolet 216 cubic-inch six-cylinder. This same casting number was used from 1941 to 1953. I have not seen any Chevrolet engine listings that associate a given engine number with a specific body style. Some engine numbers were used only with cars and some with both cars and trucks. Other engine numbers were used in conjunction with Chevrolet's Powerglide transmission. The casting number you list would be appropriate for your truck. The fact that the last two digits in the serial and engine casting numbers match on your truck is coincidental. Matching numbers refer to cases where the serial number contains digits from the engine number and where various casting numbers match those correct for a given production year, as is the case with your truck's engine block casting number.

Q. I am wondering if a 1936 or 1937 Plymouth coupe came with a rumble seat? It seems to me I've seen one, years ago. J.M., New York.

A. Yes, Plymouth did offer a rumble seat coupe in its deluxe P2 line in 1936 and in both the standard P3 and deluxe P4 lines in 1937. The domestic market only saw the rumble seat coupe in the deluxe cars, however, as all standard rumble seat coupes were destined for export.

27

Q. I ran across a brochure dated August 10, 1934, by a person who watched a 1934 Chevrolet being assembled at the Century of Progress exhibition in Chicago. I had never heard about the assembly of Chevrolet cars at the Century of Progress fair. When was assembly (there) started and stopped? What body styles were produced? What serial numbers were produced? Would a 1934 Chevrolet assembled at the Century of Progress be worth more than one built in an assembly plant? Were these cars sold to special buyers? D.R., Kentucky.

A. Photos of 1934 Chevrolets built at the Century of Progress Exposition (Chicago World's Fair) appear in *CHEVROLET 1911-1985* by Richard Langworth and Jan Norbye and *CHEVROLET CHRONICLE: A PICTORIAL HISTORY FROM 1904* by Arch Brown, Pat Chappell and Bob Hall. The first book states, "An undetermined number of 1933-1934 Chevrolets were assembled ... on the grounds of Chicago's Century of Progress exposition. The General Motors exhibit there included a functional Chevrolet assembly line. The finished vehicles were available for purchase and had a small plaque identifying them as Century of Progress cars on their instrument panels." Hobbyist Jean Allan told us, "I remember dad mentioning that he saw cars assembled at the Century of Progress. He doesn't remember specific details, except that he thought he actually saw complete cars coming off the assembly line." Car buff Tom Conron actually went to the Century of Progress as a high school senior. "We viewed the assembly line from a balcony," he recalls. "They were piecing together the wood framework of the sedan bodies and then placing them on 1934 Chevrolet frames. I doubt the assembly line was longer than 125 feet." Historian David Cole says that Chevrolets were assembled there in both 1933 and 1934. It was the main exhibit in the General Motors building both years. The *OFFICIAL GUIDE BOOK* of the World's Fair described the automobile assembly line and General Motors published folders giving considerable detail of the operation. Cole believes that the assembly line was operated whenever the building was open. Cars were turned out at a rate of 18 per day. Photos in the folders show only four-door sedans and two-door coaches. Bodies for both were built right there, although the hardwood framing of these Fisher bodies (and steel panels, too) were cut and formed elsewhere. Workers at the fair building actually assembled the wood framing, sheathed it with the steel body panels, and primered and painted the bodies, which were lifted across the room and chassis-dropped on a little assembly line. Building the bodies limited production to just 18 units per day. Industrial architect Albert Kahn designed the General Motors building, which measured 429 feet by 306 feet. There were actually two assembly lines inside. One was for building the Fisher bodies and another was for assembling complete Chevrolet cars. A brochure stated, "From a balcony a fifth of a mile long, 1,000 visitors at a time may watch the entire process, from the first step of the assemblage of a Chevrolet car until the finished car is driven off at the end under its own power." Two hundred, white uniformed workmen assembled the cars. Old car fan Chuck Jensen was nine-years-old in 1933, when he visited the exhibit and viewed the assembly line from the elevated platform. One of his neighbors had a 1934 Chevrolet Deluxe coach that had been built at the fair. It had a plaque on the dashboard indicating that the car was assembled there. Hobbyist Art Baske remembers that customers could order a world's fair car through their local Chevrolet dealer. They would arrange to take delivery at the fair, then drive the new car home. Robert Hensel, the owner of Chevy Acres, has a friend who owns a car that was assembled at the fair. He adds that the serial numbers used at the fair were Janesville, Wisconsin assembly plant numbers. George Singer photocopied the pages of the souvenir *GUIDE BOOK* to the Chevrolet-Fisher Manufacturing Exhibit and Bill Colford loaned us a copy of the original. In its introduction, the *GUIDE BOOK* states, "Of all the brilliant spectacles in the drama of modern industry, none is so fascinating to watch as the making of a motor car." The book goes on to state that assembly activities encompassed the final 24 operations required in building a car. Hundreds of other operations, such as stamping out the fenders and fabricating the crankshafts, occurred elsewhere. The book shows, scene-by-scene, all 24 assembly operations performed on the two lines. The lines ran up one side of the building and back down the other. The bodies were welded, primered, painted, striped and assembled on chassis that began as bare frames, just like in a real car factory.

Some 1934 Chevrolets were built at the Chicago World's Fair.

Q. I enjoyed your coverage of the Chevrolet Fisher assembly line at the Chicago World's Fair of 1933-1934. A little known fact is that General Motors gave serious consideration to replacing this wonderful exhibit with something else for 1934. In fact, anything else was, apparently, being considered at one point. The powers that be deemed that this assembly line had to go. Chrysler Corporation, in the summer of 1933, began turning on the heat with a slam-bang advertising campaign for its new all-steel body. Dodges were shown rolling down hills. Yet, the doors still opened and closed. Diagrams depicted Plymouths rolling over in horror accidents with passengers surviving. By 1934, Airflow models were depicted crashing down 100-foot cliffs, only to be driven away. This was heavy-duty promotion and almost frightening; it made most effective advertising. Fisher bodies, splendidly made as they were, still had a wooden structure. Presumably, this could break up under crash or collision circumstances. At Chrysler's worlds fair exhibit, the relentless message was that only all-steel bodies were safe for human occupancy. Meanwhile, across the street at the General Motors pavilion, the public could clearly see the vast amount of wood going into the

29

Fisher-bodied Chevrolets. General Motors had a problem. In 1934, the first indication of concern was a brochure stating that "wood and steel" were best for body construction. A man was shown bending a flimsy steel tube over his knee. Then, when a piece of form-fitting wood was placed inside the tube, he could not bend it. This was absurd! Nowhere in the Chevrolet body structure were similar components used. But, clearly General Motors was admitting it had a problem. In 1935, the corporation's A-Body cars got "Solid Steel Turret Top" bodies by Fisher. This sounds like a reference to all-steel bodies. This was not so, however. Only the top itself was "solid steel." The same wood structure was beneath the skin. In 1936, the big Buicks and Cadillacs received the same treatment. Not until 1937, at long last, did the "Uni-steel Turret Top" Fisher body appear. General Motors termed Chrysler's slam-bang advertising campaign "disgraceful," but as a result of it, Chrysler climbed to second place in the industry. The whole episode really began to rumble with the threat to abandon the assembly line exhibit in 1934. Dick Stout, Delray Beach, Florida.

A. Our thanks to Mr. Stout for shedding light on little-known facts. He reports this episode in his book *MAKE 'EM SHOUT HOORAY*, which is an excellent inside history of the American automotive industry from its founding to the 1980s. Those who want to understand the real reasons that the American auto companies were so badly overrun by foreign manufacturers should read Mr. Stout's book.

Q. I read with interest the article on the Doble steam car. If this car worked so well, why wasn't it developed by someone to use during World War II when gasoline was being rationed? Where can I find further information on this seemingly exceptional car? J.R.R., Connecticut.

A. The answer to your first question is that manufacturing activities during World War II were under the strict control of federal government boards that allocated materials and coordinated the production to meet the needs of the war effort. The Doble was indeed superbly engineered. The Series E cars built after 1923 were able to develop a working head of steam in just one-and-a-half minutes. They were capable of reaching speeds in excess of 90 miles per hour. There were several flaws in the Doble venture. The cars were priced in the high brackets. Production was also extremely small, totalling no more than 45 cars during the company's 17-year lifespan. You will find additional information on the Doble in the *STANDARD CATALOG OF AMERICAN CARS 1805-1942*. There was an eight-page "Drive Report" of a Doble model E-14 in issue number 71 of *SPECIAL INTEREST AUTOS* magazine.

Q. Can you tell me anything about a Daniels Special? When I was a kid around nine- or 10-years-old (about 60 years ago), I remember riding in a yellow roadster that reminded me of a Kissel Gold Bug or Stutz Bearcat. The gentleman who owned it cut the back off and made a tow truck out of it. They had trouble building the springs up to carry the heavy load. It had an aluminum body and was easy to cut. It was a beautiful car. I would like any information you can give me about it. J.H., Delaware.

A. According to the *STANDARD CATALOG OF AMERICAN CARS 1805-1942*, the Daniels was built between 1916 and 1924. It was a very impressive car. The model you refer to was probably a Submarine Speedster, which had top bows that draped down on the body when the top was folded down. It looked similar to a Kissel Gold Bug. The Daniels was powered by a 90-horsepower, 404-cubic-inch engine. This may be one reason that the unfortunate car you recall was converted into a tow truck. It had plenty of power for the job. Three of the remaining Daniels cars are on display in the Boyertown, Pennsylvania Museum of Historical Vehicles. You may wish to rekindle your fond thoughts of these fine cars by visiting the museum. We suggest that you call or write first, though, to find out the hours the museum is open.

Q. I am inquiring about Rickenbacker cars. Is there a club or newsletter connected with these cars? My father owns one and we would like to find out the history of the manufacturer. Also, we have been told there is a club and newsletter called "*HAT IN THE RING.*" Any information you could furnish us would be appreciated. S.H., Maine.
A. Rickenbacker cars carried the name of America's World War I flying ace Captain Eddie Rickenbacker. They were built between 1922 and 1927 by the Rickenbacker Motor Company of Detroit, Michigan. Among the Rickenbacker's features were four-wheel brakes. It was the first medium-priced car to be so-equipped. The Rickenbacker emblem showed a top hat in a ring. You can contact the Rickenbacker club by writing to: Rickenbacker Car Club of America, 82 South Ellicott Street, Williamsville, New York 14221.

Q. I have an interest in three-wheel cars. Were any three-wheel cars built after World War II? A.D., Michigan.
A. Two notable post-war three-wheel cars are the Bond, which was built in England, and the Davis, which was built in very limited production in the United States. Bond three-wheelers were produced in the mid-to-late 1950s and are an ungainly looking vehicle shaped like a rowboat. Only 17 Davis three-wheel coupes were built by Gordon Davis in Van Nuys, California, around 1950. These cars had rounded lines and were quite attractive. Three-wheel enthusiasts will be interested to know that the Davis 3-Wheel Club of America, New Frazer Farm, Rural Route 1, Dundee, Michigan 48131, publishes a quarterly newsletter of historical, technical and contemporary material on the Davis and other three-wheelers. You will also find a chapter on three-wheel cars in the book *WEIRD CARS* available from Krause Publications, 700 East State Street, Iola, Wisconsin 54990.

Q. I can't locate any information on a 1974 Jensen Interceptor. Is this the only year the car was manufactured? Is this an American car? I would appreciate any information you are able to provide regarding its present range of values. R.O., New York.
A. Jensens are a low-production British-built hybrid of English design and styling and American engineering. The company was started by two brothers, Alan and Richard Jensen, using their own bodywork on an Austin Seven. Initially, the company was basically a body building firm. The first real Jensens were built in 1936. They used a Ford V-8. The Jensen Interceptor you refer to was built from 1966 to 1976 and revived a name first used in 1949. These later Interceptors used a Chrysler drivetrain. The coupe body is of Italian design and was first built by Vignale. Later, Jensen itself built the bodies. Before 1971, Interceptors were imported into the United States on an individual basis. In 1971, Jensen Interceptors began to be imported in some volume. Most of these cars carried a Chrysler 440 cubic-inch engine. Later, a very low production convertible model was added to the series. Because of the Chrysler drivetrains, Jensen Interceptors are fast and easily serviced. On the minus side, their fuel consumption is heavy. You will find pricing information in the *STANDARD CATALOG OF IMPORTED CARS* by Krause Publications, 700 East State Street, Iola, Wisconsin 54990.

Q. I teach in Rochelle, Illinois. In helping students with local history projects, we came across references to a Partin-Palmer automobile that was assembled here for several years in the early 1900s. However, my students and I have been unable to find much information or even a photograph of the car. Do you know where I might find information or a photograph of one? Also, do you know if any of these automobiles still exist? R.M., Illinois.

A. According to our *STANDARD CATALOG OF AMERICAN CARS 1805-1942*, by Beverly Rae Kimes and Henry Austin Clark, Jr., the Partin-Palmer was built in Chicago and Rochelle between 1913 and 1917. The car resulted from the Palmer Motor Car Company of Detroit joining with the Partin Manufacturing Company, a large automobile sales agency in Chicago. The first Partin-Palmers may have been built in Detroit, but early production centered in the old Staver automobile plant in Chicago. The manufacturing operation was moved to Rochelle in 1915. There the cars were put together by the George B. Whitcomb Company. The Partin-Palmer name continued to be used through 1917. Then, the car's name was changed to Commonwealth. The Commonwealth became the forerunner of the Checker Cab. The entry shows three Partin-Palmer automobiles: A model 38 touring, model 20 roadster and model 32 touring. Hobbyist Chuck Westcott of Apache Junction, Arizona, advises us he owns a Partin-Palmer. It is a boattail roadster racer. As far as he knows, it is the only one still around. The identification plate on the cowl, under the hood, reads: Mason Motor Company, Flint, MI Model #30, Ser. 141. The headlights are removable for racing. (They lift up and unplug). The *AUTO MUSEUM DIRECTORY USA*, 1009 Placer Street, Butte, Montana 59701 lists cars in different auto museums. You may be able to locate a museum with a Partin-Palmer car if you check this book.

Q. I have a 1917 Master Junior truck. I have been unable to find information on it. Specifically, I would like to know what years this truck was in production? How many were built? I need parts books, advertisements and a source for solid rubber tires. T.W., Minnesota.

A. According to G. N. Georgano's *COMPLETE ENCYCLOPEDIA OF COMMERCIAL VEHICLES*, Master trucks were built from 1917 to 1929 by Master Trucks Corporation (later called Master Motor Corporation and Master Motor Truck Company) of Chicago. Models ranged from 1-1/4 ton to 6-tons capacity and used mainly Buda engines. The American Truck Historical Society, Saunders Building 201 Office Park Drive, Birmingham, Alabama 35223 or the Antique Truck Club of America, PO Box 291, Hershey, Pennsylvania 17033 may be able to help you locate the needed parts books and literature and should be able to refer you to a source for solid rubber tires.

Q. While on vacation in Booth Bay Harbor, Maine a couple of years ago, I visited a small antique car museum. On the wall of one of the buildings was a big poster containing all the names and companies that have made cars in this country since whenever. I have searched all over since then and have not seen another chart like this one anywhere. Can you help me find this poster or a listing of any kind? E.D., Connecticut.

A. Floyd Clymer was one of the first to publish such a list in the old car history books he penned in the early 1950s. Car collector Richard Rairden believes, however, that you probably saw the *SATURDAY EVENING POST* "Roll Call." This is a chart or poster containing 2,726 names of automobiles sold in America during the time period of approximately 1900 to 1950. Rairden saw such a poster in 1955, sent away for a copy, and was delighted to receive a packet, which not only included the poster on automobiles, but also another on trucks. It lists 1,801 trucks and buses sold in America between the same time period. The charts are in color and measure 25 by 39 inches. The automobile chart lists all manufacturers alphabetically, with the 21 survivors (as of 1950) shown in red and enlarged. This chart also has a copy of the first automobile advertisement to appear in the *SATURDAY EVENING POST.* It was dated March 31,

1900 and showed a W. E. Roach (successor to Roach and Barnes) horseless carriage. The truck chart also listed manufacturers alphabetically. In addition, it gave the years production started and ended. Both charts have many copies of original *SATURDAY EVENING POST* covers done by Norman Rockwell over the years. According to another hobbyist, George Ives, the chart was prepared by the magazine's advertising sales department for distribution to advertising prospects and agencies. Its message was: "When you don't advertise you are soon forgotten." Hobbyist Al Lendzian has a similar poster similar in his collection that was distributed by White Post Restorations. It was given away, years ago, as a premium from White Post. You might be able to find such items at a large automotive swap meet. If you are looking for a listing of automotive names and companies, you will find the most complete information in our *STANDARD CATALOG OF AMERICAN CARS 1805-1942*. Over 5,500 brands of cars are included in this thick book.

Factory photo of Franklin's 1929 Model 135 Sport Phaeton.

Q. Our firm, an art and photography studio in Chicago, purchased what used to be the Locomobile and Franklin automobile showrooms. Originally, the building was built in the 1920s for Locomobile. Later, the H.H. Franklin Manufacturing Company of Syracuse, New York took over the building and had their autos shipped here to be sold to the public. We are very interested in any data you could provide regarding these companies and their products, particularly any photos that we might copy. We have restored the first floor display room and would like to display any memorabilia that is available. To date we have photos of a 1924 Locomobile Sportif 48, 1931 Franklin sport phaeton, 1931 Franklin Dietrich speedster, 1929 Franklin sport touring and 1933 Franklin Olympic convertible coupe. Where can we get more? J.C., Illinois.
A. You should be able to obtain photos of 1920s and 1930s vintage Locomobiles and Franklins from Applegate & Applegate, Box 1, Annville, Pennsylvania 17003. You may also want to contact the H. H. Franklin Club, Cazenovia College, Cazenovia, New York 13035 and the Vintage Motor Car Club of America, 18840 Pearl Road, PO Box 36788, Strongsville, Ohio 44136 for sources of photos and other memorabilia.

Q. Just before World War II, I took a tool and die course. Part of the course included a study of the history of precision measurement where I learned of a machinist by the name of Johannsson. In some circles he was regarded as the father of the assembly line, since without using the same inch universally, interchangeability of component parts was an impossible dream. Johannsson was, I believe, an early partner or collabo-

33

rator with Henry Ford. His techniques and innovations for controlling precision were really the backbone of Henry's assembly line. The measurement blocks used to set the gauges for controlling precision are still called, if I recall rightly, "Jo-blocks" in memory of this man. Why have Ford historians failed to note his importance to the development of the modern automobile? I cannot find any mention of his name in my reading. H.H., Minnesota.

A. It is true that the Johannsson gauge blocks enabled the exact measurements necessary for interchangeable parts and the assembly line. I'm told that the surfaces of the Johannsson blocks were so perfect that if two blocks were put together and the top block lifted, it would pick up the block below. In a mass production setting, all gauges and tools would be checked against the Johannsson gauge blocks to assure uniformity. Beverly Rae Kimes, president of the Society of Automotive Historians (SAH), responded to your question about the oversight of important contributors to the development of the automobile by saying that most writers have concentrated on the automobiles themselves. We need more biographies, she emphasized, and noted that the SAH is attempting to build a library of oral histories of important automotive personalities. Those interested in working on an oral history project related to the automotive industry should contact the Society of Automotive Historians, Box 514, Mount Gretna, Pennsylvania 17064.

Q. The book section of the December 1986, issue of *THE READER'S DIGEST* contained the story "Ford, the Man Behind the Machine." It tells about Joseph Galamb who "devised the light and durable planetary transmission." To me this is one of the great inventions of this century. It is used in all automatic transmissions in cars and trucks and all types of earth moving equipment due to its ease in shifting both up and down and forward and reverse. I have checked all the encyclopedias. I can find nothing about Galamb. Could you enlighten me? L.G., New York.

A. While researching articles on Henry Ford and the Ford Motor Company historian Beverly Rae Kimes came across two books. Both *HENRY FORD* and *GRASS ROOTS AMERICA* by Wiks and *FORD, THE MAN BEHIND THE MACHINE* by Lacey paint a rather complete picture of Joseph Galamb. According to Kimes, when Henry Ford was planning new facilities in Highland Park, Michigan, he hired a pattern maker named Charles E. Sorensen and a Hungarian-born, German-trained engineer named Joesph Galamb. Kimes reports that when Ford began planning the Model T, Joe Galamb worked as chief draftsman under Childe Harold Wills' supervision. Wills, who was assigned initially to metallurgical work for the Model T Ford, is also credited with much of the work that went into the planetary transmission. According to Kimes, Joesph Galamb also contributed to the development of the Model A Ford, persuading Henry Ford to substitute malleable castings and stampings for the forged parts found on his early models. This change resulted in the Model A becoming profitable by 1929. Kimes states that Joesph Galamb played an important role with the single-block V-8. She writes, "So I went back to my old trade of patternmaking, production Chief Sorensen remembered later, and received from Joe Galamb a layout that I could adapt to our Rouge foundries." Wiks tells of Joseph Galamb and C. J. Smith being assigned to build a light tractor in three days using a Model B engine and Model T rear axle. On the planetary transmission, Lacey states that Joseph Galamb refined a quite old, pre-automatic gearing system which Ford had already been using on previous models. The team of Ford, Wills, Galamb and Sorensen, notes Lacey, "were like children as they sniffed out new machine tools that could cut out a manufacturing stage, or increase the accuracy of milling." Galamb was one of several highly creative people in a dynamic setting.

HOBBY BASICS

Q. I recently became interested in vintage sports cars and find *OLD CARS WEEKLY* one of the best places to look for information. My friends and I have a little argument going about what it means when a car is described as a 2-liter model. Can you explain it more fully? J.H.P., Pennsylvania.
A. The liter designations refer to the displacement of the car's engine in metric terms. A 2-liter car has an engine with a swept volume of 2 liters or 2,000 cubic centimeters, which equates to 124 cubic inches under the English measure system. If you check your 1993 *OLD CARS* calendar, you'll find a chart showing metric equivalents. It tells us that one cubic inch is equal to 16.39 cubic centimeters. Going the other way, one cubic centimeter equates to 0.062 cubic inch. Therefore, a 2-liter car with 2,000 cubic centimeters would be converted into cubic inches by the formula 2000 x 0.062 = 124. By the way, some automakers spell it litre and some use the Anglicized spelling liter.

Q. What is a 2+2? We have asked car salesmen, but they don't know. Each has a different explanation. Does a 2+2 have a certain body style, a certain number of seats or do the back seats have to be bucket type? J.V.H., Indiana.
A. Let's look at two very different cars called 2+2s to answer this question: The 1965-1966 Pontiac Catalina and the E-Type Jaguar. Both have two doors, but there the similarity ends. In building the E-Type 2+2 Jaguar stretched its sports coupe to accommodate two additional (though not "Mr. T" sized) adult passengers. Due to the lengthened passenger envelope, the 2+2 Jaguar E-Type can be readily distinguished from the standard coupe. Needless to say, Pontiac did not have to lengthen the Catalina two-door to accommodate rear seat passengers. Therefore, we'd say that a 2+2 is a two-door sports model that can hold four adults. To our thinking, the actual design of the seats is immaterial. Of course, another difference between the classic European view of a 2+2 and the American translation by Pontiac is the fact that the Catalina 2+2 came in both sport coupe and convertible body styles.

Q. Would you please explain the terms NORS, NOS and SASE that are frequently seen in classified ads in old car bobby publications? H.H., Jr., California.
A. The terms seen in the classified ads are abbreviations commonly used in the old car hobby. An NORS auto part is a new-old-replacement-stock component. This means it is a brand new part for an older car manufactured by a firm other than the original automaker. The term NOS refers to a new-old-stock part, which is a new part for an old car that was produced by the original automaker. However, the part was not sold over the years and has been stored, rather than used. In some cases, the NOS part will still be wrapped or packaged in its original wrapper or box bearing factory markings. (Save the packaging if you can, since it may be collectible, too!) Those involved in supplying both NORS and NOS parts often request that a self-addressed stamped envelope (SASE) accompany orders. If the part is sold before your order arrives, the SASE will be used to return your check.

Q. I would like to know how old a car has to be to receive antique or collector status? E.R., Illinois.
A. Traditionally, it was thought that a car had to be 25 years old to earn antique or collector status. Today, however, interest has become more of a factor in a car or truck's attainment of collector status. Less emphasis is put on the year that it was built. For example, Chevrolet pickup trucks of 1969-1972 vintages are already desirable collec-

35

tor vehicles, despite the fact that they have yet to celebrate their silver anniversary. When Cadillac stopped convertible production in 1976, there were many speculators who tried to make this last convertible an instant collector vehicle. A vehicle's distinctiveness makes it desirable to collectors. Today, we tend to reserve the antique classification for very early vehicles.

Q. I was speaking with a friend and the question of whether the Ford Mustang is a classic was brought up. Has any model or any year of this car ever been declared a classic car? F.D., New York.

A. The quick answer is no. Although it was a sales success when new and is still very popular with collectors, the Mustang does not meet the criteria that have been adopted by the Classic Car Club of America (CCCA) to determine true Classics. Among these criteria are unusual engineering (the Mustangs used existing Ford Falcon drive train and suspension components); extremely high quality workmanship (most mass-produced cars cannot come up to such craftsmanship standards); and innovative styling. Although the Mustang led the so-called pony car stampede, its long nose and short rear deck were not a styling innovation.

This 25-year-old 1968 Mustang is an antique auto.

Q. I am interested in getting involved with auto collecting and investing. I have checked our library and cannot find information detailing the number of cars manufactured by make and model. Can you help me in locating this information? J.R., Illinois.

A. Our *STANDARD CATALOG OF AMERICAN CARS* series of books (there are seven volumes) and our *STANDARD CATALOG OF AMERICAN LIGHT-DUTY TRUCKS* are an excellent source of the information you are seeking. These books are available from Krause Publications, 700 E. State St., Iola, Wisconsin 54990. If you can locate a copy, *THE PRODUCTION FIGURE BOOK* for U.S. CARS by Jerry Heasley is a quite comprehensive source of production data. I believe, however, that this book is out of print. You might find a copy at a used bookstore, but more likely would have success getting a pre-owned copy from: Automotive Books, Lumberyard Shops. Marine-on-Saint-Croix, Minnesota 55047.

Q. Could you put me in touch with any "454 Chevy" truck clubs in the U.S. or Canada or both? T.H., California.
A. To my knowledge there are no truck clubs dedicated specifically to Chevrolet trucks with 454 cubic-inch V-8 engines. The National Chevy/GMC Truck Association caters to trucks of 1947-1972 vintage, which doesn't include the SS 454 model years. I'd suggest that you contact the Light Commercial Vehicle Association, 316 Berkeley Court, Jonesborough, Tennessee 37659. This club supports all makes and models of light trucks and featured the Chevrolet 454 SS in one of its recent newsletters.

Q. I am writing to you in hopes that you can settle an argument between a friend and myself concerning the current value of antique and classic cars. I own a 1957 Chevrolet and drive it every day to work. My friend also has a 1957 two-door Chevrolet sedan sitting at home collecting dust. One day last week my friend mentioned how companies are reproducing just about every part you would want to restore a 1955 to 1957 Chevrolet. He said that the new-old-stock parts and the cars would soon peak in value, then hit rock bottom. His closing sentence was that our cars would be worth twice as much if they never started reproducing parts and accessories to restore them. What is your opinion on this? T.M., Nebraska.
A. I can remember having a similar discussion with friends who owned Model A Fords when reproduction parts for these cars first began appearing. Actually, reproduction parts boost the value of original cars like yours for a couple of reasons. First, by making it possible for more 1955 to 1957 Chevrolets to be restored, these cars become more popular and therefore more sought after and expensive to buy. Second, because of their relative scarcity, original cars command premium prices. Using the Model A Ford as an example, reproduction parts helped the value of these cars increase one hundredfold between the years 1960 and 1980. The leveling out of the value of these cars has to do with a new generation of collectors showing interest in postwar cars like your mid-1950s Chevrolets and not the existence of reproduction parts.

Q. I would like to find a job, either full- or part-time, which relates directly to the old car business. I believe I have a fairly good working knowledge of old cars, since I've been collecting from the age of 16. My interests are mainly in 1955 and newer Chevrolets. I am 38 years of age and I have worked in car sales for the past year. My previous work experience includes 10 years with the Wisconsin Dairy Herd Improvement Corporation. I have also worked as an auto mechanic and auto body repairman. How do I go about getting a job in the old car field? D.S., Wisconsin.
A. There are jobs that relate to the old car hobby in everything from restoration shop work to sales and marketing positions in the parts supply and manufacturing industries. Collector car sales is another possibility. However, most of the job openings are never advertised. To find a job in an old car business, you've got to market yourself by preparing a professional quality resume, writing inquiry letters and making contact with prospective employers. If you need help preparing a good resume, there are services that can help. You can also sign up for job placement training provided by adult education classes in local high schools or skill centers. You can also make personal contact with old car businesses at car shows and swap meets. Activity in 1955 and newer col-

lectible cars is brisk and, with some effort on your part, you should find a job that matches your talents, experience and interest.

Q. Some time ago, I read in your publication that Oldsmobile's 4-4-2 designation stood for a four-speed transmission, four-barrel carburetor and dual exhausts. However, I also heard about a newly discovered 1972 Oldsmobile 4-4-2 with a three-speed transmission being located in a New Jersey garage. What does the 4-4-2 actually stand for if not a four-speed transmission? K.M., Michigan.
A. According to Oldsmobile expert Bob Bakinowski the 4-4-2 began as a midyear option (B09) in the 1964 model year. Oldsmobile sales and advertising literature for 1964 defined the meaning of 4-4-2 as a four-barrel carburetor fitted to a 330 cubic-inch V-8 with "four-on-the-floor" (a four-speed gear box was the only transmission available with the B09 package) and dual exhaust. However, for 1965 Oldsmobile upgraded its 4-4-2 package by using the 408 cubic-inch engine. Since Oldsmobile wanted to offer more than just a four-speed transmission, the company revised the explanation of the 4-4-2 designation to mean 400 cubic-inch engine, four-barrel carburetor and two (dual) exhausts. This allowed them to offer three- or four-speed manual transmissions and the two-speed Jetaway automatic. After 1965, the 4-4-2 underwent several more upgrades: A new four-speed WR manual transmission in 1966; the TH400 automatic transmission replacing the Jetaway automatic in 1966; 4-4-2 becoming a model series in 1968; and the new Rocket 455 cubic-inch engine replacing the 400 cubic-inch V-8 in 1970. By late 1972, it was clear that big-block intermediates were not the popular items they had been just a few years before. Therefore, the 4-4-2 became an option package again. Interestingly, sales and advertising literature only defined the meaning of the 4-4-2 model designation in 1964 and 1965. No matter what the definition may be today, it is a fact that when you add up the numbers, the 4-4-2 is still a "perfect 10."

Q. I have a 1979 Eldorado in number three condition. I was thinking of having the car repainted and the chrome replaced or replated. My question is, were these cars very popular when new and how many were built? I never see them for sale. Mine has a 350 Oldsmobile engine with fuel-injection. I would be grateful for any information you could give me on this car. C.F.M., Pennsylvania.
A. Cadillac built 67,436 Eldorado coupes in 1979. In this year, GM's luxury models were down-sized somewhat and given a more angular shape. Although the diesel V-8 was touted as an answer to the high fuel consumption of the gasoline-powered V-8s of the era, noise and reliability problems caused the public to shy away from the diesel as a passenger car engine. If you enjoy the car and can live with its diesel engine, there is no reason not to refurbish it some and continue to drive it. The car's value is not high, however. Our *OLD CARS PRICE GUIDE* shows the value of a 1979 Eldorado in number 3 condition to be $2,350

Q. I have a 1961 Ford two-door sedan which, when new, was a county police car in South Carolina. The body style code on the plate says 64F, which is not listed for passenger cars in your *STANDARD CATALOG*. The serial number is 1N31Z124360. The car has a high-performance 390 cubic-inch V-8 with four-barrel carburetor, heavy-duty brakes and automatic transmission. Is it rare? Do you know if there is any collector interest in it? J.P., Georgia.
A. Your serial number decodes as follows: First digit indicates the year, 1961; second digit indicates the manufacturing plant, Norfolk; third and fourth digits indicate the body type, 31 for two-door sedan; fifth digit indicates the engine, 390 four-barrel V-8; and the remaining digits are the sequential production number for this unit at the Nor-

folk factory. As you surmised, the 64F designates a police car. Judging from strong sales of our book *POLICE CARS: A PHOTOGRAPHIC HISTORY*, there is quite a bit of collector interest in police cars. Author Monty McCord says they are collectible, particularly when restored with original paint schemes and equipment. You may want to contact a club that caters to these cars. It's the Police Car Collectors, P.O. Box 112256, Tacoma, Washington 98411-2256.

Q. Could you please tell me where I can get a list of recognized appraiser associations and where I might take some classes to become a certified appraiser? T.S., Tennessee.
A. This question comes up periodically and it is important to note that certification, as it exists in the appraisal business, is only through the professional appraiser organizations. It is not given by any governmental agency. One organization you will want to contact is the American Society of Appraisers, P.O. Box 1765, Washington, DC 20041. Their phone number is (800) 272-8258. This society is highly regarded and has quite rigid certification standards. It also offers classes on appraisal procedures in various locations throughout the year. There is also another personal property certifying appraiser association which is the International Society of Appraisers, P.O. Box 726, Hoffman Estates, Illinois 60195. Their phone number is (800) 948-3868.

Q. Several years ago I purchased a 1956 Ford Crown Victoria. I am new at collector or classic cars and was told by the owner that the car was in number 3 condition and could be upgraded to number 2 condition with a little work. I don't understand the numbering system. Could you explain it? Is this car considered rare? Also, the car has patch panels in the lower front fenders and rear quarters. Considering this fact, could the car ever be a number 2? Could you tell what its value in number 2 condition would be? W.D., Michigan.
A. The 1-to-6 condition rating system was developed to provide an objective manner in which to convey a car's physical condition using universal standards. This aids collectors in establishing values and prices on old cars. If you purchase a copy of the *OLD CARS PRICE GUIDE*, you will find a written description of the six conditions and illustrations that represent the various categories. A number 3 rating represents a car in very good condition as indicated by the following description: "Completely operable original or older restoration showing wear. Also a good amateur restoration, all presentable and serviceable inside and out. Plus, combinations of well-done restoration and good operable components or a partially restored car with all parts necessary to complete it and/or valuable new-old-stock parts." A number 2 rating represents a car in fine condition, described as follows: "Well-restored or a combination of superior restoration and excellent original. Also an extremely well maintained original showing very minimal wear." Patch panels would not automatically exclude your car from a number 2 condition rating if they were professionally installed with little or no body filler used. Ford built only 9,209 Crown Victorias in 1956 and according to our current *OLD CARS PRICE GUIDE*, if brought to number 2 condition, your car would have a value of $21,000.
Q. I have learned that there is a classic Thunderbird club. How old is this club? Do you have to have a car to be a member? I can not find many clubs for the 1955-1957 Thunderbirds. What's the address of this club? R.C., New York.
A. The latest address we have for the Classic T-Bird Club International is PO Box 4148 Sante Fe Springs, California 90670-1148. The phone number we have is (213) 945-6836. This club was founded in 1961 and has 8,000 members. You do not have to own a 1955-1957 Thunderbird as a prerequisite for membership in this organization.

Q. I'm interested in vintage Volkswagens. Do you have the correct address for the Volkswagen Club of America? T.B., New York.

A. This organization often refers to itself as "The" Volkswagen Club, due to its longevity. The Volkswagen Club of America was founded in 1955 in New Jersey. It maintained national headquarters there for many years. In 1987, the club moved its official mailing address to the Midwest to be geographically closer to the center of its membership. Those interested in receiving a club brochure and the next issue of its bi-monthly magazine can write to: The Volkswagen Club of America, PO Box 154, North Aurora, Illinois 60542.

Q. I would like to know how many 1968 Cadillac DeVille convertibles were built in that year? I would also like to know what condition code would apply to a car that has been restored with new leather, new paint, exhaust, brakes, a reconditioned engine, a good top and 48,000 miles? R.M., Michigan.

A. Cadillac's distinctive terminology would describe this model as a Convertible De-Ville, as opposed to a Coupe DeVille or Sedan DeVille. The company built 18,025 Convertible DeVilles to 1968 model specifications. Of course, all of them were not produced in the 1968 calendar year, since the official dealer introduction date for these models was September 21, 1967. Depending on the quality of the work, most cars in the condition you describe would probably fall into the number 2 category. However, they could possibly rate as high as number 1 if the work is of top quality and the car has been extremely well-preserved.

Q. Could you tell me where I can find parts catalogs or price lists for a 1935 Rolls-Royce 20.25 model limousine with right-hand drive? I've been trying for over a year to restore this car and have called and written many letters, but received no responses. H.T., Missouri.

A. Usually the best source of parts information is a club for your make and model car. In your case, the organization to contact is the Rolls-Royce Owners Club, PO Box 2001, Mechanicsburg, Pennsylvania 17055.

Q. I recently purchased a 1953 Studebaker Commander deluxe V-8 Starlight coupe with the early serial number of 1453. This car bears the tri-star identification, which I've been told brought about a lawsuit from Mercedes Benz. Most recently, I read in a Studebaker-oriented publication that the 1953 and 1954 model coupes and hardtops were among the first cars recognized as postwar classics by the Milestone Car Society. I find it difficult to believe that any postwar cars are recognized as classics. I thought the newest classics were some 1941 Cadillac models and the 1942 Packard Darrin. I called a prominent member of the Packard club and asked him if my Studebaker was a classic and he said it was. If so, has this honor been extended to the Hawk series? What other postwar automobiles share this honor? K.N., Arkansas.

A. The article you read was correct in identifying the Studebaker Starlight coupe as a Milestone car. However, it is not "classic" in the sense of being recognized by the Classic Car Club of America. The Milestone Car Society was organized to identify postwar cars with the same characteristics as classics; cars that made conspicuous contributions to automotive development in styling, engineering and other categories. Both Studebakers you mention have received Milestone status. For the most part, World War II marks the end of the classic era, but postwar Lincoln Continental V-12s have also been granted classic status.

Q. I have an interest in replicars, particularly those replicating 1953 to 1955 Corvettes, 1955 to 1957 Thunderbirds and Cobra roadsters. Where can I receive an informative package on the above kit cars? R.G.C., Connecticut.

A. The appeal of modern replicas of popular vintage cars is that these are cars you can drive and enjoy. The drawbacks are that replicas with any degree of authenticity are expensive and quality standards can vary greatly depending on the manufacturer. For anyone seriously considering building a replica, I have this advice. First, take careful appraisal of your mechanical skills. Are you equipped to build a car from the ground up and, if not, do you have the finances to pay someone to do the job for you? Some kit car builders will sell assembled products at a price substantially higher than the kit. Second, be sure to inspect a completed kit before you buy. Remember that the parts that go into making the kit are not the same as those on the original car. From the mechanical standpoint, the engineering is usually improved and the fiberglass bodies are typically stronger and more damage resistant than the steel originals. Check to see if trim parts are steel (preferable) or chrome-plated plastic. Inspect the design of the frame and suspension. Is the chassis engineered to handle the more modern engine? My favorite kit car is the MG TF replica built by Noble Motor Cars Corp., 1112 Pre Emption Road, Penn Yan, New York 14572. I have watched this car through its development and am impressed not only with its well-engineered design, but also its faithful copy of the original. This replica remains true to its MG heritage by using an MG B engine and drivetrain, as well as seats and instruments. Further, the re-manufactured parts used on this car are so authentic that they are also used to restore original cars. This kind of integrity is what you are looking for when considering purchase of a kit car. The Import Auto Festival held in the spring at the Carlisle Fairgrounds in Carlisle, Pennsylvania features replicas and kit cars. A show like this is an ideal place to talk to manufacturers and inspect the cars first hand. There is a group called the Association of Handcrafted Automobiles, 7593 Satin Wood Court, Highland, California 92346 which may be of help in gathering facts about kits. Call Dan Barbee at (714) 862-6698 for information. You may also wish to subscribe to *KIT CAR ILLUSTRATED*, PO Box 70015, Anaheim, California 92825-0015.

Q. Could you please explain how the manufacturers come to assign gross vehicle weight (GVW) ratings to pickup trucks. I realize that the higher ratings indicate heavier suspensions and drive lines, but the load ratings don't seem to reflect the truck's ability to carry weight. A 1-ton truck can safely carry more than 1-ton just as a 1/2-ton pickup can safely carry more than 1,000 pounds. J.N., Illinois.

A. The 1/2-, 3/4- and 1-ton ratings we are familiar with on pickup trucks are partly historical. They have been used for years and, even though today's light trucks are capable of carrying heavier loads, the ratings are still used because they have earned such widespread recognition and acceptance. There is also another reason that light trucks are assigned load ratings lower than their actual load-carrying capacity. It has to do with the loads they are equipped to carry on a continuous basis. Keep in mind that it's not just the suspensions and drive lines that are more heavy-duty in trucks with higher load ratings. The brakes also have greater capacity and tires, too, must be capable of carrying greater weight.

Q. I have read and enjoyed the book *POLICE CARS: A PHOTOGRAPHIC HISTORY* produced by Krause Publications. Is there a club for police car collectors? B.T., Florida.

A. The Police Car Owners of America has over 250 members from all over the country, plus Germany, Scotland, Canada and Japan. For information, those interested can contact James Post, PO Box 480021, Kansas City, Missouri 64148-0021 or call (816) 941-7358.

Q. I am a relative newcomer to the old car hobby and would like an explanation of the term "matching numbers." Specifically, what are the locations of these numbers and how does one determine a match? I am particularly interested in determining my engine's originality. I own a 1970 Oldsmobile Cutlass Supreme convertible. I believe this definition will be of use to other readers. J.G., New York.

A. In a basic sense, "matching numbers" means that the vehicle identification number (VIN) codes stamped on a vehicle, engine, body or other parts conform to the numbers that the manufacturer used on vehicles of a particular year. Some cars of specific model years have identical numbers stamped in different places. For instance, a Corvette of the 1950s will have a VIN that matches the engine's sequential unit production code. My 1953 Pontiac also has a VIN that's identical to the engine serial number. In other cases, the numbers do not match in the sense of being identical, but they "match" codes that are correct for a vehicle of a certain year. This would be true for your 1970 Oldsmobile which has a VIN that is different from the engine code. The VIN still tells you the car-line, the trim level, the body style, the model year, and the assembly plant, though it does not indicate type of engine. However, the engine will have a prefix and a production number. These do not match the digits in the VIN, but they should conform to the prefixes and production numbers that Oldsmobile used in 1970 models. Let's interpret your VIN and your engine code based on information in the new third edition of the *STANDARD CATALOG OF AMERICAN CARS 1946-1976*. The VIN on your Oldsmobile should be on the top left of the dashboard, visible through the windshield. The first symbol should be a 3 for Oldsmobile Division. The second through sixth symbols indicate the car-line and body style. They should be C4267 for a Cutlass Supreme convertible. The sixth symbol indicates the model year. For 1970, the correct code is 0. The seventh indicates the assembly plant. Plants that built Oldsmobiles (not just Cutlasses) were coded as follows: C=Southgate, California; D=Doraville (Atlanta), Georgia; E=Linden, New Jersey; G=Framingham, Massachusetts; M=Lansing, Michigan; Z=Fremont, California; and X=Fairfax (Kansas City), Kansas. The remaining symbols are the sequential production number, telling you what order your car was constructed in at the assembly plant. Correct engine codes (stamped on the engine) should consist of an alphabetical prefix and a production sequence number. Prefixes for 1970 Oldsmobile engines were VB or VF for a 250 cubic-inch/155-horsepower six-cylinder; QI, QA, QJ, TC, TD or TL for a 350 cubic-inch/250-horsepower V-8; QN, QP or QV for a 350 cubic-inch/310-horsepower V-8; QD or QX for a 350 cubic-inch/325-horsepower V-8; UC, UD or UJ for a 455 cubic-inch/310-horsepower V-8; TX or TY for a 455 cubic-inch/320-horsepower V-8; TP, TQ, TU, TV, TW, UN or UO for a 455 cubic-inch/365-horsepower V-8; TS or TT for a 455 cubic-inch/370-horsepower V-8; US or UT for a 455 cubic-inch/375-horsepower V-8; UL for a 455 cubic-inch/390-horsepower V-8; and UV or UW for a 455 cubic-inch/400-horsepower V-8. If your car has a correct-for-1970 engine, one of these prefixes should appear. Again, notice that there is no code within the VIN to identify the engine used in a particular body. It wasn't until 1972 that Oldsmobile began using the fifth symbol of its VIN to denote the engine installed in a particular unit. Some cars also have body numbers, parts numbers, casting numbers and other numbers that can be used to determine correct dating or applications. An *OLDSMOBILE MASTER PARTS CATALOG* would have to be referred to for checking casting numbers and parts numbers to verify if vehicle or engine parts were correct for a certain year. Matching numbers seem to be of most importance to collectors of 1960s and 1970s cars, particularly sports and high-performance models.

1970 Oldsmobile Cutlass Supreme convertible.

Q. Some years ago I read an article about an Idaho man who drove his unregistered and uninsured car everywhere without a driver's license. He had been hauled to court 33 times and had walked out 33 times because he knew his rights and showed the judge that he knew them. Briefly, his defense was that our individual rights stem from Common Law, on which our United States Constitution is based, and that all unconstitutional statutes have no power to steal away these rights. One of these is the right, not the privilege, to drive and to drive where and what we will. J.L., Colorado.
A. State laws have made driving on a public highway a privilege and not a right. It's true that English Common Law does apply in American jurisprudence, but in areas where constitutional or statutory law does not speak. Your question brings up one interesting point: Why did states decide to license and tax automobiles? Horse drawn buggies and carriages were not licensed and, in fact, if attempts had been made to do so, there probably would have been a public outcry. The reasoning that I've heard on this question is that early cars were considered toys of the rich and, as such, were an ideal revenue source. Hence licensing fees appeared very early in the automobile's history.

Q. Earlier this year, I purchased a 1954 Buick Skylark. It has an unusual dashboard color consisting of three shades of blue on the top, center and bottom of the panel. The car has a Marlin Blue body, paint code number 330. Its title has been traced to two prior owners in Mobile, Alabama in 1970. I have some information indicating that the car may have been originally owned by Jackie Gleason. Any information about this rare car would be appreciated. Dr. F.L., Florida.
A. All Buick Skylarks I have seen had solid color dashboards. This includes one car that belonged to dream car collector Joe Bortz, which was originally owned by radio personality Arthur Godfrey. This indicates only that personalities purchased Skylarks and that some of the cars they purchased were finished in stock trim. Of course, many famous people enjoyed personalizing or customizing their cars. Certainly, for a few

dollars extra, Buick may have done custom painting of the instrument panel on a special-order vehicle. Documenting such variations is often a case of writing letters and researching old magazines or automotive history books. Most car factories do not have detailed documentation dating as far back as the mid-1950s.

Q. I recently purchased a two-door Star car. The gentleman that I bought it from believed it was a 1923 model. He purchased it in 1955 in Canada. The car is rough, but is complete. It has suicide doors and a rumble seat. It doesn't have a top. I'm not sure whether it is a coupe or not. The Continental engine has number 240435. The body number is 270187. I believe it's a model F. The body tag is scratched up and hard to read. I have two parts cars that were manufactured in Flint, Michigan. This car was manufactured in Ontario, Canada. The only difference I have found is that this car has 20-inch tires while the other two cars have 21-inch tires. Can you help identify this car? D.M., Michigan.

A. According to Grace Brigham's *SERIAL NUMBER BOOK FOR U.S. CARS 1900 TO 1975* (now out of print) Stars built in Toronto, Canada used serial numbers T-206,109 to T-277,533 in 1925. Since your car's numbers fall in this range, I would assume it is a 1925. The Model F was built in 1924 and the model FA in 1925. Since the body tag is scratched, possibly the A (in FA) is not visible. A dilemma about your car's body, our *STANDARD CATALOG OF AMERICAN CARS 1805-1942* does not show a Star rumble seat coupe until 1927. That coupe has standard-opening doors.

The 1957 Chevrolet is not covered by the Classic Car Club of America.

Q. Would you please define the following terms used commonly in the old car hobby: Classic and antique? Doesn't a classic have to be recognized by the Classic Car Club of America? Is a 1950 to 1966 model an antique? What is a roadster and convertible? I always thought that a roadster had side curtains and a convertible had windows. What is a touring car and phaeton? I thought a touring car had side curtains, while a phaeton (four-door convertible) had windows. H.W., Michigan.

A. There has been lively debate over the term classic as applied to collector cars. You're correct that the Classic Car Club of America recognizes as Classics only elite

44

cars with exceptional styling and engineering features that were built during the Classic Era; namely the decade leading up to World War II. However, the term classic, in popular culture, refers to many items and art objects that would not be considered classics in the traditional sense. Coke Classic is a classic case in point. It is in this wider view that 1955-1957 Chevrolets and Thunderbirds, various pickup trucks and other popular collectible cars are called classics. Likewise, an antique can be anything older than you are. To my 21-year-old son, a 1965 Mustang is an antique. Your definitions of roadster and convertible match my understanding of the meaning of these terms. I have considered touring car and phaeton to be one and the same, open four-door models with side curtains. An open four door model with windows is a convertible sedan. Actually, the word phaeton has its origins in the buggy era. Keep in mind that manufacturers use these terms largely for their own descriptive purposes. For example, Ford resurrected the term phaeton in 1956 and applied it to its new four-door hardtops.

Q. My 1963 Chrysler Imperial Custom four-door hardtop is a very strong number two condition car with only 36,000 miles. The interior is actually mint (I removed the clear plastic dealer covers myself last year). A few areas of the exterior have been repainted and I have had the engine compartment detailed. The mechanicals were brought up to peak condition. How is the originality of this car calculated, along with its low mileage, to figure its value? Chrysler made only 3,280 Custom Imperials in 1963 and just about 14,000 Imperials the entire year. R.S., New York.
A. An old car's primary value reference is condition, not originality. It can be argued that originality should be the most important criteria for determining value. Since any car can be restored, an original is an extremely well-cared for car that cannot be duplicated by the restoration process. Often, a car's originality is a factor between the parties in a sale. It has been encouraging to see the Antique Automobile Club of America establish a special category for original cars. Our new latest *OLD CARS PRICE GUIDE* shows your car to have a value of $5,500.

Q. I just acquired a 1941 Plymouth pickup. I have never seen a Plymouth pickup in the *OLD CARS PRICE GUIDE*. Would it be worth more to restore it to original condition? My thoughts are to customize it with a chopped top, lowered height, custom interior and paint, etc. Would I lose going this way? T.R., Oregon.
A. This was the last year for Plymouth pickups and only a little over 6,000 were built. Perhaps two percent remain. This means that there is slightly over 100 of these trucks left. Recently the Plymouth Owner's Club listed only about a dozen 1941 Plymouth pickups in its membership roster. The new third edition of the *STANDARD CATALOG OF AMERICAN LIGHT-DUTY TRUCKS* says your truck is worth $8,700 in top shape. Possibly, you might receive more for the truck if it were tastefully customized, but again that is an if. You are also likely to invest more in the truck to customize it than to restore it. Obviously the choice is yours, but it seems desirable to preserve such a rare and unusual truck in stock condition.

Q. What is the definition of a pace car? I am aware that each year a car is selected to lead off the Indianapolis 500. These vehicles are the well-known "Indianapolis 500 Official Pace Cars" or "Indy Pace Cars." In 1973, the Indy Pace Car was a Cadillac Eldorado convertible with white interior, white top and a red leather interior. I own such a car in those exact colors. Does that make it an Indy Pace Car? Does the factory make a certain number of identical cars and in some way mark them to identify them as Indy Pace Cars? I have asked this question of many people but get mixed answers. H.B., Arizona.

A. Pace cars are used at many auto races. The Indianapolis 500 and Daytona 500 Official Pace Cars are best known, but even local racetracks use pace cars. There are not set rules as far as Indy Pace Cars go. Some of them, such as the 1953 Ford, had medallions embedded in the floor pan; others had no special identification. Indy Pace Cars are usually historically interesting models. For example, you may enjoy the fact that the Cotillion White Fleetwood Eldorado convertible that paced the 57th Indianapolis 500 on May 28, 1973 was the second front-wheel drive car to do so. The other was a 1930 Cord. There is the specific car used to start the race and several back up cars are required. Additionally, the supplier provides dozens of replicas for use by Indianapolis Motor Speedway officials, 500 Festival officials, VIPs and members of the press. Sometimes the company supplying the Indianapolis 500 Official Pace Car also builds replicas that it sells to the public in special sales promotions. Often, these come with Indy Pace Car decals that the buyer can leave off or have installed by the dealer. I am not aware of Cadillac's selling a 1973 Fleetwood Eldorado convertible with Indy Pace Car markings. I feel that doing so would have detracted from the car's elegance. However, cars matching the pace car color scheme were built and these would qualify as Indy Pace Car replicas. A book about Indy Pace Cars was published several years ago, but we have never seen a copy and do not know if it's still available. However, we do have a copy of the Chevrolet Pace Car Book available from the International Camaro Club, Inc., 2001 Pittston Avenue, Scranton, Pennsylvania 18505-3233. Even if you do not collect Chevrolets, this book presents a vast amount of fascinating research into the background of Official Pace Cars and Indy Pace Car Replicas. In fact, it should be "must" reading for anyone who wants a better understanding of pace car history. There used to be a general pace car club, which we do not find in *OLD CARS*' annual club list today. One group that is listed is the Indy Pace Car Registry of 1979 Mustangs, PO Box 261251, Lakewood, Colorado 80226.

Q. Where can I get books about 1929, 1930 and 1931 Ford one-ton trucks? T.M., Idaho.
A. You should find the book *MODEL A/AA TRUCK OWNER* by **A.** G. McMillan helpful. You will also find the section on Heavy Commercial Vehicles in the *MODEL A JUDGING STANDARDS AND RESTORATION GUIDELINES* to be very informative. I also suggest that you contact either or both Model A clubs listed elsewhere in this book.

Q. I own a 1968 Chevrolet convertible which needs work. Because I am a woman and work two jobs, I don't know if I should try to restore the car. I've put a new floor in and new brakes. This costs a lot. The car is outside with a cover on it. I do not use it at all in the winter. Do you have any suggestions? K.D., Illinois.
A. Chevrolet convertibles of this vintage are extremely reliable and excellent road cars. Your 1968 convertible certainly deserves care and would be a very enjoyable car to own. The problem, as I see it, is your storage situation. Sitting outside invites deterioration almost as fast as you make repairs. I would advise trying to find indoor storage for preservation. Then enjoy and upgrade it as you have time and money.

Q. I am about to acquire two 1967 Mustangs, a convertible and a hardtop. Both are in running order. The convertible is highly restorable. I am hoping that you can direct me to informational resources such as Mustang Clubs, parts brokers and value guides. I read about your *OLD CARS* newspaper in *THE FORD MUSTANG BOOK* by Jerry Heasley. M.B., Wisconsin.

A. A newcomer to the old car hobby's first stopping point should be a club dedicated to his or her make and model car. In your case, there are two Mustang clubs you might want to contact. They are: The Mustang Club of America, PO Box 447, Lithonia, Georgia 30058 and the Mustang Owner's Club, 2720 Tennessee Northeast, Albuquerque, New Mexico 87110. When more than one club serves your vehicle, I recommend contacting each club and requesting a copy of its publication. From this, you will get a sense of the club's helpfulness and the value you will receive for your membership fee. As to values of your cars, this information is contained in the *OLD CARS PRICE GUIDE*, available from Krause Publications.

Q. THE *STANDARD CATALOG OF AMERICAN CARS 1946-1975* reports that Cadillac built 47,316 Series 62 four-door sedans in 1953. It then lists another production figure of 324 for the same car. Is the lower figure the number produced with Dynaflow transmission? If not, what is the meaning of the lower figure? B.C., Colorado.
A. The lower production figure is the number of Series 62 four-door sedans built for export. These cars were shipped overseas in knocked-down form. They were then assembled at their destination. This was the basic manner in which cars were exported to many overseas nations. This provided jobs for local workers who assembled the cars at the point of destination. General Motors referred to these as CKD (completely knocked-down) vehicles.

Q. Is the WPC Club a specific club for Dodge Brothers car owners? G.P., Illinois.
A. The WPC (Walter P. Chrysler's initials) Club covers all cars made by Chrysler Corporation divisions. The Dodge Brothers Club was formed in 1983 for the owners of Dodge Brothers vehicles made from 1914 through 1938 and Graham Brothers trucks. The club now has over 800 members worldwide. It has had national meets in Detroit, Michigan, Reno, Nevada and North Conway, New Hampshire. This club publishes a bi-monthly magazine containing historical articles, technical information and a classified ad section. The address to write is Dodge Brothers Club, 2881 County Line, Big Flats, New York 14814.

Q. I have run across an old Lincoln in a barn. I may have the opportunity to purchase it if the year of manufacture can be established. I believe it to be either a 1941 or 1942 model. The only numbers that I have been able to obtain from the vehicle are as follows: In the engine compartment, on the firewall: 876H-73-27730; on the V-12 engine's left-hand cylinder head: 26H8050; on the right-hand cylinder head: 26H8049. K.K., Kansas.
A. The *STANDARD CATALOG OF AMERICAN CARS 1946-1975* is the basic guide available to hobbyists for answering questions such as this one. According to the latest (third edition) of the catalog, serial numbers for Lincolns were the same as the engine number. Serial numbers for 1948 ranged from 8H174,290 upwards. The model number code 876H indicates that the Lincoln you have found is a 1948 model. The symbols 73 indicate the four-door sedan body style. I hope this helps you with your purchase. It's nice to know that there are still old cars setting in barns waiting to be discovered and restored.

Q. I recently acquired a 1965 Plymouth Sport Fury convertible. In the glove box I found the following typewritten letter. "This is the only one left of the 1965 Indianapolis Pace Cars for 1965 that we at Indianapolis Speedway know of. Three cars only that year were made. One went to the winner, one back to Chrysler and one to the owner of the Speedway." The following items are on the car: A 383 cubic-inch engine, power steering, console, radio, special marking side panels, a "383" designation on the hood emblems and holes in the rear bumper for flags. How on earth can I verify the statement in the letter? M.H., New York.

A. It sounds as though your car may be an Official Indy Pace Car model that was owned by the Indianapolis Motor Speedway. If memory serves correctly, there was a pace car package available to the public that year on any Plymouth, including plain-Jane four-door sedans. This was an unusual way to market such an extra. The rationale was that Chrysler desperately needed sales, after suffering through a management scandal in the early 1960s. The pace car package was viewed as a way to boost sales. The cars actually used at Indianapolis Motor Speedway on race day were Sport Fury convertibles. I suggest that you call Nancy Cox, curator of the Chrysler Historical Collection to see what information might be on file for the 1965 Indianapolis Pace Cars. The phone number at Chrysler Historical is (313) 956-2149. You can also purchase pictures of one of the actual 1965 pace cars from the Indianapolis Motor Speedway photographic department at (317) 241-2501 at reasonable cost. It's possible that something in the photographs of the pace car may prove that it's the one you own.

Q. I have a 1962 Thunderbird that is all original except for the engine. The engine is still a factory-installed 390 cubic-inch V-8, but the numbers do not match. The car is in number 3 condition. How much has the car depreciated because the engine that came off the assembly line is not in it? G.R., North Carolina.

A. Absence of the original engine will affect the car's value, but it's hard to say by how much. Prices that collectors pay for old cars are ultimately reflective of the buyer's interest or the seller's desire to let the car go. In addition, the value penalty of a replacement engine would be less on a car in number 3 condition than a number 1 condition car.

Q. I am restoring two vintage automobiles. I would like to restore them to be competitive in shows. Where would I obtain a book similar to the one that car show judges use to determine quality judging points? T.C., Texas.

A. The Antique Automobile Club of America (AACA), 501 West Governor Road, Hershey, Pennsylvania 17033 regularly publishes its *AACA JUDGES HANDBOOK*, which gives complete guidelines for evaluating vintage cars under AACA judging rules. This book contains sample copies of the AACA judging sheets that are used to rate different aspects of a vehicle and grade it on a quality points system. You can also obtain AACA and Classic Car Club of America (CCCA) judging sheets, along with tips for preparing a show winner, in the book *HOW TO RESTORE YOUR COLLECTOR CAR*. It's available from Classic Motorbooks. You will also find it very helpful and informative to talk to other restorers whose cars and trucks have competed successfully in show competition.

Q. I would like to know if you have the address of a club that specializes in AMXs. B.B., Vermont.

A. There are two clubs devoted to the AMX. They are the Classic AMX Club International, 7963 Depew Street, Arvada, Colorado 80003 and the AMX Javelin Club of America, PO Box 9307, Daytona Beach, Florida 32020.

Q. I would like to inquire about the makes and models of Canadian cars and slightly altered models of domestic cars and trucks manufactured in Canada, assembled in the United States, and imported into Canada. Where can I locate this information? J.B., Missouri.

A. To my knowledge, there is no single book dealing with Canadian cars and trucks. However, you will find information of Canadian versions of cars and trucks in a variety of sources. You may want to contact the Reynolds Museum, 4110 57th Street, Wetaskiwin, Alberta, Canada T9A 2B6 to see if they have a library and research service through which information could be obtained. Their telephone number is (403) 352-6201.

Q. I have a 1930 Chevrolet coupe which I want to restore. Where can I get technical information relating to original color schemes? Darren Hettinger.
A. I receive numerous questions of this sort. The quickest, easiest and most enjoyable way to learn parts sources, restoration information and historical background, plus become knowledgeable about your car, is to join a club relating to your brand of car or truck. Chevrolet owners will find great assistance and support from the Vintage Chevrolet Club of America, PO Box 5387, Orange, California 92667.

Q. Where can I get restoration information on a 1965 Tempest convertible? T.J., Missouri.
A. For Pontiac owners, the largest club is the Pontiac Oakland Club International, PO Box 4789, Culver City, California 90230. Every year, in late April, *OLD CARS*, 700 East State Street, Iola, Wisconsin 54990 publishes an annual list of clubs.

Q. What's the derivation of Henry Ford's pride and joy the "Tin Lizzy?" How was this label born? Secondly, how is it that the tag "lemon" was given to any auto poorly built and in need of constant repairs? A.S., Illinois.
A. Historian Beverly Rae Kimes tells us that early Ford jokes referred to the Model T as a Tin Lizzy. We do not know of a specific event that gave the Model T its Tin Lizzy tag? Henry Austin Clark, Jr., the great automotive historian, used to say that a lemon leaves a sour taste in your mouth, hence the application of this term to sour automobiles.

Q. How can I go about finding my first automobile? In 1964, I sold my 1953 Chevrolet convertible to a dealer in Indiana. The dealership has since gone out of business. We contacted relatives who said there are no records. I have contacted car clubs, some museums, some salvage yards, the Secretaries of States of various states and so on. I've had no luck so far. I won't give up. I feel the car is out there somewhere. Where do I go from here? C.P., Illinois.
A. First of all, convertibles do not have a high survival rate. Therefore, the likelihood of your car having escaped the crusher is not good. As to trying to locate it, we are aware that Secretary of State or Motor Vehicle offices can trace former owners from a title, but we don't know how you would go about tracing sales from the time you sold the car to the dealership. If you have the serial number data for the vehicle, you might be able to run a low-cost classified advertisement in hobby publications, such as *OLD CARS*, seeking the current owner.

Q. I am considering the purchase of one of two late-model Volvos. One is a 1971 P1800E coupe, the other is a 1973 P1800ES wagon. Both are in superb condition. The owner of the coupe is asking $4,500 and the owner of the wagon is asking $6,000. The owners assure me that each is a classic due to their limited production, etc. I would appreciate your expertise in helping me. Are their asking prices fair? Which model should appreciate fastest in value? Which will become a collector's item in the near future? F.F., Jr., Maryland.

A. The *OLD CARS PRICE GUIDE* assigns a value of $7,000 to a 1971 Volvo P1800E coupe in number 2 condition and $3,950 in number three condition. The 1973 P1800ES wagon is assigned values of $7,700 and $4,400 respectively. In case you are not familiar with our 1 to 5 value rating scheme, number 2 condition refers to an excellent condition (extremely well maintained original or very sharp restoration) and number 3 refers to an above average original or an older restoration showing wear. From the figures noted, the coupe seems to be a better buy, if the condition of both cars is equal. Personally we favor the wagon's styling, but that is a matter of preference. Appreciation in value relates to many factors among which are nostalgia, desirability of current models of the same make and peoples' willingness to invest money in collectibles. Regarding the first two factors, attractive as they are we would give the Volvo E models an average rating. Regarding the last factor, collectibles rise most rapidly in value during times of inflation. You may be interested to know that a club exists for the promotion and preservation of these vehicles. Contacting other owners may also help you in your decision. The club is: Volvo Sports America 1800, 1203 West Cheltenham Avenue, Melrose Park, Pennsylvania 19126.

Q. What has happened to the Towe Ford Collection? Would you tell me something about the collection? Is part of it still in the old Territorial Prison in Montana or has it all been moved to California? What are the days and hours of operation? How many Fords are included? What condition are these vehicles in? Are there any plans for sales? V.G., Egypt.

A. The Towe Ford collection is now in the hands of the California Vehicle Foundation. It is housed in Sacramento, California. This is still the most comprehensive collection of antique Fords in the world. Every year and model produced by Ford between 1903 and 1953 is on display. The museum is open daily all year long, except for Thanksgiving, Christmas and New Year's Day. The collection has been in the California location since May 1987. Some cars are sold at the museum, but these do not appear be part of the collection. If you want to keep in touch with what is going on in the Towe Ford collection you can subscribe to the California Vehicle Foundation's newsletter by sending a check for $25 to the CVF, 2200 Front Street, Sacramento, California 95818. General information about all the automotive museums in the United States is available in several guides published by William R. Taylor of Editorial Review Press, 1009 Placer Street, Butte, Montana 59701. Call (406) 782-2546.

Q. I am seeking information on getting a collector's license plate for my vehicle. Looking at the motor vehicle forms, I see the statement that you can't alter or modify your car. What does this mean? How can I find out if the car has been changed from the way it was new? I see many old cars with chrome wheels, engines and other things changed. J.A.F., Wisconsin.

A. Each state that issues antique, historical and collector license plates has its own rules and regulations. Typically, these plates are issued to restored or original cars or trucks 25-years-old or older. Modified cars and trucks do not qualify because the purpose of the historical plate is to allow limited driving mainly for display purposes. If you take your car's most recent registration or title and proof of insurance to the Department of Transportation or Motor Vehicle Department, you should be able to obtain a collector car license plate, providing your car meets the state's criteria. With an antique or historical license plate, you may find that the license plate is only issued for driving in and to shows and parades. However, the Wisconsin Collector Plate allows broader use, with only some minor restrictions. At the same time, even with a

Collector Plate registration, insurance companies that specialize in collector car coverage may have annual mileage restrictions or require that the car be regularly garaged.

"Historic" license plates are available in Maryland.

Q. Here is a challenge to your readers. Why is the 1957 Chevrolet worth about twice as much now as the 1957 Ford? The 1957 Bel Air two-door hardtop in top condition is worth $25,700 verses $13,800 for a comparable Ford. The 1957 Chevrolet was a warmed-over 1955 model, while the Ford was entirely new. In tune with the times, the Ford was longer, lower and wider. In 1957, Ford also outsold Chevrolet for the first time in 25 years. J.C., California.

A. You've hit on an enigma. What makes any collectible more desirable than another? My answer to your question is that, for some reason, the 1957 Chevrolet stirs greater nostalgia than the 1957 Ford. I was a teenager at the time these cars were new. While I would have given most anything for a 1955-1957 Chevrolet, I didn't have much interest in same vintage Fords. In fact, a friend offered to swap me his year-old 1956 Ford hardtop for a Model A Ford roadster that I was driving at the time. I refused. (He might have been surprised if I'd accepted.) On the other side of the coin, editor John Gunnell (whose first car was a 1955 Chevrolet) always preferred the 1955-1957 Fords back when they were new. Where he lived, in Staten Island, New York, a Ford was the popular car to have at that time. He remembers General Motors cars becoming more popular, there, after 1957.

Q. I have recently purchased a 1961 Chevrolet station wagon from a fire department. The vehicle is equipped for emergency use, having a siren, red light, dual spotlights and complete emergency vehicle markings. I would like to keep the emergency equipment on the car and use it for shows, parades and an occasional drive around town. I have two questions. First, can a vehicle of this type be kept with the emergency equipment in place? Second, are there any clubs for collectors of emergency/fire vehicles? M.B., Wisconsin.
A. Regarding the emergency equipment, you will want to check with your state motor vehicle department and the state police. In my state, Michigan, I am told that if you registered the fire department car as an historic vehicle and used it (as the law allows) for club events and parades, you could keep the emergency equipment on the car. I was further advised that in Michigan an owner of an emergency vehicle used for historic purposes should contact the State Police about also registering it with them. They issue permits for emergency equipment. If the State Police deemed a permit necessary and allowable, they would issue a permit which would be carried in the car in the event you were stopped. I was also told that operating a vehicle with emergency equipment is cause for being pulled over on the highway by law enforcement officials, so you will want to look into the permit question. The Emergency Vehicle Collectors Club, 118 Highway 101 West, Port Angeles, Washington 98362 should also be able to give you tips on registering your bright red Chevrolet.

Q. I noted an article in *OLD CARS* stating that classic cars are appreciating at a minimum of 15 to 20 percent a year, with some cars going up 300 percent. I have subscribed to your *OLD CARS PRICE GUIDE* for more than two years and have been following your values placed on some classic cars in which I have a particular interest. I noted that your values remained exactly the same over this time period. Can you explain this apparent discrepancy? B.P., Indiana.
A. Although market highs make news, they do not determine fair market price levels. If you compare prices listed in the *OLD CARS PRICE GUIDE* for cars where there is a definite upward trend, muscle cars of the 1960s for example, you'll see a rise that reflects the percentages talked about. But this rise does not apply across the board. Keep in mind, too, that the price guide is a guide and that cars do sell for prices over and under those listed.

Q. Could you publish a definition for OBO? I have seen this abbreviation listed recently and am not sure what it means. J.R., Indiana.
A. Old car hobbyists use several abbreviations in their ads that sometimes puzzle newcomers to the hobby. OBO stands for "or best offer." Other commonly seen abbreviations are NOS for new-old-stock (non-used factory parts); NORS for new-old-replacement-stock (non-used aftermarket parts); and SASE for self-addressed stamped envelope.

Q. I hope that you can answer my insurance question. I have added vintage speed equipment (aluminum heads, a four-barrel carburetor, an Isky cam, Fenton headers, etc.) to the original flathead engine in my 1953 Ford F-100 pickup. I have also added a 12-volt alternator system, which I feel is much safer. I know there are original cars with more horsepower then my truck now has. I've got a bunch of money in this 100-

plus horsepower, three-on-a-tree "screamer." I'm 42 years old and my wife says I drive like a little old lady. Where can I get insurance? G.T., Ohio.

A. I suspect that the problem you report resulted from your checking yes to the question in the antique insurance forms that asks if the engine has been modified. At that point your application was probably rejected. The same thing recently happened to a friend of mine. He replaced the original 259 cubic-inch V-8 in his Studebaker with a later R-2 engine. After years of loving care and restoration, he also drives his prize very carefully. However, his application for antique insurance was rejected due to the non-stock engine. If you speak to your local insurance agent about availability of collector vehicle insurance, I believe you will not find the modified engine to be a problem. Your agent may not be able to sell you the policy as inexpensively as the mail-order antique insurance companies. Any policy with restricted use clauses will be considerably cheaper than regular insurance. However, another vintage truck collector reports that his agent gave him a 10 percent discount on the insurance premium for belonging to a club promoting the preservation of vintage trucks. If you belong to a club, you might mention this to your agent. You may also want to check some of the newer insurance plans advertised in *OLD CARS* newspaper, which are geared towards modified vehicles that are driven more than antique show cars.

Q. I have 17 cars in my collection. It includes all types and makes from the 1940s to the early 1970s. Is there a car club for collectors like myself? J.M., Texas.
A. The Contemporary Historical Vehicle Association, 16944 Dearborn Street, Sepulveda, California 91343 is designed for collectors like yourself who own and are interested in a variety of later vintage vehicles.

Q. Do any states specify an age other than 25 years to qualify for antique, collector or horseless carriage license plates? D.M., Michigan.
A. Hobbyist Bill Johnston says New Mexico issues only one type of plate for this category of vehicles. It is called a Horseless Carriage license plate. The vehicle must be at least 35 years old to register it as such. This means, for example, that a 1956 Chevrolet can carry a Horseless Carriage plate in this state, which hardly seems appropriate but meets the criteria. Lawrence Fullington, Jr. adds that Florida has a Horseless Carriage license plate for a one-time fee. When he applied for an "antique" plate for his 1947 Citroen, the application specified 25 years. However, a form received in the fall of 1990 (when Fullington licensed a 1923 Stanley Steamer) stated that the age requirement had been increased to 35 years and the fee had been raised to $18.

Q. I have purchased a 1953 Pontiac Chief with an eight-cylinder engine. I would like to have an owner's manual or a book which would mention details about the car such as hood ornament, tune-up specifications, etc. I would appreciate any information regarding the possibility of obtaining such data. E.D., California
A. Inquiries concerning sources of old manuals are the most frequent questions we receive. Anyone starting in the old car hobby can save a lot of frustration by following a few suggestions. First, subscribe to a hobby publication like *OLD CARS* newspaper that has both news and articles. Vendors and suppliers advertise regularly in these magazines. Second, join an active club catering to your make and model vehicle. Third, attend swap meets and flea markets; look at the cars and make the rounds of the vendors to see what is available. It is wise to buy owners and service manuals. In addition to originals, reproduction manuals can sometimes be purchased. Specifically, the 1949-*1953 PONTIAC SHOP MANUAL* was reprinted by Don Bougher, Route 1 Box 42, Dayton, Oregon 97114 and may still be available. You'll have to look for originals

when it comes to sales brochures and an owner's manual for your car. Other desirable items to own are the *PONTIAC MASTER PARTS CATALOG*, the *1953 SALESMAN'S HANDBOOK* and the *1953 PONTIAC DEALER PRESENTATION ALBUM*. Also look for old issues of Pontiac's *SERVICE CRAFTSMAN NEWS*, a monthly bulletin for factory servicemen. The old car hobby is meant to be enjoyed and will give you the pleasure it has afforded thousands of others, if you draw on others' experience, encouragement and help.

Q. Why aren't people more accurate in dating their vehicles? Recently a local resident has come back from America with what he was sold as a 1902 Schacht high wheeler. It obviously is not a 1902 model, as they were not even made that early. The very earliest is 1904, of which there is some doubt. As far as I can see, earlier models tend to fetch less money in your country, thus the incentive for inaccurate dating would not appear to exist. R.J.E., Crosby, Isle of Man, United Kingdom.
A. Nothing is gained by representing a vehicle as something it is not. More commonly, and without misguided motives, many of our older vehicles were mis-titled in reference to their actual year of manufacture. This occurred quite frequently with high-wheel cars. These cars became popular in the United States during the 1908-1912 period because of two factors. First, auto travel was catching on nationwide. Second, the high-wheel vehicles were able to move more reliably on the unimproved roads in rural areas. Most high-wheel vehicles looked older than they were, since they were designed very much along the lines of wagons. By the time states began titling motor vehicles, the agencies that did the titling had no way to accurately date the high-wheel cars. Therefore, the ages of many were estimated, based on their appearance. Since they looked old-fashioned and wagon-like, many were estimated to be older than they actually were. A good example of this was the Pontiac made before the General Motors Pontiac. Only a handful of these high-wheel cars still survive. Nearly all of them were once thought to be 1902 or 1903 models. Later, it was discovered that they had been built at later dates (around 1908). In other cases, inaccurate dating results from dealers and factories carrying over stock and titling it as new the next calendar year. Studebaker historian, Fred K. Fox, has written about the South Bend manufacturer's policy of declaring trucks with serial numbers after a given cut-off to be next year's models and dealers titling them accordingly when sold. As an example of the confusion that results from such practices, we recently met a Studebaker owner who purchased his 2R series pickup as a 1949 model. He discovered that, based on investigation of serial numbers, it was more likely built in 1952 and was probably originally titled as a 1953 model.

Q. Our Detroit Area Corvair Club has some 300 plus Corvairs. I plan to write an article for our club newsletter on ownership versus the number produced. I have seen reference to survival rates. Do you have any generalizations for unit-body vehicles in the periods of 1960 through 1969? The Corvair seems to be exceptionally tough in that, even with severe rust, the car remains a solid driver. R.K., Michigan.
A. Three factors affect a vehicle's survival rate. They are: Toughness or stamina of the original construction; collector desirability; and body style. As you note, though it carried a unit-body at a time when this construction was extremely rust-prone, the Corvair was a well-built automobile. Its survival potential gets a plus in this category. As a desirable collector car, the Corvair is a mixed entity. Corvairs haven't attracted the widespread popularity of the Mustang, but devotees to these little air-cooled cars take to them with a passion. As to body style, working models (vans and station wagons) have the lowest survival rates. Convertibles are also casualty-prone (when the top

goes, so does the rest of the car). However, these are also the models that collectors work the hardest to preserve. While I haven't seen published figures on Corvair survival rates, probably no more than 10 percent of the original production still exists ... possibly less.

The 1961 Corvair Lakewood wagon probably has low survival.

Q. Would you please be kind enough to supply me with the necessary information on how to become a car appraiser? C.S., Oklahoma.

A. Several readers have asked this question. In gathering information for an answer, I called the American Society of Appraisers, 535 Herndon Parkway, Herndon, Virginia 22070. This organization has a certification procedure for antique car appraisers. To become an appraiser under the ASA's auspices, one first makes application to become an appraiser candidate. A fee payment must accompany this application. The candidate's application is then sent to a local chapter. It reviews the would-be appraiser's background. This is followed by an interview and ethics examination. If the candidate passes these hurdles, the application is returned to the ASA headquarters recommending the candidate. To progress from candidate to member and eventually to senior member status, it is necessary to: 1) Take an eight-hour exam in your specialty; 2) Complete five years of appraising experience or; 3) Show proof of having completed four years of college and submit two appraisal reports. There are several advantages to establishing your credentials as a collector car appraiser through the American Society of Appraisers. By becoming a member of the society, you will receive referrals from purchasers, banks, insurance companies and others interested in collector car values. Since, your credentials as an appraiser are established and affirmed by the society, your authority will be recognized by financial institutions nationwide. In addition, you can receive assistance from other members in preparing your appraisal reports and learning the trade. I checked with authorities in my local area and learned there were no governmental rules regarding appraiser certification. The ASA said that anyone interested in establishing themselves as an antique auto appraiser should check with their state and county governmental agencies regarding possible certification. Local chapters would also be able to provide information on this.

55

RESTORATION

Q. I've been trying to rebuild my 1977 Pontiac Trans Am. She's gone 186,000 miles and numerous problems have crept up, so I decided to restore her. I own the Pontiac body manuals and shop manuals. This brings me to the question, are there really factory assembly manuals that show cars being constructed? Are there other manuals of disassembly? M.C., Illinois.

A. Mechanical disassembly should be covered in your shop manual, at least on an individual component basis. According to Roy R. Nagel of Metamora, Michigan, who works at GM, a number of other manuals did exist as production aids. However, they are not publicly available. A Product Description Manual (PDM) spelled out the features and options released for each specific style of GM car and included illustrations. Another type of publication is the Vehicle Description Summary (VDS). It performed a function similar to a PDM. GM also printed Operation Description (OD) sheets. These described the manner in which various assembly operations were to be performed. There are other manuals used in the planning, design and later production process for each GM car. They include program plan books, weld studies and other such specialized books. However, as far as books available to the general public, about the only additional one to look for is a parts manual. These are large publications, often organized with multiple sections. A text is usually in one section, with illustrations and parts breakouts in other sections. As people and groups in the old car hobby become familiar with the publications that were printed, the amount of information available to GM collectors tends to grow. The Classic Chevy Club International, of Orlando, Florida obtained the rights to reprint factory assembly manuals for 1955-1957 Chevrolets. More recently, the Pontiac, Cadillac and Oldsmobile Divisions have established independent research services that allow access to some GM publications. For a reasonable fee, these research services can provide hobbyists with much more information than they had available in the past. The PDM and VDS publications for Chevrolet trucks are now available in photocopy form to individuals restoring such vehicles. We've been told that they can be obtained by calling Chevrolet's toll-free Customer Assistance Center number. The current number for this service can be obtained through any local Chevrolet dealer. GM is doing a lot to help car collectors today.

Q. My antique car uses Delco Lovejoy inertia type shock absorbers. These units are leaking badly. How do I go about fixings them? F.R., Wisconsin.

A. First remove them from the car. The disassembly procedure is practically the same for all Delco single- and double-acting types. First, drain all fluid from the shock. Then remove the cover screws and cover. On single-acting models, hold the piston down while taking out the cam set screw and tapping the arm out lightly. After the arm has been removed, let the piston up slowly until spring tension is fully released. The piston and spring can then be removed. On double-acting models, remove cover screws and cover. Center punch the cam arm to ensure correct reinstallation. Remove the cylinder nuts at each end of the unit and loosen the intake valve assembly. Press out the camshaft, while making sure the cam lines up with the opening on the cover plate side of the shock. Then, remove the piston, packing gland and washer and the compression and relief valves. To reassemble, reverse these procedures. The installation of new-old-stock shock absorber arm packing gland assemblies (available from hobby parts vendors) should solve your problem and help to prevent future leakage.

Q. I am new to the antique car restoration business, so this question may be rather basic, but no one has yet told me what I want to know. How did the factory apply woodgraining to dashes and window frames? Does anyone offer this process to restorers today? J.P., Texas.

A. In some cases, woodgraining the interior trim of old cars was achieved by applying various shades of pigments over a primer base. The resulting simulated wood finish was protected by a final clear coat. Burt Mills, who writes the "Restoration Basics" column for *the OLD CARS* newspaper, described this process. He also covers the topic of restoring woodgrained parts in his book *AUTO RESTORATION: FROM JUNKER TO JEWEL.* Dennis Bickford, the owner of Vintage Woodworks, in Iola, Wisconsin specializes in woodgraining by the painting and clear coating process and has successfully duplicated and documented the patterns used in many specific models of cars. His phone number is (715) 445-3791. Still, if you look very closely at some of the original woodgraining in cars of the 1930s, you will find that the patterns are printed as a photographic reproduction, made up of tiny dots like the photos in a newspaper or magazines. From 1938 on, Di Noc employed a decal-like system to woodgrain dashboards and window sashes. A lacquer transfer or decal was used over a base color on a sanded, unprimed, flat piece of sheet metal. The sheet metal was then die-cut and formed. The woodgrain was touched up and clear coated before assembly and installation in the car. Gerry Lilian uses a Simu-Process photographic dot reproduction system to produce the woodgrain pattern exactly like the Di Noc factory originals. He can be contacted at 5929 West 89th Terrace, Overland Park, Kansas 66207, phone number (913) 648-1986. Other restorers are experimenting with the duplication of woodgraining via computers using the same CAD-CAM (computer-aided-design/computer-aided-manufacturing) systems that create graphics for modern vehicles like Pierce fire trucks. However, it is very unlikely that computers will replace artisans when it comes to reproducing the woodgrains for cars that are nearly one-of-a-kind vehicles. There would have to be a big demand for a specific woodgrain pattern to make it cost effective to use a CAD-CAM system to recreate it.

Q. I recently purchased a 1931 Model A Ford coupe. I am writing to ask if you have anything to help me in restoring this car? I am particularly interested in pictures of the back end where the rumble seat should be. It was removed and was not in the car when I bought it. I need information on parts, original colors, seat coverings, head liner, roof, bumpers, etc. K.M., California.

A. There is no shortage of information on Model A Fords. I'd suggest that before starting your restoration project, you invest a few dollars in books and join one of the Model A Ford clubs. One of the most helpful books you can buy is the *NEW MODEL A JUDGING STANDARDS AND RESTORATION GUIDELINES* (available from either of the two major Model A clubs). This incredibly detailed and authoritative book will give you color options, upholstery information, and countless details to make an authentic restoration. As a guide to the mechanical aspects of your car's restoration, the book *RESTORER'S MODEL A SHOP MANUAL* (available from Classic Motorbooks) can't be beat. The two major Model A clubs are the Model A Ford Club of America, 250 S. Cypress, La Habra, California 90631 and the Model A Ford Restorers Club, 24822 Michigan Ave., Dearborn, Michigan 48121. New rumble seat cushions are available from a number of Model A parts suppliers including Snyder's Antique Auto Parts Incorporated, 12925 Woodworth Road, New Springfield, Ohio 44443.

Q. Do you agree with me that there is no such thing as a "frame-off" restoration? This is like saying you just finished a basement-off-your-house home restoration. I am retired, but still do a body-off restoration about once a year. What takes the most time is removing the body from the paint. S.B., Wisconsin.

A. Technically, you're right. The term frame-off is not logical. A frame-up restoration or a body-off restoration are terms that can be used to describe the car rebuilding process more accurately. In a frame-up restoration you would disassemble the car down to the frame and restore it "up" from that point. A body-off restoration would be another way to describe the same procedure. However, you can assume that anyone talking about a frame-off restoration is really talking about a body-off-the-frame job. As we know from the publicity that always accompanies the release of a new edition of *WEBSTER'S DICTIONARY,* common usage of a word or phrase can lead to its being accepted as proper English. Given the widespread use of the term frame-off, it seems to be a term that everyone understands to mean the same thing as a frame-up or body-off restoration. While we're at it, how about debating the correctness of other hobby terms, such as "mid-year" to describe 1963-1967 Corvettes? These cars were actually built in the middle of a decade, not the middle of a year. It seems that people involved in just about any special interest field like to invent words that they understand, but novices don't.

Q. We recently purchased a 1929 Model A Ford two-door sedan. We are very interested in restoring it to all-original condition. Any help you can provide for us would be greatly appreciated. Where can we order parts? We were also wondering about the original color of this automobile. The car is black, but there is an undercoating of green. Could green be the original color? D.E., Arkansas.

A. My first advice to anyone new to the old car hobby or who has acquired a car with which they are not familiar is to join a club dedicated to your make of car or hobby interest. In your case there are two well established Model A Ford clubs, which are listed elsewhere in this section. Belonging to a club has many benefits. You have a chance to meet owners of cars similar to yours, make new friends, learn about parts sources and receive help with mechanical and technical questions. Either club will surely direct you to reliable Model A parts suppliers. As a Model A owner myself, one of the suppliers that I have found to be completely honest, with excellent service, is Snyder's Antique Auto Parts, 12925 Woodworth Road, New Springfield, Ohio 44443. Snyder's is a family-owned business that has been in existence since the early 1960s. Regarding your 1929 two-door sedan's original color, according to the *MODEL A JUDGING STANDARDS AND RESTORATION GUIDELINES* published by the clubs mentioned above, your car was originally available in Vagabond green upper and lower body with Rock Moss Green on the beltline and moldings. This is an attractive color combination and one you might want to use in restoring your car.

Q. I read an article on the "Final Finish" touch-up system offered by The Eastwood Company, but found no address to order it from. Do you have any information on the kit and an address to write to? Dr. L.S., Ohio.

A. The Eastwood Company is a major supplier of restoration tools and supplies. They will be happy to send you a complete catalog of their products. They also have an automobilia branch that sells automotive collectibles. A separate catalog is available for those lines. Their address is: The Eastwood Company, 580 Lancaster Ave., Box 296, Malvern, Pennsylvania 19355. The toll-free order line is (800) 345-1178. The specific kit that you are referring to contains a number of fine abrasives to repair scratch and chip damage to a car's finish.

Q. I am restoring a 1962 Oldsmobile Starfire convertible. The car has 68,000 miles on it and the original upholstery is real good. I want to repaint the car with a nice urethane paint job. Would this deduct from the vehicle as compared to a lacquer paint job? G.H., Florida.

A. General Motors would have used an acrylic lacquer on your car when new. Like the modern urethanes, this is a synthetic paint and very different from the old nitrocellulose lacquers used on cars in the 1920s and 1930s. It is not uncommon for show cars to be painted with modern urethane paint systems. As long as the color is authentic, this should not cause any loss of value. Actually, lacquer paints are rapidly being phased out of large-scale use due to environmental hazards associated with them. Some restoration industry suppliers, such as Hibernia Auto Restorations of Hibernia, New Jersey still manufacture and sell nitrocellulose and acrylic lacquers. They ship the paints to every part of the United States. They also use this paint on their prize-winning restorations. Having checked both federal and local levels, at this time no legislation has been enacted to make the manufacture, use or sale of nitrocellulose lacquer illegal. The tiny amount of nitrocellulose original finish sold and used in the United States is only a drop in the bucket compared to the untold gallons of nitrocellulose nail polish and fast-drying lacquers used in commercial applications. As far as can be determined, the restrictions on using lacquer paints that we have heard about do not apply to the paints themselves. They apply to the thinner that is used to dilute the paint in order to spray it on a car. Environmental concerns arise with the thinner solvents. One auto paint authority believes that New York and California may have legislation restricting the use of lacquer thinner for painting entire cars in commercial paint shops. This legislation does not, it appears, restrict the hobbyist who is doing his own painting nor does it restrict the sale of nitrocellulose or acrylic lacquer paints. The issue is not the paint, but the solvents in the thinner used to apply the paint. There is definite environmental concern over the affects of these solvents on our atmosphere. Paint company representatives I have talked to say that they expect lacquer paints to disappear from the general market. At that point, more restorers will be prompted to use modern paints as an alternative. The paint company representatives also say that tomorrow's aftermarket automotive finishes will be water based and require drying ovens that are out of the financial reach of most hobbyists.

Acrylic lacquer was used on the 1962 Olds Starfire ragtop.

Q. A hobby magazine had an article about powder coating. I am interested in learning more about how this process is used in old car restoration work. Can you tell me more? G.A., Wisconsin.

A. Powder paint is not really a paint. It is a dry, granular material that is sprayed into a compartment holding the parts to be finished. The parts are negatively charged. The powder is attracted to and adheres to the electrically charged metal, which is then baked for several hours at around 500-degree temperatures. The resulting finish is much harder than regular paint. To locate a power painting service check your local Yellow Pages or the advertisements in *OLD CARS* newspaper.

Q. I have recently acquired a 1974 Chevelle Laguna S-3 with the rubber nose and the original 454 cubic-inch engine. This is an absolutely rust-free Arizona car and the restoration begins soon. I've been told that only 1,000 of these were produced in 1974. Is this true? We were in the middle of the oil crisis and not many people wanted the monster motors. Why did Chevrolet pick this time to make the Chevelle so much bigger? Could you also tell me the options this car came with, since I intend to load it up as I restore it. Who makes restoration parts like rubber seals and interior material? Where in the world can I get the original side roof window louvers? J.H., Wisconsin.

A. We don't show a production figure breakdown for the 1974 Laguna S-3, although our *STANDARD GUIDE TO AMERICAN MUSCLE CARS* says that only 6,714 were made in 1975 and 9,100 in 1976. Very likely, the total for first-year 1974 editions was also in the below-10,000 unit bracket and could well have been as low as 1,000. The S-3 was a race-image coupe with the trick urethane front end. As to why GM boosted the size of its cars at the time of the oil crisis, it's possible that design decisions were made earlier when manufacturers (GM in particular) believed that the public still wanted big cars. The new up-sized models of the mid-1970s must have been in development before the oil crisis occurred. The question of timing product releases could be raised in relation to GM's whale-sized station wagons of the early 1990s, whose debut coincided with the recent Middle East crisis. In any case, the Laguna should make an interesting restoration project. Options for the S-3 included power steering, power brakes, air conditioning, power seats, AM-FM stereo with cassette and others you'll find listed in a sales brochure for this model. The first place to check for rubber weather seal would be your Chevrolet dealer, who can put you in touch with the new GM Restoration Parts service. C.A.R.S. Incorporated, 1964 W. Eleven Mile Road, Berkley, Michigan 48072 has perhaps the widest line of upholstery kits for Chevrolet vehicles. They may be able to help you with new interior material. Swap meets and new-old-stock Chevrolet parts vendors would probably be the best source for the side window louvers.

Q. I am restoring a 1932 Ford Model B pickup truck and am having trouble with the placement and method of installing the wood blocking under the cab. I've tried several restoration books, but none have any diagrams that will help me. Can you help me or lead me in the right direction? H.M., Massachusetts.

A. Bob Seville, owner of Wood Art (a company that makes replacement wood for 1932-1936 Ford cars and pickups), says that the Model B Ford pickup cab is supported with six blocks of wood. Two long blocks go under the cowl runners at the front of the cab and four short blocks go under the cab support rail at the back. He says that it should be quite easy to figure out the correct location of these blocks by aligning holes in the frame with the blocks and cab. The biggest concern with cab alignment, he says, is making sure the top of the cowl and radiator shell are the same height so that the hood does not appear to tip up in front and down in back (or vice versa). Usually when restorers place a pickup cab or car body back on the frame, they want to make sure the body is level at all four corners. To do this, it is important to first make sure the four corners of the frame are level. If the frame has a slight sag in any of the body mount locations, a shim is placed between the frame and body mount at that point. Bob Seville recommends using small chunks of fiber impregnated rubber for these shims (a piece of rubber cut from a tire sidewall works well).

Q. I am restoring a 1920 Model T touring car. In putting the transmission back together, I could not find any markings on the triple gears of the driven gear. I simply turned the triple gears until they slipped in to match the driven gear. Is this okay? Will I have to come up with the correct mesh of the gears? Will they tear up the transmission when I try to turn the engine over? G.S., Tennessee.
A. I spoke with Dick Weiss in Marion, New York about your question. Dick is a noted Model T restorer who runs a service station that cares for vintage cars. Dick says that the triple gears would not go in if they didn't mesh. Typically, he notes, it takes two people to install these gears. One person has to hold the triple gears and a helper has to turn the gears until they will mesh and fit in place. What is important, he says, is to make sure that the thrust surface on the bushing is against the flywheel. Milton Webb of Lake View Terrace, California advises that the *MODEL T FORD SERVICE MAN-UAL* provides detailed instructions for servicing Ford cars and that reprinted copies are available through most Model T parts stores. This manual has excellent how-to text and lots of pictures on disassembling, assembling, overhauling, repairing and adjusting all Model T components. Another excellent source of transmission repair information is a 50-page manual titled *THE MODEL T TRANSMISSION* published by the Model T Ford Club of America, Box 579, Ramona, California 92065. This club also publishes *THE VINTAGE FORD* magazine. All past issues have excellent, authentic restoration articles. There are tons of information available for Model T restorers, both of show cars and drivers.

Q. I am trying to restore a white 1961 Valiant four-door sedan to its original condition. Where can I find parts and materials? E.W.N., Florida.
A. I suggest that you contact Roberts Motor Parts, 17 Prospect Street, West Newbury, Massachusetts 01985 at (508) 363-5407 or Andy Bernbaum Auto Parts, 315 Franklin Street, Newton, Massachusetts 02161 at (617) 244-1118. Both of these suppliers specialize in parts for Chrysler products automobiles and both have extensive inventories. You should also contact the Plymouth 4 and 6 Cylinder Owners Club, 203 Main Street East, Box 416, Cavalier, North Dakota 58220. This group has technical advisers for most Plymouth models and should be able to help you with parts information for your Valiant. Another group that may be able to help is the Slant 6 Club of America, PO Box 4414, Salem, Oregon 97302. The small investment in membership with a quality club is a value far exceeding its cost in information and friendships.

Q. I am in need of a convertible top pump actuator for my 1967 Buick Skylark convertible. Where can I locate one? K.K., Hawaii.
A. Kanter Auto Products, 76 Monroe St., Boonton, New Jersey 07005 is a supplier of power cylinders and pumps for convertibles of your Buick Skylark's vintage. These cylinders can also be rebuilt. Several firms specialize in rebuilding top cylinders. Among them are: Hydro-E-Lectric, 48 Appleton Road, Auburn, Massachusetts 01501, telephone (508) 832-3081; Convertible Top Specialists, Incorporated, 1250 Commerce Boulevard, Sarasota, Florida 34243, telephone (813) 351-0788; and Convertible Service, Walnut Grove Avenue, San Gabriel, California 91776, telephone (818) 285-2255.

Q. I have been involved in the old car hobby for years and would like to turn it into my career. I understand that there is a strong need for upholsterers who can redo antique and classic car interiors and install convertible tops. How can I learn skills in the upholstery trade? S.G., Arizona.
A. People who do auto upholstery and convertible tops are known as trimmers. The modern industry has a publication called *AUTO TRIM & RESTYLING NEWS* which was founded 41 years ago by Nat Danas. Today, Mr. Danas is retired and has started a business that publishes books and booklets about the various skills involved in the auto trim industry. Information about his "Business Booster Books" can be obtained from: The Danas Group, 3804 Gunn Highway, Tampa, Florida 33624 or by calling (813) 960-1203.

Q. After looking for many years, I finally located and acquired a 1940 Ford standard business coupe. It is exactly like the car I had when I was 16 years old. I want to restore this Ford properly and I need some guidance such as how to do a "frame-off" restoration. What type of paint should I use on the frame? What how-to books are available? Where can I locate parts sources for this kind of restoration? D.C., California.
A. You will get a lot of tips on the right way to proceed through a "frame-up" restoration in *THE STANDARD GUIDE TO AUTOMOTIVE RESTORATION* by Matt Joseph. It is available from Krause Publications, 700 East State Street, Iola, Wisconsin 54945 for $24.95. Call (715) 445-2214 to obtain a free hobby book catalog or to order this title. Another book that would be very helpful is *THE 1940 FORD BOOK: A COMPENDIUM OF CURRENT RESTORATION PRACTICES*, compiled by the Early Ford V-8 Club. To make contact with other 1940 Ford owners, you may want to join the Early Ford V-8 Club of America, PO Box 2122 San Leandro, California 94577. This group can also assist you with parts sources.

Q. I have a 1960 Lincoln four-door Landau. It has a black and white cloth and leather interior. I plan to have the interior redone. My first question has to do with the Lincoln emblem pressed into the center of the front seatback. Is there a source for a new piece of leather embossed with this emblem or do I have to use what I have? Since I am planning a full-leather interior, I want to do it in all-black. The sales brochure shows the full-leather convertible interior in a solid color and the steering wheel all one color (not ivory). In an article about a 1960 Lincoln Formal Sedan, I noticed that the steering wheel in the car was black and ivory. Does this mean that, while the sales brochure shows a solid-color steering wheel, the cars had a different type? Finally, in the event that I do an all-black interior, should the headliner be black or were all car headliners white? B.J., Arizona.
A. Chet Handley of Morristown, New Jersey restored a 1954 Cadillac Eldorado convertible that needed the embossed leather on the front seats replaced. The back seat was in good shape and the emblems embossed on it were quite distinct. Handley went to a local hobby shop that sells artist supplies and purchased a piece of carving linoleum. He then carved the embossed Cadillac emblem into the linoleum in reverse (the raised portions of the emblem were carved into the linoleum). The linoleum emblem must be carved a bit wider than the finished size to allow for expansion of the linoleum. The linoleum was then mounted on a 3/4-inch piece of wood. An upholsterer cut the leather seat panels. Handley took the two that required embossed emblems. He soaked the leather in water, until it was quite wet. He next laid the "face" side of the leather panel over the carving. He then put a 1/4-inch piece of soft sponge rubber on the back of the leather panel and placed a flat piece of 3/4-inch plywood over the rubber, essentially making a "sandwich." The parts of the sandwich were clamped

together with C-clamps closed as tightly as possible to force the leather into the carving. Handley then placed the assembly into an oven at 200 degrees F. for a couple of hours to dry the leather out. When it finally dried out, there was the Cadillac emblem looking as if the factory had stamped it into the seats. The linoleum is good for 3 to 4 impressions. After that, the repeated application of pressure deforms it and the embossment loses clarity. Brian Cowdery of Long Prairie, Minnesota uses a slightly different process based on letter press printing to reproduce emblems and other special markings on automotive upholstery. He creates precise, exact-size black-and-white art and has a printing cut of the original embossment ordered by someone who manufactures rubber stamps. He then wets the leather and clamps it in a vise with the printer's cut pressed into the surface." As for details about steering wheel colors and whether or not the headliner should be white, we would refer you to the Lincoln and Continental Owners Club, PO Box 68308, Portland, Oregon 97268-0308.

Q. During Thanksgiving weekend in 1926, my father took delivery of a 1927 Dodge Brothers station wagon. Many years ago the top was taken off and the vehicle was converted into a pickup truck. It is still registered, safety inspected and running as strong as ever. My question is, where might I find specifications for a wood body? The original body was made somewhere on Long Island. The top bows with the manufacturer's nameplate are long gone. J.M., Vermont.
A. Dodge called its woodie wagons Suburbans. They were actually Commercial Car models fitted with bodies built by J. T. Cantrell of Huntington, Long Island, New York. One prospect for rebuilding the body on your 1927 Dodge Brothers station wagon would be locating the owner of a similar car and taking photos and measurements of the portions of the body that are missing from yours. You may also want to try to locate a copy of the book *WOODIES AND WAGONS* published by Crestline Publishing Company. Although it is now out-of-print, you may be able to purchase a copy of this book from Tom Warth's Automotive Books, Lumberyard Shops, Judd Street, Marine-on-St. Croix, Minnesota 55047. In this book you should find numerous photos of Cantrell-bodied Dodge station wagons. It's feasible that you may be able to rebuild your woodie from these photos alone. Another possibility would be obtaining copies of original patent drawings from the United States Patent Office in Washington, D.C. Some years ago, we heard from an old car hobbyist who obtained copies of original patent drawings for antique touring car tops from the patent office. Since you know the manufacturer of the wood bodies for Dodge commercial cars, tracking down the patent drawings is a very realistic possibility.

Q. I am considering having my 1962 Buick Skylark chemically stripped to prepare it for restoration and repainting. I have some concerns. One is the fact that, after stripping, the body will have totally bare steel with only a water soluble protective coating. What happens to those places that I cannot get to for painting, such as inside the frame? This Buick essentially has unit-body construction that cannot withstand having body parts weakened by rust. Also, there are a lot of places where it has been sprayed with sound-deadening materials, such as inside the door panels. What material do I use to replace this coating? Finally, what is the recommended process for painting a car that has been totally stripped? D.S., Wisconsin.
A. You are right to be concerned about stripping inner body and unit-frame surfaces to bare metal and leaving them unprotected. A few years ago, the owner of a stripping business said that he recommended that the inner panels of doors, hoods, and trunks be protected by pouring zinc chromate through the openings in the inner panel, holding the part horizontally, and moving it back and forth to slosh the protective primer

around until all surfaces are covered. This method would not work, obviously, with an entire body. Since many of the inner panels were not protective-coated on cars like your Skylark when they were new, you would be wise in taking the unit-body to a Ziebart franchise or similar shop and having a protective coating sprayed into inner panels. Some coatings applied by rust-proofing franchises have a heavy consistency and could serve as substitutes for factory sound-deadeners.

Q. Could you help me on original colors on my car and truck? Was green a color for a 1937 International pickup? I have a 1936 Chevrolet four-door sedan. The original color is unknown. How can I determine what color it was painted? B.S., Kansas.
A. Yes, International did offer green as one of its colors on its 1937 D series trucks. The original paint combination codes for color schemes available on your 1936 Chevrolet are stamped on the Fisher Body tag. Combination numbers listed on a sheet covering Ditzler's Ditz-Lac intermix system for body colors of that year are: 196 = Black; 197 = Navy Blue; 198 = Regent Maroon; 199 = Willow Green; 200 = Kingswood Gray; 201 = Hollywood Tan; 202 = Taupe Metallic; 203 = Regatta Red; and 204 = Cabana Cream. The colors Cranbrook Gray, Frosty Green Poly and New Tampa Metallic are also listed on the same sheet without combination codes. Note that the combination code is not a paint formula (intermix number), since it also reveals fender color, wheel color and pinstripe color. Each color in each different type of paint (enamel or lacquer) had its own intermix number, such as IM-1558 for the Navy Blue. These intermix numbers don't mean too much today, except to a handful of vendors who specialize in selling old type paints. Most restorers go with a near-matching modern color as a simpler and less expensive compromise. However, you will have to find a paint chip sheet or book showing the original colors to help you "eyeball" the best match in a modern color. Paint chip references can be found at swap meets or ordered through literature dealers. You can also get information on Chevrolet paint colors through membership in the Vintage Chevrolet Club of America, PO Box 5387, Orange, California 92613-5387.

Q. What can an amateur restorer do to prevent rust on hardware? In the past, I have had my hardware cadmium-plated, but now I find that this process has a negative environmental impact and is hard to get done. I sandblast my rusted hardware to clean it up. However, I have not found a realistic method to prevent future rust. Are there any paints or processes that are available to the amateur that will provide a coating that is tough enough to use the hardware and still prevent future rusting? D.S., Wisconsin.
A. Your question points to a common problem: How to protect unpainted metal parts from rusting. In the humid Midwest, this is a real problem. It's not uncommon for a collector to put a meticulously restored car into winter storage, only to find that unpainted bolts, brake lines and exhaust manifolds have turned rust orange by spring. There are several ways of protecting bare metal parts. One is to spray them with a clear coat. Mike Cavey of Kalamazoo, Michigan, reports that he painted the brake lines on his national prize-winning 1951 Chevrolet pickup with a clear coat. Three years after the truck's restoration, the lines still look as though they were installed yesterday. The Eastwood Company sells a second product useful for clear coating. This Nyalic comes in an aerosol can. Another approach is to use a coating that duplicates the bare metal finish. The Eastwood Company also markets paints that look like the fresh metal finish of cast steel and stamped and aluminum parts. The product names are Spray Gray, Detail Gray and Aluma Blast. This company also markets a paint that can be applied to exhaust manifolds that gives a fresh cast finish and withstands high temperatures. The number to call for Eastwood information is (800) 345-1178. POR-15 is another prod-

uct that's helpful. It is a rust stabilizer and comes in clear, gray and black formulations. After even a quick clean up with a wire brush, POR-15 can be brushed or sprayed on a part to stop old rust and protect against further oxidation in the future. Call POR-15 at (800) 526-0796.

Q. I am an owner of a 1972 Buick Skylark and am in the process of restoring the interior and exterior of this car. The local Buick dealer referred me to you for parts and information. I am looking for exterior moldings, a dashboard, cigarette lighter, grille and other miscellaneous parts. J.Y., Hawaii.

A. Buick Motor Division recommends *OLD CARS* to Buick restorers so we receive letters of this sort frequently. To locate parts of the type that you are seeking, place an ad in the *OLD CARS* classified ad section or contact Buick parts vendors whose ads appear in display advertisements. To get a free sample copy of the weekly magazine write: *OLD CARS*, 700 East State Street, Iola, Wisconsin 54990. You can contact owners of cars similar to yours through membership in the Buick Club of America, PO Box 898, Garden Grove, California 92642.

Q. I just acquired a 1941 Plymouth pickup. It has been dismantled and the frame redone plus the drivetrain and the engine rebuilt. My first question, the dash is quite rusty with heavy surface rust. Would it be better to remove it and have it glass beaded or sandblasted? Everything else had only light rust so it was easy to do and primer. T.R., Oregon.

A. I'd recommend removing and bead blasting the dash. Sandblasting will leave a rougher texture.

The 1941 Plymouth Pickup looks great when restored.

Q. I am restoring a 1960 Impala convertible. I have learned how to find and read various codes. They tell me that my car was number 54,408 produced that year (out of a total of 79,903) at Tarrytown, New York. The engine stamping is F0225E, a February 25 date, which seems correct for a car numbered 54,408, but the city is Flint, Michigan. Could a Tarrytown assembled convertible have a Flint engine? (The Turboglide transmission matches the engine.) Do I have a matching numbers or non-matching numbers Impala? T.L., Texas.

A. In your Vehicle Identification Number 01867T154408 the T stands for the Tarrytown assembly plant. As you stated, the first letter in the engine number stands for Flint Motor, one of two Chevrolet engine plants in 1960. Engines were also built at Tonawanda Forge in Tonawanda, New York. To my knowledge, assembly plants such as Tarrytown used engines built in both the Tonawanda and Flint plants, so the engine in your car appears to be correct, giving you a matching numbers car.

Q. I am restoring a 1950 Chevrolet two-door hardtop. I need to know if a light blue with a white top is an original color combination for that year car. A friend of mine told me that it was, but paint dealers can't seem to find it. Where can I find pictures or color chips of that year? E.T., Minnesota.

A. None of my literature shows Chevrolet using a light blue color on its car for 1950 nor do I remember a light blue. A very attractive dark blue, however, was available. My father owned a four-door in that color. During my senior year in college, I drove a 1950 Chevrolet convertible that had originally been painted the dark blue. To determine whether light blue had been available as a special Chevrolet color in 1950, I put your question to vintage Chevrolet expert Robert Hensel of Brillion, Wisconsin. He writes, "I do not find any light blue for Chevrolet passenger cars for 1950; only a dark blue. It was not until 1952 that a light blue was available on a Chevrolet passenger car. The blue that was available for 1950 was called Windsor Blue "Metali-Chrome." The only two-tone combination using Windsor Blue was on the Bel Air hardtop where it was used with Grecian Gray as the upper body color. White was not an optional color for 1950. Grecian Gray may be the color. It is a very light color. Another light color was Moonlight Cream, a light yellow. It was only available on the convertible and Bel Air hardtop. On the Bel Air you could get the car as a solid Moonlight Cream with a Falcon Gray top. Falcon Gray was a dark color. An interesting side note for 1950 color combinations is that there were two demonstrator color combinations. These appeared on Styleline and Fleetline DeLuxe sedans and consisted of a Grecian Gray body with Empire Red wheels or as a two tone combination of Grecian Gray lower body and an Empire Red top and wheels on the Styleline DeLuxe sedan only. The Empire Red wheels had Argent Silver stripes around them. Cars with these colors were built in very limited numbers and had the new Powerglide transmission. This is the only use of Empire Red in 1950. I have a color chip of this color. It is lighter than Oxford Maroon, which was used in 1950. When a person is looking for information about any Chevrolet car or truck, I suggest that they contact the Vintage Chevrolet Club of America (VCCA). We have advisors who can help them and there is a lot of valuable information available from the club. The address to write is VCCA, c/o Membership Secretary Shirley Whitesell, PO Box 5387, Orange, California 92613-5387. As far as paint colors, the car is the owner's to do as he or she wishes, but the way the VCCA looks at it, the car should at least be painted a color combination that was available when the vehicle was produced. Personally, I think the car's color should match the paint codes on the data plate."

Q. We are in the process of restoring a 1950 Ford pickup. The model designation is F-47 and the truck is a half-ton model. According to the serial number plate and the cylinder heads, this truck was made in Canada. There are some minor differences compared to my 1949 Ford F-1, including die cast door handles, instead of stainless steel door handles. There's a different oil filter assembly, no hole for the optional right-side wiper and an added serial number plate on the firewall. I know that the Mercury pickups were designated M-47s and that domestic Ford pickups were called F-1s. Also, we found that Fords were built in Canada to export to other countries, but no one we talked to has ever heard of an F-47. Can you please help us on the problem of the F-47 designation? G.D., New Hampshire.

A. According to Paul McLaughlin's book *FORD PICKUP TRUCKS: DEVELOPMENTAL HISTORY AND RESTORATION GUIDE 1948-1956,* Canadian truck buyers could choose between Ford trucks carrying the Ford nameplate and a virtually identical truck line carrying the Mercury nameplate from 1946 through 1956. McLaughlin goes on to say that though the two versions had different trim and were sold through different dealers, both "makes" of trucks were built at the same assembly plant in Windsor, Ontario. The wrinkle here comes with McLaughlin's statement that Canadian Ford trucks used the same model designations (F-1, F-2, F-3, etc.) as their domestic counterparts. As you point out, the Mercury line designated its half-ton model as the M-47. That still leaves the mystery of the F-47 designation. I would speculate that it applied to Ford trucks built for export. Do any of our readers know the circumstances in which Ford used the F-47 model designation for its 1948-1952 "Bonus Built" series half-ton trucks?

Q. I recently purchased a 1949 or 1950 Ford F-6 truck for restoration. It has no title. The firewall tag has engine number 98RTH494672 KC. There is a tag on the inside of the glovebox door with the same engine number and the letters WBTH. The previous owner and Ford Motor Company Customer Service say it's a 1949 model due to the first digit in the engine number. The Henry Ford Museum says it is a 1950 due to the "M" six-cylinder engine and the 16,000-pounds maximum gross weight (first offered in 1950) stated on the glove box tag. What year is it? G.S., New Jersey.

A. Ford created a problem for restorers in dating these Bonus Built trucks by continuing the 1949 serial numbers through 1951. Because of a styling change, 1951 trucks are easy to identify. The 1949s and 1950s have an extremely close appearance, though. As your truck's previous owner explained, the first digit of the serial/engine number usually indicates the year. However, Ford used this same first digit for 1950 and 1951. The next digit and letter, 8R in your truck's number, indicate engine type (eight-cylinder in this case). Six-cylinder engines were coded 7H. The fourth digit tells the model. I assume that the TH combination in your truck's serial number stands for the heavier-duty F-6 model. The remaining six digits are the production sequence number. The Henry Ford Museum was correct in identifying M as the code for the larger 254 cubic-inch six-cylinder engine, but I do not see this code on your firewall identification or glove box tag numbers. The museum is probably correct in tagging your truck as a 1950 model. Besides their statement that F-6 models first appeared in 1950, the production sequence number is higher than Ford's 1949 truck output, which totalled 244,613 units. Ford truck production for 1950 reached a high of 345,801 units. Assuming that Ford's 1950 production sequence numbers begin where 1949 ended, your truck would have been built about mid-year 1950. Ford truck expert Chuck Mantiglia confirms this dating. He notes that there are several ways to tell a 1949 from a 1950. The first thing to look at is the running boards. All 1949 models have running boards that are bolted not only to the running board supports, but also to the frame rails. The running boards on 1950 Ford trucks end at the edge of the cab and don't continue across to the frame. Another thing to look at is the F series emblems on the cowl sides. If they are die-cast and chrome-plated, the truck is a 1949. If they are stamped stainless steel, it's a very late 1949 or a 1950. There are many other ways to tell between 1949 and 1950 Ford trucks. The absence of brackets under the dash for the factory radio (discontinued in 1949) and two horizontal ribs stamped in the center of the firewall (1950). Also, the big six or "M" engine came out in 1950 and was only available in the F-6 series.

Q. When you answered the reader's question about the Star car you cited well known sources of information but failed to mention perhaps the best source, the Durant Family Registry. I'd like to correct some misstatements in your answer. The reader mentioned that his parts cars were built in Flint. Either the reader is in error as to the city of manufacture or the cars are not Stars. Flint cars were built in Flint; Star cars were built in Lansing, Michigan. The body identification tag may say Durant Motor Company of Michigan. If it does, then the cars were built in Lansing. As to the body style, there were two coupe type cars (the reader's car is clearly a coupe and not a two-door sedan), the "Coupster" and the coupe. The coupe has a fixed top, metal and fabric, with doors which contain a full window frame. The Coupster, on the other hand, featured a full fabric, fixed top, but used roadster doors. Side curtains were provided which rode on channels that extended up into the top. It was a unique but useless idea. When you got in or out of the car you had to shove up the curtains to open the door. The Coupster lasted two years and died. No one to my knowledge copied it either. We owners of more obscure makes find little published about our cars and when we do, we like to know it's accurate. Owners of Durant, Star, Flint, Rugby (commercial or export), DeVaux, Canadian Frontenac and the Continental may want to know more about our publication. They can contact us by writing the Durant Family Registry, 2700 Timber Lane, Green Bay, Wisconsin 54313-5899. Jeff Gillis, Green Bay, Wisconsin.

Q. My current restoration project is a 1948 Cadillac series 62 fastback. Here are some specifics: Motor No. 486212213, Style No. 48-6207, Body No. FW-1223. My questions are: 1) how many of this model were made?; 2) approximately how many remain today?; 3) is it an early production model?; Is there any way to pinpoint what month it was made in? When I disassembled the 62,000-mile original car, I found a help wanted section of the *DETROIT TIMES* dated March 18, 1948 stuffed in the front corner of one rear fender chrome spear. Would this be the approximate assembly date?; 4) was the car built in Detroit?; 5) what would be a good source for detailed restoration data, clubs to join, etc? I want to restore this car authentically to the last detail. J.C., Massachusetts.

A. Cadillac built 4,764 series 62 Club Coupes in 1948. Perhaps fewer than 10 percent remain today. Your car's engine number, 486212213, is at the low end of the number sequence which ran from 486200001 to 486252704. The March date on the newspaper is very likely when the car was assembled in Detroit. For restoration help, I suggest you contact the Cadillac LaSalle Club, Incorporated, 3083 Howard Road, Petoskey, Michigan 49770. You might enjoy a book called *CADILLACS OF THE FORTIES.*

Q. I have just purchased a 1939 Chevrolet Master Deluxe that needs a ground-up restoration. The car itself needs about three or four years of work, but the body is sound. My problem is that it has a lot of surface rust. It will be stored and repaired outside. Should I prime the whole car to keep the rusting process at bay until such time as money and time permit me to get the body work and painting done ? R.K., Minnesota.

A. You can protect the body from further rusting by applying a coat of epoxy primer like DP-40 by PPG-Ditzler. Do not use a lacquer-based primer, as this coating will be water porous and allow rusting to occur under the primer layer. When using modern epoxy paints, be sure to follow all the safety warnings on the container. These paints must not be sprayed without wearing proper respirator.

Q. I have a 1960 Dodge Dart that I am interested in restoring. I would like to know how much it will cost and how much it will be worth after restoration? D.S., California.

A. With a California car, presumably you will not be dealing with extensive rust, but rather the standard mechanical work of brakes, engine overhaul, cosmetic repairs to the body, repainting and upholstery work. The cost of this will depend on how much you do yourself and the extent of the repairs needed. If your Dart is powered by Chrysler's famous slant six, an engine that holds the acclaim of being in continuous production in its original displacement configuration longer than any other, you will want to contact the Slant 6 Club of America, PO Box 4414, Salem, Oregon 97302. This group has three California chapters and a large membership base in that state. What you might find most interesting is this club's publication (which is mailed four times a year). It includes listings of slant six powered cars that have exceeded 200,000 miles of use. The longest running slant six in the club's most recent publication had logged 580,000 miles. These engines have almost legendary reliability. Restored, your car would have a value in the $5,000 range, about 40 percent more if it is a hardtop and approximately double that amount if it is a convertible.

Q. I'm restoring a 1970 Dodge with the factory 340 T/A six pack. Since buying the car I have purchased the 1970 *CHALLENGER-DART SERVICE MANUAL*, a data book and a price guide covering 1964 to 1974 Barracudas and Challengers. In none of these can I find any information on a 1970 Dodge Challenger T/A with the 340 six pack option. Even the vehicle identification number doesn't show up as a production car. Can you tell me why I can't find my car listed in the literature I have purchased? What was the number of Challenger T/A 340 six pack cars produced in 1970? S.O., Colorado.

A. Tom Quadrini of Legendary Interiors supplies upholstery kits for vintage Chrysler products and reminded me that the Challenger T/A was a midyear model introduced in March or April. It is covered specifically in the 1971 *DODGE SERVICE MANUAL*, as well as by several special factory service bulletins. The data books were written in advance of this model's introduction. They do not include it. According to some sources, less than 1,000 Challenger T/As were produced in the 1970 model year. Other sources pinpoint a figure of 2,500 units being scheduled for production. Perhaps Chrysler couldn't hit plan on that model. More information may be available through the Challenger/'Cuda Owner's Association, Rural Route 3, Lachute, Quebec, Canada J8H 3W7.

Q. I am restoring a Cockshutt tractor and need parts. Do you know of a Cockshutt club? A.G., Pennsylvania.

A. We list a publication called the *GOLDEN ARROW* for Cockshutt-Coop-Blackhawk tractor collectors. The address in our listing is c/o John Kasmiski, N7209 State Highway 67, Mayville, Wisconsin 53050.

Q. Recently my wife inherited a 1945 Willys Jeep which was used by the Navy in World War II. We have the engine restored and are working on the body. What is the exact color of the Jeep in its original state? Where can we buy the canvas top, side doors and seats. H.T., Illinois.

A. Anyone restoring a World War II Jeep should purchase the book *ALL-AMERICAN WONDER: THE MILITARY JEEP 1941-1945* by Ray Cowdery. It's available from Northstar Books, Box 803, Lakeville, Minnesota 55044 and other book sellers. This book covers virtually every detail, including restoration sequences, for Ford, Willys and Bantam Jeeps of World War II vintage. For those who still believe that it's possible to buy surplus Jeeps in a crate for $50, a chapter in this book debunks this myth. Of interest to those who wish to restore their military Jeep complete with correct ID numbers and markings, the book shows the correct marking schemes. The correct color for a U.S. Navy Jeep is gray. This is discussed in the painting chapter. The details in this book are incredible. No military Jeep owner should be without it. The best parts source for these vehicles is Willys Worldwide, Incorporated, PO Box 298, Lakeville, Minnesota 55044.

Q. Recently, I purchased a 1941 Ford pickup that I intend to restore. Where can I get parts or maintenance manuals for this model? G.D., Michigan.
A. Your best source of parts and service manuals for your 1941 Ford pickup is through literature vendors or at old car flea markets. In addition to the manuals, we recommend that you purchase Howard Towne's excellent little book *TWO GREAT TRUCKS: 1940, 1941 FORD*. It's available by writing Howard Towne, RFD 1, Box 479A, North Dorchester Road, Rumney, New Hampshire 03226. You may also enjoy the book *FORD PICKUPS 1932-1952* by Mack Hils. It's available from Mack Products, PO Box 278, Moberly, Missouri 65270. Towne's book is especially valuable because it shows the various changes in the 1940-1941 models with different engine options. The book also shows a complete range of accessories for these trucks. It is well-illustrated with photos and drawings and even has a place to record notes on your truck. Hils' book has almost 30 photos of the 1940-1941 Ford pickups. Most are 8 x 10s obtained from the Ford archives. We also recommend that you join a club to help you locate parts and answer questions you may have as you restore your truck. A club will also put you in contact with others of like interest. The Light Commercial Vehicle Association, Route 14, Box 468, Jonesboro, Tennessee 37659 covers pickups of all models and years.

Q. I recently acquired a 1933 Ford 1/2-ton pickup with a four-cylinder engine. Can you provide me with some needed information on this unit? The serial number is 85218812. Were these units called the Model C or were they called series 46? Was this the last year Ford made the four-cylinder engine or were they still produced in 1934? If so, in what series? Can you tell me how many four-cylinder pickups were made in 1933 and 1934? Did this motor have a balanced crankshaft? How did this motor differ from the Model A and Model B power plants? Do you know if a four-speed transmission was available for these pickups? Can you tell me what body colors were available? Does the *STANDARD CATALOG OF AMERICAN LIGHT-DUTY TRUCKS* that you have give detailed information on this model? A.O.L., Wisconsin.
A. The Model C is a mythical designation never used by Ford. It has come about, most feel, because later Model B four-cylinder engines had a C stamped on the cylinder head. Your truck is a Model 46 and as a pickup it is body type 830. We have conflicting advice on the last year Ford used the four-cylinder engine in its light trucks. The *FORD CHASSIS PARTS AND ACCESSORIES CATALOG* covering 1928-1947 lists a four-cylinder engine for the 1934 commercial models, which are also designated Model 46. Mack Hils' book, referred to in the previous answer, states that 1933 was the last year for the four-cylinder engine. The differences between 1932, 1933 and 1934 Ford pickups are subtle. One way to recognize a 1934 model is by an oval Ford insignia on the

side of the hood above the louvers. We have production figures for the 1933 Ford pickup, but not by engine. In 1933, Ford built 33,748 open cab pickups and in 1934, Ford built 66,922. As a 1933 model, your four-cylinder engine should have the balanced crankshaft. You can check by removing the fuel pump and shining a flashlight into the crankcase. This way you should be able to see the counter balance weights on the crankshaft. This engine differed from the B and A primarily by having the counterbalanced crankshaft. The B engine differed from the A in several ways, most noticeably by a different three-bolt water pump and fuel pump. These later engines can be installed in a Model A by changing the bellhousing and bolting a plate over the fuel pump opening. Since the four-cylinder pickup chassis is the same as that of a passenger car, the four-speed transmission was not available. We do not have a listing of colors for your truck, but you should be able to get this information easily from a paint vendor specializing in vintage autos. Our catalog gives an overview of Ford's 1933 pickups. You can find additional information in Mack Hils book, mentioned earlier.

Q. A few months ago you had an article about a Willys-Knight which was donated to McPherson College's restoration technology program. I would be interested in contacting this college about their program and curriculum. Would you print their address so that I can contact them? T.E., Oregon.

A. McPherson College, PO Box 1402, McPherson, Kansas 67460 operates a unique antique auto restoration program which leads to a two-year associates degree in restoration technology. The phone number for the school is (316) 241-0731.

Q. I recently purchased a 1936 Buick Roadmaster, model number 81, style number 36-4819, body number 5195. The car has only 16,400 miles on the odometer and all parts are intact. During the process of restoring the car, I have discovered eight 1/8-inch diameter holes in the roof. Four holes are across the roof, approximately six inches ahead of the center pillar. The other holes are across the roof approximately two inches behind the rear door hinge pillar. The distance between the two groups of holes is 39-1/2 inches. The holes are eight inches apart within each group of four. Assuming there was a roof rack on this car, I would like any information, a photo or sales literature so I can reconstruct the roof rack. D.M., Ohio.

A. We are advised by members of the Buick Club of America that Buick did not offer an accessory roof rack in your car's vintage. A photo of a Buick station wagon, equipped with a roof rack that appears to be mounted in the same location as the holes on your car, is shown on page 402 of the book called *THE BUICK: A COMPLETE HISTORY*. Perhaps this photograph will assist you in reconstructing the rack.

Q. I recently purchased a 1939 Buick Special four-door sedan, model number 41, style number 39-4419, body number 20 224, trim number 700, paint number 536. What color paint and upholstery do these codes indicate? P.M., Arkansas.

A. We asked members of the Buick Club of America for assistance with the information you requested. They said that trim number 700 refers to Tan Novelty Bedford cord which has a stripe in it. The paint is Yosemite Gray light. The Buick Club members stated that color and upholstery information can be found in a chassis or body book. Since these reference books are getting hard to locate for older models, our advice to readers looking for this information is to join a club where reference data like this can be gotten from other members. The Buick Club's address is Buick Club of America, PO Box 898, Garden Grove, California 92642.

71

Q. Some years ago you discussed the use of a product called RSP (Rapid Setting Polyester) in your column. In the short term, I'm sure it is a good product. However, I am concerned about long term durability. Does it really strengthen bad wood with durability that is long lasting? Is there a new and better (longer lasting or easier to use) product on the market now? J.C., Texas.

A. I think you are referring to Kwik-Poly available from T Distributing Incorporated, 24 Saint Henry Court, Saint Charles, Missouri 63301. In demonstrations I have seen of this product, it was used to restore cars that suffered from wood rot. The soft and rotted wood appeared to have been given the strength of new wood. I have no direct experience with the product's long term durability. However, it came out of the aircraft repair industry and has been used there for years. That suggests that it lasts awhile. I do not believe that the polyester product deteriorates. Since it is used as a filler over deteriorated wooden parts, it should protect the old wood from further decay.

Q. I'm in my 14th year of restoring a 1963 Falcon Sport Futura convertible and desperately need a step-by-step, illustrated instruction manual for installing a new convertible top. The scant instructions which came with a new top I purchased are useless. I can't go by the top that was on the car (as the instructions suggest), since there wasn't one on it. It didn't even have the top pads. I've seen such a manual for Fisher Body vehicles, but I don't have the name of the publisher. My local Ford dealer gave me a brochure from Helm, Incorporated and I wrote to them, telling them exactly what I was looking for. Their only answer was to send a printed copy of their list/order blank which doesn't contain one single mention of the sort of manual I specifically asked them about. Hasn't anyone published a manual for the Ford top I want to install? A.S.H., Louisiana.

A. A few years ago, *AUTO TRIM & RESTYLING NEWS* magazine published an issue with an article giving step-by-step, illustrated instructions covering the installation of a convertible top on a late-1950s Ford. It was simple and concise, but comprehensive. Perhaps you can order a back issue from them or get a photocopy of the old article. Write to: Shore Communications, 6255 Barfield Road, Suite 200, Atlanta, Georgia 30328-4300. The book *HOW TO RESTORE YOUR COLLECTOR CAR* also has a chapter on replacing a convertible top with sequence photos of a new top being installed on a 1971 Mustang convertible. This book may be helpful to you. It is available from Classic Motorbooks and can be ordered through your local book store.

Q. I would like to know where I can find information about how one can redo a vinyl dashboard? Is there a book I can purchase on how to do this? Also, I have a car 25-years-old that has only light rust on its frame. Should I spray it with new motor oil to prevent further rust? If so, how often? Is it better to spray on used motor oil than to now have it undercoated where the slight rust appears? I have always noted, on cars where oil drips on the frame at the front, the oil prevents the frame from rusting. C.W., Massachusetts.

A. In his book *CAR INTERIOR RESTORATION* (Tab Books), Terry Boyce has a short section about restoring vinyl dash pads, but it isn't a how-to section. There have been articles published on this process, but I haven't seen a step-by-step description of how to replace a vinyl dashboard in any book. Just Dashes, Incorporated, 5945 Hazeltine Avenue, Van Nuys, California 91401 will replace the vinyl dashboard covering, but you will have to remove the dashboard from your car. They also sell reproduction dash pads for some models. Regarding your question about protecting the frame, I recommend used motor oil for this purpose since the acids in the oil will help clean the rust. The oil coating will give excellent rust prevention protection. Ziebart also offers a special "Used Car Rust Protection" plan offering four different systems for rust-proofing older models. Posters promoting this plan featured an early postwar Packard and the company maintains that the systems can work for collector cars, too.

A restored 1965 Chevrolet Impala SS vinyl dashboard.

Q. As the years of restoring our various antiques have rolled by, our skills at metal working and fabrication have become more sophisticated. As time went by, we acquired many fine metal-working machines: breaks, folders, shears, nibblers, saws, etc. All of these do a fine job. We go to shows where tool dealers sell various small and medium tools. These are limited in their working range to small jobs. Our skills have marched on, but we can't find more sophisticated machines to make use of our skills. We need sources for larger metal-working machines and reference books about them. I am not referring to flat metal-working machines or machine shop equipment, but specifically to automotive sheet metal forming machines. As an example, an auto magazine article about an old time custom body builder mentioned that he used a machine called a Petingale Hammer. This remarkable machine was so good it could form nose cones for airplanes. I have heard mention of fender rolling machines as well. I am aware of stamping and metal spinning machinery, both of which we already use here. It is these larger custom body part formers that we seek. I have the distinct feeling that there is a whole world of these machines out there. Certainly Detroit does not go out and make a $100,000 die to produce the prototype of each body part for every new model. Can you help us? C.H., New Jersey.

A. English Wheels have been used for years to form compound curves on sleek custom and low production car bodies. Such a machine was once featured in the *OLD CARS* "Business Pages" section, so they are available. Several years ago, we encountered a restoration shop in Western Wisconsin that was rebuilding bodies for rare and exotic European classics. They had purchased used metal-working machinery from the

73

deHavilland Aircraft Company to create the missing body parts. Also, the Classic Car Centre in Warsaw, Indiana had installed quite a high-tech machine and metal-working shop using brand new machinery that was imported from Italy. It is our understanding that this facility no longer handles restorations, though collector car sales are continuing there. In any case, the machines you seek are available. However, they are quite expensive and beyond the reach of most "shade tree" mechanics. The Eastwood Company, 580 Lancaster Avenue, Malvern, Pennsylvania 19355 does offer a catalog including several metal-working tools geared to hobby applications. You can send for a free copy of this 100-page booklet.

Q. I have a question about a project. I am making a street rod from a 1940 Chevrolet business coupe that's too far gone to restore. Years ago, I saw ads for striping entire car bodies. I live in north central Arkansas. Where is the nearest metal stripping facility? J.B., Sr., Arkansas.
A. To locate a metal stripping laundry, I'd suggest that you look in the "Yellow Pages" of telephone books for the larger cities within convenient driving distance. Local libraries often have these telephone directories. You might also want to contact Redi Strip, 9910 Jordan Circle, PO Box 2745, Sante Fe Springs, California 90670. Their latest listing does not show a metal stripping franchise in Arkansas, but they can give you information on which of their franchise operations would be nearest to you.

Q. I have owned a 1950 Mercury coupe for 20 years. The car has been under cover the last 15 years. The body is fair. The trunk needs a floor welded in. The motor is frozen and the transmission needs work. I don't want to make this car into a rod or custom. I would like to keep it original. However, I would like to remove the body and mount it on a 1980s model, such as a Cutlass or any full- or medium-size chassis. Could you refer me to someone who has done this? G.L., Michigan.
A. Although mounting your 1950 Mercury body on a later model chassis can be done, I would discourage you from doing this for two reasons. First, it's a lot of work. You'll have the problem of trying to find a chassis with a wheelbase that fits the Mercury body. Then, you'll have to fabricate body mounts and other hardware, make new wiring, and so on. Your original-condition car is rising in value. Putting the body on a more modern chassis will lower its value and create a lot of expense. A better approach would be to update the drive train. This can be done quite easily following instructions in the *1949-50-51 FORD OWNER'S HANDBOOKLET* published by the 1949-50-51 Ford Owner's Newsletter, PO Box 30647, Midwest City, Oklahoma 73140.

Q. I purchased a very nice original 1958 Mercury Medalist last summer. This car was the cheapest Mercury made that year. I have a question about the paint offered on the Medalist. Could you tell me if they were offered in solid colors only? This is the only Medalist I can remember seeing and it is all black. I am thinking about a two-tone paint job. Would this be correct for a Medalist? B.H., Pearl, Mississippi.
A. Our *STANDARD CATALOG OF AMERICAN CARS 1946-1975* lists two-tone paint as a $17.20 option for 1958 Mercurys. Presumably, this applies to the Medalist model. For more information on your Medalist, you might want to contact The Big M Mercury Club, 5 Robinson Road, West Woburn, Massachusetts 01801 or the Mid-Century Mercury Car Club, 5707 35th Avenue, Kenosha, Wisconsin 53142.

Q. I have a 1955 Oldsmobile 88 two-door hardtop that I am in the process of restoring. My problem is that I have received a headliner with only generalized instructions. The original headliner was removed from the car before I bought it. I have the bows and the side retainer strips, but I don't have the retainers that hold the bows at one end. One bow, which it is the first one from the front of the car, has an up-turn on each side that fits into holes on the either side of the inside of the roof. The other bows have an up-turn on only one side of each of them. Is there a publication that shows detailed instructions for headliner installation on this car? Also, the bows are mixed up, so I don't know which one goes where. Can you help? J.P., New York.

A. *AUTOMOTIVE UPHOLSTERY HANDBOOK* by Don Taylor is a just released book. It has an entire chapter devoted to the installation of headliners, door panels and carpets. There are six pages and 15 clear photos showing hobbyists how to install a headliner. The book is available from Fisher Books, PO Box 38040, Tucson, Arizona 85740-8040. You can order it by phoning (602) 292-9080. The price (less shipping) is $19.95. Literature vendors, such as Walter Miller who lives near you in Syracuse, New York, should be able to provide a body service manual for your 1955 Oldsmobile. This shop book should show the location of the bows. Your best bet for the missing retainers will be to scout out an Oldsmobile or Buick hardtop (1954-1956 should work) in a salvage yard.

Q. Could you give your opinion as to the most suitable welding method (gas or arc) for an amateur like myself? Most of the welding I'll attempt would be unseen under-body work (floors, inner fenders, etc.) Second, I have been advised that to minimize distortion, brazing is the best approach. However, others have warned that brazing can and will fracture, due to flexing in service. E.P.B.

A. First, I recommend that anyone planning on taking up welding for old car repair enroll in a welding class at a high school skill center or technical college. There are too many dangers associated with welding to learn how to do it from a book. For sheet metal repair, including the under-body work you describe, I recommend investing in a MIG (Metal Inert Gas) outfit which will run two or three times the price of a gas welder or regular arc welding unit. MIG is a form of arc welding that is very easy to use, even for beginners. It minimizes metal distortion, due to heat build up. Brazing is not a suitable method for the metal repairs you describe, since it does not make a steel-to-steel bond. Besides, brazing has the disadvantage in that it is very difficult to wash out all of the flux used to etch the metal. Often, trapped flux will seep out of the seam, raise the paint and eat the metal. After taking a welding class, if you don't elect to invest in an MIG welding outfit, you will find that gas welding is usually the next most preferable system for repairing thin automotive metal. However, as you point out, heat distortion can be a problem.

Q. I own a 1948 Cadillac that was in storage for over 20 years in a heated garage. Careful storage really saved this car, but the rubber strips around the doors have melted into a hard, black crystal-like substance. It is almost impossible to remove this substance without taking off the original paint. Some of this stuff is also like tar or goo. Can you help with something to remove the weather stripping? I have new rubber weather seal to install. B.H., Pennsylvania.

A. You might try using a heat gun on the hardened weather stripping. Look for the type of gun used to strip paint from houses. If you take this approach, set the gun on the low setting and keep moving it over the rubber one area at a time. Using this technique will not raise the old paint. The heat should soften the rubber enough that it can be pried loose. You may still have a small residue of old rubber that needs to be cleaned off. You can do this by working gently with a putty knife.

Q. Last summer I purchased a Packard 120 convertible coupe. I am having trouble determining whether it is a 1936 or 1937 model. The car is in all-original, unrestored condition. The odometer reads 30,000 miles, which I believe to be correct due to the car's condition. The wheelbase is 120 inches. A Packard firewall tag gives the vehicle number as 10-99-2749 and indicates that it was delivered by W. R. Frisbie, Norwich, 4-27-37. The body number embossed on the firewall is 377475. The engine serial number is X71299. I do not see any indication of body or frame damage, so I have ruled out the possibility of the car being in a serious accident. I believe it's a 1937 model. However, the hood, grille and grille shell parts and engine serial number are definitely from 1936, while the dash is definitely a 1937 item. Could this car have been a late 1936 production car which had a 1936 nose installed on a 1937 car at the factory? I wish to start restoring it to original condition, but am not sure which way to go. Should it have a 1936 dash or a 1937 nose? Should I leave it the way it is? D.P., Massachusetts.

A. George Hamlin of the Packard club notes that the firewall on the car tag checks out to be from 1937. He suggests that the car has received a 1936 front clip (front fenders and grille) at some time in its life. If you want to restore the car as a 1937, you would have to replace the front clip. If you are not already a member, you may want to join the Packard Club, PO Box 1347, Orinda, California 94563 and enjoy its fine publication *THE CORMORANT.*

Q. My wife has a 1966 Lincoln Continental that she refuses to part with because she likes it better than any other car she has seen. The original upholstery of this car is worn. For the past several months, a local automobile upholsterer has been trying to find replacement fabric. The Lincoln factory reports that it does not have the fabric. There are firms which specialize in parts for older cars. Can you guide us to a possible source for upholstery fabrics which might duplicate the original? This is a one-owner four-door Continental which has had excellent care. G.W.P., Tennessee.

A. LeBaron Bonney Company, the Ford and Mercury upholstery kit manufacturer in Amesbury, Massachusetts, has collected stocks of old-stock upholstery material. Possibly, they can match your Continental's interior. Write to them at LeBaron Bonney, 6 Chestnut Street, Amesbury, Massachusetts 01913 or call (508) 388-3811.

Q. I have a 1938 Plymouth. The plate on the firewall reads number 416-1845. Briggs Corporation, Evansville, Indiana is also marked on the plate. Is this a clue as to the original color of the car? It has been repainted light blue. What is the correct color for the motor? R.G., Illinois.

A. Jim Benjaminson, membership secretary for the Plymouth 4 & 6 Cylinder Owner's Club, 203 Main Street East, Cavalier, North Dakota 58220, fielded questions. Jim notes, "Body number 416-1845 indicates a two-door slantback sedan, but I can't tell from that number if it's a P5 Roadking or P6 Deluxe. As to the paint, there is nothing on the car that would indicate its original color. Chrysler always advised, "If you need to know, contact the factory!" To check for original color, look in spots like the firewall and trunk which are unlikely to have been repainted. DuPont paint charts indicate the following colors were available: Gunmetal Gray, Middy Blue, Garfield Green, Mercury Blue, Stone Beige, Avon Green and Silverwing Gray number 3. West Coast manufactured cars had metallic colors, but in the same shades. The engine was silver (aluminum) with starter, generator and other accessories done in black. The carburetor, distributor, etc. were natural color. The club can send you a paint interchange for these colors." (Note: With his letter, R.G. sent a copy of the *CHRYSLER RESTORER'S GUIDE*, published by the Chrysler Corporation's Historical Collection. This publication, which lists clubs related to MoPar products, serial number locations, assembly plants and related data, is available for a small charge from the Chrysler Historical Collection, Department CIMS 416-02-46, PO Box 1919, Detroit, Michigan 48288.

Q. I have a 1970 Pontiac Lemans Sport with original engine and transmission. The car now has over 200,000 miles and does need some body work. I would rather not take it to the junkyard and was wondering if you could suggest someone who might want to refurbish the car. Wayne E. Williams, Boulder Creek, California.
A. Guessing that the car hails from California, we'll presume that the body is basically sound. On that premise, you might be able to interest car clubs or a technical college auto repair program in accepting the car as a donation. You could begin by contacting the Pontiac Oakland Club International, PO Box 4789, Culver City, California 90230. Your local *YELLOW PAGES* will give a list of vocational schools and technical colleges in your area. They might be interested in restoring the car as a class project. In order to receive tax credit for the donation, you will have to have the car appraised by a competent auto appraiser.

Q. Could you tell me if the headliner for my 1946 Chevrolet panel truck should cover the passenger or cargo area or both? What is the proper material for the interior? The vehicle was purchased mostly restored with a headliner of brown cloth over the cargo area only. It has a bare roof exposed over the passenger area. Our local upholstery shop cannot get kits or patterns. L.B., Mount Airy, Maryland.
A. The Chevrolet dealer's *SALESMAN'S DATA BOOK* for 1946 states that the panel truck body was fitted with "form-fitting insulation top and sides" and that the "driver's compartment (was) completely trimmed." My understanding is that the form-fitting insulation is a Masonite type of panel board. The completely trimmed driver's compartment refers to an embossed cardboard headliner. Headliner kits for 1946 Chevrolet pickups and panels are available from Jim Carter, 1508 East Alton, Independence, Missouri 64055. Jim also provides instructions for installing the headliner. This operation is a little tricky. The problem arises in getting the cardboard formed to the correct bends.

Q. I have a 1970 yellow Cougar convertible. It has a rusty bottom and is a monstrous oil eater. I love it as if it were my own child. What should I do about it? It drives beautifully if I feed it lots of oil and I do. But my mechanic says he can't do anything about the rust. Any suggestions? S.E., Florida.
A. These cars can be repaired, but it's the kind of work that needs to be done in a restoration shop. Depending on the extent of rust damage to the structural members of the body, the engine and interior would be removed. Next, the car would be mounted on a cradle and tipped on its side for repair of floors, body support members, etc. The process is labor-intensive and expensive for that reason. The *OLD CARS PRICE GUIDE* shows the value of a 1970 Cougar convertible to be between $5,000 in solid, driveable, number 3 condition and $10,000 in number 1 show-quality condition. Perhaps knowing something of your car's potential value will help you decide whether you want to make the investment which will allow you to drive it in the future.

Q. I have a 1925 Maxwell four-door. The wood is bad. I would like to know where I could send for a manual so I could start working on it? J.M., Illinois.
A. The book *HOW TO RESTORE WOODEN BODY FRAMING* by Alan Alderwyck should supply the information you need. This is an Osprey book, published in England and distributed in the United States by Classic Motorbooks, Route 1, Osceola, Wisconsin 54020.

Q. I just bought a 1929 Ford Model A Tudor sedan. I am trying to restore it, but haven't too much information. This hobby is not very common in Chile. What I need is a complete restoration manual for this car and, if possible, a full parts list. How could I buy these publications? J.J.L., Chile.

A. A good book for anyone restoring a Model A is Jim Schild's *RESTORER'S MODEL A SHOP MANUAL*. It's available from Classic Motorbooks, (715) 294-3345. What makes Schild's book so helpful is that he describes how to restore a Model A from worn and weary condition. Numerous photos in the book show parts as they are found and what they should look like. The restoration steps then explain how to bring the parts back to proper shape and condition. In addition, Jim Schild provides a collection of tips on such simple, but difficult tasks as compressing and retaining the gearshift lever spring in order to install a rechromed shift lever. He also shows how to make special tools such as a jig to hold wheels for painting. Any full catalog from a Model A parts supplier will give you the parts list you need. Schild's book gives names and addresses of major Model A parts suppliers. In addition, you may want to contact either the Model A Ford Club of America, 250 South Cyprus, La Habra, California 90631 or the Model A Ford Restorers Club, 24822 Michigan Avenue, Dearborn, Michigan 48121. Both clubs provide their members with informative and interesting to read publications.

Q. I am the proud owner and driver of a 1952 Mercury sedan. I have enjoyed driving the car and receive many compliments on it, but a problem has developed. The rubber gusset surrounding the rear window has deteriorated. The chrome trim is supposed to fit into the rubber and rest in it. Due to the lack of elasticity of the rubber, the chrome piece raises up and remains several inches above the window at the center of the window on the upper edge. Could you tell me where I might obtain a new piece of rubber? It is embarrassing to drive the car this way. E.M., Iowa.

A. I suggest that you contact Dennis Carpenter Ford Restorations, PO Box 26398, Charlotte, North Carolina 28221. A comment is in order here for hobbyists who are plagued by hard-to-find replacement window rubber. Salvage yards in the upper Midwest (Michigan in particular) can be a source of sound, resilient window moldings, especially from cars parked among trees. A friend, who is a professional body man, ordered replacement rear window rubber for his Studebaker. However, he was not able to make the reproduction rubber parts fit. A few weeks later, while scouting parts in a salvage yard, he came across a Studebaker of similar vintage with all glass intact. He asked the yard owner if he could remove the rear window to see if the rubber was usable and found it to be soft as new.

Q. My husband and I are restoring my father's first farm truck. We believe it to be between 1936 and 1945. Where can we get information? There are many details that we are not sure about. The one delaying us now is the original engine color. I am in hopes that you have a book on older trucks that we may purchase. J.T.C., Texas.

A. You don't state the make of truck, but during these years Chevrolet truck engines were painted gray, Dodge engines were painted silver, Studebaker and International engines were finished in green and Ford engines were done in green or blue. Ford used green for their engines up to 1941 and blue for several years thereafter. Ford returned to green for the flathead V-8 in the 1950s. You also don't specify the size of the truck. If you are restoring a light truck, you may wish to order the *STANDARD CATALOG OF AMERICAN LIGHT-DUTY TRUCKS*.

Q. I am trying to restore a 1929 Model A Ford station wagon. All the wood is bad or missing. Do you have any idea where I can find plans to build the wood body? C.B., Wisconsin.

A. The last time I visited his shop in Fishers, New York (a tiny village near Rochester), Richie Colombo was still tooled up and producing superb quality, absolutely accurate wood bodies for 1929 Model A Ford station wagons. At the time, Colombo was also producing replica MG-TF roadsters. His business was called Great Lakes Motor Cars. You might call directory assistance for a Victor, New York listing for this company or its proprietor. These bodies have been installed on a number of show winning cars. They are flawless. Even if you are a master woodworker, you would be hard-pressed to duplicate the complicated joints used in these bodies. My suggestion is to buy Colombo's replacement body, if they are still available.

Q. Where can I find original color schemes for 1930-1931 Ford Model A roadsters? J.S., South Dakota.

A. The source of this information is the *ANTIQUE FORD REPAINT MANUAL* 1928-1936. This little book contains authentic color paint chips and color schemes for Fords between the years in the title and gives tips for applying a show-winning finish. Since you are concerned with returning your Model A to authentic standards, you may also want to purchase the *MODEL A FORD JUDGING STANDARDS* jointly published by the Model A Restorers Club and Model A Ford Club of America. Both books are available from Classic Motorbooks and many Ford parts suppliers.

Colors for Ford Model A convertibles are available in a book.

PROBLEMS and CURES

Q. My collector car has been stored in a garage and not used for several months. I noticed that a lot of gum formed in the carburetor. Why did a car that was clean when it was put in storage develop gum in the fuel system? Is there some way to remove it? A.H., New York.

A. Most likely, you failed to remove all gasoline from the car before storing it. As gasoline oxidizes, it forms a hard varnish which is often called gum. While the car is being used, this deposit doesn't form because the car is moving. During storage periods, the gum settles on various parts of the fuel system. When storing a car, you should drain the gas tank and run the engine until all remaining fuel is used up. Gum formation in a dry fuel system will be minimal or non-existent. An easy way to clean out the entire system is to add a pint of acetone, which you can purchase at a drugstore or paint store. Acetone is an effective solvent which will clean away the gum and varnish while the engine operates. If your system is heavily gummed, it may be necessary to take the works apart and scrape away the sludge.

Q. I have a 1949 Buick Roadmaster that exhibits a metallic "clacking" from within the torque tube or differential. The noise starts after driving four or five miles when the car is warmed up. It is also heard going around curves or down a bumpy road, but is not related to the shock absorbers. How can I fix it? L.K., England.

A. A seasoned mechanic explains that Buicks had a constant velocity joint inside the torque tube, just behind the transmission. He suspects your constant velocity joints are the source of the noise. Most service station owners don't know that the joint is there and fail to give it proper lubrication. You can access the grease fitting for the joint by removing a plug on the torque tube. If the constant velocity joint is badly worn, you can check for play by removing the plug and manipulating the joint with a screwdriver inserted through the hole.

Q. I have just purchased a 1936 Dodge in good condition. The problem is that someone snapped off a key in the driver's side door lock. We have not been able to get the broken key out of the lock. What can we try? E.L.R., Illinois.

A. Try using a crochet hook. In many cases, the small hooked end of the crochet hook will bring out the broken key without any difficulty. It's usually helpful to squirt a couple of drops of kerosene inside the door lock to help lubricate and free the broken key.

Q. I'm having cooling problems with my collector car. I have had it worked on by several shops without success. They have changed the thermostat and pressure cap and replaced two hoses. We have also flushed the radiator and block and added anti-rust compounds, but none of this has done any good. What do you think my problem is? L.M., Georgia.

A. There's a strong possibility that the cause of your problem is a leaky head gasket or a cracked cylinder head. If water has to be added frequently and you haven't noticed any external leaks, it is reasonable to assume that combustion gases are leaking into the cooling system. These gases heat the water and can also force it out of the overflow pipe. A quick test with a compression gauge will verify the existence of a leaky head gasket or cracked cylinder head. If the compression checks out okay, there could be a problem with your water pump. George Warner, of Roanoke, Virginia, spent about $200 making the same repairs you've done after he had installed a new water pump. Finally, on the advice of a friend, he removed the new water pump and found that the impeller inside was slipping. His parts store replaced the water pump and his overheating problem was gone.

Q. We recently purchased a 1938 Plymouth two-door sedan. The car is in practically mint condition, except for a large ink stain on the driver's seat. How can we remove such a stain? W.C., Ohio.
A. Use either a two percent solution of sodium fluoride or a number 1 ink eradicator sparingly, until the stain is removed. Allow the upholstery to dry for approximately one minute. Then, rinse it well with cold water. Use extra care in using this procedure on upholstery that shows signs of slight deterioration due to age. In such cases, be careful not to rub the upholstery too briskly.

Q. I have a 1938 Oldsmobile that has been stored for about 20 years in our neighbor's garage. Can you please advise what to do about the varnish that accumulated in the gas tank? What product should I use to clean it out? Where can I take the tank for cleaning? E.B., Wisconsin.
A. We're told a radiator shop can boil out the tank, but that the plating on the inner liner could be destroyed by this process. Therefore, solvents may work better in some cases, but mechanical cleaning could be the only solution to a severe accumulation of varnish. Truman Stockton, of Lakewood, Colorado has had good luck with the use of acetone as a solvent. He loosens the gas lines, removes the carburetor and soaks the fuel system parts in the solvent until the varnish is gone. The gas tank is drained and a half-gallon of acetone is added to loosen varnish on the bottom of the tank. The tank is drained and filled with lead-free high test gas to which one ounce of acetone is added for each gallon of gas. When the tank is clean, it must be fully drained (running an engine on a gas/acetone mixture could damage a piston). Then lead-free high test gas should be added. John Murphy, of Benton Harbor, Michigan doesn't believe in using solvents because a 1935 Chevrolet he purchased, after 27 years of being stored, couldn't be fixed that way. The previous owner had fired the car up and thoroughly clogged the entire fuel system. Murphy removed the gas filler pipe from the fuel tank and discovered an opening large enough to view a thick crust of hard material inside. He filled the tank with water and saber-sawed the top off the tank, removing a section that gave manual access to all areas. This revealed that the car had been stored with the tank three-quarters full. After mechanically removing most of the crusty material, Murphy filled it with water to a level above the "crud" line and added two or three cans of household lye. An electric charcoal lighter was used as an immersed heater. He followed standard precautions for using a caustic substance, making sure to add the caustic to the water, rather than water to the caustic. He provided good ventilation and used waterproof gloves and a wire brush to insure all materials were removed before disposing of the liquid down a toilet. The gas tank was flushed thoroughly and blown dry with a hair dryer. With all traces of petroleum vapor gone, the top panel of the tank was welded back in place. A piece of small wire was pushed through the section of gas line tubing and a piece of cotton clothesline was pulled into the tube to seal it off. The gas tank was then slushed with commercial gas tank sealing compound to take care of future rusting problems and seal any pinholes in the weld. The hair dryer was used again to accelerate sealant curing time. Murphy made sure that the gas gauge sending unit was not re-installed until there was enough gas in the tank to keep the float off the bottom. If it had hit the bottom, it would have stuck to the sealant. He said the job went easier than it sounds and that the rewelding was invisible once the tank was strapped back in place. (Editor's note: The work described above should only be done by a professional because of the danger involved in cutting or welding a gas tank. Murphy's

experience shows that a crusted old gas tank can be restored, but we do not recommend attempting this process as a home restorer).

Q. Does an oily accumulation on the top of the radiator in my 1954 Chevrolet indicate oil leaking into the cooling system due to a cracked block? P.A., New York.

A. This is a common incorrect assumption that many hobbyists make by mistake. In the great majority of cases, the oily appearance of the water is due to use of an emulsifying oil type rust inhibitor used by many motorists in the 1940s and 1950s. It is quite common to run into this type of accumulation in cars of these years. Try flushing the cooling system and using one of the modern rust inhibitors, which incorporate agents that prevent this situation.

Q. I am writing about my 1950 DeSoto Club Coupe. I was driving up a slight hill between two intersections. After I pulled away from the first stop sign and hit 20 miles per hour, I removed my foot from the gas pedal so the Fluid Drive transmission would shift. It didn't. I was approaching the next intersection where I would have to stop again, so I let the car stay in first gear. Just before I touched the brake, the engine seemed to speed up and the car lurched forward with a bellowing clunk. Needless to say, this has me worried. The car performed as it should afterwards, but I expect it to lurch and clunk at any moment. What was the cause of this? D.D.D., Jr., Ohio.

A. Carl Tatlock, a Chrysler devotee from Williamson, New York, chuckled a bit at your description. His diagnosis is simply that your DeSoto missed a shift. The cause, he notes, is either electrical or mechanical or a combination of both. Since the problem has occurred just once, he suspects an electrical problem. At the point of the shift there should have been a momentary ignition suppression. Perhaps it was missed. To prevent similar clunks, check the wiring. Follow a schematic drawing of the transmission-related circuits from any vintage Chrysler or DeSoto service manual. Clean connections and repair or replace deteriorated wiring to avoid a reoccurrence.

Q. I have a 1946 Dodge custom in very nice shape. I am thinking of altering it so it would become a four-door convertible. Can anyone tell me what reinforcements are necessary? I wouldn't want to compromise the structural integrity of the car. Also, does anyone know who could make a top for me as I would like this car to be as functional as possible. R.B., Illinois.

A. While a conversion of the type you envision is possible, given enough time, skill and money, we wouldn't advise it. You will alter a nice original car into one that is primarily of interest to you and of questionable resale value. If you decide to go ahead with the conversion, you'll need to reinforce the frame and rear door pillars. Convertibles of your car's vintage had X members in the frame for support. If you look underneath a 1940s or 1950s convertible, you'll see what we mean. On four-door convertibles, the pillar between the front and rear doors is generally supported by being tied into the back bracing for the front seat. Often the rear doors are hung from the rear quarter panel. We really don't know who could make the top mechanism, which would be quite complicated. You would also need to make support pillars to fit between the front and rear door windows, when they were rolled up, which would also lock into the top and help strengthen it. There's a lot to think about in this conversion. Four-door convertibles are attractive, desirable cars and my advice (if you really want a car of this body style) would be to look for one of the rare Kaiser four-door convertibles. These were factory converted from four-door sedans and are both attractive and functional.

Q. I have never had the willpower to let my lack of a garage keep me from owning and enjoying an old car, even though I suffer anxiety over rusty nightmares. What is the best way to protect a car that is stored outdoors, on pavement, and is not moved during the week? I want to protect it mainly from sun and moisture, but soon I'll have to consider snow and cold also. Is a cover enough and what kind/type would you recommend? J.S., New York.

A. A car cover can lead to more problems than it solves, because the cover is likely to be whipped about in the wind. Since dust can blow up from underneath as the cover whips against the car, it can abrade the paint. Also, moisture can be trapped under the cover, making those rusty nightmares come true. If outside storage is really your only option, you might consider purchasing an "instant garage." This is a fabric cover stretched over a metal frame. This cover arrangement provides the protection you are looking for from rain and snow, but the cover doesn't come in contact with the vehicle. I don't have a manufacturer's address, but there is a toll free number (800) 452-6837 that you can call for price and other information.

Q. I have a 1950 Studebaker convertible and am having problems with the top not going down. Do you have any advice on fixing this? R.K., Kansas.

A. Convertibles of your Studebaker's vintage used an electro-hydraulic system to raise and lower the top. This system consisted of a pump driven by an electric motor that resembled a car starter, a valve assembly, hydraulic tubing and the hydraulic lift cylinders that actually raise the top. You should find a description of this system and troubleshooting information in the factory's "body service manual" for your car. When the top won't operate at all, some common causes are problems with the pump motor circuit or a bad solenoid on the motor. Contamination in the hydraulic fluid can also clog hydraulic lines. Other problems include leaking seals in the cylinders or hydraulic lines that have corroded, causing the fluid to escape. Unless the car has been restored, you will probably want to inspect and troubleshoot all parts of the top-lifting system. If you need to drain the hydraulic fluid, be very careful to catch the old fluid in a container and have rags ready to absorb any overflow. This fluid can easily damage the paint on your car. The electro-hydraulic top-lifting systems are not overly complicated, but they do have a lot of plumbing, so you'll want to check carefully for leaks. A good publication for convertible owners to read is *AUTO TRIM & RESTYLING NEWS*. This monthly magazine is published for professional upholsterers and top installers and frequently prints how-to articles.

Q. I have heard that the problem with the push-button transmission controls used in cars like Chryslers, Dodges, Plymouths, DeSotos, Edsels and Mercurys in the 1950s and 1960s was engaging the wrong gear or engaging two gears at once. Do you have any information on why automakers discontinued the push-button control setup? G.L., Michigan.

A. There may have been some isolated cases of problems with push-button drives. Mercury's is the only one I remember having a stubborn Park selector. But, as a whole, push-button transmissions did not cause big problems. The 1956 Dodge (first with push-button drive) was designed well. If you hit Reverse while in Drive, it would automatically shift to Neutral. It would engage if you were still in Low range under 10 miles per hour. Also, if you pushed Low while in Drive, Low would not engage until you reached a suitable speed for downshifting. While I tried many times, I could not push two buttons at once and get "stuck" between gears. The only problem with this early push-button Dodge was that it did not have a Park selector. You simply engaged the hand brake. Later Chrysler products came out with a Park lever that moved across the top or side of the buttons and put the car into neutral. According to car collector Harvey Leners, of Omaha, Nebraska, automakers finally discontinued push-button controls for automatic transmissions because the federal government mandated that a uniform P-R-N-D-L shift pattern be adopted for 1965. Consumer confusion over the wide number of selector patterns available prompted this move. Even GM had two patterns: P-N-D-L-R for all car-lines except Chevrolet, which had P-R-N-D-L. The problem was that reverse and low were found at different places on different makes. Many accidents happened when former Buick, Oldsmobile, Pontiac or Cadillac owners drove a Chevrolet, Ford or Lincoln. Often without thinking, they pulled the shift lever all the way down to where they felt reverse was and lurched forward into their garage wall. This happened in traffic or parking situations as well. There were many more column-shift vehicles on the road when the government's decision to unify shift patterns was made. Had GM put push-button selectors in Chevrolets, they would have been more common and you would probably see all cars today having push-button drive. With today's weight-saving ideas and electronic digitals, it is surprising that this idea hasn't resurfaced. Imagine the weight saved by eliminating all the linkages. Maybe it is time to have Detroit reinvent the wheel by bringing back the old push-button drive idea. At the same time, it would bring back a bit of nostalgia to many of us.

The 1957 Chrysler had push-button transmission.

Q. What can I do to change the gear ratio to a higher speed for my 1954 Chevrolet with standard transmission? Is there an overdrive unit or some other change that I can make? J.B., Oklahoma.

A. There are several ways to check what gearing your car has. You might look for a tag on the differential which would tell the axle ratio. If this tag is missing, another way to

84

check the rear end ratio would be to pull the cover on the differential and count the teeth on the ring and pinion gears. Then, you can calculate the ratio. If your car had an exposed driveshaft (1954 Chevrolets have the driveshaft enclosed in a torque tube) you could check the rear axle ratio quite easily by jacking up the rear end so that both wheels were off the ground and counting the number of tire revolutions for one revolution of the driveshaft. The standard rear end ratio for a 1954 Chevrolet equipped with manual transmission is 3.7:1. This ratio should allow your car to cruise at legal speeds without excessive engine noise and rpms. However, if you want a higher geared (lower numeric ratio) rear end, you may want to replace your car's axle with a unit from a 1953 or 1954 Powerglide equipped Chevrolet. The standard Powerglide rear end had 3.55:1 ratio gearing. Since you are dissatisfied with your car's axle ratio, it's possible that it is lower (higher numerically) than the standard ratios mentioned. Because of the torque tube drive design, an overdrive cannot be easily fitted into your car's driveline. Besides changing to a higher (lower numeric) rear end from a Powerglide-equipped car, you can increase cruising speed somewhat by going to the next larger tire size. Your car used 6.70 x 15 tires as standard equipment. As an option, 7.10 x 15 oversize tires were available. If your car is running on the standard size tires, you might want to switch to the taller (larger diameter) 7.10 x15 size.

Q. Some time ago, I read an article about adding Tetrasodium Ethylene Diaminetetra Acetate (EDTA) to a battery to increase its service length. The article did not advise where to buy this product. I have asked for it at hardware stores and pharmacies, as well as auto and chemical supply stores. Where can I purchase this chemical? What size package does it come in? How much does it cost? R.B., Illinois.

A. The article you read may have been written by K. L. Martin of England. According to Martin, the chemical EDTA cleans the battery plates of sulfate deposits that build up during the battery's working life. The process he advises is to empty the battery of all acid. He warns against spilling the acid on clothes and cautions that goggles be worn for eye protection. If acid gets on the skin, it should be washed off immediately with large amounts of cold water. Since the electrolyte will probably be reusable, it should be poured into a plastic bowl. A metal container should not be used because the acid may react with it. Martin advises that an average-sized car battery holds about 3-1/2 pints of electrolyte. After the battery has been emptied, it should be washed out with cold water. Keep rinsing and dumping out the water until all traces of sediment are gone. The next step is to clean the plates of sulfate build up, which is what causes a battery to lose its ability to receive and hold a charge. This is where the EDTA comes in. Martin recommends dividing about a third of a tablespoon of the EDTA powder between each cell and then topping-up the battery with warm water. He states that EDTA works slowly in battery acid, but very rapidly in neutral or alkaline solutions. Therefore, EDTA should be left in the battery only for an hour or so. He advises shaking the battery occasionally during this time. At the end of the hour, the solution is poured out and the battery is again rinsed with water. Now the acid is poured back in and the battery is recharged. Martin states that this treatment should rejuvenate batteries which are completely dead or more commonly have one dead cell. Complete success, however, depends on how and why the battery failed. Martin advised that EDTA should be available from chemical supply houses. Other sources of EDTA are Courtney Classics, 18218 Auburn Drive, Tomball, Texas 77375 and Louis Truffa, RR1, 11951 South Lawler Avenue, Alsip, Illinois 60658.

Q. I am working on a Rochester Quadra Jet tune-up. I have followed the standard tune-up procedures, but still feel that I haven't obtained maximum performance and economy. What kind of advice can you give me? T.B., Michigan.

A. Carburetor rebuilder William B. Studley noted several items that are sometimes important to carburetor performance and economy. First, in many older carbs, the main throttle plate shaft can wear enough from the bearing surfaces to allow air leakage. This leakage can affect operation, particularly to the cylinders that are at the end of a long manifold run. Anyone rebuilding an older carburetor can easily check for play or bends in the throttle shaft and choke shaft. To pinpoint leaks around the throttle shaft and carburetor base, spray a squirt of carburetor cleaner around the ends of the throttle shaft with the engine running. If the engine picks up speed (due to the carburetor cleaner's being inhaled into the engine) an air leak may be present. The same test can be used to detect whether there is an air leak at the carburetor base. Ex-hot rodder Steve Kelly offers an even better method of checking for a loose throttle shaft. Disconnect all external linkage. With the car idling, attempt to pull or push the shaft back and forth in the base housing. If it is loose, then the engine will react by speeding up or slowing down. In idle position, the lower throttle plate should be firm against the inside of the carburetor and no back and forth effort should change its position. When you find a loose throttle shaft, the best fix is to properly re-bush the base shaft hole. All throttle shafts have to move smoothly within their bores. They cannot seal so tightly that no air can get in or they could not move at all. The primary throttle shafts on Quadra Jet four-barrel carburetors are notorious for being loose after many thousands of miles of use. Thankfully, re-bush kits are very available. The Quadra Jet also has a certain spot that is particularly susceptible to leakage. It is located under the float bowl. Between the base and the bowl, there is a cavity which the main jet passages go through. There are two plugs located there. They often leak. Some carburetor rebuilding kits include a formed piece which fits into this cavity and positively seals these plugs.

Q. I live right on the Gulf of Mexico. The salt air makes it unreasonable to have a classic or antique car here. If I were to rent or build a storage area to house such cars, how far from the ocean should such a building be located? Is a wood, brick or metal structure best? Should it be a combination? What's best for fire protection and insulation? I have been told that, with a high water table, the concrete floor should be poured over a half inch of gravel to keep the floor from sweating. Is this true or false? Dr. B.R., Florida.

A. There are times when the salt winds will carry 15 or more miles inland, but we're sure that there are some collectors who safely store their cars closer than that to salt-water bodies. As to construction, you want to use materials that will minimize condensation. Any well-insulated building should do this. Storing collector cars in uninsulated metal, brick or cement structures invites the risk of condensation and corrosion. As to a concrete floor, contractors will probably advise that the concrete be poured over a moisture barrier. A gravel or sand base will not keep moisture from penetrating the concrete.

Q. I own a 1974 Chevrolet 1/2-ton truck. It has been in storage and not started for three years. During storage, mice did a job on the under-dash insulation. Everything is now cleaned and sprayed with WD-40. Recently, the truck was attended to. No wiring appears to have been chewed, but some areas show corrosion. The following problems occurred: 1) When the headlights were on and the right turn signal was switched on, the high-beam indicator comes on, but only when the dash light switch is in the on position; 2) If the dash light switch is in the off position, the headlights do not come on; 3) When the four-way flashers are on, the high-beam indicator will also flash, but only when the headlight switch is in the on position; 4) With the dash light switch in the on position, only the right-hand turn indicator bulb stays (dimly) on; 5) When the dash light switch is pulled out to turn on the headlights, the lights by the fuel gauge, speedometer and automatic transmission selector go out. If the high-beams are on, the indicator bulb goes out too; 5) When the high-beams are switched on, the lights to the fuel gauge, speedometer and automatic transmission selector go on. However, with the high-beam switch in the off position, they go out; 7) The fuel gauge reading is erratic. With no ignition, the needle goes full sweep to "E" and pegs itself there. However, with the ignition on, the needle goes full sweep to "F" and stays there. The vehicle is stored in a large metal building with a floor that is part dirt and part paved. The truck is in the farthest corner of the building, with old rugs underneath. It is covered. Could the problems be due to corrosion? Could it be that the printed circuit board has gone awry? Will these problems eventually work themselves out if the truck is put back in operation? Could you help me with these problems? How do other people who store vehicles cope with these problems? D.M., Indiana.

A. You have raised good questions about proper storage as well as the wiring problems. We'll look at the wiring first, then talk about storage. I discussed the electrical problems your truck is having with Randy Rundle, owner of Fifth Avenue Antique Auto Parts, 502 Arthur Avenue, Clay Center, Kansas 67432. Randy is an expert in diagnosing and correcting electrical problems and recently conducted a seminar on this topic at Car Expo '92 in Reno, Nevada. Randy states that he believes the lighting problems are related and are probably traceable to a criss-crossed ground between circuits caused by the damage the mice did to your truck's under-dash wiring. You state that your inspection does not show any wires that have been chewed through. However, breaks in the insulation are probably letting one circuit (such as the headlights) ground against another circuit. Randy also states that the odd lighting behavior shows that the circuits do not always find the same ground. He does not believe that the problems lie with the printed circuit board nor does he believe that the problems will correct themselves. He says that to correct the lighting problems, you will need to use a test light or a VOM (Volt-Ohm meter) and a wiring diagram to check the continuity (passage of current) through each wire in the various lighting circuits. To correct corroded terminals, you should uncouple the wires and carefully clean both the wire terminals and connectors with emery cloth or fine sandpaper. You should repair any areas of damaged insulation with electrical tape or replace the wires. All this is a tedious process. It is made more difficult by the fact that most people feel very uneasy when working with electricity. However, electrical troubleshooting is really a straight-forward, easy-to-understand process. There is a discussion about how to troubleshoot electrical problems like those you are experiencing with your truck in the book *HOW TO RESTORE YOUR CHEVROLET PICKUP*. It is available from Classic Motorbooks. Regarding storage of your truck, I have a few suggestions. First, don't put rugs underneath the truck or any other vehicle. If a tiny pinhole should develop in the gas tank, gasoline will seep into the carpet. It will act like a giant wick, absorbing fuel throughout the carpet's entire area. If a spark should occur, you will have an instant conflagration which will destroy your truck and the building it is stored in, plus put you under great risk, as well. A dirt floor is not a good storage condition. However, rather than covering the dirt with carpet, you can place the vehicle in what is called an Omnibag. This is actually a giant plastic bag. It is big enough to completely envelop the truck. This product is available from Pine Ridge Enterprise, 13165 Center Road, Bath, Michigan 48808. The Omnibag comes with several large packets of desiccant which is placed inside the Omnibag with the vehicle. It absorbs all moisture present at the time of storage. Since the bag is sealed, no more moisture can ever enter. When placing a vehicle in the Omnibag, it is important to avoid tearing or poking holes in the bag. Storing your truck in an Omnibag not only eliminates the problem of moisture and corrosion, but also prevents mice or other rodents from chewing the wiring and upholstery. John Schoepke, who markets the Omnibag, says that rodents won't eat what they can't smell. With your truck sealed in an Omnibag, as far as the mice are concerned, it doesn't exist. For vehicles in dry storage, where an Omnibag is not used, another product called Pest-Away is available from B.W. Incorporated, 4th Street, 2nd Avenue South, Browns Valley, Minnesota 56219. PestAway is effective in keeping rodents out of a stored car. This product emits a sound frequency that humans and pets (such as dogs and cats) can't hear. However, the frequency is irritating to rodents. It drives them away from the storage area.

(Editors note: The following letter was received, at a later date, from the hobbyist who asked the above question: "Thank you for printing my inquiry. I deeply appreciate your advice on Omnibag and PestAway to ward off rodents. As to my truck's electrical problem, I contacted a local Chevrolet dealer and automotive electrical service center. Both advised me (as was stated in your column) that it was a grounding problem. I started searching under the dash and checking the wires. Finally, I pulled the dash out and found the problem. Mice had built a nest in an opening above the dash and all their waste had accumulated on the printed circuit. This corroded the copper that the bulbs twist into. Also, the clips on the printed circuit that hold the gauges had corroded, since the mice built their nest only on this one side. Parts of the circuit had turned black. I tested the printed circuit with an ohm meter and realized I had found the problem. A new General Motors printed circuit for my truck costs $62, but I got an entire dash at a local salvage yard for $35. This circuit had no deposits or corrosion and tested out fine.")

Q. We have experienced vapor lock problems while touring in our old car. What can be done to prevent this from occurring? R.G., Nebraska.

A. Old car buff Red Burke had a friend who toured the United States in his motorhome and experienced vapor lock trouble all the way. He had spent over $600 enroute to cure this problem. While in Texas, an old time mechanic told him to put two gallons of diesel fuel in at every fill up of gasoline. After that, he drove all the way to Fort Bragg, California with no more problems. The logical deduction is that modern gasoline is a lot more volatile and boils off at a much lower temperature than older fuels. When it vaporizes, it won't pass through a pump designed to pump a liquid. The diesel fuel raises the vaporization point to a level where the fuel mixture won't boil off at driving temperatures. Burke says he was in Reno, Nevada with a 1952 Chevrolet convertible during the summer of 1992. The car had Powerglide transmission and a new fuel pump. Due to the altitude and heat, it vapor locked. A gallon of diesel fuel and a bag of ice cubes on top of the fuel pump allowed him to cruise and parade for a week. Burke believes that 90 percent of all vapor lock problems in the old days were caused by a weak fuel pump and feels that they could easily be cured with a replacement fuel pump with good suction. Nowadays, we are dealing with completely different fuels and will have to adjust to it if we want to drive our old cars on the highway.

Q. I am writing in regard to your article on Advance-Design Chevrolet pickups. I have a 1951 model 3100. I would like to increase the road speed up to 55 miles per hour, but I do not want to change the transmission or drivetrain. Do you have any information on replacing the gears in the transmission or rear end? T.F., Indiana.

A. Your desire to keep the transmission and drive train original severely limits the higher gearing options for your truck. Your best bet, when they are available (research and development is still going on) will be buying a set of higher speed rear end gears for 1947-1954 Chevrolet 1/2-ton pickups from Patrick Dyke, Box 648, Casa Grande, Arizona 85222. Meanwhile, different gearing for the transmission won't help, unless you install an overdrive. Otherwise, all that you would change is the gear reduction. In high gear, the transmission is in direct drive. An aftermarket overdrive was available for these trucks, but it is very rare. Patrick Dykes is the only person I have talked to who has owned one of these transmissions. He said his was not complete. If you can tolerate some modification of your truck's torque tube drive line, there's another option. Overdrive Incorporated, PO Box 173, Portage, Ohio 43451 can couple a Borg-Warner overdrive transmission to the end of your torque tube. They will shorten the torque tube to the length of the overdrive. The installation will be so hygienic that it will look almost stock. The overdrive will decrease your truck's final drive ratio by 33 percent and easily allow comfortable 55 mile per hour cruising speeds.

Q. On my 1967 Mustang convertible there is a small live wire on the inside of the trunk. It is located at the driver's side along the side of the wheel well. What is this wire for? Why don't I see more 1967 Mustang convertibles at car shows? How many were made and how many are around today? J.T., Florida.

A. Most likely, the wire inside your Mustang's truck is for a light which attached to the trunk lid and went on when the trunk was raised. I see quite a few 1967 to 1968 Mustang convertibles, but one reason that you are encountering more of the earlier 1965 to 1966 cars at shows is that almost twice the number of Mustang convertibles were built in each previous production year than in 1967. Ford built 44,808 Mustang convertibles in 1967 and only 25,376 in 1968 compared to 73,112 Mustang convertibles in 1965 and 72,119 in 1966. There is no hard data on how many of these soft top models still exist, but the number probably doesn't exceed 10 to 15 percent of the original production.

Q. I would like information on installing a late-model Chevrolet V-8 engine in a 1952 Ford sedan. H.B., Missouri.

A. I'm sure our Ford enthusiasts would rather see you put an engine with the distributor in the front (meaning a later model Ford V-8) in your 1952 sedan. Chevrolet engines come with the distributor in the rear. However, Chevrolet 305- and 350-cubic-inch engines are plentiful and cheap. These factors may dictate your decision. The best source of information on the swap you are contemplating is the *1949-50-51 FORD OWNERS HANDBOOKLET* available from the 1949-50-51 Ford Owner's Newsletter, PO Box 30647, Midwest City, Oklahoma 73140. This group has installed both a Chevrolet 350 cubic-inch V-8 and a Ford 302 cubic-inch V-8 in early 1950s Ford sedans. The installations described won't be identical to yours, since Ford did a major restyling for 1952. However, the mechanical details will be very similar. If you order the Handbooklet, you will want to ask for a copy of the Chevrolet engine swap, which was printed in the newsletter. It does not appear in the handbooklet (at least not in the edition I have). The installation described in the handbooklet is for the 302 cubic-inch Ford V-8. The authors recommend this engine because it is a relatively simple conversion that does not require any cutting or major changes to the frame or steering.

According to the 302 V-8 installation chapter, engine mount conversion kits are now available to fit either a Chevrolet 350 or Ford 302 V-8 to an early 1950s Ford frame. Supplier addresses and prices are given for the various items needed for the conversion.

Storing a collector car outside is not good practice.

Q. I have a 1972 Cadillac Eldorado convertible that I put in storage from November through April. Should I leave in the battery or take it out? Should the gas tank be filled? For the six months I take it out, I have to park it on my lawn. I have a big lawn and do not park it in the same place all the time. Does parking a car on grass during those months rust out the bottom? If so, what can I do to protect my car from moisture? There is a possibility that I could park it on a sandy area in the vicinity of the house, but it is very near the road and subject to dust, flying road objects and possible vandalism. Can I have your advice about all this? B.C., New Hampshire.

A. As to whether to leave the battery in the car or take it out, I would remove the battery and store it in a cold location (garage or entrance to the house). Put it near an electrical outlet where you can plug in a charger. Every couple of weeks, plug in the charger and bring the battery up to full charge. A friend says that he has hooked his battery charger up to the automatic garage door opener circuit. Every time a car goes in or out of the garage, the battery charger comes on and gives the battery of his collector car a shot of electricity. That way he doesn't have to remember to plug in the charger. This sounds like a good trick. You'll want to be sure that you place the battery on a couple of blocks of wood. If the battery case sits on cement, moisture will collect on the case and create an electrical path which will discharge the battery. If the battery is allowed to sit discharged for any length of time, it may refuse to take a charge and be unusable when you get ready to put it back in your car. To prevent the battery from self-discharging, you will want to wipe the case clean and make sure it stays dry. Also, be sure that the electrolyte is at the proper level above the plates inside the battery. It's a good idea to keep the gasoline tank filled on any vehicle, but especially one that sees a lot of storage. Filling the tank prevents moisture from condensing on the walls of the tank on humid days and during temperature swings. Since water is heavier than gasoline, it will settle in the bottom of the tank, eventually causing rust to eat pinholes in the tank's bottom or seams. Parking your car on the lawn is not a good idea. Moisture from the earth can keep the bottom of the car permanently damp and lead to corrosion. My father stored a 1956 Cadillac on a portion of the lawn on our family homestead. After letting it sit for several months, rust began to flake from the car's underside. If you must store the car outside, my suggestion would be to lay down plastic sheeting and park the car over that. The plastic will form a moisture barrier, helping to keep the car's underside dry. Of course, the plastic will kill the grass underneath.

Q. I own a 1957 Buick Special (Model 46R). Back then, cars came with a single master cylinder. I am one of the old car enthusiasts who enjoys driving his car, rather than trailering it to shows. Could you tell me what I must do to convert my car's braking system to dual master cylinders? I wouldn't think this would be a major project. The car does not have power brakes. However, I have not been able to find out what parts would be interchangeable with the present system on the car. J.G., New York.
A. Since your Buick has swing pedals with the master cylinder mounted on the cowl, the conversion to a dual master cylinder should not be too difficult. I suggest that you purchase the master cylinder and brake pedal set up from a 1968 or later Buick with drum brakes. Adapt it to your 1957 Special. You will also need to redo the brake lines so that you separate the front brakes from the rear.

Q. I share the responsibility for the cars and preservation of a 26-car collection of antique automobiles ranging in vintage from 1909 to 1965. My questions are as follows: First, what are the merits of starting these cars on a bimonthly basis, as opposed to turning the motors over without starting on the same schedule? Second, various name brand batteries, although trickle-charged, regularly die on us after three years. Any suggestions as to a brand of battery known to have better longevity in this type of service? Third, is it better to keep gas tanks full to prevent gas spoilage? Fourth, is there a brand of gas better known for long-term stability? Fifth, is there an anti-sulfate additive for batteries that really works? S.J., New York.
A. If you start the cars during storage, you will need to run the engines until they are thoroughly warmed up. Otherwise, condensation will collect in the exhaust systems and raw fuel is likely to collect in the oil pans. If you just turn the engines over, you will have to crank for a long time to build up oil pressure to lubricate the engine. There is an alternative to either of these approaches. Dribble a light weight oil (automatic transmission fluid works well) down the carburetor the last time the engine is run before storage. Be sure the engine is warmed up before doing this and dribble (don't pour) the oil into the carburetor. There is a danger with putting oil into the engine through the air intake: pouring in so much oil that the fluid builds up in the cylinders. If this happens, a hydraulic action will occur that can quickly destroy the engine. But if a very small amount of light oil is dribbled into the air intake it will provide a lubricating film on the cylinder walls and combustion chamber. You'll see a lot of smoke coming out the tail pipe as you do this. Also, when you restart the engine after storage, it will smoke for a long time. Nevertheless, the lubricating coating will protect the engine

during prolonged storage. I am wondering if the problems you are having with battery longevity has more to do with where the batteries are stored than the brand of battery you are using. Many old car owners remove the batteries during storage and place them in a warm location (or leave them in the car if the car is parked in a heated area). They believe that batteries don't like the cold. For years my uncle would remove his boat battery and place it in his cellar next to the furnace. Even though he would charge the battery periodically, seldom did his boat batteries exceed their warranted life. The problem is that batteries will self-discharge at a fairly fast rate in a warm temperature setting. This is not a problem when the battery is in a running vehicle, because frequent driving keeps the battery recharged. But if you store a battery in a warm setting, even periodic recharging may not be enough to prevent severe discharging and consequent sulfate build-up on the battery plates. This will lead to shortened battery life. Believe it or not, the best storage for a car battery is to bring it to a fully charged state, dry the case, wrap it in plastic and put it at the bottom of the food freezer. You can leave a car battery in this condition for several months without the battery losing its charge. I recommend keeping the gas tanks full to prevent moisture condensation. You should add a fuel stabilizer to prevent gasoline spoilage. I am not aware of any particular brand of gasoline being more or less stable than others, though I am sure some are. Sulfating is a natural process that occurs in batteries as part of the electro-chemical process. Further, sulfate build up on the plates is not a problem if the battery is promptly recharged. The sulfate coating that occurs naturally as the battery discharges becomes a problem only when the battery is left in a discharged state over a long period of time. Then, the sulfate hardens and the plates are not cleaned with a recharging cycle. Also, if the electrolyte level drops below the top surface of the plates, exposing the lead plates to air, it will cause the sulfate coating to harden. There is a chemical which is claimed to clean the sulfate coating from lead/acid batteries, but this can be used only when the acid is poured out. The better approach is to control sulfate build up by promptly recharging batteries as they discharge.

Q. I have a 1946 Chevrolet 1/2-ton pickup with a 216 cubic-inch engine and four-speed transmission. My truck's highway speed is only about 40 to 45 miles per hour. If I put a three-speed transmission and rear end in my truck, can I get better highway speed? Also, my truck's speedometer doesn't work because the gear in the transmission is worn out. I have tried to remove the gear, but can't get it out. How can I get it out? If I do, where can I get a new one? R.K., Ohio.

A. Changing the transmission won't make any difference in your truck's highway speed. Top gear in both the three-speed and four-speed transmissions is direct drive. It is possible that a three-speed (torque tube drive) rear end would have slightly higher gearing (with a lower numerical ratio) than the differential gearing in your truck. However, the gain wouldn't be enough to warrant the swap. There are several ways you can raise your truck's cruising speed. None is exactly simple. One is to install a rear end from a mid-1970s Chevrolet Blazer. The Blazer rear is only a half-inch wider drum to drum. It comes with gearing as high as 3.08 or 2.73. To install the Blazer rear end, the spring pads have to be cut off your truck's rear axle and welded to the Blazer axle. The Blazer rear end can then be bolted in without modification. You will even find that the emergency brake cables hook right up. On vintage Chevrolet pickups that have the three-speed transmission and torque tube drive, conversion has to be made to open drive. Another solution for up to 1954 Chevrolet light trucks with torque tube drive is to have Overdrives Incorporated, 17518 Euler Road, Bowling Green, Ohio 43402 put a Borg-Warner overdrive unit in the differential end of the torque tube. Such an overdrive will increase the truck's cruising speed by one-third (12-15 miles per hour for

Merry Christmas

OUR HOUSE TO YOUR HOUSE

Don, Cookie,
Denny, Joan
Paul

your truck). The *CHEVROLET TRUCK SERVICE MANUAL* says that to remove the speedometer gear from your truck's four-speed transmission, you have to break the universal joint at the transmission universal joint flange. Remove the speedometer driven gear from the bearing retainer. Next, remove the universal joint flange retaining bolt, lock washer and flat washer. Remove the yoke and speedometer drive gear from the transmission main shaft. Assuming this operation works, you should be able to purchase a replacement gear from Jim Carter's Vintage Chevrolet Parts, 1508 East Alton, Independence, Missouri 64055. One way to find solutions to the kind of problems you are dealing with is to join a club for your type of vehicle. In this case, you might want to contact the Light Commercial Vehicle Association, 316 Berkley Court, Jonesboro, Tennessee 37659. Through this organization's membership roster you can contact other owners of trucks like yours, many of whom may have worked through similar problems.

Q. I have a hypothetical question. Assume a car is going up a hill at a given speed and you have a choice of using fourth or fifth gear to get over the summit. If you use fourth gear, the motor runs faster. If you use fifth gear, the throttle is depressed more, giving the motor more fuel/air mixture. Which gear would be more economical to use? J.W., Maryland.
A. I have just been watching a video tape produced by Gear Vendors, makers of electrically-controlled under/overdrive transmissions for modern and vintage pickups and recreational vehicles. The point of this tape is the need to keep the engine within a given rpm range where it develops peak torque and horsepower when climbing grades. If using fifth gear will lug the engine so that it is below the rpm range where it develops its maximum torque and horsepower, trying to get over the summit in this gear would definitely be wasteful. It would also be potentially damaging to the engine, since excess fuel would wash down the cylinder walls and dilute the oil. Assuming that fourth gear is a close enough ratio that it doesn't put the engine rpms at the other side of the power curve, using this gear would allow the engine to operate more efficiently. It would therefore be more economical and better on the engine. The real issue here is the gear ratios. With a five-speed transmission where the fifth gear is an overdrive and fourth is direct drive, there is a good likelihood that the ratios will be close enough that fourth will put the engine in an efficient operating range without having to drastically cut speed. If the hypothetical car had a three-speed transmission, third would probably be too high and second too low. That's where an under/overdrive transmission comes in. By allowing gear splitting ... a top overdrive ratio and underdrive ratios between first and second and second and third ... you wind up with six forward speeds to keep the engine in its most efficient operating range when accelerating and when climbing.

Q. I read with interest an article on proper care of convertible tops. However, the writer didn't mention the "time lapse" for keeping the top lowered or folded. I have heard pros and cons about the top being folded too long. Apparently, shrinkage can cause problems. What can you tell me about this? G.B., Wisconsin.
A. Shrinkage can occur when a vinyl convertible top is folded down on a warm day and is left that way for a period of time. If an attempt is made to raise and latch the top when the weather has turned colder, problems may arise. Vinyl shrinks when cold and stretches when warm. Usually, it is still possible to stretch the vinyl far enough to latch the convertible top, but this strains the attaching points and could cause the material to tear. Those with vinyl box covers on pickups experience the same shrinkage problem when they remove the box cover and try to reattach it on a cold day. With vinyl convertible tops, it's best to raise the top before putting the car into storage. I recently read

a tip that pickup owners can use to avoid the need to pull and stretch vinyl to make a shrunken box cover fit their truck. The vinyl cover can be stretched and made pliable by cycling it, for a few minutes, in a clothes dryer. With the fabric warmed up, the cover will snap in place easily. Unfortunately, this method can not be used with convertible tops. However it would work as well with vinyl tonneau covers used on sports cars.

Q. My brother and I are working on a 1981 DeLorean. These cars are underpowered. Have any of your readers ever replaced the DeLorean engine with a peppier engine, such as a supercharged Thunderbird SHO engine from a Super Coupe or a small turbo engine from any sort of late-model product? If this is not feasible, is there any way to bring the standard DeLorean engine up to a performance measure to make this otherwise fine car a performance sports car. Also, is there a DeLorean club for us DeLorean fans? J.H., Maryland.

A. The only methods I've seen to improve the performance of DeLorean sports cars were in the "Back to the Future" movie series and those were all Hollywood fantasies. Your best source of information on improving your DeLorean's performance is the DeLorean Owners Association (805) 964-5296.

Q. I have a 1938 Buick Special. My gas mileage is approximately 10 miles per gallon. I have replaced the original Marvel CD1B carburetor with a Stromberg AAV1. I get the same mileage with both carburetors. The car performs excellent and has good power and speed. I drove it up to 75 miles per hour and still had more throttle left. I would like to know what kind of mileage others get with their 1938 Buicks. W.S., Pennsylvania.

A. My father owned several 1938 Buicks (they were his favorite car) and I never heard him brag about gas mileage. He used to say he was glad his 1938 Buick didn't have the twin carburetor set up found on early 1940s Buick Supers. He said the cars with "Compound Carburetion" gave less than 10 miles per gallon. Given the relative inefficiency of the Buick straight eight engine, I would think that gas mileage in the low teens would have been common.

Q. I am experiencing a problem with my 1960 Chrysler 300F. It's a problem I know is common. The hood hinges won't hold the hood open. I can see why this happens. For the years and years the hood stays closed and the springs are in the fully stretched position. Now, when the hood is open, they don't want to retract sufficiently enough to hold the hood up. The safety concern is obvious. Is there a company out there somewhere that can remanufacture a small quantity of hood springs? Wouldn't this make a good club project? W.G., California.

A. The only source of replacement hood springs that I know of would be suppliers of New Old Stock (NOS) parts. For later model collector cars, some springs may still be available from the factory.

Q. In October I purchased a 1963 Mercury Monterey convertible. The car was perfectly dry. Since getting the car home to New York City, whenever I open the trunk compartment there are droplets of water hanging from the inside of the trunk lid. The longer I wait between trunk openings, the wetter the car. Can you tell me what is happening and what can be done to cure this? A.V., New York.

A. You don't describe the car's storage setting. However, it sounds like condensation is forming on the metal. You can see this as water droplets on the inside of the trunk lid. Probably, if you looked at the chassis, engine or drivetrain parts, you would see water droplets there, too. The condensation problem you describe can result from a dirt or unsealed concrete floor that allows moisture to seep into the storage area. Sudden temperature rises in a high humidity environment will also cause the colder metal to sweat droplets of water. The best solution I know is to store the vehicle in an Omnibag. That is the trade name for a giant plastic bag which you can push your car into to seal it off from the elements. The Omnibag provides an air-tight seal against moisture. It comes with several packets of desiccant. These are tossed into the bag before sealing to absorb whatever moisture is present inside. The result is a hermetically sealed, dry storage environment; the equivalent of desert conditions. This prevents dust from settling on the paint and sunlight from attacking the rubber parts. The Omnibag's supplier is given elsewhere in this book.

Q. Could you please advise me as to what should be done to old cars that have been stored inside for years? What can be done with others that have remained out in the weather? Storage times range from five to 20 years. Each of these cars was simply parked for storage. No special lubricant was added to the engines or other parts prior to storage. No attempt has since been made to turn over their engines or tow them. I am particularly concerned with engine damage if an attempt is made to start an engine that might be frozen. Could just towing a car without fresh lubrication damage wheel bearings, etc.? H.B., Illinois.
A. Generally, with engines that have sat for a long time without being started or turned over, it's a good policy to remove the spark plugs and pour enough light oil (automatic transmission fluid works well) into the cylinders to cover the entire piston area. The oil will seep down around the rings, often freeing engines that are stuck and providing cylinder wall lubrication when the engine is first turned over. The spark plugs should be not be replaced until the engine has turned over several revolutions and all excess oil has been expelled from the cylinders. If the engines are set up or frozen, they won't be damaged by trying to turn them over since the internal parts simply won't move. If that's the case, you will need to apply some of the techniques for freeing stuck engines discussed in other questions in this book. Chances are good that the wheel bearings were lubricated when the cars were placed in storage. It should be possible to tow the cars a short distance without repacking the bearings. However, the wheel bearings and all other lubrication points, including fluids in the transmission, engine and differential, should be serviced before the cars are considered roadworthy.

Q. I gave my daughter a number 1 condition 1964-1/2 Mustang with a 170 cubic-inch engine and three-speed transmission. She just drives the car in the summer and is a very easy driver. The problem she is having is with the clutch. It seems that 2,000 to 3,000 miles is all she can get out of a clutch. These early Mustangs had a nine-inch clutch. My mechanic, who worked on these cars when they were new, says they had clutch problems. He was wondering if it is possible to fit a larger clutch to this car?. K.W., Minnesota.
A. The 170 cubic-inch engine should not tear out clutches like this. The short clutch life your daughter is experiencing in her Mustang results from one of three causes (or a combination). The first could be her driving habits. Does she ride the clutch. That is, does she drive with one foot on the clutch pedal, keeping it partially depressed? You should be able to detect this by riding with her. The second cause could be with the linkage. Ford mechanics I have talked with tell me that the nylon bushings in the clutch

linkage wear out, causing the clutch arm to bend. This often results in a clutch with no free travel. I am told that Ford supplied a heavier clutch arm to replace the original. The third cause could be a heat cracked or checked pressure plate or flywheel that could tear up the clutch. The most likely problem is a bent clutch arm which, if it caused the clutch not to engage fully, would be the source of the problem.

Q. Here's my problem. At present I own a 1959 Cadillac Sedan DeVille and a 1977 Cadillac Fleetwood Brougham (with 425 cubic-inch engine). The 1959 is in excellent shape, except for the engine and transmission. The 1977 has front end damage, but it runs very well. How difficult would putting the 1977 engine and transmission into the 1959 body be? Could you give an idea of what would be involved? How about costs? I would like to bring another grand old car back to life. I.S., Florida.

A. In making this swap, you would encounter the usual problems of engine mounts, linkages, exhaust hookups and so on, plus a change from a generator-powered electrical system to an alternator. In addition, since the Turbo-Hydramatic 400 transmission on the later engine is less bulky (and probably shorter) than the Hydra-Matic in the 1959, you will most likely need to have the driveshaft lengthened. There would be another small change; the newer transmission uses an electrical kick-down switch, whereas the earlier Hydra-Matic handles this via mechanical linkage. You can keep the kick-down feature by purchasing an electrical switch and installing it under the accelerator. If you do the work yourself, the cost should be minimal in comparison with rebuilding the 1959 engine.

Q. I need some advice as to how to remove masking tape glue. My 1964 Cadillac had some paint work done and the tape and glue have hardened on the car. I have tried four glue and spot removers. These help a little, but I am afraid to try other removers for fear of also removing the paint. J.F., Arizona.

A. Guidelines for using masking tape say that the tape should be removed within 48 hours after painting. If left for a longer period of time, particularly if the car is parked in the sun, the tape will harden and the glue will set up making it nearly impossible to remove. 3-M Company makes an adhesive cleaner that softens and removes glues such as those on masking tape. This product will not lift paint that has dried thoroughly. When the tape is on trim only, the glue residue can be removed with gasket remover or carburetor cleaner. These solvents are harmful to paint, however. Care must be used to make sure the solvents are applied only to the trim.

Q. I have a 1972 GMC 1/2-ton pickup with a 350 cubic-inch V-8. The carburetor has just been rebuilt and I get only 11 miles per gallon of gasoline. What can I do or have done to increase the mileage? Should I put in a new 305 cubic-inch V-8 with a two-barrel carburetor? I like the truck and will do anything if it helps the mileage. J.H., Texas.

A. My experience with these trucks involves a 1972 Blazer and a 1969 C-20 Longhorn pickup. Both had 350 cubic-inch V-8s and 11 miles per gallon is about normal fuel economy. The Blazer gets between 10 and 14 miles per gallon and the Longhorn gets 10, regardless of load or terrain. The cause of poor mileage is more likely to be related to the rear end gearing than to the carburetor and engine. If your truck has standard transmission, one option is to install an overdrive. The other option could be changing to a higher speed rear end. One old truck lover, Bob Oberst has taken the hard road to conclude that a rear end change might be the answer to this problem. He owns a 1970 GMC pickup with 160,000 miles on it. It has a 307 cubic-inch V-8 and provides 10 to 12 miles per gallon, no matter how it's tuned. Putting a quick advance kit in the distributor proved to be a bad move. It caused the engine to detonate under load. Adding dual glass packs mufflers brought road mileage (with a camper back) up from 10 to 11 miles per gallon, but around town, the poor mileage persisted. Next, Oberst bought a used Quadra Jet four-barrel manifold and Holley Economiser carburetor rated at 450 cfm. In town, his gas mileage increased from about 10 to 13 miles per gallon. There were a few times that the truck even got over 17 miles per gallon on the road. With a full 8-1/2 foot overhead camper, it still provided 11 to 12 miles per gallon. At 100,000 miles, Oberst replaced the 307 cubic-inch engine with a 350 cubic-inch, but kept the old distributor and the Holley Economizer carburetor. Fuel mileage stayed about the same, but performance increased. Next, Oberst changed tire size from 7.00 x 15 to P225/R75 x 15. This seemed to make the truck roll easier, but mileage was again unaffected. The big problem seems to be lugging the engine at about 1,600 rpm at 55 miles per hour. This drops the reading on a vacuum gauge that Oberst installed. Mileage suffers if a vacuum gauge reading goes below 10 psi. Normally, at 50 to 60 miles per hour, Oberst gets a reading of 15 psi. Oberst realized that his 1963 Ford truck, with a 3.50:1 rear end ratio, was giving vacuum gauge readings of 18 to 19 psi and much better gas mileage. So, he's considering changing the rear end ratio from 3.07:1 to 3.54:1. Jon Bagley also dealt with this problem. He has a 1972 GMC with a 350 cubic-inch engine, four-speed transmission and 3.08 rear end ratio. It is a short wheelbase truck with radial tires. Bagley reports getting between 19 and 20 miles per gallon on the highway. He does his own maintenance and the engine runs like new.

Q. My 1985 Dodge 600 convertible has been an easy to drive and easy to maintain car for five years. I hope to keep it in its like-new condition for a long time. Do you know of any way to maintain the brushed aluminum trim on the interior? It is beginning to look dry and has several striations. These look like scratches, but really aren't. Do you have any advice for preserving or refinishing these areas? J.S., New York.
A. The interior aluminum trim is probably protected with a clear coat finish and the dulling and cracking you see may be on the clear coat, rather than the aluminum. In talking with automotive refinishers, the advice I get is to carefully remove the clear coat using lacquer thinner. Next, prep the aluminum with aluminum cleaner and apply a fresh clear coat. This would be a time consuming process, but should restore the aluminum trim pieces to their original bright appearance.

Q. I am currently having a problem with my 1952 Buick Roadmaster. I have been looking for a gas tank for the past 10 months and have had no luck whatsoever. There are several pinholes in the tank I have. Regardless of what I put in the tank to seal it, the tank will start to leak again. Do you have a suggestion on what to do? S.D., Pennsylvania.
A. Can any readers advise Mr. D'Ambrosio on what he can do to seal his tank, or suggest possible sources of a replacement. The only other alternative would seem to be to have a new tank fabricated.

Q. I have a 1951 Ford V-8 with overdrive. My problem occurs when the car gets warmed up to normal operating temperature and I stop it for a period of 20 minutes or so. Then, I must crank the engine quite a bit to start it. If left overnight, the engine will start immediately. If I shut it off warm and start it up, it will also start immediately. It seems like heat has something to do with this problem. The engine runs at normal heat range. The carburetor has been rebuilt with a new kit. The car runs smoothly on the road. How can I solve this problem? W.B., Michigan.
A. The hard-starting problem occurring when the engine is warm may be caused by gasoline percolating in the carburetor. This could result in a flooding condition. You

should check the manifold heat control valve on the engine (if the engine has this device) to see if it is stuck. If it is stuck, this would cause the intake manifold to over-heat and lead to the percolation problem in the carburetor. Another possible cause could be internal leaking within the carburetor. This can also lead to a flooding condition. David Cole, who owns a car like yours, has another suggestion. He thinks the real cause could be a damaged ignition coil.

Q. They say there's no use crying over spilled milk, but my wife dropped a jug of milk in my collector car last week. I have heard that it is difficult, if not impossible, to get rid of a sour milk odor in a car once the milk has permeated the carpeting or uphol-stery. Do you have any cures to my problem? F.C., New York.

A. Classic car expert Henry Jenkins has found a product that claims to cure this prob-lem. It is called Odor Neutralizer. The product reacts with the odor chemically, rather than masking it with perfume. It can be used on car upholstery. Odor Neutralizer is also helpful in destroying cigarette odors (a concern for many non-smokers when purchas-ing a car formerly owned by a smoker). A technical information sheet says that the product does not leave a residue on fabrics. Odor Neutralizer is marketed by Advanced Commercial Products, 3633 West MacArthur Boulevard, Suite 410, Santa Ana, Cali-fornia 92704.

Q. I am restoring a 1958 Ford Skyliner and am having a persistent problem with a leaking rear seal. The car has a 352 cubic-inch engine with Cruise-O-Matic transmis-sion. Virtually every part of the engine has either been replaced or reworked. The engine block has been bored .030 of an inch over-size and the crankshaft has been cut .010 of an inch under-size. However, the rear seal area has not been touched. All inter-nal parts are brand new. We are using a modern neoprene seal, as opposed to the origi-nal rope seal. However, this should not be a problem. In fact, it should be superior to the rope seal. The engine has just had its seventh seal put in and it still leaks badly. The machine shop owners are willing to stand by their work, but they are losing patience and have no idea what the problem might be. The engine runs perfectly, but leaks. Absolutely everything we can think of and check is within specifications. Both the block and heads have been magnafluxed and there are no cracks. Can you offer us any helpful advice? L.S., Florida.

A. Close inspection of the rear seal area on the crankshaft will probably reveal light grooves in a helix pattern. These grooves were cut into the seal area on engines designed to use rope-type seals. The purpose of the grooves was to draw any oil that might seep under the seal back into the engine. To work properly, a neoprene seal needs a seat against a smooth surface. So in your engine's case, the neoprene seal is not superior. If you replace the neoprene seal with the original rope-type seal, this should stop the oil leak problem.

Q. I wish you could tell me why the power steering overheats on my 1971 Lincoln Continental? I have changed the pump and checked the fan and hoses and some other parts and I still haven't cured the problem. L.T., Idaho.

A. The power steering pump on your Lincoln Continental is of the constant volume type. If there is a restriction in the lines or steering gear, the pump will increase pres-sure in an attempt to maintain volume. The overheating you are noting is the result of this pressure build up. The problem could be caused by a defective hose or the restric-tion could be in the steering gear. You should have the pump pressure tested. The pres-sure should be less than 150 psi. If the pump tests out okay, you can set about looking for the restriction that is causing the pressure build up.

Q. I had an automatic transmission on my 1964 Oldsmobile Starfire convertible completely rebuilt, largely because of a growl in low gear. When I got the car back, it still had a loud growl. The shop has been in business for 40 years and has an impeccable reputation. They even told me that I didn't need an overhaul. However, the noise was irritating (especially with the top down) so I had it done anyway. My complaints have been answered with: "These transmissions made this kind of noise when brand new. In fact Oldsmobile issued a kit to try to cut the noise or dampen it. If everything brand new was put in this transmission it would still growl." Is this true? F.R., Iowa.

A. First I contacted a long time transmission repair man about the growl in your automatic. He said the noise should not be there. He mentioned owning a new Oldsmobile convertible with this transmission, but without the noise. Diagnostic measures he recommended were listening for the noise in reverse. The planetary gear set is engaged in backing up, as well as in low gear. The noise should occur in other gears as well, until the transmission shifts into direct drive. The noise may change in pitch, but should be similar to what you hear in low. This expert suggested that the noise may be coming from a source other than the transmission. He mentioned the water pump, alternator, or air conditioner as possibilities. You can disconnect the belts to these items and drive the car briefly, checking to see if the noise goes away. If the noise is still coming from the transmission, read on. Collector Bruce Grinager contacted me and said that he wrote the Pontiac shop manual on the "Slim Jim" (Roto-Hydramatic) transmission, which is the same as yours. He advised that all Slim Jims were noisy in first gear. He road tested prototypes in 1960 cars with X-type frames and they were quiet, but when the production units were put in the new perimeter frame cars in 1961, the cross member carried the noise into the car. During 1961 (its first year), new planetary gears were developed that had small bevels cut in three or fourth tooth corners. They broke up the harmonics that were most prominent when the sun gear was being slowed down during the 1-2 shift. Dealers retrofitted these gears to many 1961 output shaft carriers to lessen the noise. The 1961s were very loud. Later cars were not so bad. Cars with rebuilds could have either gears. However, the gears never caused durability problems. The governor and the clutches were problematic, but not the gears. Hobbyist John McNerney adds some tips on rebuilding this transmission. "Check the sun gear for wear or pitting," he advises. "The dampener in this gear must be soft and pliable. If it is loose on the main shaft, it can sometimes be pressed further into the gear; this will tighten it. Check the carrier assembly for wear and/or pitting. Pay careful attention to this because these gears can wear without pitting, sometimes razor sharp. Check all thrust bearings; replace if defective. Failure of these bearings can sometimes be traced to faulty body ground. An easy way to check this is to start the engine, open the door (so that the dome light is lit) and then move the gear range selector to reverse. If the dome light flickers, you have a faulty ground. If this is the case, check all ground straps and replace as necessary."

Q. I need help. I recently acquired a 1938 Seagrave 12J1 fire truck that has been sitting in the woods here for over 15 years. The thing is nearly complete, but I haven't tried to start it. I need oil filters and information about this monster so that I don't cause any damage. Would you please send me the address of a club for fire trucks? M.M., New Mexico.

A. The club you will want to contact for information on your Seagrave fire truck is the Society for the Preservation and Appreciation of Antique Motor Fire Apparatus in America, PO Box 2005, Syracuse, New York 13220.

Q. I have a 1937 Dodge. Is there an accurate way to tell what gear ratio a car has without removing the differential cover? The gear ratio tag is missing. A.T., Pennsylvania.

A. To determine the rear end ratio, first jack up the rear end so that both wheels are off the ground. Be sure to use jack stands to support the axle so that there is no danger of the car falling on you. Then make a mark the driveshaft. This can be done with a piece of chalk. Next make a mark on one of the rear tires. Now rotate the driveshaft and count the number of turns to one revolution of the tires. For example, if the driveshaft revolves three times to one tire revolution, the rear axle ratio is 3.0:1. You are more likely to experience a ratio of slightly over or under four turns. The most common rear end ratio in your year Dodge was 4.1:1. A 3.9:1 ratio was also available.

Q. I am the owner of a 1963 Imperial LeBaron. I am in need of help solving an ongoing problem with the air conditioner. In nearly nine years of owning this fine auto, I have had an on-going problem of insufficient cooling. It has the dual air conditioner system and I have had the freon tested yearly and added when necessary. Three or four years ago, I purchased a good reconditioned compressor from my mechanic. Since then, I have had it installed. It cools, but not enough. It also takes too long to begin cooling. The control switch has the dual high and low air speeds, but only the low speed works. During the last tune up of the car, I asked for a complete check of the air conditioning systems, including checking for the doors being blocked. My mechanic reported all was working normally. I have my own copy of the 1963 *CHRYSLER-IMPERIAL SERVICE MANUAL* and my mechanic has used it, but to no avail. Is anyone knowledgeable to inform me of a way to solve this problem? F.R., Washington.

A. I presented your dilemma to instructors who teach auto air conditioning systems in Ferris State University's auto service program in Big Rapids, Michigan. They pointed to many of the areas where you already suspected problems, such as low freon. Other suggestions were valving or piston/cylinder leakage in the compressor (which should have been corrected by the reconditioned compressor), malfunction of the thermostatic expansion valve or the possibility of the blower not pulling enough air across the evaporator.

Q. I have a great deal of difficulty keeping mice out of stored autos or vehicles used sparingly. I have tried traps of various kinds and moth balls, but mice continue to be present. My storage area cannot be completely sealed to keep mice out. Please advise a product or procedure which will keep these destructive varmints outside. D.S., Nebraska.

A. The simplest and least expensive solution is liberal applications of mouse poison (Decon or a comparable commercial product). Keeping a cat in the storage area might also be effective. Car collector Harold Nassy says that the secret is to divert the mouse away from the car into a trap. His cousin developed the legendary "better mouse trap" for storage buildings. It was made from a five-gallon bucket. Two holes are punched on opposite sides, about a quarter inch below the lip of the bucket. The bucket is partially filled with five quarts of water and a half-cup of liquid soap. Next, a dowel or stiff wire is run through the center of a small waxed paper cup. This dowel is inserted through the holes at the top of the bucket, with the cup positioned so that it is over the center of the liquid. A small quantity of peanut butter is scooped into the cup. Do not use cheese for reasons that will become clear shortly. A 1x4 runway is placed against the edge of the bucket so that the mouse has to leap to the cup with the peanut butter. When it lands on the target, the cup will spin, dumping the mouse into the liquid where it drowns. The cup will then right itself due to the weight of the peanut butter in the bottom and wait for next victim. Unlike traditional mouse traps, this device does not need daily attention.

Q. I have a 1956 Ford Thunderbird. I am in the process of installing an interior kit in the car. I am sure that in the past 32 years the car has been worked on many times. As a result, the holes for the screws that hold on the inner door panels have become enlarged. To put in a bigger screw would not be correct. I would like to use the original size hardware. My question is, what can I use to make the holes smaller? I do not have any welding equipment and would like to do this myself. J.B., California.

A. I use a simple fix for your problem. Simply place a piece of soft machinists wire in the hole with the screw. The wire will conform to the threads and will take up the slack in the hole. If a single strand of wire isn't enough, use two strands. Restorer Stephen Miller has another suggestion. "Take a 3/16-inch pop rivet and drill a hole for it to fit snugly into. (I use short aluminum rivets which are soft). Pop the rivet into the hole, push out the center piece in the rivet and thread in your screw. This method works very well."

Enlarged holes in doors can be fixed to attach new inner panels.

Q. I have a 1937 Ford that I did a brake job on, including new wheel cylinders, master cylinder, brake hoses and linings, etc. Now my brakes fade-out on the freeway and go almost to the floor. The master cylinder has been adjusted. I have a repair manual which lists the length of the linings as follows, forward shoe 13.5 inches, and reverse shoe 10.25 inches. The shoes installed measure as follows, forward shoe 11-7/8 inches; reverse shoe 9-1/2 inches. I checked with a brake shop. They said I have the wrong lining lengths. A Ford repair shop said they measure that way because, when new, the truck had riveted linings. I lose no fluid and have bled the lines. How can I solve my braking problem? D.M., California.

101

A. As you know, your truck's brakes should not perform as you describe. The lining dimensions you report are short. This may be contributing to the problem, but there are other, more probable causes. First, check to see if the shoes are centered. If they aren't, only a part of the shoe will make contact when you apply the brakes. The wear pattern on the shoes should tell you whether they are adjusted to make contact the full length of the linings. Second, have you checked the thickness of the drums? If the drums have been turned repeatedly, they may be too thin to make contact without warping. Third, check to see if the brake lines are running close to the manifold or exhaust system. Heat from the exhaust system may be vaporizing the fluid. Fourth, you may have installed very poor quality linings. This, in combination with one or more of these other factors, could lead to the brake fade you're experiencing.

Q. I am having trouble with the brakes locking up on my Packard. What do you suggest that I do to remedy this? T.B., Iowa.
A. Car collector John Azzolini had a similar problem with his 1949 Chevrolet four-door. The brake pedal would be fine for 20 to 30 minutes, then the brakes would start smoking. When he carefully read his service manual, the problem was solved. The compensating port was blocked, but not by an out-of-adjustment brake pedal. The port itself was clogged shut. Azzolini bent an end of an office staple to form an L. Then, using needle nose pliers, he worked the end of the staple through the compensating port until it was totally cleaned and he could see light through it. Rebuilding the master cylinder won't fix the problem. The compensating port has to be cleaned. His brakes worked perfectly since the day he cleaned it.

FLUIDS: OIL, GAS, BRAKE FLUID

This chapter covers fluids used in autos and car parts.

Q. Where can I obtain a satisfactory and available substitute for the fluid used in the Delco-Lovejoy shock absorbers on my 1936 Plymouth and other cars of the same era? D.I., South Dakota.

A. A mixture of hydraulic jack oil and STP will do the job. Proportions are roughly two-thirds jack oil to one-third STP.

Q. I would like information on what type of lubricant to use on the inside Trico vacuum windshield wiper that I recently repaired on a 1946 Chevrolet pickup truck. The old lubricant had the consistency of tar, which was the reason the wiper failed. I hope that in the last 40 years a new and improved lubricant has been developed. D.K., Wisconsin.

A. According to two repairmen who work on vintage windshield wipers, wheel bearing grease or plain old Vaseline (in colder climates) are the best lubricants to use on old wipers.

Q. What is the normal temperature oil should be at in an engine running between 4,000 and 6,000 rpm? My present restoration is a 1971 Honda 600 coupe. Around 5,000 were built for export to the U.S. between 1971 and 1973. B.C., California.

A. According to Mike Hackman, an instructor in the automotive machinist program at Ferris State University, in Big Rapids, Michigan, the normal oil temperature in an engine is between 250 and 260 degrees Fahrenheit. If the oil reaches 290 degrees Fahrenheit there's a problem. Most old car collectors are aware of the importance of oil for lubrication to prevent friction and wear, but not everyone seems to realize that oil also acts as a coolant, particularly in the crankcase. Circulating oil helps disperse heat from moving engine parts. Running an engine while low on oil presents more of a risk that the oil will exceed its safe temperature, than that the engine will not receive adequate lubrication. Bearing surfaces are at particular risk when the oil temperature rises into the danger zone because of the soft metals used. If one is concerned about oil temperature, aftermarket gauges can be installed. However, the best way to prevent engine damage due to excessive oil temperature is to keep the oil at the full mark on the dipstick and use a quality brand of the type of oil recommended for the vehicle. Although most old car hobbyists have shied away from synthetic oils, due to greater likelihood of leakage through less effective seals in older engines, when an older engine is rebuilt and modern seals are used, synthetic oils such as Mobil 1 might be considered for their ability to withstand high engine temperatures, as well as their excellent lubricating properties.

Q. I have a 1949 Chrysler Town & Country with Fluid Drive. In 1949, Chrysler advised using "Gyrol Fluid" in the torque converter of this transmission. What would be a modern replacement fluid? S.S., New Jersey.

A. Fluid Drive users tell us 10-weight oil is a suitable replacement for the original Gyrol Fluid.

Q. I have a 1968 Cadillac with an overhauled engine. Every time I change oil, the oil pump will not pick up the new oil. I have to completely remove the oil pump and pack it with Vaseline to get it to pick up the oil. I bought a new oil pump, but installing it did not solve the problem. What can I do? E.M., Georgia.

A. Our friend the mechanic had a Cadillac owner come to him a few years ago with the same problem. He speculates that one cure could be filling the oil filter with fresh oil, rather than installing it dry. This might help the pump hold its prime. Mark Tauber, of Sante Fe, New Mexico noted the problem occurred every time the oil was changed and suggested that if the pump were at fault, changing the oil would not affect it. He pointed out that many people believe in letting old oil drip from the crankcase for hours when changing oil. This allows the oil pump pick-up to drain, causing cavitation in the pump when the engine starts up. Tauber, who is also a professional mechanic, stressed that long drain times are unnecessary. "You'll never get all the oil out," he explained. "I would suggest E.M. should drain out the bulk of the old oil until the flow drops to a trickle. Then, plug up the drain hole. Refill the crankcase and let it sit a minute so the pump can "burp." Then start the engine. Another expert, auto parts store manager Dennis Albertson, of Greene, Iowa, said that problems with pumps that don't prime have been solved by leaving the oil filter loose until the engine is started and oil starts to leak out. Then the filter should be tightened all the way and the oil level checked. Albertson added that a less messy alternative is filling the filter with oil before it's installed. A final suggestion, from Bob Carson, of North Hollywood, California, is to install a caged ball check in the pick-up line to the oil pump. He explained that this won't interfere with normal operation, but will prevent oil draining back from the pump. According to Carson, a larger diameter tube could be placed over the pick-up tube, with a couple pins to stop the ball. A short piece of the original tube can be used for the ball to check onto. It must be made to retain the original length of the pick-tip tube.

Q. My 1952 Hudson uses oil in the clutch. Do you know of any popular oil, sold today, that I can use as a replacement for Hudsonite, which was the name of the oil that the factory used back then? L.C., Ohio.
A. Jack Miller, of the Hudson-Essex-Terraplane Club, tells us that the Hudsonite clutch compound is now being made to the original Hudson/AMC formula. You can get information about how to obtain this product from Jack Miller, Hudson-Essex-Terraplane Club, 100 East Cross Street, Ypsilanti, Michigan 48197.

Q. I have a 1939 Chicago newspaper story about a man who apparently figured out a way to run an engine on a mixture of lye and water. Does anyone know what he did and whether it was a practical process? I know that any alternative fuel that the oil companies can't control wouldn't be good news for them, but that's too bad; they're rich enough. I wonder if they put the "kabosh" on this fellow back then like GM did to Preston Tucker? I think I know what the man did. He probably made a form of carbide-like gas and fed it to an engine in a manner similar to an liquid petroleum gas (LPG) setup. The article said a one-gallon mix would drive that engine as far as 2,000 gallons of gasoline would. J.J.B. Sr., Arkansas.
A. I would think that a mixture of lye and water would dilute sodium hydroxide which I have a hard time believing would work as an automotive fuel. The Chicago news story might have been a very clever publicity stunt.

Q. During a recent visit to Vermont, we heard of a technique used due to the roads being heavily salted in the Green Mountain State. It's said to prevent rust and corrosion to the underside of vehicles. They spray used motor oil onto the undercarriage in October and let dirt cake-up on the chassis. This, they say, acts to protect the metal from corrosion. They use a compressor to spray the oil. I am from Long Island. I never heard of this before. A Vermonter said it's done by people in many states, at a low cost of $10 to $20. Is there any benefit to this procedure or did the Vermonter tell me a tall tale? And is the price range accurate? T.R., New York.
A. What you heard is true. For the 10 years I lived in Vermont, I protected my vehicles against corrosion by spraying the undersides and lower outer body panels with used engine oil each October. I waited for a stretch of dry, sunny days to apply the oil treatment. Immediately afterward, I would drive the vehicle a dozen or so miles, on a dirt road, to add road dust to the oil. This made the coating less likely to wash off when driving on slushy winter roads. The treatment worked. I owned a Chevrolet Blazer during most of that period and the only rust the vehicle experienced was caused by moisture condensation that occurred inside the rocker panels and doors. Many Vermonters

even sprayed used oil on the lower outside body panels. These vehicles looked extremely unkept, particularly since brine from the road salt also settled on the oily coating. Yet, the used oil prevented rust blisters from forming in the paint. When spring finally arrived, the oil and salt coatings could be washed off with soapy water. Many service stations did a brisk "oil undercoating" business and the going rate where I lived was $20. I cut this cost by dumping the used oil from my oil changes in a five-gallon container and spraying my vehicles myself. I used a siphon gun purchased from J. C. Whitney for $8 and a Sears, Roebuck air compressor. The used oil undercoating technique really works. As I was writing this, my wife came in, stood over my shoulder reading the computer screen, and asked when I was going to oil undercoat her Tracer in preparation for winter driving. The coating of used engine oil has another advantage. Besides forming a protective barrier against road salt, the acids in the oil actually remove surface rust that has formed on the underbody metal. On modern cars, I know of no disadvantage to the used oil coating. However, if used engine oil were to be sprayed on the undercarriage of an older vehicle with fabric coated wiring, it could damage the insulation on the wiring. Of course, I would not spray old engine oil on a cleanly painted automotive chassis.

Q. Have you considered running an article about gasoline? Surely it would be of interest to know who first distilled crude oil and came up with a product we now call gasoline. Did gasoline originate as condensation in a natural gas line? What was gasoline used for before being used in internal combustion engines? Why do we use gasoline rather than some near product like naptha or benzene? Was there a company selling benzene for cars? Who were the first oil companies? What big ones failed, and which continue? Which changed names or were gobbled up? How was gasoline first distributed and marketed? What was the early dispensing equipment like? What did the numbers mean? Was Phillips 66 named for the highway or an octane rating or something else? How about Speedway 79 and Union 76? I am not a first-issue subscriber, so you may have already covered all this information. If not, why not put it on your list of projects for future publication? R.K., Michigan.
A. Your questions are interesting ones. Much information is available from the American Petroleum Institute. Although history books credit Edwin Drake with drilling the first oil well in 1859, in Titusville, Pennsylvania, our Canadian neighbors say that they were actually the first to successfully tap underground oil. The reason for oil exploration had nothing to do with cars. It was done because of an energy crisis in lamp oil. At the time, lamp oil came from whales. The chief product from the early oil refineries was kerosene. It was used principally for lighting. Gasoline and other by-products of the kerosene refining process were considered useless waste and often dumped in creeks. They created some spectacular fires when touched off by lightning. One suggested use for gasoline was as an anesthesia. No doubt it had some nasty side effects. The internal combustion engine provided a use for what was otherwise a waste product. However, for a period in Detroit, benzene (produced as a by-product in the Ford coke ovens) was also sold as a motor car fuel. One of the earliest oil companies was John D. Rockefeller's Standard Oil of Ohio. So rapid was the expansion of the petroleum industry that, only 18 years after its founding, Standard Oil had become the largest and richest company in the world. The first "drive-through" service station, opened in 1905 by the American Gasoline Company, featured a novel fill-up feature. The motorist simply parked his automobile alongside an elevated barrel and poured gasoline into his car's tank through a garden hose. The 66 in Phillips 66 stood for the octane rating of the company's product, as did the 79 in Speedway 79. There's much more to tell. For instance, the world's first oil gusher occurred in a nondescript bit of southeast

Texas landscape called Big Hill. It shot a plume of oil 175 feet into the air. Six wells pumping the fabulously rich Spindletop reserve (as Big Hill was later renamed) produced as much oil as all the rest of the world's wells combined at that time. In fact, so great was their production that by the end of 1901, oil prices had dropped to three cents a barrel, while water at the well site sold for a nickel a cup. As Henry Ford ruminated, burning petroleum as a fuel may have been one of mankind's dumbest ideas because, when we have sucked the last drop of oil liquid from the ground, we will have lost a wonder resource with applications as diverse as healing salves and hamburger wrappers, to say nothing of our chief source of lubricants.

Q. While talking shop with the owner of a repair shop that does work on my cars, the owner advised me to check the gas in my old cars by smelling to see if the odor had changed. He said that unleaded gasoline, even with additives, will turn bad. He related several experiences where unleaded gasoline was left in vehicles or engines for up to a year and a varnish residue formed. This caused some engine parts to seize up. He related a similar experience with his tractor. After rebuilding the tractor engine, it varnished up again after sitting over the winter. He related the same experience with four snowmobiles sitting over the summer. He is presently experimenting by adding some two-cycle engine oil to the gas in one of the snowmobiles. He said his most recent experience with gas going bad happened when a customer called him to look at a 1938 Chevrolet engine, which had been sitting for a year-and-one-half without being used. He checked some of the engine parts after detecting that the gas was bad. Parts of the engine had seized. Do you know of a problem with unleaded gasoline? Have any old car hobbyists experienced this same problem? Is the answer to drain the gas every six months to prevent engine overhaul? Is there a proven additive? C.G. Jr., Pennsylvania.
A. When I took my chain saw to the repair shop for a tune up last spring, I heard a similar note of caution about varnish settling out of the gas from the shop owner. He strongly advised that I pour gasoline stabilizer into the fuel tank before putting away my chain saw or parking my old cars in winter storage. (Gasoline stabilizer is available in the automotive area of most discount stores or in the fuel additive section of auto parts stores.) His cautions were directed at the problem of varnish settling in the fuel tank and clogging the carburetor. I don't see how varnish settling out of the gasoline could do damage to the internal parts of the engine, since whatever unburned gasoline might remain in the intake manifold or cylinders when you shut the engine off would soon evaporate. If you are concerned with protecting an engine's mechanical parts, you can pour light weight engine oil into the carburetor as you run the engine the last time before storage. When the engine stalls, shut off the ignition and finish your storage preparations. The oil will coat the cylinder walls and prevent rust from forming during storage.

Q. Is modern Dextron II automatic transmission fluid suitable for use in 1940s-1960s Hydra-Matic transmissions? I use Dextron II in my Oldsmobile. When cold, the shift from second to third is very positive and hard. When accelerating more aggressively, it slips. However, when the transmission warms up it shifts just fine. I have not changed the transmission fluid in the 1963 yet. Is there an additive that I can use to give the Dextron the same properties as the A type fluid? J.P., New York.
A. Type A automatic transmission fluid was recommended by GM, Chrysler and AMC between about 1956 and 1967. Dextron superseded Type A. It was recommended by the same manufacturers from 1967 to 1975 and for any other automatic transmission that had previously specified Type A. For 1975 and later cars using this type fluid, Dextron II has superseded Dextron. There should be no problem with compatibility

between Dextron II and Type A automatic transmission fluid and to my knowledge no additive is necessary. I would not think that the slippage you experience on hard shifting when your Oldsmobile's transmission is cold is caused by the Dextron II fluid.

Q. What can you tell me about the use of engine oil additives such as Teflon, graphite, Moly, QMI, Exxceed, Slick 50 and the thicker types of so-called oil stabilizers? H.P., Oregon.
A. Such products claim to reduce friction, prevent dry starts and make engines run cooler with better gasoline mileage. All of these product use Teflon in their formulas. An article titled "Snake Oil! Is that Additive Really a Negative?" appeared in the August 1992 issue of *ROAD RIDER*, a motorcycle enthusiast magazine. It used a very plain-talk writing style to present information based on reports and studies by the University of Nevada Desert Research Center, DuPont Chemical Company and many other well regarded labs and institutions. Concerning products using the PTFE (commonly known as Teflon) additive, the article presents a quote by DuPont Chemical Corporation's Fluoropolymers Division (inventor of Teflon) which states, "Teflon is not useful as an ingredient in oil additives or oils used for internal combustion engine." The article goes on to discuss that statement in light of the use of PTFE in additive products. The conclusion of the additive article is that, when it comes to engine oil additives, hard facts are almost impossible to come by. Countering the testimonials for the additives is a substantial volume of evidence against such claims. Some of the evidence suggests that the additives actually could be harmful. There is a company on the West Coast that focuses on the marketing of special conventional lubricants for collector vehicles and vintage racing cars. Penrite, The Classic Oil Company, 1330 Galaxy Way, Concord, California 94520 has informational literature available on its veteran-vintage-classic lubricants line. The company also has a technical hot line to handle questions from enthusiasts. Call (510) 798-8500 to utilize it.

Q. Can anyone tell me if Fram, AC or anyone else ever made an adapter kit to convert a 1959 Plymouth 318 cubic-inch V-8 from a canister type oil filter to a spin-on type? G.B., Wisconsin.
A. All of us who have done oil changes on cars with canister type filters can appreciate your interest in the more convenient spin-on type. According to car collector George Hillman, the 1992 Purolator Filter Master Catalog says the following about conversion to a spin-on filter: Remove entire (canister filter) housing. Clean surfaces. Service with specified spin-on filter (which in this case is Purolator number PER1-A, new part number L30001). This particular filter has many usable substitutes to facilitate outer dimension restrictions.

Q. I have two Chevrolet trucks. Both have sat for 20 years. One is a 1942 and the other is a 1952 Cab-over-engine tractor with a 24-foot trailer. Both ran when parked. The 1942 has a rebuilt 235 cubic-inch engine in it. I think that 20 years is too long for an engine to sit and still be free. What is best to put in the cylinders so that the engine will turn over without breaking the rings? L.C., Missouri.
A. The best lubricant for freeing an engine with seized rings is automatic transmission fluid. Remove the spark plugs and pour the bright red transmission fluid into the cylinders. Let it work for several weeks. Chances are the engine will come free when you turn it over.

Q. I have just received a 1979-1980 AMC Concord six-cylinder with 90,000 miles. I don't know how well it has been kept up with oil and filter changes. I have heard that you can clean out an engine by adding Rislone and driving the vehicle on the highway, changing the oil and filter at 3,000-mile intervals. Most of my driving is done on the highway at 55 to 60 miles per hour and consists of 40 minute runs for a distance of 40 to 50 miles. All of my vehicles have been subject to this kind of driving, with oil changes as mentioned. I have obtained 200,000 to 300,000 miles on the engines. Can I use the Rislone engine treatment to clean out the engine? Would this have adverse effects on the rings, valves and lifters? D.M., Indiana.

A. The engine cleaner you refer to contains a high content of solvents and detergents. If the engine in your Concord is exceptionally dirty, you risk gumming up the rings, valves and lifters. The oil pump can get gummed up, too. This occurs because the oil filter does not catch all the oil. A bypass valve will shunt oil past the filter, if the detergent picks up enough gunk to clog the filter. Then, the gunk circulates with the oil. I put your question to an experienced professional mechanic. He said he would hesitate using an engine cleaning agent in a high-mileage engine that you do not know the history of.

Q. It is my understanding that gas line antifreeze is primarily alcohol (methanol) and that it works by making the water miscible with the gasoline. It basically dissolves the gas so that it is not subject to freezing. Does this mean that gasoline with ethanol in it is already de-iced and doesn't need de-icing additives? J.A., Indiana.

A. A chemist tells me that ethanol (grain alcohol) is soluble in both gasoline and water and could therefore could act as a de-icing agent. However, in a blended pump fuel, ethanol is already in solution with the gasoline. It would have to come out of solution to mix with water. The chemist did not think this would happen. When you pour a deicer into your gasoline tank, the alcohol in the additive is a separate agent. It is not pre-blended with the gasoline. Therefore, it is free to form a solution with the water.

Q. I recently rebuilt the engine of my 1966 GTO. I have always changed the oil and filter every 3,000 miles. Now I am reducing the mileage to 2,000 miles per year or less. Last year I changed the oil twice, every six months, but only after 800 to 1,000 miles of driving. Is this wasting oil? The oil still looked pretty good. What would you recommend for oil and filter changes on low mileage vehicles? D.H., California.

A. Mileage is not the only factor that determines when the oil should be changed. The oil is actually less likely to build up contaminants if a car is driven long distances at highway speeds than if it is subjected to numerous short drives. Given the number of miles you now put on your GTO, I recommend that you change the oil at least once a year. If the car sits in storage for any length of time, I suggest that the oil change be done before this storage period.

Q. Six years ago I purchased a 1928 Durant with the standard four cylinder W-5 Continental engine. Just prior to my purchase, the engine had been rebuilt. Since then, I have driven the car a total of only 4,650 miles. I change the 20W-50 weight oil in the spring and fall and occasionally after long tours. I have been told that using detergent oil in a car that has no oil filter can be harmful, since dirt and small metal particles stay in suspension. I am now wondering if I should go to a non-detergent oil with the option of adding something like Slick-50 to increase its protection. I don't feel I have the knowledge to install an oil filter system and would just as soon keep the engine original. F.K., Ohio.

A. Authorities recommend detergent oil for use in a vintage engines that have been rebuilt, if the engines are cleaned thoroughly in the rebuilding process. The 20W-50 oil you are using is designed for today's high-performance engines. Hopefully, you are not starting your car in cold weather with this oil. It becomes very viscous in cold temperatures. A friend reports that he put 20W-50 in his 1970s era Cadillac just before the car went into winter storage. He started the car one mid-winter day and destroyed the oil pump. As long as the engine seals are good, you will experience proper lubrication from a good quality 10W-30 or 10W-40 oil. There is quite a bit of controversy over the actual benefits of products like Slick-50.

Q. I recently purchased a 1939 Buick Special four-door sedan. Where can I find a safe additive to add to the present unleaded fuel? P.M., Arkansas.

A. Lubrizol Corporation was producing an additive called PowerShield. It could be added to unleaded gasoline to prevent premature valve seat wear. For information on PowerShield you should write: The Lubrizol Corporation, Wickliffe, Ohio 44092.

Changing the oil in your Shelby frequently is a great idea.

Q. I have a 1969 Thunderbird that I bought in 1983. I have put 100,000 miles on it in 10 years. I bought it with 69,000 miles on the odometer and now have 176,845 miles on it. My boyfriend changes the oil every 2,000 miles. He also changes the filter with the oil. It does not burn oil at all. Is that because I have the oil changed more often than most people do? A.K., Michigan.

A. Changing the oil at 2,000 to 2,500-mile intervals is definitely beneficial to an engine for the reasons mentioned above. It is very important to replace the filter when changing the oil, because the filter traps metal particles and other impurities that could damage the engine. I believe that the main reason manufacturers talk about 6,000-mile oil change intervals is to give owners a false sense of maintenance economy. However, a few gallons of oil and several filters purchased over 10 years is far less expensive than the cost of an engine overhaul.

Q. Lately, I've been seeing many articles about synthetic oils and their use in collector cars. As the owner of eight collector cars from the mid-1950s to the early 1970s, my question concerns the use of these products. Can synthetic oil, such as Castrol Syntex 5W-50 extend the interval between oil and filter changes on vehicles that are seldom used? The maximum annual mileage on any one of my vehicles is 500 miles, which consists mainly of highway driving. The minimum mileage is zero with show cars being driven only on and off the trailer and then to the show grounds. I have been changing the oil and filter every 12 months in these vehicles. This year, I decided to try synthetic oil in the vehicles which have newly rebuilt engines. They've accumulated between 200 and 1,800 miles. Will the use of this oil allow me to extend the oil change interval to 24 months? It is also my understanding that synthetic oils should not be used in engines which have not been rebuilt. Is this correct? T.A., New Jersey.
A. The principal reason for annual oil changes on collector cars that are driven fewer miles than normal is that this practice prevent contaminants from accumulating in the crankcase. A lubricants expert I talked to said that synthetic oils are of much higher quality than natural oils, but that the key factor in a decision to extend oil change intervals should be whether or not the engines are operated long enough to boil out contaminants (water and gas) that accumulates in the oil when the engine runs for only short periods. Since you describe your use as mostly highway driving and since you are considering using synthetic oil only in rebuilt engines (and wear metals are not likely to be present), you should be able to extend your oil change intervals. However, the warning to rid the crankcase of water and gasoline by driving the car enough to boil out contaminants needs to be heeded. The only reason I know of for not using synthetic oil in engines that have been rebuilt is that these oils have greater slickness (ability to decrease friction). This characteristic can allow the lubricant to seep past poorly sealing gaskets. Synthetics may also lack some gasket-swelling additives found in natural oils.

Q. Do classic vehicles require special oils and lubricants? R.B., California.
A. Modern oils are sophisticated products, but old car engines have special needs. Many factors impact the correct choice of lubricants for a collector car. Older engines were designed to use thicker oil. The typical signs of using too thin an oil is low, hot oil pressure, high oil consumption and lack of oil film protection while the engine is standing. Older vehicles can benefit from the major changes in additive technology made recently and incorporated in modern lubricants. These have virtually eliminated engine wear and the build up of deposits inside the motor. Penrite Oil Company of Australia has brought out a line of classic car lubricants that combine the high-tech additives with thicker viscosity ratings. You can obtain information on them from the Classic Oil Company by calling 1-800-PENRITE or (510) 798-8500.

Q. Can you advise of any helpful guide for those of us who wish to continue to use non-detergent oil in our older car and truck engines? B.O., New York.
A. Restorer Jim Banach was in the lubricating oil business for 20 years. He made and tested motor oils from bottom line economy grades to top line oils used in the Antarctic. Banach says there are non-detergent multi-grade oils on the market. National 10W-30 and 10W-40 for service classification SA are made from superior base oils refined by major oil companies. National SA grades do not contain any detergent additives.

National is manufactured by Pinnacle Oil Company, 5009 West 81st Street, Indianapolis, Indiana 46268. Pinnacle markets through various distributors and chain stores. The key to telling if a motor oil is detergent lies in the service classification. Current classification is SG. Prior classifications, which started in the late 1960s with SC, evolved to SE in the 1970s and SF in the 1980s. Each subsequent classification required ever more detergent to meet increasing demands. Major branded companies generally market products formulated to the current service classifications only. Therefore, one will need to look over the multitude of non-major brand products on the market to find non-detergent oils. I think it would be safe to assume that any oil that does not have service classifications SC or SD, SE, SF or SG probably does not contain any detergent additives. The description "heavy-duty" means nothing. The last comment that should be made is that a top quality non-detergent motor oil will be honey colored and crystal clear with a slight petroleum odor. Dark color oils, opaque oils or oils that smell burned were probably manufactured with poorly refined oil or blended with inferior base stocks. In his studies of competitor products, Banach even found used crankcase oil repackaged in a nice container with the statement "meets all manufacturer's specifications." This product was sold by a major chain store. In a nutshell, buyer beware.

Q. Is it better to use detergent or non-detergent oil in old flathead engines? I've heard that non-detergent is best, but can you get non-detergent multi-viscosity oils for winter use? I like to run 10W-30 in the winter. If I can't get non-detergent 10W-30, would it be worth going with straight 10 weight oil in the winter? Are all straight weight oils non-detergent? I have a 1959 Dodge 1/2-ton pickup with the 230 cubic-inch flathead six and a 1952 Ford pickup with a 239 cubic-inch flathead V-8. I've had both engines rebuilt. The Dodge has 34,000 miles on it since rebuild and the Ford 8,000 miles. In the winter here it often goes to -20 degrees Fahrenheit. I drive both trucks in the winter (especially the Dodge). Last winter I drove the Ford a few times just to exercise it when the roads were dry during thaws. I've been using 10W-30 so that I can start the trucks in the winter. I don't have a garage for my Dodge so it sits out in the cold all the time. B.O., New York.

A. Non-detergent oils are recommended for all older engines (not just flatheads) operated consistently with this type of oil, which have not been rebuilt. The problem with using detergent oils in an older engine is the possibility of loosening deposits which could then clog oil passages or score the bearings. Since both of your engines have been rebuilt and you are using detergent oils in them, there is no reason not to continue to do so for the reasons you mention. Also, detergent oil will keep the engines clean. Straight weight detergent oils are available, but these would not be a benefit to you since a multiple viscosity oil provides the starting and driving flexibility in temperature extremes that you are looking for. I have not seen non-detergent oils with multiple viscosity ratings. Before multiple viscosity oils appeared on the market, it was not uncommon to use 10W oil in the winter (owners sometimes mixed in a quart or two of 20W). However, use of the light weight oil did pose the risk of inadequate engine lubrication on occasional warm days (i.e. a January thaw) and in the type of heavier use that pickups often encounter.

Q. I am restoring a 1939 Chevrolet Master Deluxe and my question is whether I should be using non-detergent or detergent oil in this engine. There is no oil filter on this car and I have heard of people switching to detergent oil and clogging up all the oil passages. Please advise. R.K., Minnesota.

112

A. If the engine has not been rebuilt, it's advisable to continue using non-detergent oil for the reason you mention. In an older engine that's been rebuilt so that everything is clean, detergent oil would be preferable to prevent sludge and deposit buildup.

Q. I have a 1934 Chevrolet and a 1947 Ford six-cylinder. On the issue of gasoline, what is your opinion on unleaded gasoline for these old engines. Should an additive be added to the unleaded gas mixture? Would the engine be damaged over time without an additive? What octane should be used? F.J., New Jersey.

A. Basically the answer to the question of whether unleaded gasoline will cause engine damage over time is "yes." That damage will occur in the form of premature valve seat wear. Using a lead supplement additive will protect against valve seat wear. The octane of standard grade unleaded gasoline should be more than adequate for the engines in your cars, however.

Q. Recently a 1966 Volvo owned by Irv Gordon hit the million mile mark. The owner claims the car went 675,000 miles before the engine was rebuilt. Is this possible? I find this hard to believe even if the oil was changed once a week. J.D., Washington.

A. Seeing as the engine on our 1983 Oldsmobile has been burning oil since 24,000 miles and probably won't make 90,000, we asked friends in the automotive service program of the university where we teach this same question. We were told that two factors led to the engine longevity Irv Gordon experienced with his Volvo. The first is a good engine from the factory. One of the automotive service instructors we spoke with now has over 200,000 miles on a Ford Granada with no engine overhaul. This car is running strong. It is not used to commute a short distance to work, but is used for 240-mile weekend round-trips to the Army Reserve air base where he is a helicopter pilot. This is the second factor in engine longevity. From our reading of Gordon's feat, his Volvo received similar driving. An engine that never warms up in its short hops to work or in town driving will have a markedly shorter life than an engine that gets out on the highway and goes. In short start and stop commutes, the oil becomes contaminated with raw gas. It washes down the cylinder walls while the automatic choke is on, increasing wear and contaminating the oil in the crank case. Carbon build-up and other problems also result from short hop driving. And, of course, we know that some engines come together on the assembly line better than others. Put these two factors together, add the care Gordon clearly gave his Volvo, and the mileage figure you read about is possible.

Q. Could you tell me what is the general practice for storing old cars? Do you drain the radiator before storing, or do you store with water? What coolant or mixture is recommended for aluminum, cast iron and brass engines? What do you recommend to stop electrolysis? B.D., California.

A. Most collectors store their old cars with a 50/50 mixture of quality anti-freeze and water. Modern name-brand anti-freeze (Prestone, for example) contains anti-corrosion ingredients to protect aluminum as well as iron blocks and engine components from oxidizing. The coolant should be drained, the cooling system flushed and new anti-freeze added every couple years. To prevent build-up inside the water jackets from chemicals in the water, distilled water can be used.

Q. Where can I get magnetic oil plugs? I never see them any more. I have two cars, a 1974 Ford LTD with 400 cubic-inch engine and a 1973 Mercury with a 460 cubic-inch V-8. Both need magnetic oil plugs, but I need help to find them. H.W., Arkansas.

113

A. Advertisements for magnetic oil plugs used to appear in virtually all automotive magazines. The concept behind these plugs was that they picked up metal debris that would accumulate in the oil, thereby preventing these pieces from circulating through the engine where they could cause damage. At the time, many older cars were not equipped with oil filters. When filters were fitted to them, the pick up line running to the filter often ran from the valve galleys. These add-on filters were not part of the main oil circulation system and did not clean the oil as effectively as a system where oil flows through the filter on its way to the oil pump. Both of your cars are fitted with full-flow oil filters. If changed at recommended intervals, they will trap any metal debris. Therefore, you really don't need the magnetic oil plugs, which I have not seen advertised anywhere for a number of years.

Q. Back in 1981, *OLD CARS* had an article by John Lane regarding mixing of unleaded gas with regular gas to supplement the loss of lead in regular gas. Now that there is even less lead in regular, I need to know if mixing unleaded with regular is better than lead additives? If so, what ratio would be best? J.W., Kansas.

A. The leaded gasoline you can buy at pumps today (where it is available) bears little resemblance to the leaded gasoline available in 1981. At the time, mixing leaded and unleaded was recommended to give the unleaded stock an octane boost. There is no longer enough tetraethyl lead in leaded gasoline for this trick to work. Today, the maximum tetraethyl lead content in a gallon of "leaded" gasoline is .1 gram. This is the maximum and much leaded gasoline stock runs significantly below this figure. This is because refineries must pay substantial fines if their leaded gasoline stock tests out at more than the .1 gram limit. Fortunately, lead substitute additives are becoming readily available and the advice relating to older engines today is to use an additive.

Q. With all the controversy about leaded or unleaded gasoline, I don't remember reading anything about Amoco white gas that was sold back in the 1930s and 1940s. It was unleaded and many people used it in all types of cars. Was that gas different from the unleaded gas of today? Were there any reports of damage to valves back then? F.K., Florida.

A. The reason Amoco white gas didn't bring reports of valve damage is that true leaded gasoline had a residual lubricating effect that would last through several tanks of white gas. In other words, if you were one of the diehards who always filled up with Amoco white gas, it's likely that from time to time you would be away from an Amoco station, need a refill and pull in at another station where leaded was the only option. That tank would provide adequate valve lubrication through the next several fill ups of white gas. Also, if there were other drivers in the family, chances are they would fill up with leaded from time to time. The result was that most cars got enough valve lubricant from the high tetraethyl lead-content gasolines to make premature valve wear uncommon. Today, of course, even leaded gasolines have only marginally sufficient tetraethyl lead to lubricate valves. That's why a valve lubrication additive is good insurance against premature valve seat wear.

Q. Can you comment on Unocal's "Valve Saver" product? The manufacturer's literature indicates that this valve lubrication product does not contain the PowerShield additive. I use the amount recommended for non-leaded gasoline with leaded gasoline in my old cars. O.H., California.

A. After receiving Mr. O.H.'s letter, I talked with Don Chaffin, Manager of Petroleum Products at Unocal. Mr. Chaffin explained that Unocal's Valve Saver contains a specially formulated valve lubricant which extensive testing has shown to be as effective in preventing premature valve wear as PowerShield. The testing process was quite ingenious. Chaffin explained that the tests were run on Chevrolet 350 cubic-inch V-8 engines with special manifolding that fed the cylinders on one bank with plain unleaded gasoline and the cylinders on the other bank with unleaded plus Valve Saver. The engines were then torn down and inspected. The bank run on unleaded gasoline showed significant valve seat damage while the side protected by Valve Saver showed none. According to Chaffin, what actually happens when engines designed to run on leaded gasoline are fueled with unleaded and operated under heavy loads is that heat build-up actually causes the valves to weld to the valve seats. The problem with today's leaded gasoline, Chaffin explained, is that the legal tetraethyl lead amount gives only borderline protection against valve wear. Therefore, only a few refineries actually produce gasoline blends with up to the maximum lead content. As a result, the unleaded gasoline you buy at the pumps is likely to contain virtually no lead additive. The reason for this is that the EPA does spot checks of leaded stock to make sure that the tetraethyl lead content does not exceed legal concentration. Heavy fines can be imposed if it does. So to be safe, the refineries stay well below the lead maximum. Leisurely cruising is not likely to cause valve wear on most older engines. However, some older engines (like flatheads that normally ran hot) can experience valve wear when operated on today's unleaded. Therefore, valve lubrication products are sometimes a good idea.

Q. Several years ago I bought a 1964 Buick Electra with 65,000 miles on the odometer. I used the highest octane gas available and it still had a bad pre-ignition knock. Through the mail, I purchased a water and alcohol injection kit that sucks in this half-and-half mixture by way of the vacuum advance hose. It solved the spark knock problem and the car is now an excellent performer. About 10,000 miles after installing the water-injection unit, I had to remove one head. I found the entire combustion chamber was clean as new. Will this accessory also protect the valve seats when using the present low-lead gas? E.M., Florida.
A. To the extent that the water/alcohol-injection may cool the combustion, some valve protection could result. However, a safer plan is to add a valve lubricant.

Q. Old car hobbyists and restorers seem to take better than average cars of their vehicles, both old and new. They change oil more frequently and are careful about what brand and grade of gasoline they use. Do you have any interesting stories to tell concerning their experiences in realizing many miles of trouble-free driving? G.J., Wisconsin.
A. One hobbyist, James Steele of Walpole, New Hampshire has a 1969 Toyota Corona deluxe sedan on which he ran up some 376,000 miles (mostly stop-and-go delivery work) between 1969 and 1992. The only significant repairs during that time were a transmission rebuild at around 300,000 miles; a new radiator, distributor, starter; and replacement of a cracked cylinder head. The fan clutch was troublesome and had to be replaced at intervals of about 50,000 miles. He said his secrets were regular maintenance, daily checks and a relaxed driving style. He avoided hard acceleration, excessive speed and panic stops. Steele tends to shift up to higher gears sooner than most people and downshifts a bit slower, thus lowering engine rpms. He also makes oil changes with lubrication every 2,000 to 3,000 miles. In the past 25 years he's owned Ford, General Motors, Studebaker, Chrysler and Japanese products. With one exception (a Model A Ford) the hands-down winners for durability and ease of maintenance have been his Toyota, Datsun and Subaru. Ed Higgins of Sidney, New York, also notes his high mileage experiences. He has a 1967 Ford Ranch Wagon that he purchased

new. It now has over 226,000 miles. It has a 289 cubic-inch engine coupled to a three-speed transmission with overdrive. No motor work has been done. The valve covers haven't even been off and the original ball joints are still good. In its prime, this heavy wagon would get 22 miles per gallon in interstate driving at 65 miles per hour. There have been problems: The overdrive was not one of Ford's better ideas and after rebuilding it three times in 50,000 miles, Higgins substituted a Mustang transmission. He has also installed three fuel pumps and several rear wheel bearings. The roll pin in the distributor shaft disintegrated and salt on the highways in winter has taken its toll on the body. However, Higgins says, "If I had known the car would last this long, I would have taken better care of the body." He also has a 1976 Plymouth Volare (slant six) with 205,000 miles on it. He also knows of a 1964 Plymouth Sport Fury with 454,000 miles. It has had a valve and ring job and fuel pumps replaced as a precaution every 100,000 miles.

Q. In the July 21 column a product called Unocal Valve Saver was discussed. Can you furnish an address to which I can write to get information concerning mail order purchasing of this product? C.A.S., Virginia.
A. When I talked to a marketing representative at Unocal, nothing was mentioned about mail order distribution. However, you might check to see if case lot purchases can be made. The product is currently available mainly in the West, with distribution spreading East. The address to contact is Unocal Refining and Marketing Division, Unocal Corporation, 911 Wilshire Boulevard, PO Box 7600, Los Angeles, California 90051.

Q. I have a car that has been in storage for awhile. No gasoline has been running through the engine in years. The oil has not been changed. What is the best way to start the engine, since it hasn't been run in quite a time? J.B., Iowa.
A. First, check to see that the motor has oil in it. Top off the gas tank with fresh fuel. Assuming that your car's engine has suffered no electrical deterioration while in storage (corrosion can form on the points and contacts to the ignition wires), you can aid the starting process by spraying some carburetor cleaner into the air intake as the engine cranks over. Carburetor cleaner won't damage the engine. Such ether products will give the engine a little boost to get running.

Q. I understand that the Environmental Protection Agency has "called off the dogs" on the subject of eliminating lead from regular gas. I have been using lead additives with regular gas to protect the valve seats on my pre-1972 engines since they started phasing out the lead. Now that they have stopped the lead phase-out process, is there enough lead left in regular gas to protect my valve seats? Should I continue using lead additives? G.O., California.
A. The present maximum lead content of 0.1 grams per gallon is not considered sufficient to afford full protection against valve seat wear. Therefore I would recommend that you continue to use the lead additives. An official at Lubrizol Corporation, which manufactures PowerShield (the active ingredient in most lead supplement products) told me that he considers leaded gas and a lead supplement necessary to insure against premature valve seat wear. He uses this combination in his Corvair.

Q. How much did oil cost back when the first automobiles were being made? N.B., Illinois.
A. In the early 1900s, when the automobile manufacturing industry was just getting rolling, no one could anticipate what petroleum products like gasoline and oil would be

116

selling for in 1993. Specifically, 90 years ago, the price being paid for crude oil was less than five cents per barrel.

Q. Is there a book that shows the gas mileage of all types of older cars from the 1920s? I own models from that era and I've looked high and low to find records of their original fuel economy ratings? G.B., Georgia.

A. A hardcover volume called the *LESTER-STEELE HANDBOOK: AUTOMOBILE SPECIFICATIONS 1915-1942* was produced for the hobbyist during 1984. It reprinted technical information from original industry trade journals for the years it covered. For the years 1922-24, some fuel economy figures are given in the charts in the book. For example, the average miles per gallon of gas (as well as the average miles per quart of oil) are listed for many 1922 cars. The Chevrolet 490 was recorded at 22 average miles per gallon of gas/170 miles per quart of oil. Using the same format, the figures for some other cars were: Dodge - 19/100; Durant A22 - 17/230; Kissel CB6 - 15/175; Packard Single Six - 19/500; Rickenbacker Six - 18/375; Studebaker Big Six - 15/175; and Wills Sainte Claire - 16/125. The coverage is extensive, but not complete. There is no listing for the 1922 Model T Ford. In other cases, only one or the other rating is given. As we all know, fuel and oil economy depends a lot upon the car's mechanical condition and the operator's driving habits. It appears that the trade journals stopped recording fuel and oil economy figures after 1925. The handbook was marketed by Lester-Steele Publishing Company, PO Box 1580, Cashiers, North Carolina 28717.

Q. A recent article on metal fluid lines and fittings was informative, but did not answer the big question. How do you bend the tubes in a different direction? It's easy to bend the tubes in one plane, but the minute I have to go off in a different direction the tube squirms, twists and crushes if I try to hold it too firmly. I'm working on replacing the lines on a 1953 Nash-Healey. I want to make them exactly as they were installed. H.S., New Jersey.

A. If you will purchase a tubing bender tool at a local auto supply store your brake tube bending problems should be solved. The tube bender holds the tube by clamping it between two guides and a bending die. To bend the tube in a different direction, you simply orient the tube differently in the bending tool. The only difficulty in changing direction comes if you are trying to make two different direction bends in very close proximity to each other.

Q. Why does the carburetor on my Packard Six have a vent which allows fuel to evaporate out of the reservoir when the car sits for several hours? This necessitates running the starter for several seconds, while the fuel pump gets enough gas back into the dry carburetor to finally start the engine. Is there any reason I shouldn't plug the vent to eliminate the evaporation? S.J., Kansas.

A. The vent keeps pressure from building up inside the carburetor. Fuel will evaporate out of a carburetor, but usually over the period of a week, not hours. You shouldn't plug the vent. If you do, pressure build up inside the carburetor could force the fuel out through the main metering jet accelerating the car.

Q. I am about to start the restoration of my 1953 Studebaker. After putting on new brake lines, wheel cylinders and master cylinder, I was going to fill the system with silicone fluid. We have all read that the traditional fluid attracts moisture and will eventually rust through the lines. Now I am reading that silicone fluid seems to destroy brake light switches. What is one to do? D.M.

A. I, too, have heard reports that silicone brake fluid eats up hydraulic stoplight switches. However, it has no effect on a mechanical stoplight switch. In the days of vented hydraulic brake systems (like the one on your 1953 Studebaker) owner and service manuals advised to flush the system and replace with fresh fluid every 12 to 24 months. This was to prevent the fluid from becoming water-bound. This is what leads to corrosion of the brake lines, wheel cylinders and master cylinder. Presumably, if one followed the flush-and-refill recommendation, traditional polyglycol brake fluid could be used with minimal internal corrosion problems. However, few brake systems were flushed and refilled on an annual or bi-annual basis. When I rebuilt my Studebaker pickup's brake system, I had the wheel cylinders relined with stainless steel sleeves so that I could use polyglycol fluid and not fear corrosion damage to the wheel cylinders. I decided, however, to fill the brake system with DOT 5 silicone fluid. This has been coursing through my pickup's brake lines for three years now, with no leaks and no deterioration of the stoplight switch. Personally, I'd recommend using polyglycol brake fluid if you flush the system every year or two, but using silicone fluid and replacing the brake light switch (if need be) when you don't follow such a maintenance schedule. This view seems to be backed up by the experience of Terry Quesnel, a 1950 Nash owner. He feels that silicone brake fluid froze up the hydraulic light switches on his car. To alleviate the problem, he mounted a mechanical stoplight switch from a motorcycle down by the master cylinder and spliced in the wire leads. His problem was solved. However, for complete peace of mind, Quesnel ran a wire from the cold side of the switch to a small pilot light mounted under the dash. Now he always knows exactly when his brake lights are on, which isn't a bad idea for an old car that's driven a lot. There are other opinions on using silicone brake fluid, however. Car collector Malvin Hawkins reports that he has a 1946 Jeep, 1950 Buick and 1953 Dodge pickup. All had their brake systems purged and silicone brake fluid installed in 1980. He has not needed to replace any brake light switches since then. They all function the same as before the installation of silicone brake fluid. As noted above, it is cars with hydraulic stoplight switches that may encounter problems. Therefore, anyone who is using silicone brake fluid and feels concerned about the stoplight switch failing might consider adapting a mechanical switch. I have also been told that deterioration of an hydraulic stoplight switch seems to correlate with the amount of driving the vehicle receives. Remember, when any stoplight switch fails, the system does not lose fluid. The big danger is that the brake lights are not working. There are definite advantages to using silicone brake fluid in automotive brake systems, even those with hydraulic stoplight switches. However, if you go this route, monitor the performance of your vehicle's brake lights and stock up on a few extra stoplight switches.

Q. I have a 1940 four-door DeSoto and am having trouble getting the brakes bled. I went through everything the repair manual mentioned and also used a bleeder. The master cylinder has been rebuilt according to specifications and all the wheel cylinders have been rebuilt with new rubber boots. What am I doing wrong? P.W., Wisconsin.
A. The master mechanics I put your question to said that if you used a pressure bleeder, you should have quickly spotted the problem with any leaks in the lines or wheel cylinders. One mentioned that brakes should bleed themselves if all the bleeder screws are opened and let stand overnight. If you are using regular polyglycol brake fluid, you will want to attach short lengths of hose to the bleeder screws to prevent the fluid from running down over the backing plates as the polyglycol fluid is destructive of paint. Possible problems suggested were caps not sealing in the master cylinder or wheel cylinders. Hobbyist Mike Schmander feels that since the whole system was done (cylinders rebuilt, shoes relined, drums turned) there all sorts of causes for brake fade

118

problems. Your DeSoto uses Lockheed brakes. They had an adjustable anchor at the heel. With this arrangement, a simple relining of the brake shoes was no problem. The brake shop riveted on new linings of the required thickness, per factory specs. However, if the drums had to be turned, shims had to be riveted under the lining and/or the anchors had to be adjusted. This required a special tool called a drum micrometer to measure the diameter of the drums. Using this measurement, the needed added diameter for the brake shoes could be determined. Failing to "mike the drums" resulted in a spongy brake pedal and lousy braking with the same symptoms as air in the lines. Some Chrysler products, mostly trucks with floating axles, had a slit on the outer side of the drum to insert a feeler gauge to aid in adjusting the anchor. Another problem that was uncommon in the old days, but all too common today involves the check valve in the master cylinder. A faulty check valve can leak on the initial thrust, then hold partially or completely. However, these same symptoms could indicate air in the system, a low brake fluid level or bad adjustment techniques. A quick check for the problems this DeSoto owner is experiencing would start by pulling off the brake drums, leaving the adjustments as they are and lightly coating the brake shoes (don't rub) with soft chalk. Then, re-install the brake drums, drive a few miles braking easily a few times and remove the brake drums. If there is chalk on the heel (bottom) on even one set, anchor adjustment is the problem. As an added note, Chrysler Corporation used Lockheed brakes into the mid- or late-1960s, while Ford and Mercury switched from Lockheed to Bendix in 1949. Bendix brakes, in the early days, had an anchor adjustment at the toe. A more positive pedal feel could be obtained by loosening the large nut/anchor, adjusting the ratchet until snug, locking the anchor, then backing off the adjustment until the wheel spun freely.

Q. I have an engine that I believe to be a 265 cubic-inch V-8 made by Chevrolet. It was installed in a 1955 two-door sedan. I believe it to be the original motor. One notable feature of it is an unusual oil filter. It is painted blue with an orange cap. Can you confirm that I have identified the engine correctly? R.K., New York.
A. According to Chevrolet buff Steve Pratt, this could only be a 1955 engine. A nonpressurized canister-type oil filter was an option that year. It attached to the intake manifold with a bracket that used the same bolts as the water jacket. If ordered from the factory, the whole unit was painted semi-gloss black. However, if the dealer installed this item, the canister housing was blue and the lid a bright yellow-orange. In 1956, Chevrolet machined the 265 block to accept an upside down canister-type filter. It mated to the underside of the block. This unit was fully pressurized. The 265 cubic-inch was also installed in some 1957 Chevrolets with overdrive or three-speed manual transmissions. These late 265 cubic-inch V-8s were painted light green, as opposed to the standard orange.

Q. I have a 1948 Buick Roadmaster with the straight eight. This engine is good. However, when I purchased the car no oil was getting to the value train. It had a clogged filter and some clogging of an oil line. I was told never to use detergent motor oil, unless it had been used previously. I have been using 30W oil of the non-detergent type and have had no problems. I'm inclined to leave well enough alone, but what do you think about adding a small amount of Marvel Mystery Oil or one pint of detergent oil to the non-detergent when changing oil? As it stands, there is no sludge on the valve train or valve cover. V.R., New York.
A. I asked an old-time mechanic for his advice on the oil for your Buick eight. He heard of the filter clogging you reported and said that since the oil passages were now open and you were not seeing sludge in the valve train, that he would continue doing as

you are. In other words, keep using non-detergent oil with frequent oil changes. You will not need to supplement this with Marvel Mystery Oil or detergent oil.

Q. I own a 1973 Corvette that I have had to run unleaded fuel in. I have experienced no problems. Were engines adapted to burn unleaded gasoline before catalytic converters? H.K., Florida.
A. It is my understanding that domestic manufacturers began installing hardened valve seats (the wear point with unleaded fuel) about 1969. Engines built after that date can be run on unleaded gasoline without concern for engine damage.

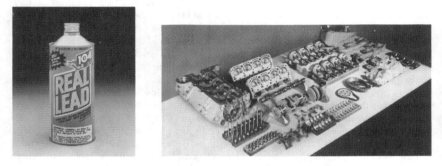

Lead additives (left) and hardened valve seats (right) protect engines.

Q. It is becoming almost impossible to find leaded regular gasoline at any station and I have been told that this type of gasoline is no longer being made. Mechanics have also told me that unleaded gasoline will ruin the valves in older cars in only a few miles. The additive containing lead is very expensive. Can you give me some options? I own a 1937 Cadillac flathead V-8 and a 1942 Willys Jeep. R.D., Texas.
A. The fact that leaded gasoline is being phased out is not a big problem, since the amount of tetraethyl lead in current stocks of leaded gasoline is so minimal as to do very little in the way of protecting older engines. The absence of tetraethyl lead does not ruin the valves, rather it causes premature valve seat wear. Studies on the use of unleaded gasoline in older engines (without hardened valves and seats) show that rapid wear occurs only when the engine is under a heavy load, as in pulling a travel trailer through the mountains. Normal highway driving does not cause rapid valve seat wear. In response to the phase out of leaded gasoline, you have three options. 1) Use unleaded gasoline and drive your collector vehicles as you normally do and expect not to have any noticeable engine deterioration for years to come; 2) Use one of the lead supplement products (which act as a valve lubricant) with unleaded gasoline. This option should forestall any valve seat wear. However, I have received one report from an old car hobbyist who believes that the lead additive supplement caused a build up on the valves, necessitating engine overhaul; 3) Have the engines in your collector vehicles rebuilt with hardened valves and seats. This is a sure-fire, long range solution that will bring your older engines up to modern standards and allow you to use unleaded gasoline with no problems whatsoever.

Q. I own a 1964 Riviera originally purchased by my Dad new in 1964. I use this car as my primary vehicle (not to work) and now have 125,000 miles on it. It is in very good condition. I guess you could call it a "driver," but it is garaged when not used for errands or visiting. In 1988, I purchased six gallons of a gas additive that was advertised to boost octane, protect valves, and provide tetraethyl lead (2 grams of lead per 12 fluid ounces). I cannot tell you if this product contained what was advertised; I can only assume it did as the car ran well while using it. I am now out of the product and would like to purchase something similar. I do not have the means nor the background to distinguish a good chemical additive from a fraud. Can you help me? W.F., New York.

A. I have seen no recent ads for this product. Regarding other lead replacement products, I would like to refer you and other interested readers to an excellent article, titled "Gasoline Update," which appeared in the Winter 1990 issue of *THE 9N-2N-8N NEWSLETTER* for owners and admirers of 1939-early 1950s Ford tractors. It is published by Gerard Rinaldi, 154 Blackwood Lane, Stamford, Connecticut 06903. Tractor owners are particularly concerned about lead replacement additives, because older farm equipment engines are very susceptible to valve seat wear without the protection of Tetraethyl lead. In the article, Rinaldi reports on a USDA study concerning the effect of using low lead and unleaded fuels in gasoline-powered agricultural machinery. Seven agricultural engines were tested on leaded (1.20 grams of lead per gallon), low lead (0.10 glpg) and unleaded gasoline. In addition, two lead replacement additives were tested with the unleaded gasoline. These were PowerShield, manufactured by the Lubrizol Corporation and another additive manufactured by E. I Dupont de Nemours & Company. Used at four times the manufacturer's normally-recommended amount, PowerShield proved effective in eliminating valve seat wear, but at this concentration it also produced engine deposits. The Dupont product gave some, but not total, engine protection. It also produced engine deposits. The article further reports that the EPA has done no follow-up testing. I have spoken to Lubrizol representatives who state that their own testing shows PowerShield to be effective against valve seat wear. They further report that the additive helps clean carburetors and fuel systems. Their study makes no comment on engine deposits. Recently, I received a letter from the owner of a 1946 Chevrolet pickup. He stated that, after using a lead supplement, the valves in his truck's engine began sticking. Upon pulling the head, he noticed extensive build up on the valves, particularly those nearest the carburetor. He says that he has no proof that the build up is traceable to the valve lubricant, but he suspects that to be the cause. He has had the engine upgraded to hardened valves and seats. Contacting Lubrizol Corporation, 29400 Lakeland Boulevard, Wickliffe, Ohio 44092 (216) 943-4200 should get you a list of valve supplement additives available today. With the miles now on your car, you may want to consider doing the valve and valve seat upgrade thereby eliminating the need for gasoline supplements. For health reasons I certainly urge you not to fool with real lead, assuming this product is actually available.

Q. What type of lubricant should I be using in the three-speed manual transmission in my collectible cars? I currently own 21 cars and two old pickup trucks. T.T., Georgia.

A. According to Glenn Abbey of The Classic Oil Company in Concord, California, the lubrication needs of gear boxes may appear relatively straightforward, but individual designs have very specific requirements which can only be catered for with an extensive range of lubricants. Prewar gear boxes generally used relatively thick oils, for two reasons. First, sealing arrangements were often inadequate and thin oils could leak right through transmission seals. Second, thick oils helped to slow down heavy gear wheels to provide better gear-changing. Abbey recommends Penrite's Transoil in SAE 90, 140 and 250 weights for such vehicles. Postwar gear boxes are a different story. These often used SAE 30 or SAE 40 engine oils for lubrication. Others used rear axle oils with similar viscosities, such as EP80 or EP90. However, EP additives are specifically designed for hypoid axles and are out of place in most gear boxes. Abbey recommends Penrite's GearOil 30 and 40 for better additive protection and smoother gear-shifting. These are also compatible with overdrives, pre-selector type transmissions and fluid drive transmissions.

Q. I am among the many owners of mid-1970s cars who want to boost their engine's fuel economy above the 10 to 12 miles per gallon level. Do you have any suggestions? J.B., Wisconsin.

A. Professionals who did engine building on 1970s to 1980s cars say the problem relates to the de-tuning of car engines during this era of early pollution devices and oil shortages. My father worked as an engineer for General Motors during this period and puzzled over the logic of how increasing gasoline consumption by 100 percent or more cut down on pollution. Certainly the emissions standards reduced specific pollutants such as nitrous oxides, but it would seem that burning twice the amount of hydrocarbons would result in a net gain in overall atmospheric pollution. There were several fixes for those gas-guzzling 1972 to 1975 bombs. The biggest thing automakers did in 1972 was to retard the cams in their engines. This killed horsepower dramatically and gas mileage as well. The quickest and easiest fix was a Cloyes True Roller timing gear/chain set. It had different key ways to time the cam back in stock position or advanced or retarded position. By setting it in an advanced position, you could gain back most of what Detroit lost. A better fix was one of the mileage cams that the reputable cam companies were making. You could buy several different grinds. Then, you could tailor the engine for the kind of driving you did (i.e. city, city/highway or highway only). These cams are probably still available. Car manufacturers also dropped the compression in their engines during this time. This also hurt economy and power, but not to the degree that the cam change did. In fact, you need the lower compression nowadays with the lower octane gasoline in use.

Q. A little over a year ago I bought a 1929 Packard with a "Standard 8" engine. I used it all last summer without any problems. The engine ran very well, although the carburetor did run rich. I was unsuccessful at trying to lean-out the fuel/air mixture. Before putting the car away for the winter, I changed the oil (non-detergent) in the engine. At this time the old oil was very dirty and I found some very small pieces of metal in the oil. During the winter, I have removed the valve cover to see what was involved in adjusting the valves. This was one of the first things I wanted to do this spring, after the car was running again. When I removed the valve cover, I found a considerable amount of sludge in this area. I am very concerned now that I may have a partially blocked or totally blocked oil passage. Therefore I am afraid to run the engine for fear of wiping out a bearing or worse. I am trying to figure out the best way to get rid of the sludge without rebuilding the engine or damaging it. The best way I have come up with so far is to remove the valve cover and the oil pan to physically clean out as much of the sludge as possible. I have even thought of removing the oil pump and trying to blow a degreasing agent through the engine with compressed air. I have also thought of dropping the crankshaft to inspect the bearings and to rod out the oil passage. After reassembling the engine, I would start it and use an engine oil flush to further clean out the oil passages. At this point, if I felt the engine was fairly clean, I would use a detergent oil and would change the oil and filter after a few hours of operation and continue very frequent oil changes until I felt the engine was clean. I am very concerned about the possibility of loosening some sludge and then blocking an oil passage and ruining the engine. What do you suggest? J.O., Pennsylvania.

A. I put your question to an old-time engine rebuilder. He said that sludge build up in the valve tray is not at all unusual on older engines that have been operated with non-detergent oil. In fact, he related an experience with a "stovebolt" Chevrolet six where the valve cover was completely caked with sludge. The sludge accumulates in this area, he explained, because the oil is cooler. Where the oil is hot (pan, bearings and passages to and from) little or no sludge should accumulate. He suggested that you mop out the sludge in the valve tray area. He advises that you do go ahead and drop the pan, clean out any sediment you find there, and make sure the oil pump pick up screen is clean. He advised against flushing the oil passages with a degreaser. If you do a thorough cleaning, when you start the engine (with the valve covers still removed) you can watch to see if oil is getting through the passages. From your letter, the rebuilder feels that the metal particles you found in the may actually be bits of hard carbon. If something was disintegrating, you'd hear it.

ENGINES

Q. My 1949 Ford V-8 misses and backfires, especially after starting. The ignition, carburetion and compression seem okay. The miss seems to be coming from just the first few cylinders, but we can't pinpoint the cause. What do you think the problem is? V.M., Oklahoma.
A. On 1949 Fords, it was common for the front half of both cylinder heads to run cooler than the rear half. This could cause exactly the type of problem you're experiencing. To compensate for the variation, old-time mechanics changed the front two cylinders on each bank to higher heat range spark plugs. This little trick often caused the missing and backfiring to disappear.

Q. What are the correct engine paint colors to use on a 1959 Edsel 332 cubic-inch V-8 and a 1964 Ford Falcon 260 cubic-inch V-8? I need to know. J.P., Michigan.
A. International Edsel Club secretary Paul Yount says that the 332 cubic inch Edsel engine should have a black engine block, silver valve covers and a silver air cleaner. The Falcon 260 cubic-inch V-8 should have a black engine block, blue valve covers and blue air cleaner. The oil filter on this motor should also be black. In most cases, one-marque clubs are the best source of information about engine color details. Hobby suppliers who source such paints can be helpful, too. Sometimes technical literature and manuals produced for automakers will include engine color data. However, original sales literature can be an unreliable source of this type of information. The illustrators who created sales brochures years ago often took "artistic license" when depicting technical features in color. Late-model sales literature, illustrated with photographs, is somewhat more reliable for pinpointing correct colors. However, it's still possible that some of the engines photographed were display units that did not look identical to production power plants.

Q. I purchased a 1972 Oldsmobile Cutlass Supreme two-door hardtop equipped with a 350 cubic-inch V-8 at the Spring Carlisle show in Carlisle, Pennsylvania. Can it be operated on today's unleaded gasolines? G.B., Pennsylvania.
A. It's our understanding that 1969 marks the point when American automobile manufacturers began fitting engines with hardened valve seats so that they could be operated on unleaded gasoline. Therefore, it should be safe to operate your Oldsmobile on such fuels today.

Q. I own a 1929 DeSoto. I have a puzzling problem and hope you can help me. I had the engine rebuilt and drove the car for two summers. It drove like a new car. However, one day while driving along, the engine began to miss. It floods. Four spark plugs out of six get flooded with gas, which runs down the cylinders into the oil. This creates black smoke which comes out of the exhaust. I installed a new coil, points, rotor and adjusted the points to "spec" at .020 in. The new spark plugs are adjusted to .027-.030 in. according to the manual. I bought two used updraft carburetors. I started the car after installing and adjusting each carburetor and the car ran perfectly for about one minute, then began to miss. I bought a third new carburetor. I started the car and the same thing happened. It runs very good for about one minute, then begins to miss. I hired a professional mechanic who spent one hour adjusting the carburetor with the same results. While the engine was missing, he lifted each individual spark plug wire. The spark jumped an eighth inch on each plug. What else should I do? P.G., Massachusetts.

A. The problem could be with the valves. The flooding condition suggests that the valves aren't closing properly after the engine warms up causing the engine to lose compression and flood the cylinders. Weak valve springs could be the cause of the problem. Al Zamba, of Ambridge, Pennsylvania is convinced that the problem you're experiencing lies in the vacuum tank. The float inside the vacuum tank may not be functioning properly or has a hole in it (causing the float to fill with gas and remain at the bottom of the tank). As a result, the gas is vacuumed directly into the intake manifold, bypassing the carburetor. Many times owners of cars become weary of vacuum tanks and bypass them with electric fuel pumps. This is okay, but there is nothing wrong with vacuum tanks if they function properly and the owner understands them thoroughly. Electric pumps can be installed, but should be operated by a separate switch and used as an auxiliary pump only when needed. Old car expert John Koll of Colorado Springs, Colorado also tags the vacuum tank as the source of your problem.

Q. Why is low oil pressure so common with Ford flathead V-8s? What can be done to prevent the valves sticking on these engines? On my 1942 Ford, the identification number on the frame does not match the vehicle identification number on the title. Is there any other number on the car that I can use for identification? E.P.R., Louisiana.
A. The most common reason for low oil pressure in Ford flathead V-8s is worn camshaft bearings. Due to the difficulty of removing and replacing the valve train to facilitate removal of the camshaft when installing and fitting new bearings, many rebuilders wind up with sloppy cam bearings and low oil pressure. High-volume oil pumps are available to help alleviate the problem, but the real answer is doing a thorough job. A total engine rebuild done the right way will include removal of the valve gear and replacement of the camshaft bearings. This should also solve the sticking valves problem. There are other causes of low oil pressure. Al Easley, of Yucca Valley, California remembers owning a new 1941 Ford V-8 that suffered such problems. His oil pump was found to be loose in the block. This allowed the oil to return directly to the pan. A pressure pot can be used to check for this once the car's oil pan is removed. In fact, with the pan removed, a loose oil pump could probably be detected manually, although this would not detect a gasket leak. As for identification codes, sometimes the Ford flathead V-8s have identification numbers stamped on the clutch housing.

Q. My car is a 1955 Ford with a 272 cubic-inch two-barrel V-8 and manual choke. I installed a rebuilt carburetor. When the motor was turned off, I had a leak on the control side. I installed a new Holley carburetor, but have the same problem. There is no leak when the car is running. A new fuel pump and inline filter were also installed. What is the problem? Colonel L.L.J., Georgia.
A. It is difficult to diagnose mechanical problems by mail, but we have a few suggestions. Check float adjustment and the needle seat. Possibly, you are getting dirt from the fuel line into the carburetor and it is holding the needle valve open. This may be flooding the carburetor with gas, which leaks out when the motor is shut off. Ford restorer Sam Busse, of Montello, Wisconsin says that carburetor overflow leaks were very common in 1955 because the fuel pump put out more pressure than the carburetor, needle valve and seat could handle. A factory bulletin was issued on how to fix this. It advised shimming the fuel pump from the block to reduce stroke pressure. Busse says another problem was that gasoline would expand in the line over a warm engine causing fuel to percolate into the carburetor. He suggests that the surest fix for both problems is to install a fuel pressure regulator (rated for no more than three pounds per square inch) at or near the carburetor. A fuel pressure regulator does not reduce volume a measurable amount, but will solve the problem of excessive pressure.

Q. Late in the 1961 model year, my brother-in-law bought a Buick Special with a V-6. Dad liked it so much that he acquired a 1962 Buick Special with a V-8 as soon as they came out. Dad was pleased that his 1962 V-8 got the same gas mileage as Dave's 1961 V-6 with zippier performance. My 1961 *MOTOR'S MANUAL* concurs with the statement that Buick offered only the V-8 in 1961 and not a V-6. Could my brother-in-law's car be a case of the last of the run getting the new V-6? Maybe this was like the 1956 Chevrolet with a 283 cubic-inch V-8 that I once had. I remember the engine air cleaner had 283/220 horsepower decals. The valve cover screws were directly opposite each other, instead of the upper pair being slightly inboard as on 265 cubic-inch V-8s. The "ram horn" exhaust manifolds were used. They exited into separate systems. The car's original owner said that he had ordered it special, perhaps through some sort of clearance sale on 1956s. There's no question in my mind that the 283 in that car had been factory installed. J.L., Colorado.

A. Our opinion is that it would have been impossible to order a 1961 Buick Special with a V-6. The *STANDARD CATALOG OF AMERICAN CARS 1946-1975* shows the 1961 Buick Special being equipped with the aluminum 215 cubic-inch V-8 and the 198 cubic-inch V-6 debuting in the 1962 models. This is backed by information in *WARD'S 1962 AUTOMOTIVE YEARBOOK*, which reported, "At the outset of the 1962 model year, Buick scored the engineering coup of the year with a peppy V-6 engine, the industry's first (Editor's note: This was not accurate) for passenger car use. As the new standard engine in the basic Special series, the V-6 quickly proved its merits and gave the small Buick a new edge in price competition, although the aluminum V-8 was retained in this series and as standard power plant for Deluxe and Skylark models." *WARD'S 1962 AUTOMOTIVE YEARBOOK* also includes a chart listing GM engine production for model year 1962 by cubic inch displacement. The chart shows that no 198 cubic inch engines were produced. Another source, the December 1961 issue of *MOTOR TREND*, says, "One of the first 1962 Buick Specials powered by the new V-6 engine to leave the Southern California assembly plant was assigned to *MOTOR TREND*'s testing group." Thanks for providing us with the additional detail on your family's 1956 Chevrolet with a 283 V-8 engine. In this case, we also have doubts that a 283 cubic-inch V-8 was available in 1956 Chevrolets, though you could get a 265 cubic-inch engine in some 1957 models. However, we have to admit that we do not have any way to back our opinion with figures from trade publications, since they did not record engine production by cubic inches back in model year 1956.

Q. I have a 1936 Graham with a six-cylinder engine and need to do a valve job. I do not know the proper valve settings. Do you know any place I could find this information? I have the *STANDARD CATALOG OF AMERICAN CARS 1805-1942*. It tells the history of Graham, but does not give service information. R.K., Kansas.

A. You will find the specifications and other service information you need to do a valve job on your 1936 Graham in an old *MOTOR'S AUTO REPAIR MANUAL* or *CHILTON MANUAL* covering cars of that year. These books can often be found at swap meets. They are also available from literature vendors who advertise in hobby magazines. Regarding the valve settings for your 1936 Graham, according John Dillon, of Zion, Illinois, *MOTOR*'s called for hot tappet clearances, on both intake and exhaust valves, of .010 inch. Joe Perkins, of Cincinnati, Ohio adds that if you set the valves at .012 on the intake and .014 on the exhaust cold, then start the engine and run it until it's at operating temperature, you won't have much additional adjusting to do. When adjusting valves at the cold setting, you always go by the firing order, 1-5-3-6-2-4.

126

Q. I would like to know who has information or a kit to put a Pinto engine in a 1930 Model A Ford? I saw an ad listing once, but can't find it now. C.P., Rhode Island.
A. Personally, I wouldn't recommend this swap. You will be substantially lessening the Model A's value. All of the advantages you would gain from the Pinto engine swap can be gained in more authentic ways. Have the Model A engine rebuilt with a counter-balanced crankshaft. If higher road speed is a goal (keep those mechanical brakes in mind) you can install an overdrive transmission. A supplier named Over Drive Inc. has one that fits right into the Model A torque tube.

Q. I am restoring a 1930 Model A Ford and need the name and address of someone who can recondition my engine. I would like someone in the Midwest as I do not want to travel too far. When I was at the Iola Old Car Show last summer there were Model A parts dealers with reconditioned engines, but I have lost their cards. E.H., Michigan.
A. At the same Iola show I talked to Dick Knapp of Country Classic Engines, 1608 Bellevue Boulevard North, Bellevue, Nebraska 68005. This company's literature states that it can do a complete rebuild on Model A engines, including balancing the crankshaft and installing hardened valves and seats in order to use unleaded gasoline. If you plan to attend Iola again, you might contact Country Classic Engines ahead of time. You can arrange to bring your block and pick up an exchange engine. If you want your block rebuilt, you could ship it to them and have it delivered at Iola. Either of these practices should save you hassles and shipping fees.

Q. I have a four-cylinder flathead engine and transmission, serial number PB23342. Cast in the head is the word "Silverdome." The distributor is on the front and the throw out bearing greases through a hole in the bell housing. What is it? J.R., Wisconsin.
A. Grace Brigham's *SERIAL NUMBER BOOK FOR U.S. CARS 1900 TO 1975* is one good source to use when attempting to identify old car engines by the codes stamped on them. This book shows that Plymouth four-cylinder engines in 1932 used the numbers PB1001 and up.

Q. I recently noticed an advertisement that listed a Ford with a 312 cubic-inch engine and two-barrel carburetor. Later, I was at a farm auction that was selling a 1957 Ford. It was represented to be all original and had a 312 cubic-inch engine with a two-barrel carburetor. I am curious to know if Ford offered a two-barrel carburetor on their 312 engines by special order or if, in these instances, the manifolds had been changed? D.W., Iowa.
A. According to Ford fan T.W. Ulrich, Ford fitted all of its 312 cubic-inch engines "Thunderbird Special" V-8s with either a single Holley four-barrel carburetor or dual Holley four-barrel carburetors. Also, at least some of the 1957 Fords with 312 cubic-inch engines came equipped with Ford Autolite or Carter carburetors. This was true at least for the single four-barrel engines. Either the ads you saw were in error or the manifolds where changed. The availability of a two-barrel is not listed in general literature.

Q. A compression check on my 1937 Ford V-8 was done by a local mechanic about five years ago. It showed about 90 pounds of compression pressure per cylinder. In 1990, the fellow who removed the body of the car to paint it also removed the headers and pan. He supposedly cleaned the pan and said everything looked like it had recently been rebuilt. The ridge above the top ring, the valves, and so on looked good. I drove the car about 300 miles last summer at speeds up to 50 miles per hour. It consumed about four quarts of oil in the process. Most of it exited via the valve chamber vent that opens on the right side and front area of the block. This plastered the underside of the motor and frame with oil. Almost none came through the oil filler opening. I took the heads off, removed the pistons and dropped the oil pan. Two spark plugs were oily, but the motor ran really well and started fine. On most oily cylinders, the ring gaps were all nicely lined up. There was no baffle in the pan. I can probably take care of the missing baffle myself, but I can't find a good picture of the baffle. There are a couple of flat pieces left on the pan and what seem to be spot welds broken loose. Could the lack of this baffle cause the oil to blow out the vent? Could the lined up ring gaps account for this much oil usage? Could the rings have been installed upside down in the cylinders that are wet with oil? Could it be that installing rings without removing the glaze from the cylinders is the cause of all this? If the baffle is necessary to prevent excessive oil use, is it possible someone could supply a drawing so I could make one? Would it be best to get a different pan? Incidentally, there is no knocking and the oil pressure runs over 20 pounds all the time on 10W-30 oil. There was a good cup full of glop in the bottom of the pan. I'm sure that this was due to detergent oil being used. Would 15W-40 or straight 40W oil be best? Or can I assume most of the crud is now flushed out of its hiding places and continue to use detergent oil? M.C., New York.

A. Although lined up oil rings or rings installed upside down could increase oil consumption somewhat, I don't think these are your problems. If you take a careful look at the pan, you will see that the oil vent hole, located as you describe at the right front side of the block, has a lip all the way around it. This lip mates against the bottom of the block. When your mechanic replaced the pan, he may have misaligned the gasket that sandwiches between the pan and block along the inside of this vent. This would allow oil to pour through the opening and run out the vent and would explain the heavy oil usage and oil coating on the underside of the engine and frame. The purpose of the baffle is to keep oil from sloshing about on cornering. The baffle is placed across the pan just to the rear of the oil pump. You can see its location on your pan from the spot welds. It has a height of about two inches and is positioned so that there is about 3/8-inch clearance between the bottom of the baffle and pan. Two notches, approximately 1 x 3/8 inch high, are cut in the bottom of the baffle to allow oil movement at the bottom of the pan. You could make this baffle quite easily yourself. Regarding oils, I use straight viscosity oil in older engines. This is simply my own preference. In my judgement, the detergent oil has probably cleaned most of the build up from the oil passages and can be continued. Replace the pan, making sure there is a good gasket seal around the vent. This should cure your oil consumption problem.

Q. In 1947 I purchased a 1917 Packard Twin-Six Cloverleaf Runabout Second Series. It is a Model 2-25, body style 167. It was stored on blocks in a heated coach-house since 1927. This car is entirely original and is in running condition, but needs a few things for completion. It is my retirement project. I dearly want to get it back on the road. Unfortunately, the previous owners did not drain the cooling system when they stored it. When I put it back on the road in 1947, the entire system (radiator, block channels, water manifolds and water pump) was badly obstructed by rust. The rust was often in large chunks. I replaced the original radiator when the fan blew up and shredded the core. I drove it for six years with much enjoyment. I then put it up on blocks again until last year. Then, I discovered Hershey and began getting the car ready for restoration. The block still contains large chunks of rust and the replacement radiator is blocked. This latter can be flushed out without problem, but will be replaced with an authentic honeycomb core. As you perhaps know, these Twin-Six engines have cast iron blocks with steel water manifolds and water inlet and outlet pipes running to the radiator. The remainder of the engine (crankcase, water pump and intake manifold) is cast aluminum and also contains water channels. This is the problem. Is there any way

I can dissolve/flush out/remove the rust in the water channels without harming the aluminum parts? There are, of course, large clean-out plates bolted onto the ends of both blocks and "freeze-out plugs" elsewhere along the sides, but while the rear plates can be removed by working from the sides, access to the rear interiors is almost impossible. There is only a few inches between the blocks and the wooden instrument panel. If there is no way of cleaning the engine out short of removing it from the car, I can handle this despite the tremendous weight. I really would prefer not to do this since the car has only about 12,000 miles on it and hasn't been disturbed since Packard put it together. The best the local radiator shops could suggest was to pickle the rust out with muriatic acid. They said that I could get away with this if I didn't leave it in the engine too long. Although this car is my retirement project, I dearly want to get it back on the road and drive it for a few months before I start in. Dr. J.H.S., Virginia.

A. Hobbyist Dave Phinney restored a third series Twin Six in the early 1970s. He believes it hadn't been run since the early 1940s. It had substantial rust accumulation in the cooling system. Phinney spent considerable time checking out the best information on how to repair the system. He discovered that the job cannot be done effectively with the engine assembled and in the car. If the whole engine cannot be removed, the individual blocks and be extracted using suitable guide equipment. A Volkswagen ring compressor can be used for reassembly. Phinney described the repair process in a detailed restoration article that appeared in the May-June 1977 issue of *BULB HORN*, a magazine produced by the Veteran Motor Car Club of America (VMCCA). A copy of this article should be available from Walter McIlvain, editor, 17 Bonnet Road, Manchester, Connecticut 06040. Another collector, Dan Long, has a technique that he has used many times to clean rust and debris out of an engine. He first checks to ensure that the radiator has good flow and isn't clogged. He then obtains some copper screening (the same kind you would use when replacing the screens on your house). From the piece of screening, he fashions a cup-like filter to place over the inlet pipe to the radiator. He then slides the regular radiator hose over the screening and inlet pipe. The hose needs to extend onto the inlet pipe a bit further than the filter, so that the connection won't leak when it is tightly clamped. This filter will stop the circulation of anything large enough to clog the system. The filter can be cleaned and inspected quite easily by removing the upper radiator hose. A replacement will usually have to be fashioned following inspection. Although this filter catches loose material, Long has never seen one plug up and stop the normal flow of the system.

Q. In the summer of 1990, I took my 1967 Mustang with a 289 cubic-inch V-8 off blocks to begin a complete restoration. After checking out the fuel pump and carburetor, I got the car started. The engine ran well, but it had no power. I took the valve covers off and found out that I had bent the push rods on five of the eight intake valves. Since the motor had only 50,000 miles on it, I felt that my problem was the year it had set before I started it. I did a complete cleaning job on the heads, rebuilt the carburetor and put in new hydraulic valve lifters, push rods, a new fuel pump and a new gas filter. The gasoline had a funny smell. I drained the tank and the line that connected the tank to the fuel pump. The old gasoline was leaded, but it was clear with no sediment build up. I put five gallons of unleaded gasoline in the tank and started the motor. After a final adjustment to the carburetor and automatic choke, the car ran well and the motor sounded great. I ran the car very little from November 1990 to September 1991. During this time I put an additional 10 gallons of unleaded gasoline in the tank. One morning, while working on the car, I tried starting it to move it to another location. As the motor turned over, a banging sound developed and it would not start. I took the valve covers off and found that the intake valves on cylinders one and eight were stuck open.

At this time I determined the possibility that the unleaded gasoline might be the cause of the problem. I took the heads to a machine shop where they were completely done over including new valves, inserts and valve guides so that car could run on unleaded gas. The motor was reassembled and ready to run. Before I started it, I detected a funny smell to the gasoline that was present when I removed the original leaded gas from the tank. I ruled out the possibility that the gas was bad because it was only in the tank for a relatively short period of time (less than a year). When I started the engine, it fired immediately. I retuned the carburetor. The engine sounded great. I ran the engine no longer than 15 minutes and turned it off. The next morning, I started the engine to see if everything was fine. When I turned the engine over, the same banging sound occurred. The engine never started. I took the valve covers off and again found that the intake valves on cylinders two, three, five, six and seven were stuck either open or closed. I had three bent pushrods and on two other cylinders the pushrods had come off the rocker arms. All five intake valves were stuck so bad they moved the valve guides and the rocker arm studs from the head. When I dismantled the engine for the third time, I discovered a thick varnish substance around the intake valve stems, on the valves and cylinder heads and in the ports of the intake manifold. I have since gotten the heads repaired and the motor reassembled. The machinist who did the repair work was surprised to see such a high build up of varnish on the heads from the short period the engine was run. I have not started the car since this work was done. The only thing I can figure out that is causing me trouble is the gasoline. I have ruled out someone putting a foreign substance in the gas tank, because the car was secured and in a safe location where the gas tank could not be reached. One thing that I suspect could have happened is that the gas tank is impregnated with a substance left by the old gasoline that is dissolving in the unleaded gas causing the varnish build up in the engine. I was also told that the additives in gasoline being manufactured today could be breaking down causing the problem. In any case I am completely baffled by what has happened and appreciate any comments on the matter. F.W., Maryland.

A. I talked about your problem with a friend who has a large collection of old cars and trucks and is employed as a research historian by a major restoration shop. He confirms that gasoline being refined today is much less stable than that which was available just a few years ago. He reported that the gasoline in one of his shop's recent restorations had started to break down (indicated by the funny smell you report) after several months of storage. In this case, no engine damage resulted, but the gasoline tank had to be pulled off and cleaned. Your problems sound extreme, but should serve as a warning to old car collectors not to neglect adding gasoline stabilizer (available at auto supply stores) to fuel tanks of gasoline powered vehicles that will be stored even for just a few months.

Q. Can you help me decode the engine, Fisher Body tag and vehicle identification number numbers on a 1959 Chevrolet? C.T., Utah.

A. Chevrolet expert Bob Hensel, of Brillion, Wisconsin helped us decode your engine number T1211C. The T indicates that the Tonawanda Engine Plant built the engine. The symbols 12 indicate that the engine was built in December. The symbols 11 indicate the engine was built on the 11th day of that month. The C indicates that the engine is a 348 cubic-inch V-8 that was attached to a Powerglide transmission. Regarding the body style 59-1837, 59 is the model year and 18 means Impala V-8 and 37 means two-door Sport Coupe. The body number OA-2800 uses OA to tell that Oakland (California) body plant built the body and that it was the 2,800 built. Trim number 852 is a combination of light, medium and dark turquoise cloth and light and medium turquoise imitation leather upholstery. Also, the interior is painted turquoise. The ACC (accessory) code EZ indicates Easy-Eye glass. The paint number 936A is solid Snowcrest White with the accent strip on the rear quarter painted Tuxedo Black. The serial number (VIN) F590015033 decodes as follows: F stands for Impala eight-cylinder with 119-inch wheelbase and 590015033 means this was the 15,033 car off the assembly line for the Oakland plant in the model year 1959. Hensel has provided this thorough decoding of numbers from a 1959 Chevrolet Impala by researching his extensive library of Chevrolet data, sales and service literature. Readers who want to decode their own car's serial number, color and trim codes and other numbers should be aware that Motorbooks International distributes a series of *CARS & PARTS* books including car and truck identification numbers.

The 348 cubic-inch Chevrolet V-8 engine.

Q. Can you tell me how to install a full-flow oil filter on my LaSalle? E.S., Florida.
A. According to hobbyist Bill Atwood, installing a full-flow oil filter on a 1937 to 1948 Cadillac or LaSalle flathead V-8 is extremely easy. The modification can be done without showing in a conspicuous way. On the bottom left side of the engine, at the rear, you will see where the oil pump feeds in. This cast-in hole was accessed from the bottom at the factory with a drill. The drilled hole was then filled at the very bottom with a tapped pipe 3/8-inch pipe plug. All that is necessary to change to a full-flow filter is to take a standard 5/8-inch straight tap (the same thread count as the 3/8-inch pipe) and tap down beyond the oil inlet cross hole. Now, make a plug from a bolt. Liberally apply sealant and run the plug down below the oil pump inlet hole. Stake it in place. Now you can install a fitting where the original pipe plug was. Modify the edge of the oil pan to clear and add a fitting to the front of the engine where the main oil galley has a 3/8-inch plug. With this simple change, all oil from the pump comes out the bottom of the block at the back, through your filter (which you can locate anywhere you like) and enters the block at the front near the fuel pump. This modification is very simple and very effective.

131

Q. I have a 1940 Buick Model 46-S bought from its original owner. I have the original bill of sale, all tag receipts and the original owner's manual. The engine has never been out of the car. It is black. Most Buick people (I'm a member of the Buick Club of America) say that Buicks had only gray engine paint. I have taken this engine out to restore it and taken off all accessories. I looked in the normal places for gray paint and found none. I talked to a fellow at the Hershey, Pennsylvania Antique Automobile Club of America Fall Meet last year. He had a 1940 Buick with only 33,000 miles and said that his car had a black engine. What is the engine color for my car? H.B., Ohio.
A. The engines were painted gray. However, they were black underneath the gray. After the passage of time and repeated engine washings, the gray paint frequently disappears, leaving the engine looking as if it was painted entirely black.

Q. Last year I had the engine in my 1947 Hudson eight rebuilt. The company that did the work recommended 20 weight non-detergent oil. My jobber recommended 10W-40 or 20W-50 SF oil for the film strength and cold flow needed for a splash oil system. I went with 20W-50 and in less than 1,200 miles the engine developed a rod knock. When dismantled, all the bearings, the rod bearings and the main bearings were burned out. The shop blamed it on the detergent oil and also told me that similar problems had occurred during last year's Great American Race in cars using detergent (SF) oil. I now have the car on the road using 20W non-detergent oil. Was the detergent oil a factor in the failure of this particular engine or simply a ploy for another $1,500? I've had similar problems from different shops on larger vintage engines, Packards, a Cadillac and a Hudson 308. Is this the normal case? If so, is the reason that the parts supplied aren't quite what the originals were? Is it a lack of knowledge or lost art in this type of work? With the limited warranties offered, a make-good can cost as much as the original job. It seems that my Model T fours and vintage Chevrolet sixes can be just slapped together by anybody and run fine forever. D.D., Connecticut.
A. Detergent oil becomes a problem in an engine that has not been thoroughly boiled and rodded while being rebuilt. What detergent oil, if the oil passages are left with the deposits that have built up over the years the detergents will loosen these deposits and circulate them with the oil. This can often cause blockage at key points. If the engine has been thoroughly cleaned during the rebuild, then the detergent oil is a plus. It will keep deposits from settling (as it does with modern engines). I suspect that your Hudson block had not been cleaned and rodded (metal rods are actually used to push the sediment out of the oil passages). As a result, the detergent oil loosened these old sediments and deposits. Then, the deposits lodged in smaller passages, cutting off oil flow to the bearings.

Q. My 1949 Buick Super convertible had 150,000 miles on the original engine. She used one quart of oil every 800 miles and was getting a little slow. After a complete engine rebuild, it no longer used oil. However, it suffered from severe blow-by and poor gas mileage. It also had a fine knock from the front of the engine at idle. This wasn't a desirable trade off. Wouldn't you think that a vintage engine rebuilt with today's modern alloys in rings and bearings would be superior to original? D.D., Connecticut.
A. I have experienced some of the same frustration on having a rebuilt engine perform below my expectations. I blame this on the rebuilder's lack of knowledge or care in the rebuilding process. In one experience, the rebuilder didn't bother to check the rods to ensure they were "true." This was overlooked even though the reason that the engine needed rebuilding was that it kept chewing up the number five rod bearing. A bent rod that caused the earlier failures wasn't detected and continued to chew up bearings until

132

the rod was checked and straightened. In another experience, a machine shop used a dull stone to grind the crankshaft. As a result, the crank journals had a cup shape and the crank seized when the bearings were fitted. These things shouldn't happen. In the case of your Buick's blow-by problem, usually the cause there is taper in the cylinders. An engine of your Buick's mileage would normally be bored as part of the rebuild. For whatever reason, the rebuilder may have skipped this step. I suspect that old time mechanics and machinists paid closer attention to details and got the job done right the first time. In some cases, it's also possible that they had more firsthand familiarity with the unique characteristics of specific old engines, since they were dealing with those motors on a more regular basis.

Q. Two years ago I acquired a 1971 Mercedes 250C in excellent shape. I drive it approximately 30,000 miles per year. It has 187,000 miles. In the interest of longevity and ecology, I would like to convert it to operate on Liquid Petroleum Gas (LPG). Are such conversion kits readily available? What difficulties would I encounter in such a job? Can a propane tank be installed in the spacious trunk behind the back seat? If so, how might one have an external filler without changing the car's graceful lines? D.H., California.

A. Engine swapper Bob Brown has detailed facts about a vehicle with a V-8 that he converted to LPG propulsion at 100,000 miles. It now has 142,000 miles and very few mechanical difficulties. Brown likes the conversion so well that he is considering converting his restored 1964 Oldsmobile 98 Luxury Sedan to LPG propulsion. He drives the Oldsmobile every day. With such a large car, the 40- or 60-gallon LPG fuel tank will fit easily inside the trunk. A dealer advised that the trunk must be separated from the car's passenger compartment by an air-tight, welded metal bulkhead for safety reasons. This requirement is stated in literature that LPG dealers have. The compartment containing the gas cylinder must be ventilated and have a pop-off valve exiting the outside. It is possible to place the filler to the gas canister inside the vehicle, thereby avoiding having to mount a filler door on the outside of the vehicle.

Brown recommends keeping the regular gas tank. The LPG conversion kit has a cut-off. It allows the carburetor to be fueled by either LPG fuel or gasoline. If you experience trouble finding LP gas, you can switch to gasoline and continue down the road. The major cost is acquisition of the LPG conversion unit. Brown was able to locate a used unit for about $250. He had to replace gaskets in the device that delivers gas to the carburetor. Outside of that repair, he has had no trouble. He estimates the cost of conversion with a new unit to be about $1,000. In his state, vehicles converted to LP gas must have a permit. This costs him about $85 a year for some 15,000 miles of driving. The permit sticker goes on the windshield. A bumper sticker is also required stating that the vehicle runs on LP gas. Brown buys LP gas for about one-half the price of gasoline. Since an intake device on the unit mounts on top of the carburetor, some clearance is needed between the carburetor and hood. LPG fuel does not contaminate engine oil and spark plugs last longer. A local LP gas dealer can provide information on what's required and probably recommend a shop to do the conversion. Ak Miller Enterprises, Incorporated, 9236 Bermudez, Pico Rivera, California 90660 specializes in LP gas conversions. The proprietor is Ak (Akton) Miller, a name famous in the racing and hot rodding hobbies. He is over 70 years old and has a wealth of information on fueling automobiles with LP gas. About 30 years ago, vintage parts vendor Ed Jacobwitz converted a 1955 Buick Special convertible to propane gas. He recalls that the car was quite a disappointment to him. A 30-gallon fuel tank all but totally occupied the front and center of the spacious trunk space. Installing a conversion kit he had on hand was inexpensive. However, the switches and solenoids necessary to start the engine on gasoline and switch over to propane were overly-complex. In addition, the normal 20-plus miles per gallon gasoline mileage dropped to a disappointing 10 miles per gallon with propane. He found the car to operate sluggishly while running on propane. Jacobwitz also felt that incorporating a remote external filler on the body shell's extremity increased the danger and vulnerability from possible collisions.

Q. I have a 1940 Chevrolet coupe which I want to restore to original condition. It has been sitting idle for years and the engine is stuck. How would I get it unstuck? Should I take the head off or the pan off to work the pistons loose? E.N., Florida.
A. Often you can free a stuck engine by removing the spark plugs and pouring automatic transmission fluid into the cylinders. You will want to let the fluid work for several weeks. This light weight, highly penetrating oil will often loosen the rings from the cylinder bores. Then the engine will turn over. If this method doesn't work, you may have to remove the head and pan, disconnect the connecting rods from the crankshaft and drive the pistons out of the cylinders using a hammer and block of wood. Hopefully the hydraulic transmission fluid will work and more drastic measures won't be necessary. Model T Ford owner Roger Gore once left the cylinder head off his car all winter. The cylinders filled with water, which froze on and off all winter. By spring the motor was stuck. Soaking the cylinders in penetrating oil for several weeks didn't help. Then, Gore disconnected the con rods on the down-stroke. The other two pistons moved. He then reconnected the two con rods and the engine was free.

Q. I would like information on installing a late-model Chevrolet 350 or 305 cubic-inch V-8 in a 1951 Chevrolet pickup. B.B., Mississippi.
A. This swap is very common and can be done without too much complication. You can read about a similar swap (a 327 cubic-inch Chevrolet V-8 in a 1947 Chevrolet pickup) in the September/October 1992 publication of the Light Commercial Vehicle Association. The owner of that truck used a late model General Motors four-speed transmission and 1986 Blazer 3.08 rear end. You can contact this old truck Association by writing to the Light Commercial Vehicle Association, PO Box 838, Yellow Springs, Ohio 45387.

Q. Some years ago a company called J. C. Whitney advertised parts that would allow you to install a modern V-8 engine in older cars such as the 1940 Ford Tudor sedan that I own. They sold motor mounts and adapters to bolt the modern engine to the original transmission. Is there any company that sells this type of equipment now? I want to do an economical conversion of my car from original to street rod. I don't want a high-powered machine, just something that will run and still look like the old-time street rods. R.S., Iowa.
A. Numerous companies sell engine conversion kits. Butch's Rod Shop, 2853 Northlawn Avenue, Dayton, Ohio 45439 makes conversion kits for both Ford 302 cubic-inch and Chevrolet 350 cubic-inch V-8s. In the last information I have, the kit for either conversion sold for just under $90. Another conversion kit manufacturer you may want to contact is Fat Man Fabrications, 8621-C Fairview Road, Highway 218, Charlotte, North Carolina 28227.

Q. I have a Cadillac diesel with about 110,000 miles on it. It has the GM converted 350 diesel engine and I would like to have a genuine diesel engine of an advanced design. I would like to buy a 1989 Fleetwood Brougham Cadillac or a Silver Shadow Rolls-Royce (1965-1980) with the body and interior in good shape. I would then like to put in a 5.9-liter Cummins turbo diesel engine with an overdrive transmission so I could get good mileage. I would not want a truck transmission, because they provide lugging power and deliver poor fuel economy. Is it possible to do this on a technical and mechanical level without excessive cost? Could I match the 5.9 liter Cummins diesel engine with a car transmission? Who in Wisconsin could do this type of conversion for me? What type of special problems would I encounter by switching engines in a vehicle originally designed for a gas engine? L.S., Wisconsin.

A. Although we have received several questions dealing with engine conversions recently, this is by far the most challenging. My first response is that any engine can be put in any vehicle, providing cost and time are no object. By time, I don't just mean the length of time required by the conversion, but the extra time needed to sort out the inevitable "bugs." A local mechanic where I live specializes in swapping General Motors 350 cubic-inch V-8 engines with Tuned-Port-Injection into cars. Currently he is doing one of these conversions in a Jeep. By specializing in one type of conversion, he has become familiar with motor mounts and transmission adapters, as well as with the extensive electronic work required to install computer-controlled engines in vehicles lacking sophisticated electronics. The Cummins diesel, however, presents another series of challenges. Possibly, you can find a mechanic capable of doing the swap you desire. My feeling is that the expense and difficulties the conversion would present will outweigh the gains. Why not consider a low-mileage, well-preserved Mercedes diesel?

Cutaway of GM diesel engine produced by Oldsmobile.

Q. The air cleaner heat stove on my 1974 Chevrolet Caprice 400 cubic-inch two-barrel engine has succumbed to age. The stove, which is comprised of two sheet metal pieces attached to the exhaust manifold, provides heated air to the air cleaner through a tube. This improves carburetor operation and engine warm-up characteristics by keeping combustion air above 100 degrees or more. The two pieces comprising the stove were

135

pinned to bosses on the manifold with some type of drive pins. I had no problem getting new parts. The Chevrolet dealer even had one of them in stock. How do I remove the old fasteners from the manifolds? The shop manual does not offer a clue. It just says remove them. I am going on the presumption that they are the original fasteners, but I don't know what they are made of. I've tried soaking them with solvent, but to no avail. I am about to try drilling them out. If they are hardened steel, that can be a real bummer. The engine is in the car and there is not a lot of room to get even an angle drill in there. R.R.J., Wisconsin.

A. Mechanic Rich Jensen specializes in retrofitting General Motors Tuned-Port-Injected engines to 1950s through 1980s collector vehicles. His trick for removing these heat stove rivets (pins) is: 1) Heat the pins with a torch until the heads are red hot; 2) Let the pins cool (this heating and cooling expands and contracts the metal, breaking the rust bond between the pin and the manifold); 3) Using a gasket scraper or similar tool with a thin, sharp edge, tap the edge of the tool under the rivet head. The head should pry up so that it can be grasped with pliers; 4) Pull the pin (rivet) out of the manifold. Rich said that you may find it easier to remove the manifolds from the engine to get full access to the pins. If the heads are rusted or have been broken off, you can drill the pins (they're soft metal). Replacements are available at your Chevrolet garage.

Q. I have tried almost everything to unscramble a Ford engine number for my 1934 three-window coupe. It is 99C 72I659. The car has a 21-stud V-8 with cast iron heads. The numbers on the heads are (right) 406049B and (left) 406050B. The serial number stamped on the frame is B5236447. I have contacted parts houses and club members to figure out the engine's origin, but got no definitive answers. The engine does not exactly fit into my 1934 coupe. Can you help? J.A., Maine.

A. According to the *FORD CHASSIS PARTS AND ACCESSORIES CATALOG 1928-1948*, the numbers on the heads show them to be from a 21-stud V-8 of 1933-1936 vintage. This catalog lists a 99T prefix for the 1939-1941 Ford 100-horsepower truck engine and a 99A prefix for the same-vintage car engine. The 99C prefix is not listed in any engine number reference. According to Ford fan Ted Masilian, the 21-stud V-8 was used until the middle of 1938. After that, Ford came out with the 24-stud flathead V-8 (still rated at 85 horsepower). In 1946, the power of the passenger car engine was upped to 100 horsepower. The only engine "fit" problem Masilian can recall would occur with a 24-stud engine's radiator. The water outlets were in the middle of the cylinder heads from 1937 to the middle of 1938. However, from 1932 to 1936 the top radiator hoses went to the water pump at the front of the engine. This changed the angle of the top radiator outlets. However, heads interchanged between these two engines. Switching heads should correct a radiator hose fit problem. Grace Brigham's *SERIAL NUMBER BOOK FOR U.S. CARS 1900 TO 1975* (now out of print) states that Canadian-built Fords used a C in their engine number prefixes. It is possible that the engine in your coupe is a 1939-1941 Ford V-8 built in Canada. There may be some fit problems associated with minor differences in a Canadian engine, but we can't say for sure.

Q. My friend says the 1932 Ford Model 18 engine (the first Ford V-8) was an 85-horsepower job. I say it had 60 horsepower and that the 85-horsepower V-8 came out in 1936 or 1937. Who's right? When did the 100-horsepower engine come out? M.R., Michigan.

A. The Model 18 Ford V-8 introduced in 1932 was rated at 65 horsepower. In 1933, the V-8's power rating was increased to 75 horsepower. It went up again to 85 horsepower in 1934. Ford introduced the 100-horsepower V-8 in its larger trucks in 1939 and in cars for 1946.

Q. In the 1960s, Studebaker had an R-4 Lark high-performance model. I also recall rumors of a special Studebaker Lark with the hotter supercharged R-3 engine. What can you tell me about it? T.P., New Jersey.

A. According to an article in *MUSCLE CAR* and *TRUCK BUYER'S GUIDE*, Studebaker's R-4 Lark recorded a top speed of 132 miles per hour and 0-to-60 acceleration of 7.8 seconds. Since the supercharged R-3 engine produced 55 more horsepower than the R-4, its top speed and performance figures would have been even hotter. There was at least one R-3 supercharged Lark. Enthusiast Mike Firth once drove it. The car was a base two-door sedan with four-speed transmission. His father bought a Lincoln from Towne Lincoln-Mercury in Fremont, Ohio. This dealer also sold Studebakers. The Lincoln was in for service and the car provided as a "loaner" was the R-3 Lark. When Firth saw the Lark he laughed at the car his father was driving. Then he opened the hood! With less than a little coaxing, Firth was allowed to drive it. A friend who had a Ford with a 360 cubic-inch V-8 came whipping by as he pulled out onto the road. Not being one to let the horses stand idle when challenged, Firth stomped the Lark and beat that Ford.

Q. I recently purchased a 1968 Dodge Charger with a well running 225 cubic-inch Slant Six. The vehicle identification number is XP29B8B375501. Could this six-cylinder engine have been specially ordered? I am aware of Dodge Chargers with six-cylinder engines only from 1970. S.J., Wisconsin.

A. According to the "percent of factory installed equipment on U.S. '68 model year cars" chart included in *WARD'S 1969 AUTOMOTIVE YEARBOOK*, the exact production total for 1968 Chargers was 96,108 cars and one percent of them had six-cylinder engines. Another chart in the same source, titled "U.S. 1968 model year car output by cylinder type" shows rounded-off totals of 900 Chargers with six-cylinder engines and 95,200 Chargers with V-8s. We do not know if the eight cars that were "rounded-off" the total were sixes or V-8s, but as you can see, not very many sixes were built. Many people I have talked with were unaware of the Slant Six being available regularly or upon special order in these cars. However, the reliable figures in *WARD'S* verify that the possibility was real. MoPar enthusiast Jim Smith also purchased a six-cylinder 1968 Charger from its original owner. His car's vehicle identification number number is XP29B8B. He obtained an original window sticker listing the six-cylinder engine and indicating strongly that the Charger six was not a special-order item. Researching the car through the Walter P. Chrysler Club newsletter, Smith found that the Charger V-8 had a base price of $3,014. The base price on his window sticker is $2,934. This indicates an $80 credit for the six-cylinder engine. However, the original owner did not special order the car. He bought it off the showroom floor at City Dodge in Oakland, California in July 1968. Apparently, some Dodge dealers felt that there would be a demand for six-cylinder Chargers. This makes sense, since competing sporty cars such as Mustangs, Camaros and Barracudas came with sixes.

Q. I have a 1976 Cadillac Eldorado convertible with a 500 cubic-inch engine and fuel-injection. This was a $500 option in 1976. Can you tell me how many of the 14,000 convertibles were produced with fuel-injection? I have written Cadillac's Customer Service Department and have been told that they didn't offer fuel-injection in 1976. D.C., Wisconsin.

A. According to *WARD'S AUTOMOTIVE YEARBOOK 1976* at the beginning of the 1976 model year, full-size Cadillac models were powered by the 500 cubic-inch V-8 and the standard Seville was equipped with a 350 cubic-inch V-8 with electronic fuel-injection (EFI). The same source notes that EFI was optional on all models, except Fleetwood 75s. Unfortunately, *WARD'S AUTOMOTIVE YEARBOOK 1977* does not show the fuel-injected power plant as an "optional engine." Charts in the yearbook indicate that 100 percent of cars in all three 1976 car-lines (Cadillac, Seville and ElDorado) had "standard V-8s." Of course, standard equipment varied per car-line. This is a bit confusing. Apparently, Cadillac considered the EFI system an individual optional, but considered the engine itself a "standard" component. Qualifying the engine seems to be based on cubic-inch displacement, rather than the type of fuel delivery system. At least that is how they reported engine production to industry trade journals. Consequently, the trade journals do not show a production total break-out for fuel-injection. Cadillac fan Dave Kolovat also has a 1976 Eldorado convertible with the 500 cubic-inch engine and fuel-injection. He bought it new and still has it. Kolovat says a great deal of factory literature is available to document this option. He also does not have production figures, but from looking at a great many cars, he ventures a guess that about five percent of the full-size Cadillacs were built with fuel-injection. This excludes those Sevilles with the Oldsmobile 350 cubic-inch engine and a different type of fuel-injection system. The Cadillac fuel-injection system actually premiered on 1975 Cadillacs. It was virtually unchanged in 1976. A very similar version was also available, as an option, on the 425 cubic-inch engines in 1977 through 1979 Cadillacs. The system is a Tuned-Port-Injection (TPI) system with eight injectors, a central throttle body for air intake only and two in-line fuel pumps (one on the frame near the rear wheel and the other inside the gas tank). The pumps maintain about 35 psi whenever the engine is running. In addition to the fuel-injection components themselves (injectors, distribution rail, pressure transducer and pumps), the system uses a number of other components not shared with carburetor cars. These include an under-dash computer, throttle linkage, distributor, intake manifold and gas tank. Fuel-injection improved engine smoothness and driveability. It was also good for a substantial increase in power. Cadillac's own figures were 215 net horsepower at 3600 rpm and 400 pounds-feet of torque at 2000 rpm, compared to 190 horsepower at 3600 and 360 pounds-feet of torque at 2000 for the carburated engine. One other useful thing to know is that, even after 15 years, there are a surprising number of parts available through Cadillac dealers. These include the injectors, fuel pumps, seals, pressure regulator and distinctive distributor parts. These are not cheap to order through dealers, but the next year or two will probably be the last years to get many of these items.

Q. I have just purchased a 1964 Ford 500 XL convertible, serial number 4G69Z209469. This car has the 390 cubic-inch Thunderbird engine with gold valve covers and gold air cleaner. Can you give me any information as to how many of these cars were similar and any other information on this car? J.B., Ohio.

A. Ford built a total of 15,169 Galaxie 500 XL convertibles in 1964. The standard engine in these cars was the Challenger 289 cubic-inch V-8. According to your car's serial number, its engine is the standard Thunderbird V-8 with a 10:1:1 compression ratio. This motor was rated at 300 horsepower. Ford offered three other Thunderbird engines in 1964, the Thunderbird Special, Thunderbird High Performance and Thunderbird Super High Performance. The high-performance engines used the 427 cubic-inch block. Figures in industry trade journals indicate that 330,924 of Ford Motor Company 1964 passenger vehicles had 390 cubic-inch V-8s installed. This engine was used in 16 percent of the company's total production. This would include all Fords, Thunderbirds and Mercurys. Usage was obviously highest in Thunderbirds, where motors of this displacement were standard. The 390 cubic-inch V-8 was also used in 16 percent of Ford's 1963 products (308,549 cars), but only 8.7 percent (162,189) of 1962 models. Such percentage figures are also available for options such as a movable steering column, which 3.2 percent of all 1964 full-sized Fords featured. Your Galaxie 500 XL is a handsome car. In general, 1964 Fords are becoming more and more popular with collectors.

Ford's 390 cubic-inch V-8 with two-barrel carburetor.

Q. I would like to get some information on a car I just purchased. It is a 1969 Chevrolet Chevelle Nomad four-door station wagon. This car has a six-cylinder engine with Powerglide transmission. Is this the correct engine and transmission for this car? M.E.R., Pennsylvania.

A. According to the *STANDARD CATALOG OF AMERICAN CARS 1946-1975*, Chevrolet built 45,900 Chevelle station wagons in 1969. No car-line break-out is given, so this includes models in all Chevelle trim levels. Rounded off production figures do show that only 7,400 of these wagons were equipped with six-cylinder engines. This was the Chevrolet-built 250 cubic-inch inline six with bore and stroke dimensions of 3.875 x 3.25 inches. It had seven main bearings, an 8.5:1 compression ratio and a Rochester model 7029017 one-barrel carburetor. The factory rated it for 155 horsepower at 4200 rpm. Powerglide transmission was available with sixes and small V-8s. It was $163.70 extra with six-cylinder attachments. The 1969 factory price of Nomad wagons ranged from $2,668 to $2,758 for the standard model and $2,710 to $2,800 for the deluxe. As has been mentioned in this column before, station wagons and convertibles survive in lower numbers than sedans. In the case of station wagons this lower survival rate is due to the fact that these cars are simply worked to death. I would estimate that less than 10 percent of the original production total remains. This would put the number of cars like yours at probably less than 500.

Q. I just bought a 1951 Oldsmobile 88 two-door sedan. I found this car in a barn with 1963 tags (license plates) on it. The odometer shows 76,125 miles. The engine and transmission work great. Is this engine any different than the 1949 to 1950 Oldsmobile V-8? It looks different. I know this one hasn't been changed. I had a 1950 coupe when I was 16 years old and have been looking a long time for another. I am now almost 51 years old and have found just what I wanted, so dreams do come true. E.W., Michigan.
A. Oldsmobile used the same 303 cubic-inch V-8 in 1951 that can be found under the hood of a 1949 or 1950 Eighty-Eight. Perhaps a different air cleaner or redesigned valve covers make this engine look different than what you remember from when you owned your coupe. It may have an optional oil-bath air cleaner. The valve covers might be a different color or have distinct decals. Perhaps the spark plug wire holders have been redesigned. Small detail changes from year to year were common, although the basic engine remained the same.

Q. I have a 1950s Buick engine that was originally installed in a car that had Dynaflow automatic transmission. I would like to swap this engine into a similar Buick that has a three-speed manual gear box. Can this be done? What's involved? M.R., Wisconsin.
A. Buick lover Chris Welch says that putting a Dynaflow engine into a standard transmission car is no big deal. A machine shop can easily mount the standard pilot bushing in the back of the crank. The shop can also bore new holes in the standard flywheel and balance them. The transmission fits the bell housing, the mounts line up and you get more horsepower and go. Welch recalls once having trouble getting the transmission in the last half-inch. He succeeded after shoving the vehicle across the road and over two bumpy curbs. We would not recommend doing this with a valuable collector car.

Q. I have two questions on a late 1930 or 1931 (indented firewall) Model A Ford truck. It is rated at 1-1/2 tons with dual rear wheels and a four-speed transmission. The engine cylinder head is like no other I have seen. Printed in big bold raised letters on the raised portion of the cylinder head (the water jacket channel) is Model A. Could you tell me if this is original, aftermarket or whatever? Also, the oil fill tube pipe (breather) on this engine is the same diameter that I believe is found on late Model B Ford engines. The breather cap is also large like the later Model B engine. Can you explain this? G.W., Connecticut.
A. We are not aware of Ford ever having stamped Model A on any of the 1928 to 1931 engine cylinder heads. From the description of the breather tube, we suspect that the engine in your truck is a Model B engine. Also, the indented firewall indicates late 1931 production.

Q. While going through my archives I found some old *FLYING ACES* magazines. One has an item about the production of B-24 Liberator engines at the Buick plants of General Motors Corporation. It says that more engines were produced in the final quarter of 1943 than all of 1942. Buick built these 1,200-horsepower engines under license from Pratt & Whitney and was the major engine source for the Ford Willow Run, Douglas and Consolidated plants producing Liberator bombers. What other automakers built engines and parts for the military or completed military vehicles? D.L., Minnesota.

A. As most old car buffs are aware, the American automobile manufacturers converted entirely to production of war material in early 1942. At Chevrolet, the last passenger car left the assembly line on February 6 of that year. General Motors even went so far as to lease some of its plants to the government for war work. A partial listing of General Motors war output includes eight million shells; 500,000 cars and trucks; 60,000 Pratt & Whitney 14- and 18-cylinder aircraft engines; 3,800 armored cars and 200,000,000 pounds of aluminum forgings for propeller blades, pistons, cylinder heads, etc. Ford and Willys shared production of the famous Jeep, Studebaker built nearly 200,000 trucks (most of which went to Russia on Lend Lease), over 63,000 Wright Cyclone engines for B-17 Flying Fortress bombers, and 25,000 Weasels, an amphibious troop carrier. Without exaggeration, it was the production capacity of the automobile industry that made possible America's transformation into the "Arsenal of Democracy." One historian even went so far as to attribute the Soviet Union's defeat of the German war machine to two factors: Russian mud and the Studebaker 6 x 6 truck.

Q. Recently I bought a 1972 Marquis with 60,000 miles on it. I plan to use it as an everyday car, because it has so little pollution control equipment and electronic rubbish on it. I expected it to have a 429 cubic-inch engine, but the sticker on the valve cover said it is the 460 cubic-inch engine. When I tried to buy filters and a vacuum advance diaphragm for it, none of the parts information showed a 460 cubic-inch engine. They indicated it was not used in a Marquis until 1973. I finally called a Mercury dealer and a parts department person verified from my vehicle identification number that the car was indeed factory equipped with a 460 cubic-inch V-8. My car was manufactured in June 1972, which I believe would be near the end of the production year. Would you have any information on the number of Marquis's equipped with 460 cubic-inch engines in 1972 or if this would in some way make my car rare? E.M., Texas.

A. According to our *STANDARD CATALOG OF AMERICAN CARS 1946-1975*, the 460 cubic-inch engine was an option in the Marquis line for 1972. *WARD'S 1973 AUTOMOTIVE YEARBOOK* indicates that all full-sized Mercurys had V-8s and that 75.7 percent of the engines were the standard equipment type. This source also indicates that 4.2 percent (109,494 cars) of all 1973 FoMoCo products had 460 cubic-inch engines. The specific percentage or number of installations in Mercurys only is not given, so you will have to make estimates based on these known figures.

Q. I have a Model T Ford. I contend that every time the motor makes a complete revolution, all four cylinders have fired. My friend says no. If I am right, how about a six-, eight-, 12-, or 16-cylinder motor? C.P., Ohio.

A. A four-cycle engine takes two complete revolutions to fire. This is the case regardless of the number of cylinders. One revolution is for intake and the other for exhaust.

Q. What make of engine did Duesenberg automobiles use during their years of production? E.W., Maryland.

A. The Duesenberg brothers, Fred and Augie, used engines of their own design. These engines were racing-inspired and very advanced for their time. They featured double overhead camshafts and four valves per cylinder. Some versions put out nearly 400 horsepower. In the hands of racing driver Ab Jenkins, a supercharged Duesenberg hit 152 miles per hour. That was in 1935, not 1991. In fact, driving a Duesenberg Special known as the Mormon Meteor (Jenkins was of the Mormon faith), the speed ace set a 24-hour speed record that stood until broken by a Corvette in 1991. There are two Mormon Meteors (one roadster and one coupe) still in existence today.

Q. A recent article on the 1972 Thunderbird stated, "All 1972 engines were de-tuned to take unleaded fuel with the result being poor mileage and performance." I enjoy a 1972 Cadillac Coupe DeVille from which I can only manage 11 miles per gallon. I drive it in a car pool twice a week. Is there anything a backyard mechanic can do to improve mileage? Is an engine rebuild necessary to achieve, say, the horsepower and performance of a 1970 Cadillac? The 1970 Cadillac had a horsepower rating of 375 compared to the 1972 model's 250 horsepower. Gas mileage is similar, so why such a performance difference? Would moving the timing up or down help the stock 1972? What does the air pump do? Is it still helping our environment after 107,000 miles and 19 years later? I love this car. D.L., Indiana.

A. I've never heard of a fix for the poor mileage and lower performance ratings of the early-to-mid 1970s engines. The motivation for such engines was the legislation of stringent environmental controls. Automotive engineers met them by making patchwork modifications that cut engine horsepower and devastated mileage ratings. The air pump helps eliminate unburned hydrocarbons from the car's exhaust and does so at a small power penalty. I drive a 1969 Chevrolet Longhorn pickup to shows and collector events. This truck was built in California. It has the air pump and other anti-pollution controls required by that state at the time. Its mileage is between 10 and 11 miles per gallon regardless of whether it is loaded or empty, whether the road is flat or hilly or whether you're traveling at highway speed. In an attempt to increase mileage, I plan to install an overdrive transmission. However, even with a 22 percent decrease in engine revolutions at cruising speed, the manufacturer of the overdrive anticipates a fuel mileage increase only to 13 or 14 miles per gallon. The early 1970s brought us many great cars, but they are plagued by very poor fuel economy.

Q. My problem is a Chevrolet engine. After great tender and loving care, it rewarded me by quickly and repeatedly overheating. I have tried countless solutions to this problem. What do you recommend? R.H., Indiana.

A. C. E. Hammett, a 1940 Buick Super owner, has driven his car thousands of miles with practically no overheating problems. In December 1949, he drove it from Auburn, Alabama, to Wilmington, Delaware. He was returning on New Years Day. Hammett was driving along at 50 or 55 miles per hour. Suddenly the radiator coolant erupted and drenched the windshield. Coolant was added. A short distance down the road there was a repetition. He found he could drive at 25 miles per hour and avoid the problem. Eventually, he got back home. Hammett searched for the problem for some time. Finally, he was watching the engine while he tried increasing the revs. Water came out the overflow and the lower hose collapsed. He found that there was no supporting spring in the lower hose. A new hose with a spring inside cured the problem for as long as he drove the car. He suggests that attention also be given to the intake hose.

Q. I have recently acquired a 1957 Mercury Turnpike Cruiser convertible. What size engine does it have? D.P., Idaho.

A. The Turnpike Cruiser bowed at midyear in 1957. Initially, it came in only two models: Hardtop coupe and hardtop sedan. Since Mercury was selected to provide the pace car for the Indy 500 that year, a convertible Turnpike Cruiser was also added. Checkered flag emblems on the car commemorated its selection as Indy 500 Pace Car. Turnpike Cruisers used a 368 cubic-inch engine rated at 290 horsepower. Only 1,265

142

Turnpike Cruiser convertibles were built in 1957. Two clubs may be able to put you in touch with owners of similar cars and help you with information. They are: Ford-Mercury Club of America, P.O. Box 3661, Hayward, California 94540 and the Ford-Mercury Restorer's Club, PO Box 2133, Dearborn, Michigan 48123.

Q. Did the 1969 Pontiac Grand Prix Model J have only a 428 cubic-inch engine? How many were produced and what is one worth in number three condition? J.C., New York.

A. Our records show that the 350 horsepower 400 cubic-inch engine was standard. Two 428 cubic-inch V-8s were optional. The less expensive big engine had a four-barrel carburetor and produced 375 horsepower. The extra cost for this version started at $67 and ran as high as $105 on some Pontiacs. The more expensive 428 cubic-inch, 390 horsepower four-barrel engine had more get up and go. It sold at prices from $150 to $255. When installed in Grand Prixs, the prices charged for the engines were at the lower end of the ranges shown here. A total of 112,486 Grand Prix hardtop coupes were built in 1969. This model's current value in number three condition is $2,350.

Q. I am in the process of restoring a 1955 Ford F-100 pickup. It has the 239 cubic-inch engine. Can you tell me what color to paint the engine and valve covers? E.J., Delaware.

A. Steve Morgan, a Ford F-100 authority and collector, handled your question. He reported that all Ford truck engines used from 1954 to 1956 were painted Golden Glow Yellow (Ford part number M20J-531). This color was also used on the bellhousing and transmission. The generator, the generator bracket, the fan pulleys and the crankcase breather were all originally done in Raven Black (Ford number M20J-532).

Q. I have a 1936 Dodge pickup and two extra engines. The motor numbers are P9-171566 and D-164238. Can you tell the year of the engines from the numbers? Both are MoPar flathead sixes. D.B., Wisconsin.

A. Joel Miller, a MoPar authority, identified the P9 as originating in a 1940 Plymouth Road King and the D16 as a 1940 Canadian Dodge engine. Both, Joel notes, are 201.3 cubic-inch sixes. This means that they are of the same displacement as the engine in your truck. Both should fit fine in your pickup, if an engine swap should become necessary.

Q. I have a Model A crankshaft with balance weights I'm told were put on at the factory. I understand the weights have to be removed before the crank can be turned. The weights are round. They are held in place with three pins that go through holes drilled through the weights and into the crank. How do the weights come off? One pin could be drilled out easily enough, but there is no way to tell which way the other two pins go through the weights. I understand that this crank was used in the first Model B four-cylinder truck that also used Model C type cylinder heads. I don't know very much about Model A Fords and would appreciate any help. J.S. Indiana.

A. Your balanced crankshaft is from a 1933 or later Model B engine (sometimes called a Model C because of the C stamped on the head, though Ford never used this designation). Model A Ford crankshafts were not counter-balanced. This later Model B engine can be installed in a Model A with few alterations and makes a very nice (though non-authentic) power plant. I talked to Mrs. Richard Fallucca at Antique Engine Rebuilding, of Skokie, Illinois. She said that all the pins can be reached and drilled out. The accessible end may be peened over and not be readily visible.

143

Q. I am trying to identify an engine I recently acquired. It is a four-cylinder sold by Star Motor, Incorporated, New York, New York. The motor number is 150570. It is manufactured by Continental. What did it come from? Was it an industrial engine? It has a power take-off in place of the clutch. B.J., California.

A. The engine you have was originally installed in a Star automobile. This marque was built by a company organized by William C. Durant. It was first intended as the competitor for Chevrolet in this auto pioneer's new Durant Motors scheme. Our serial number records indicate that the engine you have is from a 1924 Star. Like many cars and trucks of the day, Stars used engines built by Continental. We suspect that the reason your engine is coupled to a power take-off is that the car in which the engine was originally installed was scrapped at some point. Then, the engine was probably adapted to some farm or industrial use.

Q. I am presently restoring a 1955 Ford F-100 pickup. The engine is a Mercury V-8. Is this the original or a replacement? Several people have told me that Mercury engines were put in Ford cars and trucks as an option in the 1950s. The only numbers are on the left side of the block. These numbers are C1AE 6015R. J.P., Pennsylvania.

A. Actually, Ford installed the larger Mercury V-8 in heavy- and light-duty trucks in the 1940s. At that time, the Ford V-8 had a horsepower rating of 85 and the Mercury V-8 had a rating of 95 horsepower. By 1955, Ford had introduced its new Y-block overhead valve V-8. It installed this engine as optional equipment in its light-duty trucks. The I-block six with overhead valves was standard equipment in 1955. The Y- and I-block descriptions were used since the engine block castings extended down past the center line of the crankshaft. In 1955, Ford installed a 239 cubic-inches V-8 in its pickups. It produced 132 horsepower at 4200 rpm.

Q. I am trying to establish the authenticity of the engine of the 1947 Chevrolet pickup I recently purchased. My engine has the serial number LEA 212330. The 1947 *CHEVROLET TRUCK SHOP MANUAL* uses the letters EEA followed by four digits. Also, the vehicle serial number plate is missing, but the title lists the manufacturer's serial number as 5EPH2311. Can this number be documented as well? J.D., Ohio.

A. The EP prefix on the serial number shows your truck to be a 1947 Advance-Design model. Production of this new style began May 1, 1947. According to Chevrolet buff Warren Rauch, the serial number 5EPH2311 decodes as follows: The first digit refers to the manufacturing plant. At the time this truck was built, Chevrolet had assembly plants in (1) Flint, Michigan; (2) Tarrytown, New York; (3) St. Louis, Missouri; (5) Kansas City, Missouri; (6) Oakland, California; (8) Atlanta, Georgia; (9) Norwood, Ohio; (14) Baltimore, Maryland; (20) Los Angeles, California; and (21) Janesville, Wisconsin. (21). As can be seen, this truck was built in Kansas City. The next two letters, EP, refer to a 1947 Chevrolet 1/2-ton. The third letter refers to the month of manufacture as follows: (A) January, (B) February, etc. The final four digits are the number of the vehicle in sequence for its assembly plant. The engine in question, LEA-212330 is a 1953 Chevrolet truck 235 cubic-inch six. The proper engine would be a Chevrolet truck 216 cubic-inch six with a serial number between EB-1001 and EB-683120. The prefixes for a 1947 Chevrolet 235 cubic-inch engine are EDA, EDM, EEA and EEM. However, these were not installed by the factory in 1/2-ton vehicles. Other prefixes used by Chevrolet in 1947 are EA (passenger car and sedan delivery) and EC (3/4-ton or larger truck with 216 cubic-inch engine).

Q. I would like to know how long Chevrolet produced the 265 cubic-inch engine. I have what I believe is such an engine. It does not have an oil filter and does not appear to have any place for it to go. Is it possible that this engine could have been a special-built or race-type engine? Also, is it possible that this engine might have been installed as factory equipment in a Corvette as late as 1960?

A. Chevrolet introduced the 265 cubic-inch engine in 1955. This was the first of its small-block V-8s. Chevrolet continued this engine through 1956. In 1957, the 283 cubic-inch small-block replaced the 265 cubic-inch small-block in Powerglide models. You could still get a 265 cubic-inch V-8 in 1957 stick shift models. In truck form, these engines were without an oil filter, as you describe.

The famous 1955 Chevrolet 265 cubic-inch "small-block" V-8.

ELECTRICAL

Q. My son and I are trying to get a 1954 Oldsmobile 88 into operating condition. Every time we start the car, the wire to the condenser burns. Could you suggest what's wrong? L.F., Nevada.
A. You must have a condenser that is shorted out. A good condenser has no direct connection inside. With one that is shorted out you should not get a reading when you test it with an ohm meter. Condensers can short out in cars with contact point distributors that haven't been started for a long time. The failure of the car to start can be traced to a film of rust developing on the contact point surfaces. This sends all the battery current to the condenser and causes it to break down. Filing the points can restore them to operational condition, but the condenser will have to be replaced. Too much voltage delivered to the condenser can also ruin it. American cars with 12-volt systems and contact point distributors have either a resistor or resistor wire to drop the 12 volts down to about seven during startup. This resistance is needed for proper operation. Without it, the points will burn and overheat, causing the condenser to short out. Make sure that you haven't bypassed the resistor or resistor wire.

Q. Would you explain the proper way to connect jumper cables from a car with negative ground to a car with positive ground? T.L., California.
A. The guidelines when connecting jumper cables is to observe battery polarity, meaning that you will connect the cables from positive to positive and negative to negative. However, as a safety precaution, it is always advised that the last connection be made to a remote ground, such as a head bolt or generator bracket. The reason for this is that if the last connection is made to the battery post and a spark occurs, it could ignite volatile hydrogen gas which is released as part of the battery's electro-chemical process. Hobbyist Gus Chompff adds two tips. First, prior to connecting the jumper cables to the respective vehicle's batteries, make certain that the cars are not touching. If the vehicles are in metal to metal contact, one or both of the eletrical systems will experience the equivalent of a direct short across the battery terminals. Second, if a 12-volt battery is being used to jump a six-volt system, connect the 12-volt battery to the six-volt system only during the actual starter engagement. If left connected to the six-volt system, the 12-volt current surge could damage wiring, gauges or other electrical components. The best advice is to keep your car's electrical system working well and repair problems at the first hint of trouble.

Q. How frequently should water be added to a car battery? The battery in my 1952 Hudson seems to need refilling about every 200 miles. Someone told me this indicates a problem. What do you think? A.Q., Vermont.
A. The frequency with which water must be added depends on how hot the weather is and how much you use the car. On average, a car battery should not need refilling more than once a month. If your battery is always fully charged, but requires lots of refilling, there's a very good chance that the generator is overcharging and causing unnecessary battery wear.

Q. I own a 1929 Ford Model A with a six-volt battery. Sometimes I leave the ignition on and the battery discharges. Is it okay to jump start a six-volt battery with a 12-volt? If not, is there a device to cut voltage down so a 12-volt battery could be used for a jump start? I've been told it's better to use an eight-volt battery than a six-volt. Is it okay to use an eight-volt battery? R.L., Wisconsin.

A. We don't advise jump starting a car equipped with a six-volt electrical system using a 12-volt battery. The danger potential and threat of harm to the six-volt electrical system is too great. If you were to jump start a six-volt car with a 12-volt battery, two people would be required. You would have to have the starter motor engaged and turning when you make the jumper connections. This is further complicated, on the Model A, by its under-the-floor battery location. We don't see why you would need an eight-volt battery. The Model A is one of the best starting cars ever made. The original Model A ignition switch was a pop-out type. With the switch on, the switch pops-out from the face of the gauge panel. When you turn the ignition off, you push the switch in flush with the panel. If your Model A does not have the original switch, why not install one? Then, you can see, at a glance, if the switch has been left on. Leaving the ignition switch on will pit the points and burn out the coil, too. Then you will have real starting problems. An alternative to 12-volt jump starting is to start the Model A with a crank. We have done this a number of times. The only trick is to avoid the spinning crank. Give it only a half-turn on the upstroke. Usually, a well-tuned Model A will start on a couple of pulls of the crank.

Q. I am rebuilding my 1939 LaSalle's engine. Do you know of anyone who converts old distributors to electronic ignition? E.S., Florida.
A. One old car hobbyist has used a system made by Per-Lux Incorporated. It is a small, self-contained system that is completely hidden inside the distributor. One restorer even converted a 1913 Delco distributor and Bosch magneto over to this system. The address is Per-Lux, 1242 East Edna Place, Covina, California 91724. In addition, restorer Dave Hall, of Tucson, Arizona, has used a GM High Energy Ignition (HEI) distributor on older eight-cylinder cars. For four cylinder cars, Hall says you can use the same distributor and put a plug wire in every other plug point in the distributor cap. Punch out the contacts in the others and fill the hole with epoxy cement. For six-cylinder cars, he uses a Buick Even Fire distributor from a 231 cubic-inch V-6. The distributor and shaft have to be machined to fit the engine. The magazine *DUNE BUGGIES & HOT VWs* carried an article on this type of conversion in their December 1989 issue. This article stresses that the actual conversion is not for a hobbyist or do-it-yourselfer, because machining work is required to the distributor shaft and housing. It refers to a service that converts HEI distributors (for VWs at least) at a cost of $325 for a ready-to-install unit. The service is Precision Products, 4320 North Effie, Fresno, California 93726. The result of the conversion is impressive, giving 45,000 volts of ignition firing power.

Q. I recently found a new six-volt coil (no brand name on it) in my garage and am confused on hooking it up. One terminal has a "+ BATT" marking and the other has "-DIST" marking. But, with a positive ground system (which most six-volt cars are), the minus is the hot wire (battery) and the plus is the ground (distributor). What do you make of it and how would you hook it up? T.Q., Wisconsin.
A. Generalizing that six-volt cars have positive ground electrical systems is inaccurate. Many cars, including numerous General Motors models, used six-volt negative ground electrical systems. The markings on the coil you found indicate that it was designed for a negative ground system. For a positive ground system, disregard the BATT and DIST legends and use the plus and minus marks to connect the coil. The plus terminal should be connected to the distributor and the minus terminal to the ignition switch for correct coil polarity. Since the coil's original application is unknown, you should measure the primary circuit current flow. This should not exceed 2.5 amps with the engine running or 4.5 amps with the engine at rest. Current flow which is too high will cause short

point life. If the current reading is above the values listed, you can still use the coil if you use a resistor in line with the distributor. Hobbyist Dave Weber adds that checking coil polarity can be accomplished in two easy ways. The first method uses a volt-ohm meter (VOM), while the other uses a common lead pencil. Check coil polarity with the engine running. Touch the negative lead from the volt-ohm-meter to the spark plug terminal. If the coil polarity is correct, the needle will swing upscale. If the polarity is reversed, the needle will swing down. For those who don't have a VOM in their tool kit, a lead pencil can be used to make a second test. Do not hold the pencil by the metal ferrule with the eraser. Hold the pencil on the wood. Remove one of the spark leads and place it so there is about a 1/4-inch gap between the end of the plug wire and the spark plug terminal. Place the point of the sharpened lead pencil in this gap. With the engine running, if the spark "feathers" on the spark plug side, the coil polarity is correct. If the spark feathers on the terminal side, the polarity is reversed. When coil polarity is reversed, there is approximately a 25 percent loss in voltage.

Q. I am wondering why American automakers favored six-volt electric systems. Also, when did the American car makers convert to 12-volt electric systems? What are the pitfalls to putting a 12-volt battery into a six-volt car, besides burning out light bulbs? Are there any step-down devices commercially available that would allow one to use a 12-volt battery in a six-volt car? Dr. T.P., Texas.
A. A six-volt electrical system gives much longer cranking power, something that seemed beneficial for starting the older long-stroke engines. Voltage is often represented as electrical pressure and modern high-compression V-8s require a hotter ignition and faster cranking speed, which can be better supplied by 12-volt electrical systems. An increase in electrical accessories also led to the changeover. Most domestic manufacturers switched to 12-volt electrical systems between 1954 and 1956. I remember the contrast in a 1954 DeSoto owned by my uncle and a 1955 Oldsmobile that was my father's car. The DeSoto, with its hemi V-8 and six-volt electric system, would crank and crank and crank in an effort to get the engine started on a hot summer day. Sometimes it went for as long as 15 minutes. The Oldsmobile, with its 12-volt system, would just snap into life. Converting to 12-volts requires a different generator and starter, as well as step-down converters for electrical accessories. These converters are available.

Q. How can I convert my old car from a DC generator to an AC alternator electrical system? J.B., New York.
A. Hobbyist Julius Borri replaced the stock generator in his 275-horsepower fuel-injected 1960 Corvette with an alternator. He followed a schematic he found in an old issue of *HOT ROD* magazine. The trigger from the push-in connector was connected to the ignition switch side of the ballast resistor through a standard alternator diode from an old mid-1960s alternator. The diode cost $1 from a local engine rebuilder. He put it in the wire harness and could hardly tell it was there. It only allowed the current to flow to the trigger circuit for operation. This prevented run-on. This is necessary for cars with ammeters. Cars with idiot lights have enough resistance to prevent the run-on phenomenon. Since the "Batt" wire of the old regulator goes to the battery through the ammeter (this goes to the hot output of the alternator), connect the other side of the push-in connector to the big post on the starter solenoid (where the main battery cable is located). The theory in doing this is that this connection monitors the voltage level in and out of the battery without loss. This is the basic way an alternator is installed in all new cars. Borri's installation works great and he replaced the clock with a big voltmeter so he can instantly check both voltage and current draw at any time, under all loads.

Incidentally, the volt meter is very important. Alternators can fail in the over-charge mode as easily as in the under-charge mode.

Q. Could you tell me the original color of the battery caps for the Chrysler automobiles of the 1950s, 1960s and 1970s. The colors on the current battery caps are red and green. Is this correct? J.K., Pennsylvania.

A. I talked to Delores and Dave Lane at the Antique Auto Battery Company, in Hudson, Ohio. They sell original-type batteries for Ford, General Motors and Chrysler automobiles. Regarding the colors for battery caps on original-type Chrysler products batteries, the Lanes stated that on 12-volt group 24 batteries the caps were green. On batteries used with the 1969 and later 383 cubic-inch V-8 the caps were yellow. On pre-1956 Chrysler cars with six-volt batteries, the caps were usually red. In 1941 to 1942, Chrysler products used primarily Willard batteries. These had the red caps. Some Exide batteries appear to have also been used during this time period. On these, the caps were black. After World War II, Chrysler used the MoPar trademark on the six-volt batteries in its cars and on these battery caps appear to have been red or a combination of clear and red.

Old-style batteries with original color caps and logos are available.

Q. Could you explain how a DA plug works in a six-volt to 12-volt alternator conversion? I've done a number of alternator conversions on GM products, both six- and 12-volts and never ran into the DA plug possibility. It's my understanding that a Delco alternator with internal regulation is wired as follows: Output screw stud to BAT wire of old regulator; one push-in connector jumps to output screw stud; second push-in connector goes to "run" position on ignition switch. Where does the DA plug enter the picture? B.A., New York.

A. Randy Rundle of Fifth Avenue Antique Auto Parts, 502 Arthur Avenue, Clay Center, Kansas incorporates a DA plug into the six-volt alternators his company markets. He reports that most pre-1950 cars and trucks had an ignition switch that had just two positions: off and on. This is commonly referred to as a knife switch. As many have experienced while putting alternators in old cars, the installation and basic wiring are pretty simple, except for one small problem. How come the car won't shut off with the ignition switch any more? Along with the changeover to alternators in the early 1960s came a change to a three-post "accessory" type ignition switch. The alternator was wired through this post. This isolated the ignition switch so, that when the key was turned off, the feedback from the alternator wouldn't keep the car running. A similar setup is required for antique vehicles with alternators, so that they will not keep running when the key is turned off. The reason the car keeps running is because an alternator charges at idle, while a generator doesn't. With the DA plug, the car will shut off with the original ignition switch just as before.

Q. What is your advice about making sure an electrical system has good grounds? I once owned a Corvette with completely undependable lighting. The previous owner had taken off all the chassis grounds and the lights couldn't make ground through the fiberglass body. G.P., New Jersey.

A. Anyone with auto electrical problems should go through the following procedure. First, make sure all grounds are good. These include the line from the battery to the engine and from the engine to the body. Some automakers use a pigtail body ground. This is a small wire from the battery's negative terminal direct to the body. Some have a strap from the engine to the body. If the electrical system isn't grounded properly, it will seek ground through other circuits. This will cause some real strange results. For example, switch on the turn signals and everything flashes; turn on the headlights and all the rest of the lights go out. I have seen some rather bizarre wiring repairs because the mechanic didn't have the electrical system properly grounded. My advice is to ground the system first. Then, get meters and check for problems. Remember that rust is not a good conductor of electricity. Clean all wires first. If a wire is warm at the terminal post, you can bet that there is rust or corrosion causing a bad connection at that point. I am not saying that a good ground is the cure for all problems, but it will keep you from chasing ghosts.

Q. I have a seen some very pretty rose buds and rose petals and some awful "gobeldygookey" stuff on car battery terminals. Would you please explain, chemically and mechanically, where this stuff comes from? H.F., California.

A. Batteries release a small amount of their acid in the charging/discharging process. This acid attacks and corrodes surrounding metal. Particularly prone to problems are the battery posts, cable clamps, hold-down bracket and battery case. These are the metal items nearest the battery. The festering build up you see around the battery terminals is a residue caused by this corrosion. The older style batteries with vented cell caps used on vintage cars give freer release to the corrosive acid. Thus, you're more likely to see the crud you describe on the battery terminals of your collector car than you are on a modern car with a so-called sealed battery.

Q. At the last two swap meets I've visited I have bought two sets of six-volt fog lamps which have Mazda or Mazda-GE as part of the trademark. I also have some Model A compatible headlight lenses with the Mazda trademark. Did we have a Japanese connection back in the 1930s and 1940s? If not, why Mazda of all the names in the universe? S.S., Texas.

A. Hobbyist Les Gehlsen has an ad from the May 1916 issue of *NATIONAL GEO-GRAPHIC* with the MAZDA name. The text in the ad states, "Instead of one manufacturer's spasmodic development of his product, MAZDA Service substitutes a systematic, all-inclusive study of incandescent electric lamps for several manufacturers." The ad goes on to explain the meaning of the Mazda name, which it says is "...the trademark of a worldwide service to certain lamp manufacturers. Its purpose is to collect and select scientific and practical information concerning progress and developments in the art of incandescent lamp manufacturing and to distribute this information to the companies entitled to receive this service. Mazda service is centered in the Research Laboratories of the General Electric Company at Schenectady. The mark MAZDA can appear only on lamps which meet the standards of MAZDA Service. It is thus an assurance of quality. This trademark is the property of the General Electric Company." Another hobbyist, Dave Webber, remembered that Mazda produced vacuum tubes for battery chargers, in addition to automotive light bulbs. Additionally, T. W. Jentsch pointed out that Ahura Mazda was the god of light in the ancient Persian religion of Zorastrianism. David Gracey reports that he recently purchased two strings of old Christmas tree lights in their original boxes. "Equipped with General Electric Mazda Lamps" is printed in several places on each box. Finally, car collector Jim Boyden recalled the calendars and advertising copy used by GE-Mazda lamps in the 1920s. They featured idyllic scenes that tied in with the Persian god theme. They were painted by the famous artist Maxwell Parrish. The originals of these paintings are highly collectible today, Mr. Boyden adds.

Q. I have a 1968 Ford Ranchero with the standard dash and optional clock. What I would like to do is replace the dash cluster with one from a 1968 Torino GT that has a built-in tachometer. What would I have to do to make this swap functional? Do I need to replace the under-dash wiring harness, change the alternator wiring, oil sending unit, etc.? Also, if the wiring harness needs to be changed, would one from a 1968 Mustang with a tachometer work? R.T., Vermont.

A. Trevor Berge of Ranchero Classics in Sunset Beach, California, responded to your question. He states that you will need to replace the whole cluster and cannot directly interchange the clock and tachometer, since the cluster with the clock and tachometer is completely different. It has a different circuit board. Berge says that you could make the tachometer functional simply by connecting the red wire off the tachometer in series with the ignition switch. He says that a different under-dash wiring harness is not needed, nor would you need to replace any other wiring or sending units. If you need to contact him for details as you make this swap, his address is Ranchero Classics, PO Box 1248, Sunset Beach, California 90742. Ranchero Classics manufactures parts for Fairlanes, Torinos and Rancheros. In addition to his work at Ranchero Classics, Trevor Berge also serves as a technical advisor for The Ranchero Club, 1339 Beverly Road, Port Vue, Pennsylvania 15133.

Q. We have 18 collector cars, about half with six-volt batteries and the other half with 12-volt batteries. Even with battery cut-offs, they discharge within a few weeks or months and frequently are damaged. I am considering hooking up all six-volt (and separately all 12-volt) batteries in parallel to a battery charger. Is it better to have the batteries on a constant trickle charger? If so, how low an amperage charge is appropriate (one-tenth an amp per battery or one-half)? Is it better to use a higher amperage charge on a daily timer switch? If the latter alternative is best, any guidance on time/amperage relationship? I think I read that batteries quit charging when full, but continual charging boils off water (or is it the acid)? With this many cars, batteries can be expensive. I know constant "exercise" keeps my commuting car battery good for years. I would appreciate some advice on this common problem or reference to a good technical manual. K.R., Oregon.

A. You and other collectors with several cars will be interested to know that Snap-on Tools sells a multiple battery charger. This unit is fairly expensive, running about $300 for the charger and another $200 for the several sets of cables. It is designed for the purpose you have in mind: To charge a number of batteries in parallel. A less expensive alternative would be to purchase a good quality battery charger (the type used in service shops) and convert it to a multiple battery changer. This can be done by attaching lugs at the end of the cables to which multiple cable sets can be connected. This would probably cost around $200. It's true that when batteries reach full charge a resistance builds up. The resistance usually exceeds the trickle charge input and thereby prevents further charging. However, if the charging input is able to over-ride the battery's resistance, overcharging can boil off the electrolyte. A simple way to keep the batteries to your collector cars charged would be to purchase or set up multiple battery chargers (one for the six-volt batteries and another for the 12-volts). Plug these chargers into a wall timer, such as the type you would use in your house to control lights. You could then set the timers to give the batteries a short (20 minutes or so) trickle-charge boost on a daily basis. The Snap-on multiple battery charger has settings for fast and trickle charging. The trickle-charging rate is about a half-amp (the charger has a meter that shows charging amperage). The batteries will need to be removed from the cars or else you would need lots of cable.

Battery Tender (1-800-456-7901) safely keeps batteries at full charge.

Q. I have a 1967 Morris Minor. Typical of older English cars, it has a positive ground electrical system. I would like to convert it to negative ground so I can install a modern radio and other accessories. Can you tell me how to do this? D.N., California.

A. The problem you run into in converting from positive to negative ground is with electrical components that are polarity sensitive. These include the generator, coil and gauges. Car collector M. D. Rogers reports that reversing polarity is easy to do on generator-equipped cars without transistorized accessories. First reverse the connections to the battery. This requires that the battery be repositioned and the cable clamps be re-sized to fit the opposite posts. When this is accomplished, disconnect the leads from the regulator that go to the generator. Next, take a clip-lead from the hot side of the bat-tery and quickly touch them. This will make a spark and re-polarize the generator. A coil's duty is to change the low-voltage from the battery into high-voltage to fire the spark plugs. This is done through a series of windings inside the coil. Low-voltage goes into the positive side of the coil and exits the primary windings. These primary windings then excite the secondary windings producing the high-voltage surge required for the spark plugs. When you change polarity at the battery from positive to negative ground, you must also change polarity of your original coil. Otherwise you will be trying to excite the secondary windings of the coil from the low voltage of the battery. By not reversing the wires on a positive ground coil when changing polarity, you'll experience hard starting or no starting and very poor performance. However, if you are using a new negative ground coil, the negative post of the coil would in fact go to the points. The only gauge that is polarity sensitive is the ammeter. Its sensitivity can be overcome by reversing its electrical connections. Now, put things back together and start the car. The ammeter should indicate charge. According to hobbyist Betsy Will-iams, Lucas Electric Company's Service Bulletin number 265 covers this type of con-version in detail. It is titled "Change to Negative Ground on English Vehicle Electrical Systems." This service bulletin's instructions are to re-polarize the generator (as M.D. Rogers mentioned); to reverse the connections to the ammeter and to any permanent magnet motors; and to switch the cable leads to the battery. This instruction sheet also recommends reversing the coil leads to retain "correct sparking plug polarity." Restorer Wayne Herman installed a modern negative ground radio in his 1949 Crosley (with positive ground electrical system) simply by insulating the mounting brackets and putting the hot wire to ground on the radio box. He solved the six- to 12-volt con-version problem by finding an old Sears dual voltage AM-FM radio at a thrift shop for $1. On the back of this radio there is a slide switch for selecting six- or 12-volt current.

Q. What about converting a Model T Ford to a 12-volt electrical system? Would this be a wise move? What would be the advantage? E.R., Montana.

A. Restorer W. W. Suggs Jr. says that the conversion of a Model T from six- to 12-volts can be easily accomplished. Light bulbs and the coil must be changed, but the starter works fine. Sugg's 1915 Model T speedster had higher than stock compression. It needed more "juice" to spin the engine over. With some help from his friend Max Emonds, he found a more modern 12-volt generator that was very similar to the origi-nal six-volt unit. A little machine work along with a couple of added wires put them in business. Today, he even has a 12-volt 30-ampere generator that bolts right in place of the original. This unit looks very much as if it belongs and is not like an aftermarket alternator that sticks out like an afterthought. Suggs knows of Model T owners all over the United States and Canada that have been using this generator for more than 12 years. Information about it can be obtained by writing: R.J. Restorations, 8220 Palla-day Road, Elverta, California 95626.

Q. I have been told that pre-electronic ignition coils came only in two types. One came with an external resistor. One came with internal resistor. The coils on which an exter-nal resistor is used are the same whether marked for six- or 12-volts. It is the resistor which controls the voltage to the points. Why, then, are the coils marked six- or 12-volts? G.C., New York.

A. According to hobbyist Bill Kircher, this question pops up frequently. He hears people asking for six-volt ignition coils with external resistors at old car swap meets. Kircher recalls that around 1953, when many cars switched to 12-volts, a decision was made by the parts industry. Parts makers felt that more coils could be sold if the public did not know they were switchable. Consequently, if an old car is changed from six- to 12-volts, the resistor must be changed, but not the coil. Personally, I feel there probably is an internal difference in the 12-volt coil, but Kircher is correct in that it's the current value at the primary circuit that is most important. If the value is high, you'll burn the points. If it is low, hard starting will result. The resistor is largely what controls this current value.

Q. I am restoring a 1936 Ford cabriolet. My car has the battery box under the hood. I am told all 1936s had them under the floor. It is possible that some of the late 1936s could have a 1937 firewall? R.D., New York.
A. Ford V-8 authorities we talked say that it was not uncommon for owners to relocate the battery box to the firewall for convenience. This may have happened on your car.

Q. I need wiring for a 1949 Lincoln Cosmopolitan convertible. I have tried all the ads and there is nothing listed for a 1949 Cosmopolitan. Where can I find it? T.K., Arizona.
A. Although 1950 and later Cosmopolitan wiring harnesses are listed in catalogs, I find no wiring supplier for the first year of this new top-of-the-line Lincoln. However, if you have the original harness, Rhode Island Wiring Service, Columbia Street, Box 3737, Peace Dale, Rhode Island 02883 can make you an new wiring harness using original style material. It may take two to three months to fabricate the new harness. If you lack an old harness, I suggest that you contact the Lincoln Cosmopolitan Union, 2914 Gulford, Royal Oak, Michigan 48073 to see if any of that group's members can help you with a source for replacement wiring.

Q. I have a 1954 Chrysler New Yorker and my wife has a 1953 New Yorker. Both have the original six-volt electrical systems. This morning it was three degrees below zero and I went out and started the 1954 Chrysler. It turned over so slowly. I thought it wouldn't start, but it did. Then I started the 1953. It kicked over much smoother and faster. How come so many collectors change their car's six-volt electrical systems to 12-volts? J.J., Ohio.
A. Remember the analogy of electrical energy flowing like water through a hose. Voltage is the pressure forcing the water through the hose. The water compares to electrical current (amperage). The internal hose diameter represents resistance. In the equation Volts = Amps x Ohms ($E = I \times R$) if the voltage is doubled (the pressure on the water is increased) the current (water flow) will double if the resistance (hose diameter) stays the same. Increased current was what the auto makers were looking for when they converted from six- to 12-volt systems. It is also what most hobbyists are after when they upgrade the electrical systems of their collector cars or light trucks to 12-volts. The automakers needed additional current (greater electrical flow) to power the multitude of electrical accessories from power windows to automatic headlight dimmers on the more modern cars. The advantage of the older six-volt systems is the cranking power. Think again of the water hose example. If only so much water is available, you can pump it out fast or slow. A six-volt system pumps the current more slowly, but for a longer period of time. Your Chrysler's 331 cubic-inch hemi engine may turn ever so slowly on a cold morning like the one you recently experienced, but pretty soon it catches and starts. A 12-volt system would spin the engine more rapidly, probably causing it to start more quickly, but the system's cranking potential would be of shorter

duration than your six-volt system. In most cases, the older six-volt systems served their purpose well. However, when you hook up a CB radio, AM/FM stereo, air conditioning, power seats and other modern amenities, a six-volt system isn't up to the additional current drain.

Q. Do you think the Model T Ford registered the first burglar alarm? The reason I ask this is that, when I was a kid in the 1920s, Model T Ford owners used to rig up a coil to shock you if you touched their car standing on the ground. It gave you quite a jolt. If you jumped on the running board, you wouldn't get the shock. Can you explain how it was rigged up? J.H., Delaware.

A. This trick was a favorite of Model T owners and pranksters. What they would do was run a wire grounding the coil to the body. A Model T coil could put out 6,000 or so volts and would give quite a jolt, as you say. However, the amperage was low, so no physical harm would be done. I'm not sure the intention was to keep the cars from being stolen, but more to play a prank. While on the anti-theft subject, with the Model A, Henry Ford introduced an early and highly effective armored ignition cable that virtually prevented hot wiring, at least in the short time a thief would have to get a car started.

Q. I have an old headlight lens that I found in the attic of a old house. It is 9-7/8 inches in diameter and is stamped Liberty Lens, McBeth Evans Glass Company, Dec. 8 14. Can you tell from this information what car it would have been used on? J.W., Maryland.

A. THE LESTER-STEELE HANDBOOK; AUTOMOBILE SPECIFICATIONS 1915-1942 has reprinted charts from auto industry trade journals that show the suppliers of original equipment lighting systems for many cars. However, this particular information is not presented for pre-1916 models. From the stampings on your lens, it appears to date to 1914. Although 1916 is just two years later, the handbook gives no indication that any domestic automaker used Liberty or McBeth lighting equipment that year. Your lens may be an aftermarket type. The Antique Headlamp Lens Company, 12150 Southeast 143rd Place, Portland, Oregon 97236 specializes in supplying 1912 to 1942 headlamp lenses and might be able to help with a positive identification or value estimate.

Q. I am writing to request your help in identifying a set of very old headlamps that appear to have been for some type of automobile. One of the lamps is still in its original canvas bag, which I have not opened. The material is so old, it would probably disintegrate. The following information appears on the headlamps: Model, Solarclipse 950-B, Badger Brass Mfg., Co., Kenosha, Wis. I have tried to locate Badger Brass Company, but apparently they have been out of business for many years. The headlamp that's not still wrapped in its original bag had a dent in the rim so I took it to a professional shop and had them remove the dent. The metal was "chrome" colored when I brought it in, but after removing the dent and buffing it, it turned to a gold color. The metal seems to be either bronze or brass. I would appreciate any information you can give me regarding these headlamps. Of particular interest is the year, make and model of vehicle they were for and approximate value. T.M., Wisconsin.

A. Solarclipse lights were top-of-the-line accessory items installed on cars of the 1907-1910 era. They were not associated with any particular make of car, but could be found on any of the more expensive cars as specified by the owner. The lamps were made of brass. Nickel plating would have given the chrome appearance you report. Value would be in the area of several hundred dollars.

155

Q. I recently acquired a 1935 Terraplane four-door sedan with 29,000 original miles. I have found two horns that attach to the headlights, but they are missing the trumpets and need to be rebuilt. I have found no service organizations for rebuilding horns, do you know of any? H.M., Illinois.
A. The service you are seeking is rather unique. I know of only one individual specializing in horn repair. If you contact Bill Randall at The Horn Shop, 7129 Rome-Oriskany Road, Rome, New York he should be able to help you with the missing trumpets or advise you in locating the needed parts.

Q. I recently replaced the voltage regulator on the 1949 Ford I'm restoring. Upon closer inspection, I saw the date Oct. 48 stamped on the back of the base. It is a genuine Ford regulator, but it has a stainless steel cover. The car was built on November 10, 1948. I have two questions. First, can you verify the stainless steel cover as being original? Second, does anyone rebuild old regulators? I would love to put the old regulator back on the car. R.C., Virginia.
A. Mike McCarville, editor of the '*49-50-51 FORD OWNER'S NEWSLETTER* says, "On February 15, 1949 FoMoCo announced that regulators were being produced with steel covers painted black, replacing previous aluminum covers which were not painted." This information appears in Ford factory service letter P-47 Weighing the "stainless" steel cover in your hand will probably show you that your regulator has the original aluminum cover. Mark Shields Electronics, S & T number 136, Hazen, North Dakota 58545 rebuilds vintage regulators with modern solid state parts. The solid state regulator installs exactly as the original and there are no visible external changes. The advantage of solid state is that there are no moving parts to stick or corrode.

Q. Is there any way to install a 12-volt cassette tape player in my six-volt collector car without making changes to the original electrical system? R.T., Kentucky.
A. John Bernier, a 1953 Mercury owner, wanted to keep his car original, but also wanted to add a cassette player. He solved the problem by installing a very small cassette player under the dash and powering it with a 12-volt garden tractor battery. He placed the battery in the engine compartment on a homemade battery tray. The system works great and he only has to charge the battery once a year. Bernier adds, "If one finds this unsightly, I'm sure he or she could find a place to hide the battery, while remembering to keep it well vented."

Q. A friend told me of the practice of putting an aspirin in a weak battery and trickle charge it to remove sulfate buildup. In your opinion does this work? J.W., Maryland.
A. I have heard that tetrasodium EDTA (also used as a heart medicine) can result in some sulfate reversal in conjunction with discharging and slow recharging (which in itself can have a restorative effect). However, there is no effective way to reverse extensive sulfation in a lead/acid storage battery, despite claims from "miracle" chemicals to that effect. This is the first I've heard of aspirin used to reverse sulfation. I wonder if someone hasn't confused it with the chemical mentioned earlier. My advice would be to save the aspirin for headaches and buy a new battery. The premature battery sulfation that many collectors experience results from letting the batteries in their older cars discharge and stay that way for prolonged periods. It can also result from failing to keep the electrolyte level above the plates.

Q. Chevrolet installed Impala/Nomad body trim on 1960 Chevrolet El Caminos at the customer's request. A few years ago, I took a picture of one in a salvage yard. It was not dealer retro-fitted. It must have been custom-built at the factory. The truck had electric-operated windows unlike any I have ever seen. The switches were installed in the "knee knocker" moulding, where the cruise control mechanism should be mounted. The dual/single electrical switches could only have been supplied by a Corvette or a luxury car with power vent windows. It also had an electric seat. Was this a factory prototype? T.B., California 91730.

A. Gene Skowronski, who has headed Chevrolet truck advertising for over 25 years and whose familiarity with Chevrolet's truck line has earned him the nickname "Mr. Chevrolet Truck," comments that Chevrolet built a few early El Caminos for the show circuit. These, he recalls, were fitted with Impala trim and, as the truck you found shows, other amenities. It's possible that this truck was, indeed, a factory prototype.

Q. In 1981 I purchased a new Cadillac DeVille with the problematic "8-6-4" six-liter engine. It is my understanding that it was the computer, not the engine, that caused problems. Can you comment? My 8-6-4 now has 120,000 miles and is running beautifully, but I never see other cars with this engine. C.B., Florida.

A. A mechanic who works on these engines tells me that the problems occur in the electronics system that cuts off fuel to the cylinders under varying load conditions. He said that no one wants to work on these engines (they're a profits-killer for mechanics working on a flat rate basis). He did not, however, fault the engine's mechanical design. Hobbyist Robert E. Smith recalls reading literature about this engine when it first came out. It noted that, in addition to the electronic cut-off of fuel, there was also a cam system that opened both valves to relieve compression on the two or four cylinders that weren't firing. I believe that this mechanical system for opening values on the idle cylinders was also electronically controlled.

Q. I store my cars in an old metal airplane hangar. It seems to be picking up radio signals from station KSPA. Can metal buildings become AM radio receivers? R.B., California.

A. According to electrical engineer Doug Houston, absolutely so. He says that the hangar was probably within five miles of KSPA Radio's transmitter. You were in what is known as the "near field" of the antenna, where strange phenomena of that sort commonly occur. The near field of a transmitting antenna is the first three to five miles surrounding it. This varies according to the broadcast power and absorptive objects (such as the hangar) or other items which may be near the antenna. The hangar's metallic covering absorbed some of the radio frequency (RF) from the energy from the antenna. Perhaps, overlapping plates of the metal building's covering or rusty nails acted as poor non-linear conductors. If so, they functioned much as a crystal receiver set would, with arcing at the seams or nails "singing" from the station's modulation. Auto maker Powell Crosley was also the owner of a radio station. His 500 Kilowatt WLW "superpower" transmitter went on the air in May, 1934 and ceased operating on March 1, 1939. Crosley then returned to the normal limit of 50 Kilowatts broadcast power. The phenomena you mention, plus co-channel interference problems with WOR in Newark, New Jersey and CFRB in Toronto, Canada, were the basis for shutting down Crosley's superpower transmitter. AM stations are still limited to 50 Kilowatts and this should explain why. One of the radio clubs that I am involved with had a convention in Cincinnati last year and visited the WLW transmitting site in Mason, Ohio. Parts of the 500 Kilowatts equipment are still in the building, cannibalized, and gathering dust.

Q. I own a 1956 Ford Fairlane with a 312 cubic-inch engine. When driving at normal operating temperature, the engine shuts down without an indication of trouble. The distributor has been re-wired and the car has been about 750 miles since a tune up. Even though the carburetor is getting gas and the engine is getting spark, the car will not start until it sits for a few hours. Do you have any suggestions regarding this stalling problem? K.J., Wisconsin.

A. We're not sure how you determined that the car is getting gas and spark. If this were true, the engine should run. We suspect fuel or electrical problems first. Traditional causes would be vapor lock; a bad coil; or a condenser that is breaking down with heat. Sometimes the carburetor will appear to be getting gas because the accelerator pump squirts a few streams of gas when the throttle linkage is pulled. In reality, however, the gas supply has dried up due to vapor lock. We'd suggest starting with new electrical parts. Replace the coil and condenser first. See if this makes a difference. Then re-route or shield the gas line to prevent vapor lock.

Q. My uncle, Lyle J. Hicks and a partner purchased an electrical manufacturing company named Dongan Electric Company in 1909. They moved it from Schenectady, New York to Detroit, Michigan. During the teens and 1920s, they had orders from various auto makers for ammeters and possibly other electrical devices. To date, I have purchased three ammeters bearing the name Dongan. All three are different, indicating that many specifications or brands of cars could be involved. Do you or any readers know which vehicles used ammeters made by Dongan? R.H., Oregon.

A. *THE LESTER-STEELE HANDBOOK* gives this type of information for some years and some models of cars built in the years that the hardcover book includes. For instance, the handbook indicates that a Dongan ammeter was used on the following cars: 1921 Friend, 1921 Lorraine, 1922 Ace (models F,L and C), 1922 Friend, 1922 Taxicab, 1923 Barley Six, and 1923 Roamer 6-54 and 4-75. We are not certain if copies of this source-book are still being sold by Lester-Steele Publishing Company, PO Box 1580, Cashiers, North Carolina 28717. Copies can sometimes be obtained through T.E. Warth's used automotive book store at (612) 433-5744 or at swap meets.

Q. I have heard that there is a device on the market that stops a car from rusting. To my understanding, the device puts a small electrical charge through the body of the car, but with reverse polarity. How effective is this device? K.S., Ohio.

A. It's true that metal oxidizes (rusts) as a result of an electro-chemical reaction. It is also true that older negative-ground battery systems were more prone to develop corrosion at ground contacts on the electrical systems than present day positive-ground systems. However, passing an electrical charge through a car's body won't stop corrosion. This is what an electrical system that uses the body and chassis for electrical grounding actually does. The metal also has to be sealed from exposure to air and moisture, which can't be accomplished electrically.

Q. I understand that storage batteries should never be placed on concrete. I'm told a piece of wood should be placed under the battery if it is rested on concrete. Is this correct? P.M., Illinois.

A. Wes Grant at the Reliance Battery Manufacturing Company, of Council Bluffs, Iowa advises "I don't know who came up with the rule to always put a battery on a piece of wood and not on the cement floor. Many manufacturers of battery containers in the 1930s through 1950 made a competitive container using very porous material. They coated the inside with a sealer to make the container leak-proof. However, this material could absorb exterior moisture and break down that seal. This could happen if the battery was set on a concrete floor and moisture from the floor formed under the battery. Also, if the battery was messy, like many old batteries get, it would mark the floor if set on the concrete and not on a piece of wood. Also, setting a battery on a piece of wood usually guards against the danger of resting the battery on a rock or stone that might be in the concrete and possibly damage the case. Modern materials used in making battery containers are excellent protectors against either interior or exterior moisture penetration and keeping a battery on the concrete floor causes no ill effects to the battery, and in most cases is the coolest place to store the battery, thereby reducing self-discharge." I mostly agree with Grant's analysis. It is true that a concrete floor is not a conductor of electricity, so setting the battery on concrete does not automatically cause the battery to discharge. What does happen though (Grant clarifies this may have been more of a problem with older batteries), is that a concrete floor tends to draw moisture. The moisture condenses on the case and makes a path for electricity to pass between the terminals, slowly discharging the battery. The best storage for a battery is to wipe the case clean and place it in a cool, dry place. As long as a battery is fully charged, it should be left in the garage or other unheated storage. A battery is done no favors by bringing it inside and putting it near the furnace for the winter months.

Q. I need help finding a set of double ignition points for my 1928 Dodge standard six. Where can I locate such electrical components? Is there a Dodge club or vendor that might be able to help me? L.F., Minnesota.

A. I am not aware of a specific source for points for your Dodge. Robert D. Bliss, 2 Delmar Place, Edison, New Jersey 08837 specializes in the supply of ignition parts and electrical parts for 1920 to 1970 cars. You can phone him at (908)-549-0977. Perhaps he can help. Also, check with the Dodge Club. The address is: Dodge Brothers Club, 4 Willow Street, Milford, New Hampshire 03055.

Dodge introduced its "Silent Starter" on its mid-1926 models.

Q. Did the 1926 Dodge automobile come with a silent starter? A local mechanic tells me that the silent starter had to be ordered. Is he right? M.M.M., Indiana.

A. Hobbyist Nick Corey indicates when Dodge Brothers started building cars in 1914, they used a 12-volt electrical system. The heart of this system was a starter-generator

159

combined in one unit. It was mounted on the left front of the engine. The drive for this unit was from the crankshaft via a silent chain that ran in an oil bath, hence the "silent starter" description. According to The *LESTER-STEELE HANDBOOK: AUTOMO-BILE SPECIFICATIONS 1915-1942*, when introduced in January, 1926, the 1926 Dodge Brothers car had a 55-ampere North East brand starting motor as standard equipment. It normally produced 12 pounds-feet of running torque. Static torque was 35 pounds-feet. The handbook indicates that it had chain drive and did not mesh with teeth on the flywheel, confirming that it was of the silent-engagement type. Restorer Nick Corey advises that Dodge switched to a six-volt electrical system in May, 1926. The handbook confirms this, showing that 1927 Dodges had a 130-ampere North East brand starter with Bendix-drive. It normally produced two pounds-feet of running torque and 11 pounds-feet of static torque. Normal armature speed was 1,600 rpm. It also had a front pinion mesh with 122 teeth (with an 11/16-inch face width) on the flywheel. Later Dodges also retained Bendix-drive starters.

Q. I have recently converted a Model A to a 12-volt negative-ground electrical system and installed an AM/FM radio. The ignition noise is very loud. I have installed capacitors and suppressors, but they do practically nothing. Do you have any ideas on how to solve this dilemma?. J.U., New York.

A. If you have the original ignition, the noise could be from unshielded metal spark plug leads. A mechanic suggests this test to isolate the source of the static. Get some chicken wire (light wire with inch-square holes) from a hardware store or farming supply outlet. Cut an approximately two-foot square piece of the chicken wire. Tape the edges so you don't cut yourself. Wrap a grounding wire to one edge of the chicken wire and to a ground on the Model A. Then, hold the wire over the top of the engine. Don't let the chicken wire touch any of the spark plug leads. If the static stops, you will know that the problem is in the ignition leads. You can move the chicken wire around the engine to see where the static is originating. A solution is a little more difficult. The mechanic suggested attaching the chicken wire over the noise-generating component. That will look a little unsightly. The mechanic also suggested grounding the hood. Hobbyist Paul Moller, who has spent almost 50 years working on radios for cars and homes, has additional ideas. He owns two Model As, one with an AM radio and the other with an AM/FM Citizens' Band (CB) radio. Both are noise-free. He advises replacing the coil-to-distributor wire with a modern suppression type wire and installing a condenser (obtained from a car radio shop or electronics dealer). The condenser connects to the battery terminal of the ignition coil with the condenser case grounded to the car body or firewall. The antenna needs to be as far from the motor as possible. Moller used a pair of television antenna lead-in wire stand-offs with a machine screw end. He put a hole in the running board bracket to support the insulated stand-offs. A plain solid copper wire was stretched between the round insulators, with the front of the wire bared of insulation. A modern antenna cable for a car radio was plugged into the radio and run down along the floorboards. A ground tap was soldered to the braided outside wire covering that serves as a shield for the cable. This should be carefully grounded to the frame or body, whichever is easiest. The thin wire inside the antenna cable should be soldered to the bare end of the long antenna wire attached to the runningboard mount. An old antenna cable can be stripped of outer insulation and the inner insulation discarded. This leaves a braided strap that can be used to make a ground connection between one of the bellhousing bolts and the frame. The added braided ground wire or cable serves to ground the engine for noise. It also provides a good electrical path to ground engine components. Moller's CB radio is in a coupe, on the rear package shelf. The antenna is mounted at the rear. His thinking was to get the antenna as far from the ignition system as possible. In extreme cases, the power lead for the radio can be connected directly to the battery post. (The battery acts like a capacitor that helps filter out noise). Moller adds that grounding a Model A's hood is difficult. While this is no problem on a modern car where a hole can be drilled for a sheet metal screw ground connection, it's harder on an antique car. For best results, flexible braided cable would have to be soldered to each hood panel and grounded.

Q. I have a 1898 Oldsmobile. Do you have information on it? I don't have the right lights. It has been converted to battery-operated lights. How can I restore it to original? T.R., Ohio.

A. According to the Gary Hoonsbeen of the Curved Dash Oldsmobile Club, in 1898, Ransom E. Olds was still experimenting with automotive designs. The first Curved Dash Olds appeared in 1901. Production of this model continued until 1906. The Curved Dash Oldsmobile Club, 3455 Florida Avenue North, Crystal, Minnesota 55427 should be able to help you. You will need information on converting the electric-powered lighting system back to the original system with carbide lamps.

Q. I have a 1958 Oldsmobile 98 that has a portable radio. It is locked in by a padlock in the glove box. The lock number is OM278. A locksmith here said something about pin tumblers and that it would have to be cut out. I really don't want to do that as the lock is as rare as the radio. Do you have a better idea. R.T., Wisconsin.

A. The portable radio is a rare electrical option for the 1958 Oldsmobile and we do not blame you for wanting to save the accessory locking device. We would suggest that you contact Wayne Finney at The Key Shop, 144 Crescent Drive, Akron, Ohio 44301. Finney specializes in repairing and re-keying locks for vintage cars and trucks. He may have a solution to your lock problem.

Q. I have recently acquired a 1931 Detroit Electric. As part of the restoration process, I am in dire need of a wiring arrangement of the batteries, switch box and motor. Would you be able to put me in contact with persons who have this information? J.P., Illinois.

A. I'd suggest that you contact a service offering wiring diagrams. Possibly Robert Heise, 11 Bond Street, East Norwalk, Connecticut 06855, who advertises wiring diagrams for American cars 1915 to 1967 could help.

Q. In an English automobile book, I saw numerous references to a "self-canceling trafficator." Can you tell me exactly what such a device is or does? N.L., New Jersey.

A. It indicates to traffic around you where you are planning to turn and automatically cancels the indication after you have turned your car. In other words, it is the British term for a directional signal.

Q. My 1953 Pontiac with a six-volt electrical system has a braided wire ground cable that has been severely attacked by battery acid to the point where it requires replacement. Where can I obtain a similar battery cable? J.A.G., Wisconsin.

A. Pontiac parts are not easy to come by. The Antique Auto Battery Company, 2320 Old Mill Road, Hudson, Ohio 44236 is known as a source of vintage style batteries and battery cables. It might also pay to contact companies that sell reproduction Ford, MoPar or Chevrolet parts. They handle such cables and should be able to help if you supply the measurements of your cable, which is a rather long one.

Q. I have a Telefunken car radio and would like to know the cars it was used on. It is in two separate units, one being the power supply which has a plate stating STC V611 6.3V. The chassis has a five-lever system. W.S., New York.

A. Telefunken is a German radio used in Mercedes and other European cars of the 1950s and 1960s.

TIRES

Ken Kemper "customizes" a tire at an auction.

Q. I recently purchased a 1956 Thunderbird that has four practically new whitewall tires. Unfortunately, they're not authentic "wide" whitewalls, which are, in my opinion, a must for this car. I am not anxious to spend $400 for the correct tires and seem to recall an article about people who reconditioned or widened whitewalls. Is there any system that can convert the black portion of rubber to white and make it look professional? R.O., Florida.

A. Ed Thomas, of Saint Louis, Missouri recalled a white tire paint that he used for at least 30 years, advising that he bought it at Western Auto stores and later through J.C. Whitney. He had success thinning the thick paint with water and spraying it on after the tires were mounted and masked. It was called White Stripe and made by Best Bros. Paint Manufacturing, Incorporated, 172 Shillington Road, Sinking Spring, Pennsylvania 19608. Later, Sue Nielsen, vice president of Best Brothers, wrote to advise that her company no longer manufactured White Stripe because there was not enough call for the product. Duncan Hickey, of Canoga Park, California advised that Mobile Tire Customizing Service (818) 347-4514 widened the size of the white sidewalls of the tires on his 1936 Chrysler Airflow coupe. He had 2-7/8 inch whitewalls created at a price of $10 per inch or $30 per tire. Doyle Killebrew, of Canoga Park, California operates Mobile Tire Customizing. A similar service is provided by Ken Kemper, 6725 West Colter, Glendale, AZ 85310; (602) 846-5296. Red Burke, of Fort Bragg, California advised that K Gap Automotive Parts, PO Box 3065, Sante Fe Springs, California 90670 also has a machine to make both narrow or wide whitewalls. Burke said that there is a lot of white in the sidewalls of all tires and that this grinding machine can expose it to any width. Dan Carroll, of Lubbock, Texas explained that the grinder operates like an old spin balancing machine, spinning the tire on the car at a slower speed as a tool similar to a lathe cuts the black off the top of the white rubber underneath. Carroll warned that on some makes of tires, the underlying white band is narrower than on others. He added that Goodyear makes a tire that will "buff" larger than most.

Q. Why is it that, in pictures of really old cars, the tires look as though they are anything but black? They appear gray or white to me. Were they? I have been around over 70 years and can't remember tires being any color other than black ... and I mean jet black. P.C., Michigan.

A. The color of natural rubber is gray and the earliest tires were made of natural rubber, so this may be why you've noticed that the tires on early cars have a gray look in old photos. Black wasn't added just for cosmetics. It was found that carbon black substantially increased tread life and that's why black tires quickly became popular. However, all-natural tires continued to be made until the end of World War I. Some early tires used red rubber for the tread area or sidewalls and tires combining gray, natural rubber sidewalls with black tread appeared around 1910. The next step was to add pigments to the rubber to make the sidewalls white. Photos of cars from the 1920s and 1930s also show many cars with gray-looking tires. Many photos in Krause Publication's book *ANTIQUE CAR WRECKS* seem to show gray-looking tires. We would assume that this has to do with two things. First, the quality of the pigments used in making tires at the time. Second, the fact that the roads of the era were often "unimproved" or of the cobblestone type. Apparently, tires got dirtier in normal driving back then. While the black tire dominated after 1910, attempts to market different colored tires have popped up in different eras. For example, the Packard Panther Daytona show car now owned by Joe Bortz, of Chicago, Illinois has brown tires to match its bronze and gold paint scheme. There were efforts made in the 1950s to sell color-coordinated tires like these, but they did not catch the fancy of the public. If you study the photos in *ANTIQUE CAR WRECKS* you will notice that the tires on 1955 and later cars look "blacker" than those seen in photos of earlier cars. Apparently, the synthetic rubber compounds that evolved around that time retained their black color better and longer.

Q. My 1935 Buick Model 41 is definitely in need of new tires. I have been told that radials with tubes will improve the steering. I have also heard that one should not attempt to use radials on that age of a car. Can you give me some advice as to radials versus conventional tires? The Buick's original equipment tires were 6.25 x 16. It now has 6.50 x 15 tires that are at least 20 years old and still in use. J.B., Colorado.

A. Radial tires are available for 16-inch rims, so you could replace the bias-ply tires on your car with radials. According to the tire representatives I have talked with, the major detractor of radial tires would be appearance. There is quite a clearly visible difference between radials and original-style bias-ply tires. Theoretically, radials should give better mileage, improve the ride, provide better traction, and improve handling. In actual practice, old car hobbyists have had mixed experiences with the installation of radial ply tires. Larry Larson, of Grand Rapids, Michigan advised us, "Regarding radials on vintage cars, unless the car is to be driven primarily on smooth highways and Interstate Highways, I'd advise against radials. My 1951 Mercury two-door had them on when I purchased it. The car steered like a truck and felt very heavy in town. I decided to replace the L78-15 radials with Sears 7.10 x 15s. The difference was so drastic I thought I had power steering. The ride was better, too. Gas mileage on the highway dropped about one mile per gallon. I had the same experience with a 1956 Plymouth wagon. I put on a set of inexpensive bias belted G78s and the ride is more comfortable than with radials. One must remember that older cars were turned for bias-ply tires, not for radials. One reason light, front-wheel-drive cars have power steering is that, in addition to their forward weight bias, more steering effort is needed because of the radial tires." On the opposite side of the issue, Grant Sanders of Newell, New Jersey reported, "I drove a 1956 Ford F-100 pickup from 1969 to 1975, going through two sets of bias-ply tires during this time frame. For the third go-around I decided to try radials. What an improvement! Steering, handling and ride were all much better. I bought another set and had the same experience. From 1975 to 1992 when I sold the truck I installed two more sets of radial tires." Another pro-radial fan was Thomas Conron of Danville, Illinois. He said, "I have been restoring and driving classic and milestone cars for 25 years. I just completed 3,443 miles on a trip to Florida with the Classic Car Club. I drove my 1946 Cadillac Series 75 at 60 miles per hour with radial tires. I first put radials on my 1950 Cadillac three years ago. The ride improved and it steered just as easily. The reason I changed was to eliminate the 'dancing' which I have encountered on worn black top highways with bias-belted tires. This occurs when road wear produces longitudinal ridges on the highway surface. Bias-ply tires ride in these ridges."

Q. Recently I found and bought a 1952 Chevrolet deluxe two-door sedan with a six-cylinder engine and standard shift transmission. It runs and drives good, the body has no rust and hasn't been patched. The only things I have to do is to have it reupholstered and have the grille and bumpers replated. I would like to know the correct tire size, since it has two sizes of tires on it (6.70 X 15 and 7.10 X 15). D.L., Vermont.
A. Chevrolet equipped its sedans with 6.70 X 15 tires. Convertibles came with over-size 7.10 X 15s. You will probably find that your sedan rides and handles better with the larger tires. In my college days, I owned a 1950 Chevrolet convertible that the former owner had fitted with 7.60 X 15 tires. These gave the car a rock-solid feel on the road. Since the larger tires handled the car's weight better, they also gave longer tire life and possibly even slightly better fuel mileage.

Q. Can you clear up the confusion that has arisen from some hobbyists claiming that whitewalls can be created by grinding away the black rubber on blackwall tires? Others claim that this method does not work. G.R., Iowa.
A. In response to the discussion about adding whitewalls to tires with a paint-like product, articles have stated that all tires have a layer of white rubber in the sidewalls and that white sidewalls can be created by grinding away the overlying layer of black rubber. This statement would imply that whitewalls could be created on both sidewalls. Marshall Larson of Minneapolis, Minnesota contacted Goodyear and General Tire companies about this. Both manufacturers stated that blackwall tires have no white rubber in them. Whitewall tires have white in one sidewall only. There are two exceptions: 1) Tires originally scheduled to be white and diverted to blackwall stock before the white has been exposed by grinding; 2) Tires with one sidewall white and the other in color such as red. One final point is that the width of the existing whitewall can usually increased by grinding until the entire whitewall has been exposed.

Q. I am enclosing pictures of a Johnson spare tire lock that was left to me by my great uncle some years ago. It seems to be from the early 1920s and I guess my uncle Eddie bought it new. I have never seen another like it and wondered if you had? Was spare

tire theft a problem back then? My uncle lived in Trinity, Alabama and Memphis, Tennessee. Do you have a guess at the lock's approximate value? The following printing is on the data plate, "Johnson-spare tire lock, Johnson Auto Lock Co., St. Louis, MO. Patented July 20-20. Underwriters laboratories inspected." F.Z., Florida.
A. In the 1920s, theft in general was not the problem that it is today. However, spare tires were easy game. Tires were expensive and did not have especially long lives. Many owners did protect against theft with a spare tire lock. When spare tires were carried in the front fenders, these locks often were attached to mirrors that mounted on the top of the tires and functioned like a side-view mirror on today's cars. I haven't seen a lock like that given you by your uncle and it would be speculative to state a value.

Q. It's a job dealing with the clincher tires on our Model T. What were the reasons behind these tires? R.B., Florida.
A. According to Corky Coker, vice president of the Coker Tire Company, the first pneumatic car tires were single tube tires. They combined the functions of the tube and tire. They were designed along the lines of a water hose with plies that had a valve for flotation. Glue or cleats held the tire to the rim. They tended to roll off the rim. The clincher tire, as used on Model T Fords, gave a properly inflated tire more stability on the rim.

Q. Can you date a tire according to the size of its whitewall? I purchased an old tire at a swap meet and would like to sell it to the owner of a car that it would have originally been used on. T.M., New Jersey.
A. While you cannot specifically date a tire by the width of its whitewall, some generalizations can be made. Typically, prior to 1950, from 50 to 75 percent of the sidewall of a tire was used for whitewall width. After 1950, the size of whitewalls trended downwards. They were about 2-1/2 inches wide in 1955 and about 2-1/4 inches wide in 1957. By 1962, most cars had one-inch whitewalls.

Q. Does over-inflating a tire prolong its service life? If so, by how much should a tire be over filled? P.M., California.
A. Over-inflation is used by some hobbyists to prolong tire life. This does work in a few scattered cases, but you pay for it in inferior ride quality. Most tire suppliers recommend a certain tire pressure for a reason. Their recommendations represent the best compromise between maximum comfort, safety and long tire life.

Q. I don't drive my collector cars very many miles per year, but the tires still seem to deteriorate standing still. Does storage hurt tires? What can be done to make them last longer? R.M., Arizona.
A. Rubber undergoes a continual oxidation process, whether its being used or standing still. Many vintage car tires will start to oxidize even before the tread is all used up. This is because most collector cars are driven under 2,500 miles per year (the normal insurance policy limit.) The years go by before the tread goes away. Ozone causes oxidation. Electric motors emit ozone. Therefore, old cars should not be stored near electric motors. Treat the tread and the sidewall with rubber preservative. However, do not use such a preservative on white sidewalls, as it may stain them.

Q. Why did auto manufacturers advise owners of older cars to let a few pounds of air pressure out of their tires before starting on long trips? B.D., Missouri.

A. Tires tend to experience increases in their inflation pressures due to heat being built-up during dynamic operation. Technically, this is known as pressure rise. This still occurs with modern tires. However, today's high-tech rubber compounds can tolerate pressure rise much better. That's why people years ago practiced pre-trip deflation much more frequently.

Q. When was the tubeless tire first used on American cars as original equipment? P.T., Connecticut.
A. Tubeless tires were used as original equipment as early as 1948. They were one of the highly promoted standard features of the 1948 Tucker Torpedo. Tubeless tires grew more prevalent during the early 1950s.

Q. What brand of tires did 1954 Oldsmobiles come with? Does the manufacturer of the brand still make the original type tires? How can I buy them? D.F., Ohio.
A. The most prominent brands of tires found on American cars were Firestone, Goodyear, B.F. Goodrich and U.S. Royal. Auto manufacturers required tire makers to bid on contracts for the production of a certain amount of tires. The low bidder became the supplier for that contract. If additional tires were needed, a second contract might have gone to a different supplier. Sometimes, more than one tire company supplied tires for a certain year, make and model of car. You should check factory photographs or original sales literature to see what the tires used on original 1954 Oldsmobiles looked like. Do not go according to the type of tires presently mounted on the car. Check with hobby tire suppliers such as Lucas, Coker, Universal, Kelsey, Denman or Sears to get their catalogs. These will list available sizes and show illustrations of the different tire designs they carry.

Q. What happened to the Kelly-Springfield Tire Company? Their beautiful ads from the 1920s present the picture of a well-established company with a high-quality product. E.M., Illinois.
A. During the Great Depression that began in 1929, many once-successful American companies had a hard time making ends meet. In fact, during the first full year of economic contraction in 1930, pneumatic tire production fell from more than 23 million units to less than 18 million units. For the two years thereafter, production continued to slip. It wasn't until 1933 that tire output started to climb again. Goodyear Tire & Rubber Company took some positive steps during the crisis. For example, in 1932, the company inaugurated a six-hour day to spread out work and alleviate unemployment caused by the depression. In 1935, Goodyear purchased Kelly-Springfield Tire Company. It then became a thriving Goodyear subsidiary.

Q. I saw a photo of a Model A Ford Tudor sedan with funny-looking oversized tires. They looked like rubber donuts and somewhat resembled airplane or tractor tires. Were they a factory option? J.H., New Jersey.
A. In 1927, Goodyear began development of "Airwheel" tires for airplanes. With extra-large cross-sections, they were designed to mount on a small hub with low air pressure and provide maximum cushioning and high flotation. In early 1931, Goodyear fitted these same type tires to a farm tractor in West Lake Wales, Florida. It performed so well in testing that later in 1931, Airwheels were applied to cars and trucks. By 1932, they became standard equipment on three well-known makes of automobiles. The early Airwheel tires were 9.00 x 13 size, which is probably what you saw in the old photo. Other tire companies produced similar tires, such as General Tire Company's "General Jumbo" design. There was an article about these tires, some years ago,

in *SPECIAL INTEREST AUTOS* magazine. Later, the tires were scaled down in size and adopted as either standard or optional equipment for passenger cars of the mid-1930s.

A Ford with Goodyear "Airwheel" tires.

Q. Where can I purchase "gangster" whitewalls in my area? Do they come in the old sizes (such as 7.60 x 15) that were used in the 1950s or do I have to know which new sizes will interchange? M.O., Alabama.

A. Most local tire shops or discount tire stores can special-order vintage car tires and get what you need in a few days. Sears, for example, advises that delivery is four days or less in most areas. Other tire shops usually have sourcing arrangements with antique car tire manufacturers such as Kelsey, Coker, Lucas or Universal. Sears carries modern wide whitewalls (up to 3-1/2 inches) in F78-14 to L78-15 sizes and Allstate Guardsman whitewalls in 6.50-13 to 8.20-15 sizes with whitewalls from 2.3 inches to 3.3 inches wide. The modern types are warranted for 20,000 miles, while the Guardsmans have a 12,000 mile warrantee. Both feature polyester cord and bias-ply construction. Old-size nylon cord models with whitewalls to 3-1/2 inches are also available.

Q. I'm new to the hobby. We have noticed that tire companies we never heard of supply antique car tires. Are they reliable? D.S., New York.

A. The antique car tire companies have to meet federal safety standards just like the big, name-brand companies. A catalog from Universal Tire Company describes how they make their whitewall tires by hand, with four plies of rubber-coated polyester fabric that have 23 strands to the inch for strength. They are cut on the bias, criss-crossed and layered on a steel drum. The bead is skillfully sleeved over the drum and tread stock is applied and cured for 35 minutes at 325-degrees in a steam-generated molding machine. The tires are inspected. Most are Micro-siped for extra safety. The last step is hand-buffing the whitewalls. It take 1-1/2 hours to make a single Universal tire.

Q. My hobby is the restoration of military vehicles. Who supplies tires for vintage army trucks? R.M., Ohio.

A. The Coker Tire Company has a catalog that shows that they carry at least six sizes of military vehicle tires. The sizes listed are: 7.50 x 10, 6.00 x 16, 7.00 x 16, 7.50 x 16, 9.00 x 16 and 10.5 x 16. The two smaller sizes are four-ply rated, while the 6.00 x 16 also comes in the six-ply rating of the two middle sizes. The two largest size tires come with an eight-ply rating useful on larger trucks. Possibly, other sizes are available now, since the military vehicle collecting hobby is growing very quickly.

Q. Should my 1964 Pontiac GTO have polyglas tires? Did this car come with whitewalls? My friends say red stripe tires are correct, but I would prefer whitewalls. G.S., North Carolina.

A. According to the Goodyear Tire & Rubber Company, its Custom Wide Tread Polyglas tire was first announced in 1967, some three years after the GTO was introduced. Polyglas construction combined the best characteristics of bias-ply tires, radial-ply tires and the then-popular "wide footprint" tires (radials came into general use in 1965.) By late 1968, polyglas tires were so well accepted that they were standard or optional equipment on nearly all 1969 domestic cars. The GTO package was a midyear option for the 1964 LeMans coupe, hardtop and convertible. Whitewall tires were a no-cost option on GTOs. Red stripe nylon low-profile tires were listed as standard equipment and, since they were the latest fad, they got the most attention from buyers. Also standard on GTOs were six-inch wide wheel rims.

Q. When should antique car tires be rotated? H.S., Wisconsin.

A. For a variety of reasons ranging from use patterns to construction characteristics, those expensive vintage car tires that you purchased for your collector vehicle should be rotated every 4,000 to 5,000 miles. The exception would be if you notice any unusual wear, such as caused by worn suspension components. In that case, you should get the problem fixed and rotate the tires immediately.

Q. Is there a guidebook to what whitewall widths are correct for certain cars? H.B., Massachusetts.'

A. There is no such guidebook. In general terms, research done by antique car tire companies indicates that whitewalls were three- or four-inches wide from the late 1940s to approximately 1953; 2-1/2- to three-inches wide from 1954 to 1956; two- to 2-1/2-inches wide from 1957 to 1961 and one- to 1-1/2-inches wide from 1961 to 1965. Some car clubs, notably one Chrysler 300 Club and several Corvette clubs, have done extensive newsletter articles documenting whitewall widths for specific cars. Some of the Corvette research has been reprinted in general hobby publications.

Q. How can I keep the tires on my antique car in good condition and looking their best? D.D., Ohio.

A. In a seminar presented to the Antique Automobile Club of America (AACA), the Coker Tire Company recommended Armor-All for taking care of tires and Wesley's bleech-white for whitewall cleaning. Sandpaper can be used to clean stubborn stains from whitewalls. No-Touch tire cleaner does a good job of improving the appearance of the black sections of a tire. However, it is not a whitewall cleaner. Clean the whitewalls first, then use No-Touch.

Q. Back in the old days, we never heard about snow tires. In the winter, we carried our tire chains wherever we went. When were snow tires first introduced? R.B.J., Iowa.

A. Believe it or not, Goodyear Tire & Rubber Company announced the first studded mud and snow tire almost 60 years ago in 1934. They did not come into general use until the 1950s, however. The Suburbanite winter tire was introduced in 1952 and is the first snow tire we remember hearing about.

Q. An article I read recommended inflating tires to the maximum pressure marked on the sidewall to extend the life of the tires. Does this work? How many extra miles will your tires go if this is done? B.S., New York.
A. Car hobbyist F. L. Jacobs gave us some good advice on this topic. According to his research, for maximum wear, good handling and precise stopping tires should be inflated to the auto manufacturer's original specifications. Sometimes, this isn't the "best" pressure, but it is always better than the maximum. On most cars, the maximum is much too much. At that pressure, the car will ride harder than it should, handling will be poorer, traction for going and stopping will be worse and the tires will wear improperly. With proper inflation and regular rotation, tires should wear quite evenly across the tread. Over-inflation will result in tires wearing out down the middle faster than on the outer edges. Also, it pays to keep in mind the correct tire sizes. In the 1950s, especially, many manufacturers actually "under-tired" their cars. For the best performance and wear characteristics, the next size larger was often used as a replacement. This also resulted in much longer tire life. The best pressure settings for a given car/tires combination can be determined through checking wear patterns during regular, everyday operation. In most cases, this doesn't work for older cars that are driven infrequently. Hobbyists are best advised to follow the original manufacturer's specifications. To summarize, for maximum tire wear: 1) get the right information; 2) check inflation at least monthly; 3) watch wear patterns; and 4) rotate your tires every 4,000 to 5,000 miles, again checking wear patterns.

Q. Can you tell me where I can obtain port-a-walls for a set of 6.00 x 16 inch tires? J.N., Minnesota.
A. I saw a stack of port-a-walls that appeared to fit 6.00 x 16 tires for sale at a vendor's space at the Antique Automobile Club of America Fall Meet at Hershey, Pennsylvania. The vendor wasn't representing a manufacturer, so these port-a-walls may have been new-old-stock. In recent advertisements, Coker Tire of Chattanooga, Tennessee lists these accessory-type imitation white sidewalls as being available. Why not check with them?

Q. I own a 1949 Twenty-Second Series Packard Custom. When the speedometer reads 60 miles per hour, I am going 55. My new tires are size L78-15. When the car was new it had 8.20 x 15 tires. Is the reading off because of the tires or a broken speedometer? D.M., Illinois.
A. The L78-15 tires have a lower sidewall profile than the original 8.20s and that is what is throwing off the speedometer reading. The original tires had a greater overall diameter because of the higher sidewalls. Therefore, they covered more distance with each revolution. Your smaller diameter tires cover less distance per revolution, making the speedometer optimistic.

Q. I recently purchased a 1934 Ford pickup at an auction. I am in the early stages of my first frame-up restoration. The truck was equipped with five Firestone Air Balloon wheels complete with four hubcaps proclaiming the wheel name. The wheels had 15-inch tires mounted on them. This leads me to believe they were added in the 1950s or later. The correct wire wheels for the truck have been purchased through an advertisement in *OLD CARS*, but no one I have talked to can provide any answers as to the history of the wheels. B.H., Illinois.

A. Air Balloon tires and wheels were introduced in the very late 1920s or early 1930s as an early attempt at low-pressure tires. At the time, tire pressures usually ran in the vicinity of 60 psi. This resulted in a harsh ride, regardless of suspension. High-pressure tires were one reason for the popularity of wire spoke wheels, which provided a slight springing effect. The Air Balloon tires were inflated to 30 psi or so, giving a much softer ride. This was the good side. The bad side was that they looked like huge donuts and gave the tall cars of the era a very ungainly look. *THE RESTORER*, a publication of the Model A Ford Club of America, ran an article on Air Balloon tires a few years back. Possibly back issues with this article are still available. The club's address is MAFCA, 250 South Cyprus, La Habra, California 90631.

Q. I have a 1949 Motorcycle that had Goodyear Super Eagle tires with 2-1/4 inch wide white sidewalls. I cannot obtain these wide whitewalls, but have Super Eagle black-walls. Is there some kind or paint or process by which whitewalls can be converted to blackwalls? I've tried latex paint and chalk. Neither works. These are low-pressure tires. D.S., Connecticut.

A. In the mid-1960s I bought some whitewall tire paint from an auto supply (Western Auto?) to turn the blackwall tires on my 1950 Chevrolet convertible into whitewalls. The result was far from satisfactory. The whitewalls were streaked, had uneven edges and clearly looked like painted. They did not resemble white rubber. I have not seen whitewall tire paint in a long time.

Chart shows the historical development of car tires.

PARTS

Q. I see many advertisers selling stainless steel exhaust systems with a lifetime guarantee. From your experience, what would be the "ballpark" lifespan of such a system used on a car that is driven daily? G.P., New York.

A. We put your question to Rick Rawlings at RIS Industries, a supplier of stainless steel exhaust systems for mid-1950s Fords and Chevrolets and all Corvettes. Rawlings said that his company uses 304 stainless steel for its exhaust systems, which carry a lifetime guarantee. The stainless steel exhaust system, he tells us, is totally impervious to corrosion. That includes the clamps. RIS even offers stainless steel exhaust manifold studs in the event that disconnecting the exhaust system at that point is ever necessary (such as when removing a manifold to "pull" an engine.)

Q. One of the trucks in my collection is an early 1948 Chevrolet Advance-Design pickup. According to experts, one of the identifying features of 1947-1948 models of this type is that the gas tank filler is located on the side of the pickup bed. They say that the 1949 and later models had the gas filler sticking out of the cab, rather than the bed. Well, my truck has a 1948 serial number, but a 1949 type gas filler flow can this be? J.J., Michigan.

A. In standard form, the 1947-1948 Advance-Design trucks came with a gas tank mounted under the bed and the gas filler on the right-hand side of the bed. However, according to the book *CHEVY TRUCK ID NUMBERS 1946-1972*, the inside-the-cab gas tank (that became standard in 1949) was optional in some earlier models at extra cost. Most likely, your truck has this option. As you probably know, the 1947-1953 Advance-Design trucks look almost identical to the average viewer. Because they are so similar, it is also common to find trucks fixed up or restored with parts from a different year. Therefore, trim items and even technical features were often "mixed-and-matched" over the years. Yet, it seems unlikely that anyone rebuilding such a vehicle would bother to switch gasoline tanks. Based on this likelihood, we'd assume your truck has the optional tank mounted inside the cab, with the filler tube exiting on the right-hand rear corner of the cab.

Q. Back in the early 1960s, one of my friends owned a Cadillac "LeMans" convertible. It was a true open car with a completely removable hardtop made of fiberglass. Nobody remembers such a model today. Was I dreaming? G.H., Iowa.

A. You may have been dreaming about owning a similar car, but not that it actually existed. However, the name you mention identified the top, rather than the car model. Around 1962, a San Diego, California firm called LeMans, Incorporated marketed a detachable, leather-grained, reinforced fiberglass top for General Motors convertibles. It seems to have been inspired by Cadillac's Corvette-like Motorama show car, which was named the LeMans. General Motors dealers around the country handled distribution of the 80-pound hardtop, which could be used on standard-size Chevrolet, Pontiac, Oldsmobile, Buick and Cadillac convertibles. The LeMans top sold for about $500 and was first shown at the 1962 Chicago Auto Show. It had a small plate attached to the rear quarter, which bore the LeMans name and emblem. Of course, Pontiac had a compact model called the LeMans after mid-1961, but you could not get a LeMans top for the LeMans. In case you are wondering if any of the tops are still around, about two years ago one of our staff members followed up an advertisement for a Cadillac convertible for sale in Stevens Point, Wisconsin (about 30 miles from our office.) The car was in nice shape and had a LeMans detachable hardtop. Unfortunately, our employee did not buy it, so we failed to obtain a picture of the car. We once found a lengthy article about LeMans tops in an old issue of *AUTO TOPICS* magazine, which was published by Floyd Clymer in the early 1960s.

Q. A friend of ours works for General Motors. He says the company has a special magazine in which old car hobbyists can advertise parts they have for sale. Can you tell me about it? R.D., Texas.

A. You are talking about a publication called *MOVING PARTS*. It is sent to GM dealers' parts departments each month. In addition to reports on new products, industry news and service tips, the publication has a section where one-time parts ads can be placed. However, only ads for parts wanted are printed. The purpose is to broadcast places where dealers can sell their older parts. The address we have for the publication is: *MOVING PARTS*, 465 West Milwaukee, 339-B, Detroit, Michigan 48202.

Q. I own a 1946 Chevrolet 1/2-ton pickup truck that has the original six-cylinder engine equipped with a positive crankcase ventilation (PCV) system. Someone told me that this feature wasn't used until the early 1950s, but it looks like a factory set up. Could it be original factory equipment? P.S., New York.

A. The answer is yes and no. Chevrolet introduced a PCV system for light-duty trucks in 1952. When this option was added, the company also released a service parts kit that could be used to retrofit the PCV system to any 1932 and up Chevrolet light-duty truck. Apparently, someone purchased this $15 kit and added to the truck you bought. Therefore, it is original factory equipment. However, there are some old car clubs (that also do show judging on trucks) that may not recognize this feature as original for the year of your vehicle. To avoid losing judging points in a show you might have to document that such a kit was available and that it has been properly installed according to factory instructions. This could be done by documenting the availability of the service kit through a *CHEVROLET MASTER PARTS CATALOG*.

Q. I would like information on the Columbia two-speed rear end that was offered on Ford products. What years was this option offered on Ford, Mercury, and Lincoln models? Also, can you give me the approximate cost for the Columbia? I would be interested in knowing about the company that manufactured the Columbia rear end. D.W., Iowa.

A. The Columbia two-speed rear end was made by the Columbia Axle Company of Cleveland, Ohio. The Columbia Axle Company was part of the E. L. Cord empire during its heyday and built the two-speed axle used in the 1932 Auburn. The Columbia axles were designed essentially like an overdrive transmission. However, instead of being mounted in the drive line, the gearing was placed in a housing on the passenger side axle tube. Columbia made their "Dual-Ratio Two-Power Range Axle," as it was first called, for Fords from 1933 to 1948, Mercurys from 1939 to 1948 (less the three war years) and, according to Lincoln expert Dave Cole, for Lincoln-Zephyrs from 1936 to 1941. Columbia made its first announcement of this overdrive axle in July, 1934 and the axle is described and advertised in *FORD DEALER & SERVICE FIELD* magazine for August 1934. Since the 1934 Ford V-8 rear axle was identical to the 1933 part, the kit for the overdrive would fit either one. However, there is no indication that a Columbia two-speed was made for 1932 or earlier Fords. However, I have seen a few examples of Columbia rear ends installed in Ford Model As, although they weren't originally available for these cars. (The Model A installation is done by using a later Ford rear end.) When the Lincoln-Zephyr was introduced as a 1936 model, the rear axle was nothing but a Ford V-8 component so most of the parts in a 1936 Ford Columbia set-up would work in a Zephyr, although different controls were used. In April, 1937, Lincoln made the Columbia two-speed a factory-authorized accessory and fitted some cars with the two-speed axle on the assembly line. Other Zephyrs had Columbia two-speeds installed by dealers. Oddly enough, Ford and Mercury never made the Columbia a factory-authorized accessory; it was always installed by a dealer. You do not find Columbia axle parts in Ford parts lists, but you do find them in Lincoln-Zephyr parts books. In 1941, Lincoln added the Borg-Warner transmission overdrive, but retained the Columbia as an option. It was actually possible to fit both of them in the same car. After 1941, Lincoln dropped the Columbia and only the Borg-Warner unit was available as an overdrive. In 1937, when Lincoln announced that the Columbia would be installed at the factory, the prices were given as $54.63 wholesale to the dealer and $69.50 suggested retail to the customer. This sure sounds like a deal now. Today, a good Columbia rear end fetches several hundred dollars, although bargains occasionally appear. A friend recently reported rescuing a Columbia rear end from a scrap heap at a salvage yard price of about $15.

Q. Recently you mentioned a company named Gear Vendors, Incorporated, that makes overdrive applications for vintage pickup trucks. Can you please advise me how I might contact this company? P.J., North Carolina.
A. The address for Gear Vendors, Incorporated, manufacturer of the Gear Vendors Under/Overdrive, is 1035 Pioneer Way, El Cajon, California 92020.

Q. Is it possible to install a 1936 Ford LB engine in a 1932 Ford and use the 1932 intake manifold and exhaust manifolds? J.U., New York.
A. The *FORD CHASSIS PARTS AND ACCESSORIES CATALOG 1928-1948* shows the same intake manifold part number and the same part number for the right-hand exhaust manifold. However, the left-hand exhaust manifold has a different part number for 1932. This earlier part may fit. Perhaps it was later superseded for design or durability reasons.

Q. Enormous investments in safety have been made by the Big Three and Independent automobile corporations dating back to the early 1950s. Examples include Ford's padded dash and safety belts, GM's collapsible steering column, and many attempts to place all dash controls out of harm's way by recessing them as far from both the driver and passenger as possible. So, why did Chrylser do away with the push-button automatic transmission controls first introduced in 1956 and terminated, I believe, in 1962? In the cars built since then I can think of no more dangerous protrusion emanating from both the steering column as well as the floor as the automatic shift levers. Chrysler's push-button TorqueFlite transmission controls were not only conveniently located on the left-hand side of the dash, but were out of the reach of children. With all the advanced hi-tech equipment available today, how difficult would it be to introduce the old push-button setup and go one step further by utilizing a touch-matic button arrangement similar to microwave oven controls. Someone once told me that the government had mandated a standardization of automatic transmission controls that dictated the demise of Chrysler's setup. Is that true? B.M., Pennsylvania.
A. The convenience I remember with Chrysler's push-button automatic transmission was the ease of shifting from low to reverse to get traction when stuck in snow. Jack Poehler, editor of the *SLANT SIX NEWS* for the Slant 6 Club of America advises that, in the fall of 1963, the U.S. General Services Administration (GSA) published their specifications for bidding on 1965 model cars. Among the requirements were that they be equipped with automatic transmissions that were column-shifted and had a shift

quadrant that read P-R-N-D-L (or L-2 L-1). At the time, many other makes had shift quadrants that did not conform to these guidelines. Since the government is the largest fleet buyer in the United States and since their specifications are copied by many state and local governments as well, the Big Three automakers immediately took steps to conform to the GSA specifications. Chrysler didn't have time to develop a whole new push-button shift system, so all 1965 Chrysler automatics used a column-mounted cable shift linkage. This was a one-year setup with which Chrysler adopted the push-button cables to the column. For 1966, all Chrysler cars got a positive shift linkage with their automatics. Had there been any real problems with the push-button shifters, it is doubtful that Chrysler would have continued using them in all models for the years 1956-1964 and planned to continue them for 1965 and later.

Q. I would like to install an air conditioning unit in my 1965 Chrysler Newport sedan with a 383 cubic-inch engine which did not come with factory air conditioning. Where would I buy such a unit? Who would do this type of work? Is it still possible to retrofit my Chrysler with factory air conditioning so that I might drive in relative comfort during the warmer months? N.G., Ohio.
A. Since Chrysler offered air conditioning as an option in 1965, you could obtain a unit from a salvage yard and have it installed on your car. This approach brings with it the risk that some of the parts might need servicing or replacing. Another approach would be to order a retro-fit air conditioning unit from Vintage Air, 10305 IH-35N, San Antonio, Texas 78233. Their phone number is (800) 423-4172. The sales representative at Vintage Air should be able to direct you to a qualified air conditioning shop to do the installation.

Q. We purchased an old motometer. The housing, glass and cap appear to be in excellent condition. However, the red liquid in the glass capillary has gone all the way to the top and refuses to go back down the tube. We have tried freezing, boiling and shaking it. The liquid continues to fill the entire tube. When we bought the motometer it was lying on its side. We now have it sitting upright. Can you offer suggestions on how to fix it? S. and K.L., Delaware.
A. I suspect that the liquid in the motometer's capillary tube (which I believe was alcohol, not mercury) has dried out. What you are seeing is the dye that gave the fluid its red color. "Never store a motometer flat," advises restorer Tom Herman. "I have seen a lot of them stored that way at flea markets and they all had the mercury all the way up." Herman says he ran into an old timer who had a simple fix that worked. You get a good hold on the motometer and tap the bottom gently on an inflated rubber tire. The tire will absorb the shock. It will take a while to bring the mercury down. Some require a half hour of tapping. But, it works. Several years ago, a company advertised repair kits, including new capillary tubes, for Boyce motometers. At that time, I purchased one of the kits and rebuilt a motometer I'd found. It also had the fluid "stuck" in the tube. The process of rebuilding the motometer was quite simple. It is described in a chapter of my book *HOW TO RESTORE YOUR COLLECTOR CAR*. The ad was in *OLD CARS* newspaper, but I haven't seen this motometer repair kit advertised for several years.

Q. I need a source of supply for floor boards. I am especially interested in floor boards that would fit my 1951-1954 Hudson Hornets. Where can I locate a pan that would fit over my old floors that have many holes due to rust? James H.C., Georgia.
A. Replacement sheet metal parts are not as plentiful for Hudsons, as they are for some other vintage cars. I noticed that Green Mountain Parts, Route 22A, Orwell, Vermont 05760 advertises new replacement rocker panels for Hudsons from 1948-1957. Per-

haps this company is also making floor pans. My other suggestion is to contact the Hudson-Essex-Terraplane Club, Box 715H, Milford, Indiana 46542. This group should be able to help you with parts sources for your cars.

Q. Do you know of a company that makes insignia trim for older cars? I need two front fender emblems for a 1968 Chevrolet Bel Air four-door sedan. The two emblems say Bel Air. S.K., California.

A. Numerous companies produce reproduction Chevrolet parts. Most have mail-order catalogs available. A good guide to suppliers is the *VINTAGE AUTO ALMANAC*, PO Box 945, Bennington, Vermont 05201. (Telephone 802-442-3101). Reproduction parts tend to be available for the old cars that are collected most. A certain volume of sales is needed to justify tooling up to produce a part. The reproduction parts supplier catalogs for 1960s Chevrolets that I have seen do not list 1968 Bel Air emblems. However, you should still be able to find these trim pieces at a salvage yard or swap meet.

Q. I have acquired a dual four-barrel carburetor setup including manifold, two Rochester 4GC carburetors, all linkage parts and a dual oil bath "bat wing" air cleaner. I've been trying to identify what kind of car it is from. The manifold is painted a copper/bronze color. The engine firing order stamped on the manifold is 1-8-4-3-6-5-7-2. The manifold part number is 440856. It has no water passages in it and fits a type of motor where a valley pan covers the valve lifters. The carburetors are GM Rochester models and the model numbers are 7009600 and 7009601. Each carburetor has its own automatic choke with heat tubes joining and going to the center crossover port on the intake manifold. The air cleaner is painted a cream color (although it looks like it might have been black). I have looked at literature and autos at shows all summer and checked all *MOTORS MANUALS* and *CHILTON* books from the 1950s and 1960s. I have also checked around a few of the old auto parts stores in the area trying to match the carburetor numbers. They seem to suggest that the setup is from the period of 1955 to 1958. I have read that Pontiac made a 316 cubic-inch engine with this setup in 1956 and that Cadillac El Dorados also had dual four-barrel setups. Any advice? T.G., Pennsylvania.

A. Usually, when I am stumped on the application of a vintage car part that I have acquired, I go to my local NAPA parts store and ask the friendly counter clerk for help. If the part is for a 1950s or 1960s domestic car or truck, more often than not he's able to tell me where the part is used. In the case of your dual four-barrel carburetor setup, the counter clerk first found carburetors with the 7009 leading numbers in 1957. That gave the time reference. He looked under Chevrolet, Pontiac and Cadillac, but did not find listings for carburetors with the numbers 7009600 and 7009601. He told me that he'd do some more checking. In a few hours he called to say that the numbers on your Rochester dual four-barrel carburetors were listed for a 1956 Packard. In my experience, NAPA Parts stores are not only a first stop for parts for my older cars, but also for technical help and information.

Q. You have recommended NAPA auto parts stores as an excellent source of parts and information. However, our NAPA stores have listings going back to only 1963 on MoPar parts. They have a big distribution center right here in Little Rock. In your locality, do the NAPA people go back to the 1950s in their catalogs? W.F. Jr., Arkansas.

A. My local NAPA parts store used to have a counter clerk who had worked there for years and had kept his old parts books. When I would ask for a part for my 1949 Studebaker pickup or other vintage vehicles, he would look first in his current parts book and if the part wasn't stocked, he would go to his older parts book, find a part number and put through the order. This didn't work on all occasions, but sometimes we had success that way. The store has now modernized with computers. The electronic parts inventory doesn't take parts numbers that are not on-line. I don't understand, however, the unavailability of MoPar parts prior to 1963 in your area. The store manager advised me that, while not all parts may be available, he can get Dodge tie rod ends for 1942-1952 models and many other Dodge/Plymouth/Chrysler parts of pre-1963 vintage. Some items, like exhaust systems, are dropped when current inventory runs out. However, many chassis and engine parts for Dodge and other vehicles are listed in the current parts books and can be ordered through the computer inventory system.

Q. I am restoring a 1968 Cadillac DeVille convertible and would like to know if an interior from a hardtop will fit a convertible? I am also wondering what parts from specific years and models would be interchangeable? B.C., Illinois.
A. The front seats might interchange, but convertibles have a narrower back seat due to space needed for the top retracting mechanism. You might want to obtain a copy of *AUTO TRIM & RESTYLING NEWS*, a trade publication for auto trim suppliers, to look for possible sources of specific information about auto seat interchanges. The address for this monthly publication is Shore Communications, 6255 Barfield Road, Suite 200, Atlanta, Georgia 30328-4436.

Q. I acquired a 1967 Ford Galaxie 500 XL convertible. My problem is trying to find new or remanufactured moldings for the car and rubber seals for the doors, windows, top and trunk. I have contacted some of the bigger parts dealers across the country to no avail. My questions are these. Do I have a first-grade lemon as far as restoring the car to original? Do I have a car that no one wants to rebuild? Aren't there many people rebuilding 1967 Galaxies? Where do I find weather seals and outside moldings to replace the rubber parts on my car? F.B., Sr., Alabama.
A. Have you checked with your local Ford dealer's parts department for availability of rubber parts for your car from Ford Motor Company? My local Chevrolet dealer has been able to order rubber parts that I have needed for later 1960s vehicles with no difficulty. Often, owners of collectible cars overlook the manufacturer as a parts source thinking that once their car passes the quarter-century mark, OEM parts are no longer available. Often this is not the case. Availability of parts from a manufacturer is one reason that parts may not be listed by restoration suppliers. I would suggest a word of caution when attempting to order parts for older cars from the local Ford or Chevrolet dealer, however. It has been my experience that counter clerks will tell you that parts are no longer available, when in fact they really are. The clerk sometimes gives hobbyists the cold shoulder because he does not want to take the time to look up the parts numbers and deal with small orders that are handled on a pre-paid basis and take several weeks to come in. When the parts clerk at the Chevrolet dealer in my town told me that weather seal items for a 1969 Chevrolet pickup were no longer in stock, I called a friend who works in a large Chevrolet dealership in another city. I asked him to get the parts numbers for me. When I brought the parts number with me, the local clerk ordered the parts I needed. From that time on, I have had nothing but cooperation from the parts counter people at that dealership. Another source of parts help for your car may be the Ford Galaxie Club of America, 1014 Chestnut Street, Bermerton, Washington 98310. Getting in contact with owners of similar cars is one of the best sources of parts and other helpful information.

Q. I am restoring a 1951 Chevrolet Styleline Deluxe four-door sedan. The vehicle identification number is 20JKK51510. I would like to know what this number says about this car. Also, why did some of these cars have California (one-piece) bumpers instead of the standard three-piece bumpers? W.M., Connecticut.

A. According to the new edition of THE *STANDARD CATALOG OF AMERICAN CARS 1946-1975*, Chevrolet stamped its 1951 serial numbers were stamped on a plate on the right-hand door hinge pillar. Motor numbers were stamped on the engine block, near the fuel pump. The numerical prefix in the serial number (first two digits) indicates the assembly plant. In factory literature covering 1933 to 1948, the "20" code is shown as the prefix for the Los Angeles, California assembly plant. Our car catalog does not show this code, but our new *STANDARD CATALOG OF AMERICAN LIGHT-DUTY TRUCKS* does. Researching this discrepancy, we discovered that some (but not all) historical sources list the "20" prefix for a Van Nuys, California assembly plant for only two years, 1946-1947. After that, some books show the "20" code for the Los Angeles assembly plant from 1948-1952, but several sources don't show this code after 1947. Apparently, Chevrolet confused some source book compilers by switching plant codes, then switching back, in the early postwar years. In any case, we're quite certain you car was built in Los Angeles. The car catalog tells us that JK indicates the 1951 Deluxe 2100 series. The third letter indicates the production month (K indicates November). The remaining digits are the sequential production number. Variations in Chevrolet bumper designs were related to which area of the country the parts were sourced from. Chevrolet parts expert Bob Hensel, of Brillion, Wisconsin notes that Chevrolet used three-piece bumpers (front and rear) on all Chevrolet passenger cars, except those built on the West coast and Canada, from 1949 to 1964. These three-piece bumpers consisted of two outer sections and a center section riveted together. Bumper guards hid the joint.

Fin-like chrome rear fender-top trim was optional for 1952 Chevrolets.

Q. Did any 1952 Chevrolets come from the factory with fin-like chrome trim on the tops of the rear fenders extending down almost to the taillights? A friend of mine says owners or dealers installed these. A can of Dr. Pepper is riding on your answer. A.K., Florida.

A. According to Bob Hensel, of All Chevy Acres, this trim piece was a genuine Chevrolet accessory that was intended for dealer installation. The part number is 986702. All early 1951 models had a similar die-cast trim piece, but it was dropped at mid-year due to Korean War materials restrictions. In 1952 they offered the stainless trim piece as an option. The 1951 die-cast piece was thinner and went to the top of the taillight. The 1952 piece was wider. It was made of stainless steel and stopped above the taillight. Chevrolet collector Dave Young, of Boaz, Alabama, adds that the 1951 trim piece, which is much easier to find, will fit 1952 models, although it would not be authentic. A restorer installing the stainless rear fender trim would probably need to look at a photo or an illustration from the accessory catalog to position the trim piece correctly.

Q. I have a 1958 Cadillac Hydra-Matic transmission in excellent working condition. It will be stored on a wooden pallet for an undetermined amount of years. What storage techniques can you recommend to insure the transmission will remain in decent condition for future use? J.M., Wisconsin.

A. I suggest draining and replacing the fluid to make sure that you don't store the transmission with contaminants (moisture, etc.) in the fluid. Beyond this, I talked to a transmission rebuilder who said that his major concern would be the storage environment. He cautioned against putting the transmission in a long-term storage location where humidity would settle on the case and moisture could condense inside the transmission. As an example, he spoke about the condensation that comes up through the floor of his garage during periods of high humidity and temperature swings. A setting like this, he said, could be damaging to your transmission. In dry storage, with fresh fluid, he thought your Hydra-Matic should experience no deterioration.

Q. I have a 1967 Oldsmobile Cutlass convertible. I have put a 1970 Oldsmobile 455 cubic-inch engine in it and still have the stock rear end. It doesn't have the power I thought it would have. If I changed rear ends would it make a big difference? If so, what rear end should I use? T.N., Wisconsin.

A. In 1967, Oldsmobile offered the following rear end ratios: 2.41, 2.73, 2.93, 3.08, 3.21, 3.23, 3.42, 3.55, 3.90 and 3.91. It would seem that your car has one of the higher (lower numeric) rear end ratios. You should be able to tell this by whether the engine "loafs" when cruising at highway speeds. You should also get relatively good fuel mileage (perhaps as high as 18 miles per gallon). Often, the axle ratio can be identified by locating a tag on the rear axle housing. If you determine that your car is equipped with a set of "tall" gears, you may want to go with a lower (higher numeric) ratio, perhaps a 3.42 or 3.55. To do so, you would need to find a compatible rear axle with the desired gearing and install it in your car.

Q. Could you help me find two quarter panels for a 1963 Ford Falcon two-door sedan? I can't find any place that sells them. D.F., Wisconsin.

A. You might try Northwest Classic Falcons, Incorporated, 1964 Northwest Pettygrove, Portland, Oregon 97209. This supplier's stock includes original Ford Motor Company parts. It is unlikely that anyone is stamping reproduction quarter panels for your car. In addition, check at swap meets in your area. Large meets include the spring and fall shows at Jefferson, Wisconsin, the Iola Old Car Show the second week in July and the Elkhorn show in early August.

Q. Several years ago I purchased a 1960 Cadillac Eldorado Biarritz with the bucket seat option on the car. I was told a limited number of these cars were produced with this option. I have tried to find out just how many were made with bucket seats and so far have not had any answer. Can you help? D.W., Arizona.
A. Cadillac built 1,285 Biarritz convertibles in 1960. To our knowledge, there are no factory records listing how many carried the bucket seat option. However, I have seen estimates by collectors that 10 percent of these cars were so-equipped. Industry trade books, such as *WARDS AUTOMOTIVE YEARBOOK*, did not publish the percentage of bucket seat installations until model year 1961. Only one percent of all 1961 Cadillacs had bucket seats installed. However, the percentage of sporty convertibles with this sporty option was probably somewhat higher. Our feeling, though, is that 10 percent would be too high, especially for 1960. We would guess the total to be closer to three percent.

Q. At Spring Carlisle, I purchased a 1972 Oldsmobile Cutlass Supreme hardtop coupe equipped with a 350 cubic-inch V-8. The car has 72,000 original miles and is in good condition. I have several questions. Can it be operated on today's unleaded gasoline? I would like to replace the trim items, bumpers, steering wheel, etc. What clubs can help me find parts? How many of this model were made? I know it will never be a collectible in the same league as the Chevrolet Corvette or Ford Mustang, but it appeals to me as an affordable, interesting car that is worth saving. G.B., Pennsylvania.
A. It is my understanding that 1969 marks the point when American automotive manufacturers began fitting engines with hardened valve seats to run on unleaded gasoline. As to a source for trim items like a new bumper, the first place I would check would be your Oldsmobile dealer. For parts not available through General Motors, the Oldsmobile Club of America, PO Box 16216, Lansing, Michigan 48901, should be helpful. Your 1972 Cutlass Supreme hardtop was a very popular car. Oldsmobile built 105,087 of this model. You have made a good investment in a great-looking, driveable collectible car that should increase in value.

Q. I would like to know how many 1916 Model 490 Chevrolets were made and where I can get parts? J.P., New York.
A. Chevrolet built 70,701 cars, both 490 and Model H, in 1916. We do not show a breakdown for the 490 alone. For parts help I suggest that you contact the Vintage Chevrolet Club of America PO Box 5387, Orange, California 92613-5387.

Q. Looking at back issues of the *OLD CARS* calendar, I noticed that the 1934 Chrysler Airflow Custom Imperial CW LeBaron limousine featured a one-piece curved windshield. Was this practice too costly or technologically difficult to keep it from appearing on other cars until the 1950 models from Oldsmobile, Buick, and Cadillac? J.C., California.
A. It was also my belief that there was no process to mass-produce curved glass windshields until General Motors introduced them in the early 1950s. However, Studebaker historian Fred K. Fox advises us that Studebaker was way head of General Motors in using this type of part. The South Bend manufacturer started using one-piece curved windshields on its Commander and President sedans and coupes in mid-1941. In mid-1946 (on 1947 models) Studebaker started using curved glass in large numbers on convertibles, five-passenger coupes (Starlights) and Land Cruisers. Author Bill Snyder adds that several prewar and postwar cars had curved glass before General Motors introduced it. He mentions the Chrysler Airflow, 1942 Chrysler Crown Imperial, 1942 Studebaker, 1949 Nash and 1949 Lincoln Cosmopolitan. Snyder pointed out that

curved glass was, and still is, a bit harder to install and tends to break easier during installation than flat glass. Some people claim that the severe curved glass of the 1950s gives them headaches. By the way, the *OLD CARS* calendar, which is produced annually, is available as a free premium to people subscribing to *OLD CARS* in the fall (September through December). Write to: *OLD CARS*, 700 East State Street, Iola, Wisconsin 54990 for information.

Q. I recently became the owner of a 1967 Simca model 1204 station wagon. It has been parked under a tree since 1971. This car has only 30,000 miles. The interior is immaculate. I have conquered the exterior rust and deterioration to the paint. I have the engine and oil clutch working fine, but am unable to get the brakes working. I am about to disassemble the master cylinder, but I am concerned that I may not find repair kits. Chrysler, who marketed Simcas for a short period, is no help. Can you help me locate a parts source? M.N., Alabama.
A. Usually the best source of information on parts and technical information is a club for your make of vehicle. In this case, the club is the Simca Car Club, 644 Lincoln, Amherst, Ohio 44001. The phone number is: (216) 245-1977. They publish a monthly newsletter and should be able to help you get your Simca back safely on the road. For owners of other brands of cars, *OLD CARS* publishes a complete list of clubs every April. To get a one-year subscription to *OLD CARS* send $29.95 to Krause Publications, 700 East State Street, Iola, Wisconsin 54990 or call (715) 445-2214.

Q. My parents bought a 1957 Chevrolet Bel Air with a 283 cubic-inch engine, factory power pack and Turboglide transmission. I was seldom allowed to drive this car due to what my parents called the "Trouble-glide" transmission. They liked the automatic, but said it could never be repaired and would have to be replaced with an inferior Powerglide transmission should damage occur to it. My parents always insisted Turboglide was so smooth that you could never feel it shift. I always felt I could feel it shift. Who was right? Were Turboglides impossible to repair? Is a 1957 Chevrolet with Turboglide worth more than one with Powerglide? J.F., Minnesota.
A. The Turboglide automatic transmission that Chevrolet offered as a $231 option in 1957 and built through 1961 was indeed a smooth transmission, particularly when compared with the jerky, two-speed Powerglide. One of my uncles purchased a 1961 Chevrolet with Turboglide. I can remember his inviting my father and me for a ride in his new car to experience the shifting smoothness. Like you, I could feel the shifts, but not in the jerky way felt with the Powerglide. Because of the Turboglide's greater complexity, it may have been a little more trouble-prone than the bulletproof Powerglide, but rest assured that it could be repaired. It sounds to me as though your parents concocted a line to make sure their pride and joy stayed pristine. Our *OLD CARS PRICE GUIDE* suggests adding 15 percent to the listed values of 1957 Chevrolets with power pack, but does not list a bonus for any transmission option.

Q. Why did people make a big fuss about having an overdrive transmission in their 1940s and 1950s cars? Today, people yawn when you mention that your 1990s car has overdrive. Why is this device called an overdrive? Is there such a thing as an underdrive? If so, what is it? What is overdrive good for? Both my 1983 Oldsmobile and 1985 Chevrolet and both have gone over 100,000 miles. Overdrive makes them run slower and reduces their power. What is the benefit of this? J.F., Minnesota.
A. Overdrive transmissions offered the same benefits of greater fuel economy and longer engine life to vehicles of the 1940s and 1950s as they offer in today's vehicles. The reason that owners of the older cars got more excited about overdrive is that the

auxiliary transmissions had manual controls that made their operation much more noticeable than today's overdrive gearing, which is built into the transmission. Overdrive gets its name from a step-up gearing arrangement. It allows the transmission to increase the engine revolutions transmitted to the rear end by ratio of 28 to 33 percent. With the rear wheels turning faster at a given engine speed, the engine can be throttled back and still maintain the same highway speed, thereby saving fuel and reducing engine wear. Some overdrives also give an underdrive option. Recently, I installed a Gear Vendors under/overdrive transmission in a 1969 Chevrolet pickup with 4.10 rear end gearing. The overdrive feature enables this truck to cruise at highway speeds without the engine sounding as though it is trying to launch the truck into orbit. Using overdrive has also improved the truck's fuel mileage by 50 percent. The underdrive option in this transmission results from the step-up gearing also creating intermediate ratios between the lower gears. This intermediate gearing is referred to as underdrive and has the effect of giving the truck's three speed transmission six forward gears. It works in much the same way that a dual-speed rear end works in a heavy-duty truck; it doubles the gear selection options at the transmission. In order to experience the benefits of overdrive, the engine has to have sufficient power output to handle the step-up gearing. The 1969 Chevrolet pickup I installed overdrive in is powered by a 350 cubic-inch V-8 engine that handles the under/overdrive transmission with ease. With the lower power output of your mid-1980s General Motors cars, the engine's lack the torque causes it to perform unsatisfactorily in overdrive. This is the fault of the engine, not the overdrive.

Q. I believe that early Model A wheels are not the same as Model T wheels. Is this correct? R.S., New Mexico.
A. According to Model T collector Bill Suggs, Jr. the 1928 wheel was part number AR-1015 and was definitely different than the later 21-inch Model A wheel. The 1926 and 1927 Model T wheel also differed from the early Model A variety. The hub of the Model T wheel has several bosses, whereas the Model A wheel has a smooth hub.

Q. I own a 1962 GMC Suburban which I would like to add overdrive to for open road touring. Do you have any suggestions as to how I can do this? R.C., New York.
A. If the bellhousing bolt pattern is the same used with a Chevrolet six-cylinder or V-8 engine, you should be able to replace the current transmission with a three-speed and overdrive from a Chevrolet car or light truck. Both used the same transmission and finding a car overdrive will be a lot easier than locating one from a truck. Chevrolet began offering overdrive in 1955 and continued this option until about 1965. The overdrive wiring harness and replacements for the relay and other electrical parts are still available. You may need to fabricate a kick-down switch to match the V-6 engine's throttle linkage. Before hunting for an overdrive, I advise that you check with your Chevrolet or GMC dealer to see if three-speed transmissions interchanged between Chevrolet and GMC light trucks for 1962. If they did, then you can begin your search for a replacement overdrive transmission. With the transmission installed, you will need to have the driveshaft shortened by the length of the overdrive unit. This should be done by a company that can also balance the shortened driveshaft. I have found that some of the shops which specialize in modifying larger trucks can do this work. If the overdrive installation will work on your truck, you will be pleased with the results.

Q. The 1951 Ford used a revised and different dashboard from the 1950 Ford. The major gauges and speedometer cluster are not the same for both years. However, the woody Country Squire station wagon used the 1950 dash in the 1951 model. It did not receive the 1951 revision. What is the reason for this? D.F., Pennsylvania.

A. According to Ford fan Bob Thatcher, if you look at a 1949-1950 station wagon dashboard and compare it with a passenger car dash of the same vintage, you will notice that the station wagon dash protrudes out in front near the clock and radio. In other words, a 1949-1950 passenger car dashboard will not fit in a woody. Because of this difference, Ford used the exclusive 1949-1950 woody dash in 1951 woody wagons, too.

Q. Please help settle a debate. An associate claims that the first automatic transmission available for sale to the general public was offered by either Hudson or LaSalle during the late 1930s. I am of the opinion that it was Cadillac that first offered a fully automatic transmission without a foot-operated clutch. Did Cadillac put this device into production before any other automaker? Also, was the first motorcycle made with a foot-shifter a 1930 BMW model? J.W., Pennsylvania.
A. In 1933, the Reo Royale offered an early transmission that had automatic gear changing, but used a clutch for starting and shifting into reverse. It was optional in Reo Flying Clouds. Buick Engineering worked on developing an automatic transmission during this same period. Cost projections and durability problems kept this transmission out of production. Buick's first automatic, called the Roller, used a clutch to engage reverse. General Motors continued to work on a self-shifting transmission. In 1936, Buick was asked to build a freshly designed automatic for Oldsmobile. Buick was selected partly because of its experience with the earlier Roller transmission, but also because it had the largest transmission facility of all GM car divisions. This automatic, called the "Self Shifting Transmission," appeared in 1937 as an $80 option on Oldsmobile's eight-cylinder cars. In 1938, Buick also offered the self-shifting automatic, while Oldsmobile expanded the automatic option to its six- cylinder cars. Buick, which had worked reluctantly on its development, dropped the automatic transmission option in 1939. Oldsmobile continued offering the unit in 1939 cars. Although gear changes in this transmission were made without using a clutch, stopping and starting still required the use of a manual clutch. The first fully-automatic transmission (absence of a manually engaged clutch), the famed Hydra-Matic, first appeared as an extra-cost option for Oldsmobiles in 1940 and for Cadillacs in 1941. Motorcycle buff Steven Andrews informed us that the first motorcycle produced with a foot-shifter was a works racing bike made by Velocette in 1928.

Q. My husband and I own a 1958 Ford two-door Ranch Wagon. Over the years we have been to numerous car shows and have never seen another. How many were made? How many are left? Where can we find a source for parts. P.L.M., New York.
A. Ford built 34,578 two-door Ranch Wagons in 1958. The reason that you haven't seen another is that station wagons get used hard. With such wear and tear, few survive for collectors. Probably fewer than 1,500 of these cars remain. One of the largest parts suppliers for Ford products is Dennis Carpenter Reproductions, 4140 Highway 29, Harrisburg, North Carolina 28075. You may also want to contact the Ranchero Club, 1339 Beverly Road, Port Vue, Pennsylvania 15133. This club also caters to Couriers and station wagons and can help you with parts sources for your Ranch Wagon.

Q. I own a first series 1955 Chevrolet 1/2-ton pickup with the usual rust in the cowl and floor. I'd like to replace the cab with one from a 1-1/2 ton truck. On Advance-Design trucks, the big-truck cab appears to be the same as those used on 1/2- through 1-ton pickups, but the front fenders and grille are larger. Will my pickup fenders bolt to the big truck cowl? If so, are there any other problems in making the swap? Are the hoods interchangeable? Can 3/4-ton running boards be cut and spliced for use on a 1/2-

ton truck? Starting with second series 1955, Chevrolet pickups went to a tapered frame. What problems would be encountered in swapping front and rear axles from a 1956 Chevrolet 1/2-ton to a 1954 Chevrolet 3/4-ton? Horsepower for Chevrolet passenger cars went from 115 in 1954 (solid lifters) to 145 in 1958 (hydraulic lifters) and then back down to 135 in model years 1959 through 1962. Were these horsepower changes real or did the methodology for measuring horsepower change? Are the hydraulic and solid lifter engines identical in appearance? G.C.A., Minnesota.

A. According to the *CHEVROLET MOTOR PARTS CATALOG* all Advance-Design trucks use the same cab. This suggests that the fender bolt hole pattern should be the same on both light- and heavy-duty cabs. To my knowledge, the hoods are also interchangeable. The Advanced-Design models have a tapered frame, whereas Chevrolet's 1955-1959 pickups have parallel frame rails. The parts catalog shows different front and rear axles between the 1955 first and second series truck. On 1/2-ton models, the front axle interchanges between 1941 and 1955 first series and between 1955 second series and 1959. The rear axle interchanges between 1951 and 1955 first series and between 1955 second series and 1959. On 1955 second series trucks, the rear springs are of the "outrigger" design, meaning that they are located outside the frame rails and mount to extensions riveted to the frame. On Advance-Design models (through 1955 first series), the rear springs are positioned underneath the frame rails. This means that if you attempt to use a 1956 rear axle on your 1955 second series pickup, you would at least have to cut and move the spring shackle brackets. Although you won't see noticeable external differences on pressure-oiling 235 cubic-inch engines, there were internal changes that accounted for the horsepower differences you noted. In 1954, Chevrolet's pressure-oiling engine with mechanical lifters had a compression ratio of 7.5:1. In 1958, the 235 cubic-inch six-cylinder engine had a compression ratio of 8.25:1. This compression boost accounted in large measure for the horsepower increase, though Chevrolet also made changes to the camshaft. For 1959, the engine was de-tuned for improved fuel economy with a redesigned camshaft. This accounted for the drop in horsepower rating that you cite. In 1960, Chevrolet introduced a further de-tuned six that was advertised as the Thriftmaster Economy Engine. This engine was rated for 110 horsepower, a little less than the 235 cubic-inch truck engine's 1954 rating of 112 horsepower. You can contact other owners of vintage Chevrolet trucks by joining the Light Commercial Vehicle Association (address in an earlier pages).

Q. The 1970 to 1973 body style Camaro used three different front bumper/parking light schemes: 1) Rectangular parking lights below a split bumper; 2) Rectangular parkers below a full bumper; and 3) Round parkers above a split bumper. (I've never seen round parkers above a full bumper.) Through the years I have seen 1970 Camaros with all three styles. I've seen RS, RS/Z-28, SS, SS/Z-28, Z-28 and plain-Jane Camaros with a random mix of the three styles. My 1970-1/2 Camaro RS has the round parkers. There seems to be no set style per year or sport package ordered. Your catalog pictures a 1970, 1971, and 1973 with rectangular parkers and a 1972 with round parkers. What gives? M.H., Mississippi.

A. Our information states that Camaro used the split bumper and round parking lights to give a different face to the RS Camaro in 1970. This look was retained through 1972. The Z-28 used the same bumper/parking light arrangement. In 1972, the standard Camaro got a new grille, but the earlier RS grille still appeared on the sportier models. Lacking definitive information on this, my hunch is that Chevrolet made the various front bumper and parking light packages available as extra-cost items. Perhaps some of our Camaro collectors can clear up the apparent confusion created by the different front bumper and parking light styles being applied seemingly willy-nilly to various Camaro models in the early 1970s.

Q. I have had no success whatsoever in obtaining the aluminum trim panels for my 1962 Oldsmobile Starfire. Anyone familiar with these trim panels is aware that they had very fine horizontal lines on the surface. I have written to various businesses that claim to be able to restore these panels, but when I ask if they can restore the fine horizontal lines, my question is left unanswered. I have sent panels to restoration businesses, only to have them returned telling me they can not be restored. There has to be some new old stock or perfect used panels out there somewhere. If not, can someone can tell me where to get the aluminum material to have the panels made? Does anyone know who originally made these panels for Oldsmobile? Can anyone help us? E.W., Michigan.

A. Have you contacted the Oldsmobile Club of America, PO Box 16216, Lansing, Michigan 48901 for help? Club president Dennis Casteele has close contacts with Oldsmobile and is very knowledgeable about parts sources for these cars. Either Dennis Casteele or the club may be able to help you.

Q. I recently purchased a 1961 Buick 225 convertible and an Electra 225 four-door hardtop parts car. My parts car has working factory air conditioning. I would like to install this in the convertible during restoration. Was air conditioning an option on the Electra 225 "ragtop" in 1961? Also, what color convertible top was offered with a white exterior and red leather interior? B.P., New Jersey.

A. Our convenience options listing simply states that air conditioning was available on full-size Buicks in 1961 as a $430 add on. This implies that it was available on the convertible at that price. I believe the convertible top should be white.

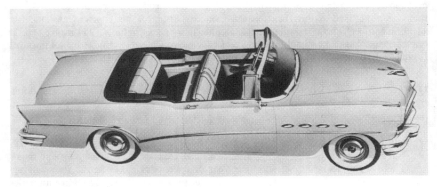

Artist's rendering of 1956 Buick emphasizes Roadmaster script on door.

Q. I am on the verge of completing restoration of a 1956 Buick Roadmaster model 73. I've been unable to find the scripts that appear on the front doors. Furthermore, I don't even know what the scripts say or how they look. Can you help me? J.P., Colorado.

A. The scripts, which attached just below the vent windows, said Roadmaster. From photos, they appear to be six- to seven-inches long. If you are not a member of the Buick Club of America (BCA), PO Box 898, Garden Grove, California 92642 you

184

should be. You may find other 1956 Roadmaster owners in BCA who could assist you in locating these scripts.

Q. I have owned a specially-striped 1976 GMC High-Sierra Custom pickup truck for several years. I have never seen another like it. I have been wanting to have it repainted, but I can not find the original stripe package. I have tried every dealer in my area. They tell me it is a discontinued part number. Someone, somewhere must have this obsolete part on a shelf. I know I can have the stripes painted on, but I would like to keep this low mileage truck as original as possible. Can you help me? S.C., Maine.

A. A GMC Wide-Side pickup with this striping package shows up in the 1975 section of the new second edition of the *STANDARD CATALOG OF AMERICAN LIGHT-DUTY TRUCKS*. It may have been offered for two years, as GMC did not follow a normal annual design change cycle. The appliques decorate the hood and side panels on your truck. They may be very difficult items to find. Most such graphics are produced by the 3M Company of Minneapolis, Minnesota. Perhaps they can help you determine if the decals are still available. Another possible source is Stencils & Stripes Unlimited, 1108 S. Crescent Avenue, number 21, Park Ridge, Illinois 60068. Although they specialize in muscle car stripes, the company may be able to give you advice. You can call them at (708) 692-6893.

Q. I have been offered a good deal on a 1962 Ford Thunderbird that has been advertised as one of the limited-production Sports Roadster models. How can I verify that this car is being accurately represented? J.B., New Jersey.
A. Thunderbird specialist Alan Tast provided details on how to identify 1962 Thunderbird Sports Roadsters. The Sports Roadster had no nameplates, but a special emblem was placed below the Thunderbird nameplate on the front fender in 1962. This additional emblem was not used with regular convertibles. The 1963 Sports Roadster used the same emblem in the same area (ahead of the front wheel cutout on the fender) but the Thunderbird nameplate was moved to the rear quarter panel. The emblem was also used on the tonneau cover between the seats. Identification of early Sports Roadsters from the vehicle identification plate is complicated by the lack of a special designation. According to the Vintage Thunderbird Club International, some hints can be used to narrow down an early Sports Roadster's authenticity. It is known that between September 13, 1961 and February 1, 1962, cars equipped with the Sports Roadster Package numbered 558 units. These were interspersed on the assembly line with convertibles, hardtops and the also-new Landau Sedan. Sports Roadsters would fall between serial numbers 2Y85Z105844 and 114640, not inclusive. The first 465 units (numbers 105844 to 109311) of this 588 were painted Rangoon Red and had black vinyl interiors. Exceptions to this were cars number 107163, 107165, 107914 and 107915, which came with red leather upholstery and car number 108297, which came with red vinyl upholstery. One way to determine if an early Sports Roadster is authentic would be to look under the rear seat for a piece of paper known as the ROT or tear sheet. At the bottom of this sheet is an area for additional comments. Early Sports Roadsters had the words "Tonneau Cover Wire Wheels" printed across the sheet to tell assembly line workers that these parts of the package were to be installed. Another telltale sign as to whether a Sports Roadster is authentic is to note whether a grab bar is installed under the dash cover on the passenger side. Note that reproductions of this part, though scarce, are available. However, if the car is missing the grab bar, chances are it's a regular convertible. From February 2, 1962 until the end of the model year, 860 units were designated with "Convertible Sports Roadster." They carried the 76B body code on the data plate and 2Y89 in the serial number. Likewise, the 1963s used the 76B/89 desig-

nations. Only 455 Sports Roadsters were invoiced for the 1963 run, but dealers and customers could order any and all parts of the Sports Roadster package at the time. However, these cars would officially be convertibles with codes of 76A and 3Y89. There are many other peculiar features of these cars: The use of vibration dampers (also known as cornering weights) on early 1962s; limited paint offerings; no hood ornamentation on very early 1962s, etc. I recommend that those interested in these collectible automobiles correspond with the Vintage Thunderbird Club International which has existed since 1968 and has 3,000 members world wide. The club publishes a bi-monthly magazine called *THUNDERBIRD SCOOP* which contains restoration and maintenance information, items of historical interest, news on meets at local, regional and national levels and free ads for members. The club also publishes a list of judging standards for the 1958 to 1966 models. The address to write is: VTCA, PO Box 2250, Dearborn, Michigan 48123.

Q. Somebody told me that sealed beam headlights were an option, at least for Packard, in 1939. All references I have read give 1940 as the introduction date of this component, without mention of make. Were sealed beams an option for Packards in 1939? C.S.K., New Jersey.
A. It has been my understanding that modification of lighting laws in some of the states was necessary before the industry could make a uniform switch to sealed beam headlights in 1940. This was also the case in 1958, when quad sealed beam headlights were introduced.

Q. I am working on a 1957 Chrysler 300C letter car that I have been told was built for racing. This would make it a Daytona Special model. The engine is a 393 cubic-inch V-8 with two four-barrel carburetors and a roller cam. The car has a standard three-speed manual transmission, no power steering or power brakes. It has a factory tachometer in place of the electric clock. It does not have electric windows or a power seat. Could you tell me how many of these cars were made and if they have a value above regular 300s? J.B., New York.
A. According to Gilbert A. Cunningham, of the Chrysler 300 Club International Incorporated (Tallahassee, Florida), "Chrysler Corporation records indicate 0.8 percent of 300C production (18 cars out of a total 2,251) was equipped with the special high-performance option package. This package consisted of: (1) The standard 392 cubic-inch hemi engine modified with a hotter cam and higher 10.0:1 compression ratio to produce 390 horsepower at 5400 rpm and 430 pounds-feet of torque at 4200 rpm; (2) A 2.5-inch diameter dual exhaust system; and (3) A three-speed manual transmission with gearshift lever on the steering column. Power steering, power brakes and air conditioning were not available, nor could one order the high-output engine or manual transmission as separate options. This high output package was released to allow stock eligibility for Daytona SpeedWeeks so the 300C could defend its Daytona Flying Mile top speed title (which it did, although not by the amount of its predecessor the 300B). It was available for purchase by the general public at $500 extra. The fact that only 18 such cars were sold probably attests to the exceptional performance available with the standard 375 horsepower engine, the desire for automatic transmission in 1957 and a warning that the 390 horsepower engine was "not recommended for the average 300C customer, as the longer duration high-speed camshaft increases idle roughness and reduces low speed engine performance." Some later 390 horsepower cars apparently had roller cams, although the Daytona ones appear not to have this part. Instead, they utilized an "Isky" ground cam with hollow "solid" flat lifters and tubular pushrods. As for value, such a car, if authentic, would tend to be worth more than a standard 300C."

Q. The convertible tops on late-model General Motors convertibles are called cantilever tops. These sometimes have an unusual appearance. Do you have any information on why they look so distinctive? H.A., Tennessee.

A. John Pildner, who dabbles in old cars today, worked on prototypes of these tops with General Motors engineers during the time they were being tested at the Ashtabula Bow Socket Company in Ashtabula, Ohio. That's where all of these tops were eventually built. The reason for the design was to create a full width rear seat, since the top was made to nest completely behind the seat instead of having bows extending at each side and behind the seat. Upon close examination, you'll notice that the right and left sides are not symmetrically opposite each other. This unusual design was adopted to facilitate the top in its folded position when retracted.

Q. I own a 1966 Oldsmobile Starfire which has a bench front seat, no console, and a column-mounted automatic transmission. Starfires came standard with bucket seats and console. I am wondering how many were produced with the parts that my car has? W.L., Ohio.

A. According to *WARD'S AUTOMOTIVE YEARBOOK 1967*, only 2.6 percent of all 1966 Oldsmobile models had bucket seats. Other production figures are given by model, but not by optional equipment installations. According to our *STANDARD CATALOG OF AMERICAN CARS 1946-1975*, Oldsmobile built 13,019 Starfires in 1966. Since the standard bucket seats and console would be more desirable, it is likely that few bench seat models were built. I am wondering if your car was fitted with a bench seat and column-shift selector for a past owner's convenience.

Q. Can you help me with any information on who is making reproduction parts for 1959-1960 Cadillacs? L.J., Minnesota.

A. Several suppliers are now featuring reproduction parts for these Cadillacs. One reliable source of both reproduction trim and replacement sheet metal, as well as other parts, is F.E.N. Enterprises, PO Box 1559, Wappingers Falls, New York 12590. For interior parts, you might want to contact: Jenkins Properties, Incorporated, PO Box 2428, North Wilkesboro, North Carolina 28659.

Q. I am writing to you in desperate need of information about my car. I own a 1970 Ford Falcon, which I am told was a midyear model. It has the identical body style of the 1970 Ford Torino. I have found that most of the body parts are interchangeable with some slight differences. The majority of the parts dealers in my area do not even believe that the car existed. I have checked many books and found very little information on this car. The engine is a 302 cubic-inch V-8 (possibly a "Boss 302") with an automatic transmission. I need to know about any body trim and where I can find parts such as the grille, fenders and rubber grommets? The only identification on the car is the Falcon name inscribed on the dash. A.D., Maryland.

A. Ford introduced the much sleeker, completely restyled Torino in 1970 and offered the Falcon in that body shell. About the only unique trim would be the Falcon script on the rear quarters. The Maverick, introduced midyear 1969, had cut deeply into Falcon sales, This last-year Falcon actually became the base model Torino. As such it is an interesting collector car. For parts help I suggest that you contact the Falcon Club of America, PO Box 113, Jacksonville, Arkansas 72076.

Q. Can a Model B Ford transmission be placed in a Model A Ford? P.A., Massachusetts.

187

A. Davis Antique Auto Parts of San Bernardino, California indicates that this swap can be done. It is necessary to use a brake and clutch pedal adapter. They have installed the Model B and so-called Model C (1933 Ford four-cylinder) transmissions in many Model As using the Model B and Model C four-cylinder engines. If the early shifter tower from a 1932-1934 Model B or early Ford V-8 is used, no emergency brake adapter is needed. All gears in the Model B and early Ford V-8 transmission are the same. The gears from later model Fords can even be used, but the shift tower forks then require reworking. A Model B transmission will bolt to the Model A torque tube, but a Model B type U-joint cover will be needed. The Model A U-joint cover has six bolts. The Model B type has four bolts. If you wish to use "float-a-motor" engine mounts, another adapter must be used. Davis Antique Auto Parts has all these adaptors in stock. Hobbyist Bill McMillan says he has used a Model B transmission in a Model A Ford for about 25 years. In his experience, the big problems are converting the pedals and wishbone. He also notes that the Model B flywheel housing bolts have different spacing.

Q. I own two antique Chevrolets, a 1937 four-door Master Deluxe and a 1948 two-door Aerosedan. Both are in need of new upholstery. I would greatly appreciate any information regarding vendors. Who sells upholstery kits with the material all cut to size that matches the original? L.W., Nebraska.
A. Hampton Coach, 70 High Street, Hampton, New Hampshire 03842 produces Chevrolet upholstery kits. These are patterned from original interiors and use original style fabrics. They are available for virtually all Chevrolets made from 1922 to 1954. If you are patient and careful, you can install these kits yourself. Ford owners are equally fortunate to be able to buy original style, quality interior kits from LeBaron Bonney Company, 6 Chestnut Street, Amesbury, Massachusetts 01913. Later model MoPar owners also have an interior kit source in Legendary Interiors, Box 358, Macedon, New York 14502. I have visited each of these companies and know that each works to the highest standards of originality and customer satisfaction. Legendary Interiors has developed a process for recreating original-style vinyl patterns so its interiors not only match exactly in color, but also in texture.

Q. Ford introduced the Crestline Skyliner Victoria two-door hardtop, along with the Mercury Sun Valley, in 1954. I remember seeing several 1954 Ford Crestline Sunliner convertibles in 1954 that had a tinted plastic insert sewn into the convertible top at the driver's seat area. This insert gave a glass-top effect when the top was up. I never saw this feature on a 1954 Mercury convertible and throughout the years I have seen many 1954 Ford convertibles, but no others with this unique feature. Was it a factory option? If so, was it also available on the 1954 Mercury? W.R., New York.
A. Ford fan Bob Thatcher recalls this factory installed option. "I sold one new," he says. "As I remember, the option was inexpensive, costing between $20 and $30. That year, Ford also offered a dealer-installed option that raised the top in case of rain. I am pretty sure Mercury did not offer the plastic insert for its convertibles." Literature collector Jim Petrik also has memories of this accessory. He saw an orange-colored Ford convertible with the plastic panel in the roof in 1954. At that time, he dismissed it as the work of a whimsical owner. A few years later, he obtained a 1954 Ford brochure showing the three sport models: Hardtop, Skyliner and Sunliner (convertible). The description under the Sunliner read, "An optional top is available with a unique tinted transparent panel over front seat. And, you can have, at extra cost, the new Automatic Rain Guard that puts the top up at the first drop of rain." No mention is made of the cost of the plastic insert. Petrik, also, has never heard of a Mercury convertible with the

plastic roof panel. He doubts that Mercury buyers ever went in for that type of thing. The Automatic Rain Guard is mentioned in the 1955 sales catalog, but no mention is made of a plastic roof panel for convertibles.

Q. I have not been able to find parts interchange information and production figures for the 1971 and 1972 "Heavy Chevy" models. Do you have information on these models? D.D., Illinois.

A. The Heavy Chevy was a somewhat stripped down economy version of the SS-454, which used the Chevelle two-door hardtop body as its base. It featured special mag wheels and an air-induction hood. It could be quickly recognized by large Heavy Chevy nameplates on the front fenders. You'll find that standard Chevelle body parts will interchange with parts for these models. As to information on the performance parts, we recommend that you look at Paul Zazarine and Greg Donahue's newly published book *HOW TO RESTORE YOUR MUSCLE CAR*. It's available from Classic Motorbooks, Route 2, 729 Prospect Avenue, Osceola, Wisconsin 54020. This book provides a detailed restoration guide for 1960s through 1970s muscle cars. The *STANDARD GUIDE TO AMERICAN MUSCLE CARS* has a complete description of the Heavy Chevy option and indicates that the production total is not available. This book is available from Krause Publications, 700 East State Street, Iola, Wisconsin 54990 for $19.95.

Q. I am seeking interior parts for several MoPar products. They include a nice 1955 DeSoto, a 1955 Chrysler New Yorker and a 1964 Plymouth Barracuda. I need some interior material. H.C.M., Alabama.

A. The address of a manufacturer of interior kits for Chrysler product cars of the late 1950s through early 1970s, is Legendary Interiors, Box 358, Macedon, New York 14502. This company has outgrown its facilities in Macedon and is building a new plant in nearby Newark, New York, so their mailing address is likely to change in a few months.

Q. I have a question which I have discussed with a number of people and have yet to arrive at a solution. With all other things being equal, is it better to have a collector car with a standard or automatic transmission? I bought a 1988 Fiero GT with automatic transmission. It broke its pressure plate at 25,000 miles. Never have I experienced such a failure on a standard transmission car, even after 100,000-plus miles. The Fiero looks as though it will become a collectible. I wonder if one is farther ahead with a standard or automatic transmission when it comes to collector value? M.C., Ohio.

A. Since value is always determined ultimately by a buyer's interest in a car, the buyer's preference for a standard or automatic transmission would be the relevant issue here. In the case of a Fiero, which is viewed as a sporty car, a manual transmission might be more desirable. However, I have heard other stories of premature clutch/transmission failure on these cars. This could make buyers wary of the manual transmission. With sports and performance cars, a manual transmission is likely to be a plus. Otherwise the type of transmission will probably have little effect on value, unless we're talking about an odd combination of a manual transmission in an otherwise well-optioned car.

Q. I always set the date for the first all-metal tops on cars at about 1932. Today, while working with old photos at the R.E. Olds Transportation Museum, I found a large photo of three Reos sitting outside the factory. Two were touring cars, but one was a fine-looking coupe. The license plate clearly reads 1915. The roof on this coupe is a solid sheet of metal. The reflection of a window above the car shows all over the roof. Was this a common thing with some of these older models with mostly flat roofs? Is there any information on this? There is no doubt that this car has a one-sheet roof with polished paint, which would have to be over metal. J.D., Michigan.

A. It's my understanding that sedans used fabric inserts in the roofs until the mid-1930s because solid metal roofs would make a drumming noise. The roof on the car in the picture you have sent is curved front to back and somewhat bowed in the center. Presumably, this compound curved shape would prevent drumming. Reo owner Randy Baker says, "I have a 1916 seven-passenger center-door sedan with a solid metal roof. My car's roof is made up in four sections. There are two pieces across the front and back that cover about 10 inches in width and two large pieces, each about 30 inches wide, making up the center section. These pieces are welded together, making a very strong roof. With this style roof, all side windows are glass panels in frames. They can be removed on pleasant days and stored in a compartment which is part of the rear seat. The windows in the doors fold down into a metal safety compartment built into the door. My car has the original paint and striping. It has the big overhead valve six cylinder engine with 16,000 original miles."

Q. I have a question about a 1928 Chrysler business coupe I purchased last year. The serial number is LR630D. I would like to know how many were made, what colors were used, and where I can obtain parts? Parts for 1928 models seem hard to find. J.A., Pennsylvania.

A. The serial number you list indicates that your business coupe is a Series 62 model. Cars in this series were distinguished by the small six-cylinder engine and a higher radiator than Series 52 models. Chrysler production figures for 1928 are only available by series. For all 1928 Chrysler Series 62 models the production total is 64,136. The WPC Club, Box 3504, Kalamazoo, Michigan 49003, should be able to provide you with parts assistance and answer other questions you will have in restoring your car.

Q. I bought a 1941 Ford pickup which had a flatbed body on it at one time. The bed is gone now. Apparently the truck came from the dealer like this. I understand that the 1940 and 1941 Ford trucks had the same size bed. Do the 1946 to 1947 trucks also have the same size flatbed body? Also, what oil should I use in the shocks? W.E.B., Illinois.

A. Ford fan Fred Edeskuty advises that all 1941 Ford trucks were available as a pickup, a flatbed, a chassis and cab, a chassis and windshield or a chassis and cowl. He says the pickup with the longer 122-inch wheelbase was called an express. Since your truck has an eight-foot bed, he assumes that it is either a 3/4- or 1-ton model with a 122-inch wheelbase. The flatbed should have a Ford script stamped on the rear of the platform frame, which would be the same back as far back as 1938. As to dimensions, the 1/2-ton pickup box was 77.7 inches long, 46 inches wide and 17.5 inches tall. The 1/2-ton stake bed measured 80 inches long by 67 inches wide. The 3/4- and 1-ton express body measured 96 inches long by 54 inches wide by 19.7 inches tall. The stake body dimensions were 90 inches long by 74 inches wide. The 3/4- and 1-ton trucks used the big truck front sheet metal with headlights mounted on pods on the fenders, while the 1/2-tons had 1940 Ford passenger car sheet metal. These dimensions were continued through 1947, so if you can find a 1946 or 1947 stake body, it can be used on your truck. Mechanics used to fill Ford lever-action shocks with hydraulic jack oil. The formula on that oil may have changed and you are advised to use the shock oil available from most vintage Ford parts suppliers.

Q. When did the shoulder/lap belt combination first appear on an American automobile? Also, when did shoulder restraints become standard equipment? I love old cars and my only complaint is that they only have lap belts on some models. W.O., Arizona.
A. Volvo, along with Saab, introduced lap belts in the late 1960s. In the United States, Ford first promoted safety restraints (in the form of lap belts) as an extra-cost item on its 1956 models. Ford also promoted safety in its 1956 models by designing a deep-dish steering wheel (to help prevent chest injuries in accidents) and stronger door locks. The safety movement picked up steam in the 1960s, as history buff Greg Nussel recalls, "In 1962, all United States sold automobiles were required to have seat belt anchors. That regulation was augmented in 1964 when the manufacturers were required to provide two front seat belts. In 1966, two rear seat belts were also required. For 1968, a host of additional safety features were required of American-sold cars, including two front shoulder belts, as well as lap belts for each passenger. Most manufacturers opted for completely separate systems and, as such, nobody ever used the clumsy shoulder belts. This regulation resulted in a spaghetti-like tangle of belts; A full-size American car would have five separate buckles (two shoulder buckles and three lap buckles) in the front seat alone. Effective January 1, 1972, cars were required to have "three- point" shoulder/lap belts (front and rear) and a warning light/buzzer for the front seat passengers. Most motorists buckled the front lap belts and buried them in the seats to disable the buzzer. For 1974, autos were required to have inertia reels on the front shoulder belts, as well as the infamous starter inter-lock system, which was mandated despite a public outcry. The inter-locks were easily thwarted by merely unplugging the two sensors located under the seat. The inter-lock was replaced, in 1975, by the current system with a 10-second buzzer/light that goes off when the ignition is started." Cord lover W.R. Osterhoudt, who works as driving examiner in New York, remembers additional early seat belt applications. He recalls, "In 1958 I purchased a new Chevrolet sedan. I do not know if seat belt equipment was available from the factory or not, but mine was ordered from the dealer after delivery. I equipped the car with a driver's side lap belt and a separate shoulder harness. The harness was a two-strap affair which was put on separately. It was quite a contraption. They were available in different colors, too. I removed the harness when I sold the car and still have it. The Chevrolet was traded in on a new 1962 Pontiac station wagon, which I chose to order without belts. I had plans to install a Volvo belt/harness combination which was then on the market. I managed to rig this on the driver's side only and used it for some years. It came only in one rather unattractive color and was rather unattractive in construction."

Q. I am looking for a source of parts for my 1959 Studebaker Lark. Do you know of a club which might be able to direct me to parts sources? R.W., California.
A. The Studebaker Driver's Club, 8330 Moberly Lane, Dallas, Texas 75227 publishes a monthly magazine that is an excellent source of parts information for Studebaker cars and trucks. This publication also contains well-written, well-documented articles on all Studebaker models.

Q. Can you or any of your readers tell me the best way to get the pistons out of a 1957 Chrysler 300 engine without breaking them? The motor has sat in a corner of the garage for the last 25 years. The engine is complete with the dual four-barrel carburetors, but everything is seized or frozen in place. The engine was in running condition when it was put into storage. J.R., New York.
A. I put your question to Pete Alley, one of the automotive rebuilding specialists in the Auto Technology program at Ferris State University in Big Rapids, Michigan. He said

191

you'll have to remove the heads and pan. With the heads off, cut the ridge at the top of the cylinders with a ridge reamer. He also suggests scouring off rust on the cylinders with a fairly coarse grit sandpaper. You'll also need to remove the crankshaft. Pete cautions to be very careful as you remove the crank, so as not to nick the bearing surfaces with the studs from the connecting rods. Since the pistons won't move, you will have to work the crank out of the engine gently and carefully. Next, turn the engine right side up and soak the cylinders with light oil (kerosene or WD-40) for about 48 hours. With that done, turn the engine over, get a piece of 2 x 2 board stock and a 48-ounce hammer. Rap sharply on the bottom of the pistons at the center of the casting over the wrist pin. You'll have to let the connecting rods drop out of the way. Once the pistons start to move, you may work them back and forth by pounding from the top and bottom. Keep soaking the penetrating oil on the cylinders and the pistons should come out without breaking. Be sure to cut the ridge off the top of the cylinders. The pistons will come out the top of the engine.

Q. I would like information on 1971 and 1972 Chevrolet trucks. Did any come with bucket seats and consoles? Could you tell me where I might purchase a book that tells how many of each vehicles were built for a given year? T.C., Texas.

A. According to the second edition of the *STANDARD CATALOG OF AMERICAN LIGHT-DUTY TRUCKS*, Chevrolet C-10 pickup production for model-year 1971 included 7,269 Step-Side and 206,313 Fleetside trucks with eight-foot beds. Bucket seats and a center console were factory options. Bucket seats were installed in three percent of all trucks that this option was offered in (apparently Cheyennes and Blazers). Chevrolet C-10 pickup production for model-year 1972 included 7,538 Step-Side and 273,249 Fleetside trucks with eight-foot beds. In 1972, the percent of qualified trucks fitted with bucket seats climbed slightly to four percent. Once again, we do not know how many trucks had center consoles.

Bucket seats for 1971-1972 Chevy pickups were same used in this 1970 CST/10.

AUTOMOBILIA

Q. Over the past 15 years, I have collected items which were giveaways at the Ford Rotunda building at the "Century of Progress" exposition in Chicago during 1934. Since I own a pair of 1934 Fords, my interest in this automobilia is explainable. Does anyone know the total list of items given away or sold at the exposition? C.J.M., Nebraska.

A. We have seen many of the interesting and very collectible memorabilia items from this Chicago World's Fair on exhibit at the Auburn-Cord-Duesenberg Museum. Thousands of promotional handouts and souvenirs are included in the permanent display, which fills an entire room of the museum's upper level. For more information about the completeness of the collection contact: ACD Museum, PO Box 271, Auburn, Indiana 46706.

Q. I ran across a gearshift knob that is black with a 1-3/8 inch brass inlay. In the center of the brass is a 1933 Ford V-8 grille with the Ford script in large letters through it. The years 1903 and 1933 are on the left and right sides of the grille, respectively. Could you give me some information on this? T.H., Wisconsin.

A. According to Bill Kueher, of Mt. Healthy, Ohio, the inlay in the gearshift knob is a commemorative coin passed out at the introduction of the 1933 Fords. It was Ford's 30th anniversary that year. The opposite side of the coin has a large V-8 insignia with the notation "30 Years of Progress."

Q. Several years ago a gentleman advertised a kit to change a mailbox so that it looked like an old car in *OLD CARS WEEKLY*. I think his company was called Paul's Products. The kit was a good one and I would like to buy another. I have not seen his ads for a long time. Is he still in business? J.N.W., Maryland.

A. A hobbyist inquired about kits to make a rural mailbox look like an old car. Raymond J. Paul is still making these kits, though he has not advertised in any old car publication for years. His main exposure is an occasional flea market spot at a car meet. In the advertisements, he used the name Paul's Products, but he has discontinued this. Four designs are available: A mail truck, a five-window coupe, a town sedan and a deluxe roadster. All are based on the Model A Ford. The antique auto mailbox kits consist of exterior plywood, wood and aluminum, with all parts cut and machined to final shape ready for assembly with glue and nails. The kit mounts on a standard (small) mailbox and requires sanding and painting. Kits and information can be obtained by writing or calling Raymond J. Paul, 402 Fifth Avenue, Lehigh Acres, Florida 33936 (813) 369-6255.

Q. I need to contact a service that restores license plates. Can you refer me to someone doing this work? W.R.A., Ohio.

A. There are several services restoring license plates. Two are Darryl's, 4505 8th Avenue South, Number A10, St. Petersburg, Florida 33711 and A. V. Polio, 746 North Greenbrier, Orange, Connecticut 06477.

Q. I have a light aqua blue transparent glass battery case. It measures 7 x 10 inches high and has raised letters cast into the glass. They spell Delco-Light Exide. Could you tell me its age and if it has any particular value? Also, could it be turned back into a working battery? W.G., Massachusetts.

A. Your Delco-Light Exide battery case was used with home electrical power plants and these were usually installed in rural settings, before rural electrification. The home I grew up in had a power plant of this type in a back annex. My father said it had powered the house in the 1920s. If you follow the instructions above for rejuvenating a battery with EDTA, you may bring the Delco-Light Exide battery back to life.

Q. Can you give me any information as to where I can find a book or magazine on old gas stations? B.F., Texas.
A. Volume 1 and Volume 4 of the *BEST OF OLD CARS* contain articles on old gas pumps and gas stations. T.E. Warth Automotive Books, Lumberyard Shops, Marine on Saint Croix, Minnesota 55047 may have copies available for the collector's market. Volume 4 has several feature stories on this topic, while Volume 1 has a single article. Classic Motorbooks, 729 Prospect Avenue, Osceola, Wisconsin 54020 sells a book titled *THE AMERICAN GAS STATION*, which was authored by Michael Witzel. You might also want to join the International Petroliana Collectors' Association, Drawer 1000, Westerville, Ohio 43081. This group publishes *CHECK THE OIL*, a bimonthly magazine featuring articles on vintage gas stations, oil company history, as well as memorabilia of the early gasoline industry, including gas pumps, road maps and gas station signs.

Q. Where can I find a publication that provides information and photographs of antique and classic automobile emblems (hood and trunk ornaments)? I want to do some research on a collection I have acquired. The majority of the 64-piece collection consists of emblems of American vehicles. Therefore I do not need information on imported makes. M.R.B., Maryland.
A. A recent book which shows and identifies these items is *ANTIQUE AUTOMOTIVE COLLECTIBLES* by Jack Martells published in 1980 by Contemporary Books of Chicago, Illinois. It contains a chapter devoted to auto nameplates and illustrates nearly 360 different American car emblems in full color. Another reference was written and privately printed by Harry Pulfer about 1968. It was titled *A MANUAL FOR OLD CAR RESTORERS AND COLLECTORS: THE AUTO NAMEPLATE COLLECTOR* and contained about 100 unnumbered pages. As originally published, the compendium cost $1. However, only about 200 copies were ever distributed. Finding one may be difficult. Automotive historian Karl S. Zahm, 4520 Edgewood Hills Drive, Rockford, Illinois 61108 may also be of assistance in identifying emblem and nameplate acquisitions. Zahm maintains a large file to help identify unusual and rare pieces. Hobbyists Von Patterson and Robert Kaiser suggest obtaining a copy of *CAR BADGES OF THE WORLD* by Tim Nicholson. It was published by American Heritage Press. Collector Ray Beardslee refers emblem collectors to a book titled *ACCESSORY MASCOTS: THE AUTOMOTIVE ACCENTS OF YESTERYEAR 1910-1940*, authored by Dan Smith. Copies of this book are available from 438 Camino Del Rio South, Suite 213, San Diego, California 92108.

Q. I am looking to purchase old car puzzles and have never found any advertised in *OLD CARS* or any other publications. Do you know of anyone who makes old car puzzles? G.P.S., Minnesota.
A. Our neighbors enjoy working puzzles which they often frame when finished. Their completed puzzles contain several showing old cars. They bought them at hobby shops, so puzzles featuring old cars are available. Years ago, *OLD CARS* actually produced and sold a puzzle picturing a rare Duesenberg. Unfortunately, sales at the time did not warrant producing additional puzzles. You may, however, stumble across one

of these at a swap meet or flea market or find one through a classified want-ad in hobby publications.

Q. Besides owning three 1950s cars, I build model cars. At one time, a book was published on professional cars of all decades. How can I locate a copy? Any leads would be helpful. I know the Indianapolis Motor Speedway has a "Hall of Fame" museum. Do they sell research material or is there a book they sell with photos of all the winning Indy cars? Do you have the address where I can write to them? J.M., New York.
A. *AMERICAN FUNERAL CARS AND AMBULANCES SINCE 1900* by Thomas A. MacPherson was published by Crestline Publishing, which is now owned by Classic Motorbooks, PO Box 1, 729 Prospect Avenue, Osceola, Wisconsin 54020. If it is no longer available, you may find a copy through used-book supplier T.E. Warth, Lumberyard Shops, Marine on Saint Croix, Minnesota 55047. The Indianapolis Motor Speedway Corporation's museum address is Indianapolis Motor Speedway and Hall of Fame Museum, 4790 West 16th Street, Speedway, Indiana 46224. Their phone number is (317) 241-2501. They have a regular photographic print service and even take credit card orders by phone. We recently purchased four rare photos from them to use in our new *WEIRD CARS* book. The cost came to a bit over $25. That seemed like quite a bargain and they have thousands of photos available.

Q. While vacationing in Hawaii, I ran across two 1937 license plates. Both were blue over beige. They were identical, except that one said Hawaii and the other Maui. How did the Hawaiian Islands issue license plates back then? If the Maui plate was from Maui, was the Hawaii plate from the big island or could it have been a common plate for all Hawaiian Islands? Additionally, were there specific plates for the other islands of Oahu, Kauai, Molokai and Lanai as well? T.P., Texas.
A. Collector Roy Ruud informs us that automobiles were first registered in Hawaii in 1906. No plates were issued until 1914. The first plates were made from porcelain enameled iron. In 1917, Hawaii's license plates were changed to embossed metal. The chief issuing office was in Honolulu and these plates carried the abbreviation "Hon." The first plate to carry the name Hawaii was in 1922. Plates were issued annually until World War II. The 1942 plate was used until 1946. It was validated annually by means of a windshield sticker. From 1922 to 1950 the first numeral denoted the county. Later, an alphabetic prefix indicating the county was adopted. Aloha first appeared on Hawaii plates in 1957. The current plate design was adopted in 1981. Hobbyist Jerry Boone recommends the book *REGISTRATION PLATES OF THE WORLD 2* by John Weeks, Reg Wilson and Neil Parker. For those interested in license plate lore, this book is available from John Weeks, 14 Manor Road, Chedzoy, Bridgewater, Somerset, England.

Q. At a tag sale, I purchased a Thermador Car Cooler. It looks to be a hanging window unit that seems to redirect outside air to the inside of a car. I'm not sure exactly what it's supposed to do. There is no electrical hook up, which might feed a fan. I have no literature. The person who sold it to me had no idea what it was. Can you or any of your readers help identify it? When would it have been used? Is it an aftermarket item or specific to a particular automobile? I thought I've seen one, or something like it, displayed in the past on a 1940 or 1941 Chrysler. J.G., Connecticut.
A. If your Thermador Car Cooler is what I'm thinking it is, it's an early form of air conditioner. In the 1930s and 1940s, several aftermarket companies sold devices that could be hung in open car windows. These coolers were filled with water. While the car traveled along, air blowing through the device evaporated some of the water. This

cooled the air in the process (remember from your high school chemistry that evaporation causes cooling). I have no idea how effective the coolers were. Often, they were manufacturer-approved accessories. They are listed in some of the facts books issued to new-car salesmen in the early 1950s. I've seen them advertised as more of a novelty accessory than a working device. Prices are usually in the $10 to $20 range.

Q. Tom McCahill, who wrote for *MECHANIX ILLUSTRATED*, was one of the greatest auto writers of the 1950s. Whatever became of old Tom? I suppose he has passed on by now, but I never remember hearing anything about him dying. B.C., Montana.

A. Tom McCahill died of a heart attack in May 1975. I remember reading of his death in *TIME* magazine. I was quite shocked not to see mention of the lovable writer's passing in *MECHANIX ILLUSTRATED*, which continued to publish his "Mail for McCahill" column and his road tests for several months after his death. Presumably, they used material that he had written before his untimely demise. Tom McCahill's writing meant a lot to *MECHANIX ILLUSTRATED* readers. I expected to see a significant eulogy acknowledging his contributions to automotive journalism and to the magazine's popularity during the nearly 30 years it published McCahill's road tests. Fortunately, a fine eulogy and fitting tribute titled "The True Tale of Uncle Tom McCahill: America's Road Tester Nonpareil," was written by automotive historian Richard Langworth. It was published in the first quarter 1976 issue of *AUTOMOBILE QUARTERLY*.

Mullins trailer rolls behind a Model A Ford.

Q. Who made the Mullins trailer of the 1930s? How many were made? What were they used for? How many were made with cream tanks? L.P., Wisconsin.

A. The Red Cap utility trailer was a depression baby that Mullins introduced with its fingers crossed in 1936. It was the only fully-engineered, all-steel, two-wheel auto trailer on the market. It had just about everything the tourist, salesman, sportsman or farmer could ask for. It was small and compact with sleeping accommodations and had a load limit of 1,200 pounds. It sold for only $119.50 f.o.b. Salem, Ohio. Hobbyist Ted Hirt recalls that the little trailers were made in Warren, Ohio by the Mullins Manufacturing Company of Warren and Salem, Ohio. Mullins was most famous for the "Youngstown Kitchen," which consisted of an all-steel kitchen including dishwasher and sink. A piece of literature Hirt sent pictures a Mullins Red Cap Trailer with its lid raised and tailgate lowered holding two golf bags and several sets of luggage. The trailer was in demand but the merchandising cost was so high that Mullins discontinued production after two years. Jerry Bengel, the owner of a Mullins that he restored in 1967 (his third) adds that the locks that latch and lock the top of the trailers are from 1935 to 1936 Ford touring sedans. Bengel sent a copy of a Mullins advertisement and an article on the Mullins Red Cap trailer that appeared in the January 1983 issue of *STREET RODDER* magazine. The ad states that a Mullins trailer is "...as important to the automobile as a baggage car is to the Pullman." It also suggests that the trailer be made into a rolling billboard for the owner's company, service or product. Ray Beardslee advised us of a Mullins trailer club which operated from 1981 to 1985. During that period, the club published a quarterly newsletter. It covered factory specifications, pictures, owner information and supply sources.

Q. I am doing research on World War II motor vehicle use stickers and ration stickers. What can you tell me about them? Do any old car hobbyists own vehicles that still have them on the windshield or in the glove box? F.L.B., Florida.

A. According to hobbyist Cliff Larson, the gas rationing coupons came in three types. The "A" stickers were available to the majority of motorists who continued to drive on the homefront. They were good for four gallons of gas per coupon per week. The "B" stickers were issued for those who needed more gas to get to work in jobs unrelated to the war effort. Allocations were determined by the mileage to and from a person's place of employment. Defense workers received "C" coupons. There were other categories, such as farmers, who received more gas to operate machinery. Each coupon, regardless of series, was worth four gallons of fuel. They had to be renewed every three months. Each county had a rationing board. Holders of "A" stickers received stickers automatically. Those who qualified for the other types had to follow the three-month renewal procedure. A figure of 15 miles per gallon was used as the basis for determining allocations. Larson has original "A" stickers on the front and rear passenger windows of his 1942 Lincoln Continental Mark I. We have seen other cars with stickers at car shows, though some of the stickers might be modern reproductions. A recent article in the *CALIFORNIA HIGHWAY PATROLMAN* magazine discussed that state's 35 miles per hour wartime speed limit, which was intended to promote fuel conservation. Tires were another item that rationing applied to and motorists of the era sometimes mounted older wood spoke wheels on cars when tires were not available. In February 1993 the Manitowoc Maritime Museum in Manitowoc, Wisconsin opened a two-year exhibit about life on the homefront during World War II. It focuses on rationing and other ways Americans conserved material for the war effort. A 1936 Pontiac is included as an example of a typical car driven during the war years. The museum is located at 75 Maritime Drive, Manitowoc, Wisconsin 54220. Their phone number is (414) 684-0218.

Q. What kind of a car is shown on the reverse side of a $10 bill? While browsing through a trivia book, I read that it is a 1926 Hupmobile. True or false? J.J., Pennsylvania.

A. It may be true that the trivia book identified the "money-mobile" as a Hupmobile, but according to Bob Lemke, who edited Krause Publication's monthly tabloid *BANK-NOTE REPORTER*, no particular year, make or model of car is depicted on the back of the U.S. $10 bill. The car shown is an artist's rendition of a typical 1920s style sedan. Somewhere along the line, the story that it is a 1926 Hupmobile was widely publicized and this speculation has been perpetuated by others referring to the same source or secondary references based on the first source. However, it is purely speculation.

Q. As a teen-ager some 50 years ago, I remember riding in a friend's low-slung, two-seat, battery-powered Red Bug. A few months ago I ran across this name in a list of "American Firsts." Can you tell me something of the history of the Red Bug? Are there still any existing? I would love to see one again, if only in picture form. T.W.J., Pennsylvania.

A. The vehicle you remember was an Auto Red Bug. There's a thorough history and photo of this buckboard-like vehicle in our *STANDARD CATALOG OF AMERICAN CARS 1805-1942*. The vehicle had several names from 1916 to about 1928. The original builder, A.O. Smith Company of Milwaukee, Wisconsin used the name Smith Flyer. This version had a gas engine driving a fifth wheel called a Smith Motor Wheel. In 1919, Smith was purchased by Briggs & Stratton. They continued building Red Bugs. Some were powered by a Briggs Motor Wheel and others by a 12-volt electric motor of the type used to start Dodge cars of the period. In 1928, Briggs parent company, Automotive Standards, Incorporated, set up a subsidiary to develop the Red Bug for amusement park use. Then, in 1930, Automotive Standards contracted with the Indian Motorcycle Company to build Red Bugs on a cost-plus basis. In May of that year, Indian was sold and no records exist to show that any Red Bugs were built thereafter. If you want to see a Red Bug in the flesh you should attend the AACA (Antique Automobile Club of America) Fall Meet in Hershey, Pennsylvania. Every year there seems to be at least one Red Bug on display. Car buff Peter Wild adds that he recently had the pleasure of viewing a Red Bug at Jekyll Island, Georgia. At one time Jekyll Island was owned by a group of wealthy people including members of the Vanderbilt family. They had a number of these Red Bugs for themselves and guests to use around the island, since no autos were allowed. In the mid-1950s, the state of Georgia bought the island and all the Red Bugs were sold. The Red Bug that Wild saw is on loan to the museum there. It is displayed along with lots of photos and history of the vehicle. The tag states that this Red Bug is a replica, but it looks like an original.

Q. I have a radiator shell from an old car which is missing the emblem. The emblem is shaped like a Phillips 66 insignia. Its measurements are three inches by two inches. Can anyone identify the emblem that belongs on this radiator shell? C.K., Minnesota.

A. Hobbyist Robert Frissore advises that an emblem such as you describe was found on the Liberty car. Only about 260 of these vehicles were built from 1920 to 1921. The emblem's colors are blue over white with red on the bottom.

Q. As I was watching the movie "Driving Miss Daisy" I noticed an obvious error in the beginning of the film. When Miss Daisy backed out her 1948 Chrysler in the opening scene, she reached down and started it with a key starter. Also, when the camera panned over the front of the car's interior, it showed a padded dash. Correct me if I am wrong, but weren't the key starter and padded dash introduced in 1949 as altogether new features? Why do you think they filmed her in a 1949 Chrysler? Why not use the 1948 model she was driving? J.V.P., Ohio.

A. Our next *QUESTIONS & ANSWERS* book may need a movie trivia section! I drove a 1948 Chrysler for a couple of years in high school and remember that it had a push-button starter. Though I also saw and enjoyed "Driving Miss Daisy," I missed the key-start scene at the beginning of the movie. Perhaps film makers think that an old car is an old car and it doesn't make any difference if they film close-up interior scenes in one vehicle and exterior scenes in another. "Driving Miss Daisy" also used two different year Cadillacs for road scenes that were supposed to occur in one car. Chrysler restoration parts supplier George Taylor notes that a 1948 C-39 New Yorker sedan was pictured in the opening scene of the movie, but says the interior shot showed a 1949 Chrysler being started. Taylor suggested a reason for the change. "The 1948 Chrysler has a key to the right of the steering column and a starter button on the left side of the dash," he pointed. "Filming the starting of a 1948 Chrysler presents problems; the steering column is in the way and camera angle becomes quite complex. By the early 1950s all car makers had abandoned the push-button start in favor of the ignition key start. This means the majority of movie goers who saw Miss Daisy have never seen a car started with a push-button. Showing a push-button start would create viewer confusion that might detract from the moment. The 1949 Chrysler had both a key start and a key located at the lower left of the dash. Filming the starting of a 1949 Chrysler provided both excellent camera angle and a normal start-up."

Q. Is there an organization of collectors who specialize in the nameplates and emblems that were on the radiator shells of automobiles built between the early 1900s and the 1930s? Back in the 1930s I put together a collection of nameplates when it was easy to find them in wrecking yards. World War II and the demand for scrap metals cleaned out most of the cars of the pre-1935 era. L.O.L., Wisconsin.

A. Our club listing does not show an organization for collectors of nameplates, emblems and related automobilia. However, this is a popular branch of the old car hobby and we're sure that the collectors of badges and nameplates "network" between themselves. You might be able to contact them through Pulfer & Williams, Forest Road, PO Box 67, Hancock, New Hampshire 03449; telephone (603) 525-3532. This company specializes in radiator emblems, nameplates and hood mascots.

Q. I have really enjoyed my copy of the *STANDARD CATALOG OF AMERICAN LIGHT-DUTY TRUCKS* and have been looking for its companion volumes on automobiles. Unfortunately, I have been unable to find these books in any local bookstore. The stores I contacted do not show them available by special order. How do I order these books? R.M., Oklahoma.

A. I'd like to expand this question somewhat to include automotive books in general, since I receive letters and phone calls asking where to locate books mentioned in this column. When you have a title you want to order, you can ask a book store (independent stores are sometimes more helpful in this than chain stores) to look the book up in *BOOKS IN PRINT*. This reference book will tell you if the book is still being published. It will list the publisher and the book's order number. A helpful local book store can then special order the book. Another alternative is to contact one of the large automotive book distributors such as Motorbooks International, PO Box 1, Osceola, Wisconsin 54020. They will send you an automotive books catalog. You can order practically any car book currently available from their catalog. If the book you are seeking is out of print, you will need to go to a second hand bookstore and ask if they will keep an eye out for the book. Many of these stores subscribe to publications that list out-of-print books and you may find the book you are seeking through this approach. T.E. Warth of Marine on Saint Croix, Minnesota specializes in out-of-print automotive books. His full address is located elsewhere in this book.

Q. I need information on where to buy an Oldsmobile "demo" stereo tape. We have a 1981 Oldsmobile Toronado with a great stereo system and the demo tape is missing. The tape had Leo Sayer singing "I love you more than I can say" on it, , among other songs. This particular cut is no longer available in stores or at "Olds" dealers. K.J., Missouri.
A. Like many items related to older cars, this is one that you may look for a long time, or may just turn up. I suggest you start by contacting old car literature and parts dealers. By the way, one such dealer is Robert A. Olds, 364 Vinewood Avenue, Tallmadge, Ohio 44278. Swap meets are another possible source of the demo tape you are seeking. (Editor's note: Later, an Oldsmobile buff named Steve Wright responded to this inquiry and offered an Oldsmobile demo stereo tape to the hobbyist who asked this question.)

Q. On "Jeopardy" a few weeks ago they asked the question, what car had the Flying Lady hood ornament? Their answer was the Rolls-Royce. I always thought it was the Cadillac. Can you tell me which is right? W.W., Texas.
A. The Rolls-Royce hood ornament is called the Flying Lady. However, the sculpture on which the ornament is based is called the Spirit of Ecstasy. Cadillac did use a winged woman for its hood ornament, but the Flying Lady belongs to Rolls Royce.

Q. I recently acquired two owner's manuals. Can you can identify the years of the cars they are for? Unless I am missing something, I can't find a year in either one. The first is for a Pontiac six. It lists the car's engine as a 186 cubic-inch six with a 3-1/4 by 3-3/4 inch bore and stroke. The wheelbase of this car is 110 inches and the tire size is 29 x 4.75. The second manual is for a Chandler Royal Eighty-Five. This car has a 340 cubic-inch straight eight with a bore and stroke of 3-3/8 by 4-3/4 inches. The wheelbase is 124 inches and the tire size is 32 x 6.00. I hope this gives you enough information to date these manuals. Also, I have the March 8, 1948 issue of LIFE magazine which contains a Tucker advertisement. Was this their only magazine ad? B.S., Florida.
A. The Pontiac manual is for a 1926 or 1927 model. The engine, wheelbase and tire size is the same for both these years. The Pontiac Oakland Club International, 286 Ahmu Terrace, Vista, California 92084 probably has a member who is looking for one of these manuals. The Chandler Royal Eighty-Five was built in 1929, the company's last year. For Chandler advice, you might try Roger Anderson, 7053 27th Avenue Northwest, Seattle, Washington 98117. Even though the Tucker venture was short lived, I don't believe the company's promotion was limited to this one ad. Certainly, the Tucker Club of America, 311 West 18th Street, Tifton, Georgia 31794 would know about any other rare ads for the 1948 Torpedo.

Q. I am an old car nut and member of the Kaiser-Frazer Club. I am interested in opening an automotive memorabilia store selling model cars, books, tapes and anything about old cars. I need information to contact wholesale suppliers. R.T., Kentucky.
A. My suggestion is that you contact the manufacturers directly. You will find that publishers like Classic Motorbooks, model makers like Ertl and other producers of old car hobby products have their own arrangements for working with retail outlets such as your proposed memorabilia store. A source book listing hobby suppliers is the *VINTAGE AUTO ALMANAC*, PO Box 945, Bennington, Vermont 05201.

Q. Twenty or so years ago, I found a bronze medallion on a sand ridge about eight miles south of Fort Pierce, Florida. The medallion has the face of an Indian with braids, cap and feathers. Under this face is the name Pathfinder. Below this appears Indianapolis. Also on the medallion are two old cars and a covered wagon. Can you give me any background on this piece and its approximate value? I.F., Florida.

A. What you have found appears to be the radiator emblem for a Pathfinder automobile, built in Indianapolis, Indiana between 1912 and 1917. The Pathfinder was a quality automobile that acquired a reputation for reliability, but sold to only a small clientele. In 1916, a 12-cylinder model called "Pathfinder the Great, King of Twelves" was introduced. This hyperbole failed to save the company from the auction block. Auto memorabilia like your Pathfinder medallion does have particular value to old car emblem collectors. Its overall condition and the buyer's desire to add this specific emblem to a collection would determine its actual value.

Q. I have a Hubley Kiddie Toy, model 509, which appears to be a 1953 or 1954 Corvette. It is made of die-cast metal and is approximately 13 inches long by five inches wide. I would like to know what year the toy was made and how much it is worth? J.M., Arizona.

A. The toy is a 1954 Hubley Corvette. It is worth between $100 and $200 and up in good to excellent condition. To keep track of such things, write for a free sample copy of *TOY SHOP* magazine. It's available from: Krause Publications, 700 East State Street, Iola, Wisconsin 54990.

Q. Can you tell me something about Ford charcoal grilles? Were they made by the car company? M.G., Michigan.

A. Ford buff Richard Grace says the Ford grille was indeed a Ford product. Not only the grille, but Ford sold charcoal, too. The charcoal was a by-product of Ford's Iron Mountain, Michigan lumber operations, which produced 55 tons of charcoal briquets daily. Beginning in the mid-1930s, Ford dealers sold charcoal for 25-cents per five-pound bag. Grilles were $2 for the standard model or $3 for the deluxe version. Ford's Iron Mountain charcoal facility closed down in June of 1946. Roger Chase adds, "Henry Ford was very frugal and was concerned about what to do with waste wood from woody wagon production at the Iron Mountain plant. His solution was to make charcoal from it and pack it in a box along with a small charcoal grille. These grilles were then sent to each Ford dealer, in large quantities, to sell. This, of course, was mandated. The dealers had no choice. Today the grilles and charcoal are rare and valuable collector items." Hobbyist Jim Nelson worked as a salesman for a Ford, Mercury and Lincoln dealer for 35 years. He says, "We sold lots of Ford charcoal and small grilles. Ford also manufactured sulfate of ammonia fertilizer, which was sold through Ford dealers. These items were more or less forced on the dealer to sell it or else!" Gerald Tobin supplied a few more details. "Dealers also sold a 78-pound stationary backyard grille," he recalls. "The purpose of all of this was to eliminate waste, which Henry Ford hated." Steve Sturim reports that though these grilles were once plentiful, he recalls seeing only one at the 1989 AACA Fall Meet in Hershey, Pennsylvania. Ford lover John J. Brown notes that Ford contracted with a company in Eden, New York to build the camping grilles stamped with the Ford logo. With the purchase of a grille came an introductory bag of charcoal. Restorer Dick Felger adds, "The charcoal production started in 1920, using a process dreamed up by Henry Ford's friend Thomas Edison. Ford named E.G. Kingsford manager of the charcoal plant." (Kingsford brand charcoal is still sold today). Finally, C.E. Thomas observes, "Today, it seems everyone has a grille of some kind in their backyard; perhaps even more than one, but grilling or barbecuing wasn't all that popular back then. The Ford dealer may have had trouble disposing of his shipments of charcoal."

Q. Can you provide any information about books on Canadian-built old cars? J.B.

A. Automotive historian Herman Sass, who lives near the Canadian border, says that he knows of two books that might be of interest to you. One is titled *CARS OF CANADA* and the other is *CANADIAN CARS 1946-84*. The first is a large coffee table book that is out of print. Copies might be available in libraries or available from out of print book sellers. Canadian Cars is available through Classic Motorbooks.

Q. Can you tell me where I can find the manufacturer for the globes for the old gas pump reproductions and who is making the old gas pumps in kits? J.S., Illinois.

A. The gas pump globes are available from several suppliers. Benkin Pump Company, 3488 Stop 8 Road, Dayton, Ohio 45414 is reproducing the early style gas pumps. Your best source of information on the items you are seeking is the International Petroliana Collectors' Association (IPCA), Drawer 1000, Westerville, Ohio 43081. This group, whose interests are similar to yours, publishes a bi-monthly magazine on petroleum industry products.

Look for vendors selling gas globes at swap meets.

Q. I have most of the issues of *THE CLASSIC CAR* magazine, including the first issue. There are 58 issues in total. All are in like-new condition. I have no idea of the value of this collection. I was wondering if you have any records that would serve as a guide? K.K., Missouri.

A. It is very difficult to attach a value to your magazine collection. If you sell to an automotive literature vendor, you may only be offered a few dollars per issue. On the other hand, a collector who is looking for a set of this magazine may pay as much as $5 (or more) per issue. Another consideration would be to donate the set to a non-profit car club, library, school or auto museum. You could then take a tax deduction for a charitable gift. If you are interested in putting the magazine collection in a library where they could be accessible to automotive researchers, you might contact The Timme Library at Ferris State University in Big Rapids, Michigan. This library is building a collection of automotive periodicals for research purposes.

Q. I am turning to you out of desperation. I went through the local library looking for a source of information. I was referred to you. I am an art teacher who sometimes gets involved in making "shadow boxes" with my advanced class. I have a senior who has a watch fob, photograph and old canceled check his grandfather gave for a Twin City motor truck. Do you have any information on this truck? R.H., Iowa.
A. As the name suggests, Twin City trucks were built in Minneapolis, Minnesota. They were made between 1917 and 1922. Two companies used the Twin City name. One started in 1917 and ceased production in 1922. Another began in 1918 and became the Minneapolis-Moline tractor company. The earlier company had factories in both Minneapolis and St. Paul. It built trucks of four-wheel drive configuration. The other Twin City trucks were conventional two-wheel drives. They were built in 2- and 3-1/2 ton models

Q. I would like any and all information on your old *OLD CARS* beer cans. I recently saw one of the Iola '90 cans. How many years has *OLD CARS* issued this can and are any still available through you or any other source? I collect beer cans and old cars and just found out about the cans issued for your show. G.K., New Jersey.
A. The beer cans sold at the Iola Old Car Show are not produced by Krause Publications, but by a local brewery. Iola Old Car Show, Incorporated, a community charitable organization, produces the annual show and oversees creation of the beer can design. The design is generally tied into the show theme, as established by the Wisconsin Chapter of the Society of Automotive Historians. A local retailer named "Grandpa's Still" sells past beer cans to collectors. They can be reached at 111 North Main Street, Iola, Wisconsin 54945 or by calling (715) 445-3707. If you attend the Iola Old Car Show, you will also find "back issues" of the *OLD CARS* beer cans available from numerous vendors.

Q. I have an old all-metal model of the 1951 MG-TD. It is red in color. It weighs four pounds and is 15-1/2 inches long by six inches wide and 5-1/2 inches tall. The windscreen is broken. It has rubber tires with Doepke and Model written on them. The front wheels steer by the removable steering wheel and the rear suspension really works. Embossed on the body behind the seat is "Model Toys Rossmoyne, Ohio, USA." Missing from the toy are the spare wheel and left front bumper guard. Can you supply me with any information about the model and the company that made it? How many were made? How much did they cost? What is the current value of one? Is it a rare toy? Could you supply me with the address of a model toy club so I can get parts and join the club. It is a nice car as is and will be a beautiful model when restored. M.B., New Jersey
A. Although not particularly rare, this very accurate MG-TD model was selling in the $100-$350 range (depending on condition). For the latest price updates, you may want to check *TOY COLLECTOR & PRICE GUIDE* magazine, published by Krause Publications, 700 East State Street, Iola, Wisconsin 54990. This hobby publisher is currently compiling a 600-page price guide that will be titled *TOYS & PRICES*. It will be available by the time you read this. A Jaguar XK-120, equally well detailed, was also built in this series of toys. Some parts for this model are available. You might want to join

the Northland Model Car Club, c/o Ben Larson, 8 Northgate Drive Albany New York 12203 or The Model Car Collectors Association, 5113 Sugar Loaf Drive, Roanoke, Virginia 24018. As with any club, send a self-addressed, stamped envelope to get up-to-date membership and activities information.

Series of metal toy cars included MG (left) and Jaguar (right).

Q. I have enclosed pictures of an antique toy car which belongs to my father. It is all-metal with metal wheels. It is about 18 inches long and approximately eight inches tall. Can you tell me any history or information concerning this toy and its approximate value? P.A., New York.
A. The toy is a sleek yellow roadster with a spare mounted on the back deck. The radiator, which appears to be painted brown, has Reo on the top. A metal roadster top with slanted oval side windows covers the driver and passenger seat. Toy collector Greg Wolf advises that Scheible friction cars were manufactured in Ohio during the early 1920s. Your toy is constructed of heavy tinplate. It has a large cast iron flywheel-type friction mechanism or a series of steel discs fastened together to make a flywheel. (Wolf has seen both types.) The toy came as both a roadster and a sedan. Yours has the original slip-over tires. These are very fragile. If this toy was played with on a hard surface, with heavy pressure applied to operate the friction motor, the steel wheels wore through the tires in no time. Antique toy buff Rick Ralston adds that this "Hill Climber" was sold by Schieble in the mid-1920s and that yours has been repainted. Finally, Harry Rosenblum sent a copy of the fall *1924 SEARS CATALOG* (courtesy of Neil McElwee of *McELWEE'S SMALL MOTOR NEWS*, 40 Fornot Lane, Pittsburgh, Pennsylvania 15212). It shows the Hill Climber painted green and orange. He says that earlier Hill Climbers and Daytons (another trade name of Scheible Toy Company) had steel wheels without rubber tires. The current retail value of this toy is approximately $75 to $250. Check the question immediately above for some sources of information that you may be interested in.

Q. Enclosed please find a photo of a hood ornament in our possession. We would appreciate the following information about this ornament: Where was it made? Who made it? What cars did it go on? How much is it worth? Does it have a name? We have tried several times to get information on this lovely hood ornament and always come to a dead end. W.L. and S.L., New York.
A. The ornament in the photo is a woman's head with the hair streaking back in a point. It appears to be made of crystal, rather than metal. It has a threaded base. The most

famous of crystal ornaments were made by Rene Lalique in France. In fact, Lalique styled a radiator ornament of a woman's head with flowing hair which was called Victorie ... Spirit of the Wind. Lalique's ornaments, however, did not have a threaded base. We believe that the ornament you have was made by Corning Glass in 1920. Two women's head hood ornaments were produced by this company. One had the head level. The other had the head tilted up. They were called Mother and Daughter. Naturally, the Mother ornament was the more "level-headed" one. The Corning ornaments featured a threaded base.

Q. I read your *OLD CARS* newspaper "Q & A" column with great interest and am usually amazed at your ability as a mystery solver. I have a mystery that has been sitting on a shelf in my home. I found it while helping to clean out an old shop some 30 years ago. It is a watch similar to a pocket watch, but designed to mount through the hole in a rear view mirror. The watch is an eight-day wind-up model with a decorative face. Written on the face near the top are the words, "Sandoz-Vuille 8 days." Near the bottom it reads, "Swiss made." Judging from the quality of this watch, it must have been the focal point of an expensive automobile. Can you identify the automobile it came from? What would be its value? D.E., Minnesota.
A. Clock mirrors were quite common on cars of the 1930s. My first car, a 1930 Model A roadster, had a rear view mirror with an eight-day clock. The clock in my Ford was a common make, Waltham, I believe. It was optional in the Model A. According to the *LESTER-STEELE HANDBOOK*, only a handful of other firms supplied American automakers of the 1930s with standard equipment clocks. They included Borg, Jaeger, Waltham, Sterling and New Haven. Instrument Services, Incorporated (ISI), 433 South Arch Street, Janesville, Wisconsin 53545 repairs all types of car clocks from wind-ups to modern quartz models. According to Frank Nocifora of ISI, there was one American car built in the 1930s that used a Sandoz-Vuille clock. It was the 1932 Buick. We would guess your clock was used on that vehicle. It should be of value to a Buick fan or an automobilia collector. I would estimate it to be worth $100-plus.

Q. I am writing to request help in finding an old book. In the late 1950s and through the mid-1960s, *POPULAR SCIENCE* magazine had a monthly column called "Model Garage." It was written by Martin Bunn. It was about automotive problems and how to solve them. Gus Wilson was the fictitious mechanic who could solve about any problem. There articles were eventually put into book form and published. I learned a great deal from these informative and entertaining articles and would like to find the book. I have written *POPULAR SCIENCE*. While they remembered the book, they could not help get me a copy as they did not have one. Can you help? H.U., Washington.
A. We remember the entertaining and informative stories of Gus Wilson's success solving the seemingly unsolvable. According to old car lover Kirk Tork, there were two such books published over the years. The early one was a paperback volume titled *GUS WILSON'S MODEL GARAGE*. It was published in 1963 by Berkly Medallion Books and copyrighted by Berkly Publishing Corporation of New York City. The book originally cost 40 cents. It contained 160 pages reprinting 25 stories originally published between 1952 and 1962. The stock number was Y722. It was of normal paperback size and had no illustrations. According to car lover Christopher Foster, this book does not contain all the Model Garage stories, since during the 10-year period, there were probably over 100 that appeared in *POPULAR SCIENCE*. Foster even has some 1946 issues of the magazine. In these, a younger Gus has a partner named Joe Clark, character Stan Hicks is more errand boy than grease monkey, and character Silas Barnstable is hardly more than middle-aged (though no less stingy). *POPULAR SCIENCE*

published the second book, which was copyrighted in 1972. It has 47 stories and 192 pages. This book was offered by *POPULAR SCIENCE* through mail order only. The cost was around $2.95. This book was the same size as the magazine. It reproduced the stories almost exactly as they were first published, complete with the original illustrations. Its title was *TALES OF A MASTER MECHANIC*. For some reason, Gus was dropped shortly after the second book was published. Tork has both books in his library. The first he found at a swap meet and the second he ordered from *POPULAR SCIENCE*. If you will go to a used and rare book store, you will find that such shops subscribe to a listing of out-of-print books. You can add your request to that listing for a nominal fee (it was $1 the last time we used this service). If a shop has the books and sees your request on the list, they will sell them by mail. Sometimes such a search takes persistence. The other option is to make the rounds of used book stores. Check their stock and ask the clerks to keep an eye out for the book you want.

Q. I have 13 *OLD CARS WEEKLY* calendars from 1966 to 1978. They are in mint condition. Do you ever get a call for back issues? Most are in the envelopes they were sent in. G.P., Maryland.

A. As far as we know, the first *OLD CARS* calendar was done in 1976 and featured artwork of older automobiles. From 1977 to 1993, the calendars featured photos of cars and trucks in a comb-bound format. The latest calendar, for 1994, has been upgraded to a stitched binding and highlights the cars of the 1950s. About 75,000 calendars are printed annually. Most of them are given away as a free premium to people who start, renew or extend a subscription to *OLD CARS* newspaper between September and December each year. Remainders are sold individually. With such a large production run each year, the old calendars can't exactly be rare, though particular editions (early ones or extremely popular ones) may be hard to obtain. We know that there are subscribers who collect the calendars. We have no idea what they are worth. If you wish to sell the calendars, you could place an ad in our classified advertising section or display them at a car show flea market.

Q. I have several old automobile hubcaps. I don't know what vehicles they came from. If I send pictures, do you know anyone who could identify them? A.S., Wisconsin.

A. Hollander Publishing Company, Incorporated, PO Box 9405, Minneapolis, Minnesota 55440 has been publishing guides to hubcaps for many years. The current edition goes quite a ways back in its coverage of designs for different postwar model years. The House of Hubcaps, 20034 Pacific Highway South, Seattle, Washington 98198 may also be able to help you. As for prewar hubcaps, you could send photos of them to the Society of Automobile Historians, c/o the Automotive History Collection, Detroit Public Library, 5201 Woodward Avenue, Detroit, Michigan 48202 for possible publication in the Society's *AUTOMOTIVE HISTORY REVIEW* magazine.

Q. Recently, while going through some of my grandmother's old phonograph records, I came across a couple that caught my eye. They are early 78 rpm records and the musicians were Henry Ford's Old Time Dance Orchestra. Is this the same Henry Ford of automobile fame? If so, do the records have any value as automotive-related collectibles? D.W., Wisconsin.

A. Yes, this is the same Henry Ford. Part of what makes Henry Ford such an interesting and legendary character are the many contrasts in his personality and interests. He was fondly attracted to a quieter, slower America that his mass-produced car swept into the dust bin of history. Henry Ford's Old Time Dance Orchestra performed a popular radio show for many years. The records may have some interest to collectors of Ford memorabilia.

Q. I have a pair of lamps that have never been lighted. I was told they are for a Hupmobile (1900 to 1910). They are in first-class condition. My question is, are they collector's items? If so, what is their value? G.P., Illinois.
A. The photo you sent with your letter shows the lamps to be rectangular in shape with a pagoda-shaped canopy on top. There are long, tapered handles extending down from the base of the lamp. These look, to me, like buggy lights. Most gas lights for early cars were round (though the cowl lights occasionally were of the rectangular, buggy light style.) They probably have some value to a collector of antiques, but do not appear to me to be automobile collectibles. Lacking a manufacturer's name on the lights, it is difficult to go farther.

Q. Some years back, I was a member of an Ertl model club. I would like to rejoin. I don't have the address. I wonder if you could supply me with it? O.S., New Jersey.
A. ERTL is a distributor of AMT and MPC model car and truck kits and has its own line of die-cast replica farm machinery, cars, trucks and vehicle banks. ERTL distributes a high-quality newsletter called *BLUEPRINTER*. A recent issue has articles on how model kits are made, new kit releases and techniques on customizing models. In addition, the newsletter includes a what's happening listing of model and toy shows and swap meets. Modelers interested in receiving the *BLUEPRINTER* (there is a nominal subscription fee) should contact Karen Sands, Associate Editor, The *ERTL BLUEPRINTER*, Highways 136 and 20, Dyersville, Iowa.

208